Building and Managing Effective Physician Organizations Under Capitation

Douglas Goldstein
President
Medical Alliances, Inc.
Alexandria, Virginia

AN ASPEN PUBLICATION®
Aspen Publishers, Inc.
Gaithersburg, Maryland
1996

This publication is designed to provide accurate and authoritative information in regard to the Subject Matter covered. It is sold with the understanding that the publisher is not engaged in rendering legal, accounting, or other professional service. If legal advice or other expert assistance is required, the service of a competent professional person should be sought. *(From a Declaration of Principles jointly adopted by a Committee of the American Bar Association and a Committee of Publishers and Associations.)*

Library of Congress Cataloging-in-Publication Data

Building and managing effective physician organizations under capitation / [edited by] Douglas Goldstein.
p. cm.
Includes bibliographical references and index.
ISBN 0-8342-0809-1
1. Health maintenance organizations—Administration. 2. Medicine—Practice. 3. Managed care plans (Medical care). 4. Integrated delivery of health care. I. Goldstein, Douglas E.
[DNLM: 1. Group Practice, Prepaid—organization & administration. 2. Capitation Fee—organization & administration. 3. Hospital-Physician Joint Ventures—organization & administration. 4. Managed Care Programs—organization & administration. W 92 B932 1996]
R729.5.H43B85 1996
362.1'0425—dc20
DNLM/DLC
for Library of Congress
96-1551
CIP

Copyright © 1996 by Aspen Publishers, Inc.
All rights reserved

Aspen Publishers, Inc., grants permission for photocopying for limited personal or internal use. This consent does not extend to other kinds of copying, such as copying for general distribution, for advertising or promotional purposes, for creating new collective works, or for resale. For information, address Aspen Publishers, Inc., Permissions Department, 200 Orchard Ridge Drive, Suite 200, Gaithersburg, Maryland 20878.

Orders: (800) 638-8437
Customer Service: (800) 234-1660

About Aspen Publishers • For more than 35 years, Aspen has been a leading professional publisher in a variety of disciplines. Aspen's vast information resources are available in both print and electronic formats. We are committed to providing the highest quality information available in the most appropriate format for our customers. Visit Aspen's Internet site for more information resources, directories, articles, and a searchable version of Aspen's full catalog, including the most recent publications: **http://www.aspenpub.com**
Aspen Publishers, Inc. • The hallmark of quality in publishing
Members of the worldwide Wolters Kluwer group.

Editorial Resources: Jane Colilla
Library of Congress Catalog Card Number: 96-1551
ISBN: 0-8342-0809-1

Printed in the United States of America

1 2 3 4 5

Contents

Contributors ix

Acknowledgments xi

Introduction—Taking Leadership To Restructure Health Care Delivery xiii

Part I—Creating the Physician Infrastructure 1

Chapter 1—Building Effective Physician Equity Alliances and
          Organizations 3
    Douglas Goldstein with Hank Fanberg, M.B.A.

    Introduction 3
    From Medical Practice to Physician Equity Alliance 3
    Six Types of Physician Equity Alliance 5
    Profiling Management Services Organizations as a Central
      Element 25
    Understanding Evolving Physician Organizations 29
    Today's Market Competition Demands Action and Merger 31

Chapter 2—System Building Blocks To Manage Capitation 33
    Douglas Goldstein

    Introduction 33
    Integrated Communications and Information Systems 34
    Process Measures and Outcomes Reporting 38
    Multispecialty Physician Networks 42
    Demand Management and Disease Management Systems 43
    Continuous Quality Improvement and Clinical Reengineering 48
    Internet and On-Line Services 49

Cost Reduction and Cost Management	54
Preventive Medicine and Empowered Consumers	55
Physician and Executive Leadership	57

Chapter 3—Strategies for Communicating with Physicians in the Era of Health Care Restructuring 58
Matthew J. Lambert III, M.D., M.B.A.

Introduction	58
Market Dynamics and the Role of Communications in Integration	58
Communication Strategies for Integration	63
Empower Communication Plan and Physician Leadership	71

Chapter 4—The Five Stages of Managed Care and Physician Organizations ... 72
Russell C. Coile Jr., Ph.D.

Introduction	72
PHOs—Are They Working and Will They Last?	73
Twenty-First-Century Health Reform Will Be Physician-Led	74
Five Stages of Managed Care	75
Three Scenarios for Integration	83
Alternative Paths to Integration	85

Chapter 5—Using Advanced Physician Management Structure To Ensure Clinical Effectiveness 87
Steven S. Lazarus, Ph.D., F.H.I.M.S.S. and John Lucas, M.D.

Executive Summary	87
Introduction	87
The LHS Implementation of Advanced Physician Management	88
The Lovelace Physician Group Population Health Model of Medical Delivery	91
Information Requirements To Support Advanced Physician Management	94
Information Systems	98
Conclusion	100

Part II—The Merger and Expansion Process 101

Chapter 6—Expansion Process for Physician Organizations 103
Douglas Goldstein

Introduction	103
Conducting Action-Oriented Research	104
Pursuing Aggressive Business Development	107
Understanding the Equity Transaction	108
Using an Aggressive Business Expansion Process	111
Implementing and Enhancing Systems for Growth	124

Chapter 7—Structuring a Physician Compensation Plan That Rewards Performance in the Managed Care Environment 127
Mark Buchanan, M.D.

Introduction 127
Getting Started 128
Criteria for a Compensation Plan 128
Building Blocks for a Compensation Plan 129
Stories from the Front Lines 134
Four Scenarios for Income Distribution 136
General Comments on the Four Plans 139
When Is Change Appropriate? 140
Income Division and the Patient 141
Conclusion 142

Chapter 8—Capital and Equity Issues in Physician Organizations and Practice Management Industry 144
Douglas Goldstein and E. James Streator III

Introduction 144
Market Realities of the Physician Practice Management Industry 144
Expansion of the Physician Practice Management Industry 145
Physicians Take Leadership 149
Financial Issues and Capital Sources Related to Growth 150
Financial Implications of Strategic Alliance Options 153
Strategic Alliance Decisions 159

Chapter 9—Legal Issues in Organizing and Expanding Physician Organizations 161
Philip B. Belcher, J.D. and S. Rogers Warner Jr., J.D.

Introduction 161
Integrated Group Practice—Merger of Medical Groups 161
Independent Practice Association 172
Other Affiliations 179

Part III—Advanced Information Systems Issues 189

Chapter 10—Selecting Information Systems for Managing MSOs and Large-Scale, Integrated Ambulatory Networks 191
Mary de Lourdes Winberry, M.P.H.

Introduction 191
A Look at the Big Picture 192
Infrastructure Needs 193
Selecting an Information System 197
Staying Competitive 201

Chapter 11—Managing the Planning and Start-Up Operations for Advanced Practice Management Information Systems 205
Steven S. Lazarus, Ph.D., F.H.I.M.S.S.

Executive Summary 205
Introduction 205
Planning the Information Systems 206
Major Information Systems Applications 208
Information Systems Budget and Financial Considerations 208
Conversion to a New Information System 210
Managing Change 213
Value Added 214
Anticipating Future Needs 215
Conclusion 216

Chapter 12—Applying Outcomes Research To Increase Quality 217
Sanford R. Hoffman, M.D. and Mary de Lourdes Winberry, M.P.H.

Introduction 217
History of Outcomes Research 217
Outcomes Research Today 218
Outcomes Data—What Are They? 219
Gathering the Data—The Survey 220
Utility Assessment—Patient Preferences 220
Accountability—Its Impact on Practice Guidelines 221
Once You Have Outcomes Measurements, What Do You
  Do with Them? 221
Who Is Collecting the Data? 223
Disease Management 223
The Demand for Outcomes Data 224
Getting Started 224
Future Trends 225

Part IV—Managing Managed Care and Capitation 229

Chapter 13—Managed Care Contracting and Reimbursement for Physician Organizations in a Capitated and Risk-Sharing Environment ... 231
Richard Ferreira, M.D., J.D.

Introduction 231
Contracts 231
Reimbursement Methodologies for Managed Care 241
Risk Sharing 248

Chapter 14—Legal Issues Associated with Managed Care Contracting 251
Irwin M. Birnbaum, J.D.

Executive Summary 251
Legal Issues Important to Competitive Policies and Procedures 251
Understanding the MCO Contract 263
Conclusion 276

Chapter 15—Critical Issues in Negotiating Capitated Contracts 278
Kerry McDonald

    Introduction 278
    The Business Environment 278
    Preparing for Negotiations 279
    Strategy for the Negotiations 280
    Negotiating the Language 280
    Negotiating the Rate 286
    Preparing the Organization for Capitation Negotiations 293
    Conclusion 300
    Appendix 15–A—Cost System Definitions 301
    Appendix 15–B—Variable Costing Income Statement Format 303
    Appendix 15–C—Data Sources, Elements, and Specific Statistics ... 304

Part V—Taking Leadership 307

Chapter 16—Developing and Operating Physician-Driven HMOs 309
John Pollard, M.D.

    Introduction 309
    Basic Requirements 310
    Initial Steps 311
    Start-Up 313
    Operational Issues 314
    Miscellaneous 316
    Conclusion 316

Chapter 17—Organizing and Managing Specialty Networks for Capitation 317
Richard W. Krohn, M.B.A.

    Introduction 317
    Specialty Networks—Development and Strategic Choices 317
    The Framework of Specialty Risk Contracting 320
    Making Risk Contracting Work in Specialty Networks 321
    Understanding the Capitation Contract 323
    Infrastructure Requirements of Successful Risk Contracting 326
    Success Factors of Risk-Based Specialty Networks 328
    The Bottom Line—What Specialists Should Expect from Their
        Network 331
    A Successful Specialty Carve-Out Network—SalickNet 334
    Winning through Adaptation 337

**Chapter 18—Multispecialty Physician Organizations: The New Force in
       Medicine** 338
*Nancy McDermott, Charles Hollander, M.D., Richard Garber, M.B.A.,
and Steven Wolfson, M.D.*

    Introduction 338
    The Benefits of a Multispecialty Organization 339
    Creating Multispecialty Organizations 341

Bridging the Gap Between Primary Care Physicians and
  Specialists 346
New Relationships Sprouting from Multispecialty Organization
  Development 347
Summary 347

Chapter 19—Creating the Future through Today's Vision and Actions 348
Douglas Goldstein

Introduction 348
Competitive Advantage through System Building Blocks 348
Track Trends and News in the External Environment 349
Competitive Advantage through Thinking and Leadership 350

Index 353

Contributors

Philip B. Belcher, J.D.
Parker, Poe, Adams & Berstein L.L.P.
Charlotte, North Carolina

Irwin M. Birnbaum, J.D.
Attorney at Law
Proskauer Rose Goetz & Mendelsohn L.L.P.
New York, New York

Mark Buchanan, M.D.
Vice President, Medical Affairs
Kelson Physician Partners
Bloomfield, Connecticut

Russell C. Coile, Jr., M.B.A.,
President
Health Forecasting Group
Santa Clarita, California

Hank Fanberg, M.B.A.
Director of Business Development
United Health Care System
Newark, New Jersey

Richard Ferreira, M.D., J.D.
Administrator, External Provider Affairs
Mullikin Medical Center
Long Beach, California

Richard Garber, M.B.A.
CEO and President
Physician Health Care Alliance
New Haven, Connecticut

Sanford R. Hoffman, M.D.
Coordinator of Clinical Improvement and Outcomes Measurement Srategies
Millard Fillmore Health System
Western, New York

Charles Hollander, M.D.
Medical Director, Physician Health Care Alliance
President, CHC Physician
New Haven, Connecticut

Richard W. Krohn, M.B.A.
Director
Medical Alliances, Inc.
Towson, Maryland

Matthew J. Lambert III, M.D., M.B.A.
Vice President for Medical Affairs
Catholic Health Partners
Chicago, Illinois

Steven S. Lazarus, Ph.D., F.H.I.M.S.S.
President
MSA Corp
Denver, Colorado

John Lucas, M.D., M.P.H.
Chief Executive Officer
Lovelace Health Systems
Albuquerque, New Mexico

Nancy McDermott
Consultant
Medical Alliances, Inc.
Alexandria, Virginia

Kerry McDonald
Consultant
Medical Alliances, Inc.
Bladensburg, Maryland

John Pollard, M.D.
Vice President-Medical Affairs
The Carle Foundation Hospital
Urbana, Illinois

E. James Streator III
Managing Director, Healthcare
  Services Group
Hambrecht & Quist, Inc.
New York, New York

S. Rogers Warner, Jr., J.D.
Parker, Poe, Adams & Berstein L.L.P.
Charlotte, North Carolina

Mary de Lourdes Winberry, M.P.H.
Vice President
Medical Alliances, Inc.
Alexandria, Virginia

Steven Wolfson, M.D.
President
Cardiology Associates of New Haven,
  P.C.
New Haven, Connecticut

Acknowledgments

Excellence is only possible through team work. This book is no exception. Special thanks to all the contributing authors who took time out of their busy schedules to share their knowledge and experience. This book would not have been possible without the dedication, hard work, editing, and contributions of Nancy McDermott, the editorial manager of the project. A final thanks goes to my wife Lorraine who supported me throughout a very challenging and exciting year and encouraged me to share my perspective and insights with the health care community.

Introduction—Taking Leadership To Restructure Health Care Delivery

Management, not the model!
Leadership, not reaction!

In this era of market-driven health care reform, new organizations being structured should not focus solely on the specific model of integration. The key to charting the turbulent seas of transition is management and leadership. Within any proposed integrated, organized, or equity delivery system, an in-depth and detailed summary of vision, principles, goals and objectives, governance, management, flow of funds, equity ownership, and service delivery must be profiled. The dynamic forces of change buffeting physicians today require aggressive action, flexibility, responsiveness, courage, experience, clinical knowledge, teamwork, and—most importantly—leaders to provide form and substance to the necessary change process. Future prosperity and success of Physician Organizations depend not on the model but on dynamic, ethical leadership.

Out of the whirlwind of change, a new industry has emerged—the Physician Practice Management industry. Although capital markets essentially ignored the development of Physician-Hospital Organizations, Physician Practice Management Organizations or Management Services Organizations (MSOs) are a completely different matter. Physicians control 80 percent of the health care dollar through their decision making. Physician networks or integrated physician practices are the single most important requirement in obtaining capitated and managed care contracts with payer groups and the predictable revenue that accompanies those contracts. Wall Street investors, institutional investors, venture capitalists, sophisticated investors, insurance companies, managed health plans, pharmaceutical companies, physician entrepreneurs, and experienced business executives are investing billions of dollars to fuel the merger, consolidation, and expansion of medical practices and health care markets.

American Health Network—a joint venture between primary care physicians and The Associated Group, a $4 billion diversified insurance company—grew from five physicians to more than 200 physicians in 18 months. MedPartners went from no revenue and no physicians under management to more than 1,000 physicians and over $1 billion in revenue in 24 months through the aggressive merger of the largest physician equity organizations in the country. These are only two examples from thousands of transactions across the country. Investigate any community in the country, and examples of physician practice integration—whether by health systems, for-profit companies, managed health plans, venture capitalists, or physician leaders—can be uncovered.

There is not just one Physician Organization or physician equity model. Dozens of variations are being touted and sold to physicians who may or may not have the information they need to make good decisions. This book provides the necessary information by describing the major variations on the physician equity model and the legal, financial, and operational issues surrounding the development and management of new integrated Physician Organizations. It explores in detail the many building block systems required for organizations to survive and prosper in a world of numerous different reimbursement schemes ranging from discount fee-for-service and primary care capitation to global capitation and percent of premium payment.

The Physician Organization of the future is multispecialty, because that is what is required to deliver quality, cost-effective care. Primary and specialty care, together, are the continuum of care that cannot be replaced. There are many paths to achieve the goal of an integrated, patient-focused continuum of health care services. Some will evolve from primary care networks, and others will come from single or multispecialty initiatives. Physician Organizations will grow and merge successfully when they define and stick to core principles and values that reflect patients' needs, sustainability, quality, and cost-effectiveness.

This resource book addresses the human, operational, and clinical support systems needed to manage a high-quality, clinically effective, patient-oriented organization, as the reimbursement system for providers moves rapidly from discount fee-for-service to various forms of capitation and risk sharing.

It may seem that power is shifting from the provider to the managed health plan. Health Maintenance Organizations (HMOs) have accumulated large stockpiles of cash, and they appear to have increasing control of the flow of patients. However, there are strong indications that the cycle will continue to evolve, with provider-based delivery systems taking a more predominant role in the twenty-first century. For example, a Minneapolis business coalition is cutting out the managed health plans from the contracting equation because of the added layer of cost and because the managed health care plans are more interested in buying managed health plans in other markets rather than caring for patients in Minneapolis. Underlying cost factors are contributing to this trend. Provider-based delivery systems have lower costs, and administrative overhead is estimated to be from 9 to 14 percent, compared with 15 to 30 percent for publicly held HMO management companies.

Many physician leaders are going beyond the practice of medicine and creating provider-sponsored HMOs. In many parts of the country, provider groups are launching and expanding their own managed care plans. The American Medical Association has developed a support program with business plans and capital sources for physicians who want the tools to develop HMOs. Fortis, a $10 billion insurance conglomerate, has developed two initiatives to support Physician Organizations. First, Fortis has developed an array of reinsurance products for the provider markets that allow an at-risk physician group to access reinsurance at more competitive rates than from the HMO directly. Under capitation, lower costs mean higher profits and more resources for patient care. Second, Fortis is making capital available to support physician-owned HMO and managed care plans. The federal government's definition of a risk-bearing provider entity called *provider service network*, which is subject to federal oversight, is another indicator of the trend toward provider-sponsored health care delivery systems.

Action is necessary. Solutions are required to deliver quality care at prices that businesses and individuals can afford. Externally driven methods of the past have failed to control cost and quality. While the focus on external utilization review (UR) in the 1980s may have squeezed some hospital days out of the system, it did little to enhance overall efficiency. Instead, external UR added significant extra costs to the system. Utilization firms spent millions of dollars on nurses and triage agents whose mission was to second-guess physicians' judgment calls. As a result, many physicians were forced to replace patient care time with as many as six to eight hours per week of unnecessary consultations addressing UR requirements.

Even more critical is the role of commitment. Physicians who operate under severe external restrictions or sanctions can never perform at the same level—and with the same passion—as physicians who are involved participants or equity owners. The delicate act of balancing quality and cost-effectiveness demands physician participation. And the most effective way for that participation to come about is for physicians to spearhead integration and restructuring of the health care system. The various forms of Physician Equity Alliance offer a framework for educating and organizing physicians to make a difference. These alliances are generally centered around a series of linked structures: a physician-owned Integrated Group Practice (IGP), a Practice Management Services Organization (MSO), and various affiliated networks or Independent Practice Associations (IPAs) that provide greater geographic access.

The major focus of this book is on managing the development and operations of large-scale Physician Organizations and Physician Equity Alliances that are dedicated to providing care in a geographical region or state or across numerous defined metropolitan statistical areas. These entities are market driven and physician led. They combine significant elements of medical practices—including their legal, operational, and financial components—yet maintain specific elements and cost-effectiveness of network structures. Long-term sustainability will depend on physician leaders and executives blending the best of centralized and decentralized organizational structures and operations for the efficient, quality delivery of health care services under various risk-sharing relationships. With the increased use of the Internet and World Wide Web and the blending of computer/communication systems, the future structure for the health care delivery system will be much more virtual than vertical.

This book is organized into five parts. Each part delivers valuable knowledge on how to organize and manage new physician-led health care delivery systems. It is intended to empower leaders, executives, and managers with intelligent approaches to reorganizing and managing the necessary human and operational systems—from communications, compensation, capitation, and capital, to information systems, legal issues, merger process, and HMO development.

Part I, Creating the Physician Infrastructure, focuses on the key aspects of business operations that physician leaders and executives must grasp in directing the rapid expansion of clinically effective and market-oriented health care systems:

- **Chapter 1—Building Effective Physician Equity Alliances and Organizations** (Douglas Goldstein with Hank Fanberg, M.B.A). Using their business development experience from across the country, the authors profile the six major types of physician equity structures used for the consolidation and merger of medical practices. The chapter also describes the key functions of Physician Practice Management Companies (also called MSOs or Management Services Organizations). Finally, it highlights several examples of how Physician Organizations are rapidly evolving in size and scope.

- **Chapter 2—System Building Blocks To Manage Capitation** (Douglas Goldstein). Goldstein delivers an overview of the nine key operational systems that integrated ambulatory delivery systems will need to manage service delivery under capitation reimbursement. These range from demand management, physician leaders, and quality, to cost management, information systems, and Internet capabilities. Many of the following chapters offer more insight and how-to information on these critical system building blocks.
- **Chapter 3—Strategies for Communicating with Physicians in the Era of Health Care Structuring** (Matthew J. Lambert III, M.D., M.B.A.). This chapter examines the issue of communicating so that the message will have its greatest impact. Lambert outlines a broad range of 20 recommendations on how to communicate more effectively so that individuals can work in teams to achieve a common vision and goals. With his diversified clinical and management experience, the author reminds the reader of critical advice and knowledge that is too often taken for granted.
- **Chapter 4—The Five Stages of Managed Care and Physician Organizations** (Russell C. Coile Jr., Ph.D.). The author, a leading health care futurist, details the predictable course of managed care evolution in markets across the country. Coile illustrates the forces that drive change and discusses the implications for Physician Organizations of the five definable stages of managed care development.
- **Chapter 5—Using Advanced Physician Management Structure To Ensure Clinical Effectiveness** (Steven S. Lazarus, Ph.D., F.H.I.M.S.S. and John Lucas, M.D.). Physician leader Lucas and management executive Lazarus discuss the systems, experiences, and philosophies that have guided Lovelace Health Systems to meet critical patient needs for care and quality under capitation. Implementation and operations of several key systems such as demand management, regional access, and integration of care delivery and financing are illustrated in detail.

Part II, The Merger and Expansion Process, charts the legal, operational, and financial standards and systems required for rapid expansion of Physician Equity Alliances. Rapid growth demands an in-depth understanding of how to merge practices in a way that addresses market requirements, physician needs, and legal issues.

- **Chapter 6—Expansion Process for Physician Organizations** (Douglas Goldstein). This chapter, based on consulting experience with numerous Physician Equity Alliances, focuses on the business issues that must be addressed in the merger and expansion process. It delivers a step-by-step summary of the growth process and lists important recommendations on how to do it right and faster than the competition.
- **Chapter 7—Structuring a Physician Compensation Plan That Rewards Performance in the Managed Care Environment** (Mark Buchanan, M.D.). Based on his experience in care delivery and building physician equity organizations, Buchanan describes how to structure compensation systems in a mixed fee-for-service and capitated environment. Several compensation models are profiled in detail, along with recommendations on how to redesign or adjust compensation systems as Physician Organizations become progressively more capitated.
- **Chapter 8—Capital and Equity Issues in Physician Organizations and Practice Management Industry** (Douglas Goldstein and E. James Streator III). The authors use their broad knowledge of

the capital markets to describe the dynamic nature of the Physician Practice Management industry, outline the reasons why billions of dollars of institutional investment money is being poured in to establish a position in this emerging industry, and profile how the flow of funds changes as physicians move assets from professional corporations to management companies.

- **Chapter 9—Legal Issues in Organizing and Expanding Physician Organizations** (Philip B. Belcher, J.D., and S. Rogers Warner Jr., J.D.). This chapter focuses on critical legal issues that must be understood, managed, and implemented accurately in the rapid growth process. It highlights important federal and state laws and their implications for corporate structuring, taxes, pensions, and contracts in the consolidation of existing medical practices.

Part III, Advanced Information Systems Issues, presents a vital development concern for Physician Organizations. Along with strong leadership and management, the effective selection and start-up of the information systems is key to support the complex financial and quality decision making needed by the Physician Organization.

- **Chapter 10—Selecting Information Systems for Managing MSOs and Large-Scale, Integrated Ambulatory Networks** (Mary de Lourdes Winberry, M.P.H.). The author describes the functional requirements for ambulatory information systems needed to manage in a capitated environment. This chapter outlines the key actions that physician leaders and executives must take in selecting new information and communication systems that will empower their organizations. It also pinpoints the pitfalls that can make information systems a "black hole" for capital.

- **Chapter 11—Managing the Planning and Start-Up Operations for Advanced Practice Management Information Systems** (Steven S. Lazarus, Ph.D., F.H.I.M.S.S.). This chapter expands on the topics addressed in Chapter 10. Selecting is one issue, but managing the start-up, staffing, and financial expenditures with a task force is a different matter. This chapter offers insights and recommendations on the proper approaches for implementing a new superpowered, capitation-ready practice management information system.

- **Chapter 12—Applying Outcomes Research To Increase Quality** (Sanford R. Hoffman, M.D., and Mary de Lourdes Winberry, M.P.H.). This chapter discusses the current status of the growing outcomes movement and outlines key clinical approaches on how Physician Organizations can distinguish themselves based on quality of care, rather than price.

As Physician Organizations go at-risk for specified health services of patients within defined populations, it is critical to understand all the implications of the managed care risk contract. **Part IV, Managing Managed Care and Capitation**, offers three how-to chapters:

- **Chapter 13—Managed Care Contracting and Reimbursement for Physician Organizations in a Capitated and Risk-Sharing Environment** (Richard Ferreira, M.D., J.D.). Ferreira provides proven approaches for managing hundreds of thousands of capitated lives from his years of leadership at Mullikin Medical Centers (since merged with MedPartners, Pacific Physician Services, and others). In articulating the position that only Physician Organizations can be Managed Care Organizations, he elaborates on critical issues for subcapitating specialists and other ancillary service providers.

- **Chapter 14—Legal Issues Associated with Managed Care Contracting** (Irwin M. Birnbaum, J.D.). This chapter provides an overview of the key legislative statutes and legal judgments that affect negotiating, signing, and implementing managed care contracts. An understanding of these key legal issues allows physician leaders and executives to ask the right questions in the contracting process.
- **Chapter 15—Critical Issues in Negotiating Capitated Contracts** (Kerry McDonald). This chapter delivers practical, hard-hitting advice in the dos and don'ts of negotiating and managing managed care contracts. Various negotiating strategies are described, along with a rigorous example of how to price a capitation contract. Finally, the chapter outlines the operational requirements for managing the contract, including the need to use an accrual method of accounting.

Part V, Taking Leadership, examines key issues being faced by Physician Organizations as they move into the future.

- **Chapter 16—Developing and Operating Physician-Driven HMOs** (John Pollard, M.D.). From his years of leadership at the Carle Clinic and Health Plan, Pollard provides valuable insights about the process and issues that must be considered when a Physician Organization is investigating whether market circumstances will support a physician-driven HMO and the feasibility of moving from providing care to financing care via an HMO.
- **Chapter 17—Organizing and Managing Specialty Networks for Capitation** (Richard W. Krohn, M.B.A.). This chapter discusses the role of single-specialty networks in the capitated delivery of care. The public funding and growth of single-specialty networks in oncology, cardiology, mental health, and other fields is reviewed, along with the success factors necessary for these organizations.
- **Chapter 18—Multispecialty Physician Organizations: The New Force in Medicine** (Nancy McDermott, Charles Hollander, M.D., Richard Garber, M.B.A., and Steven Wolfson, M.D.). This chapter points out the need for a multispecialty integrated and contractually coordinated continuum of care. It points out the weaknesses of primary care or specialist-only approaches, emphasizing patients' fundamental needs for choice and quality care.
- **Chapter 19—Creating The Future through Today's Vision and Actions** (Douglas Goldstein). In this chapter, Goldstein highlights today's market opportunities and national trends in the health care market. He discusses the interplay of national, regional, and local trends along with the critical balance between physician leadership, an alliance attitude, and the system "Building Blocks" which are necessary to survive and prosper in a health care world characterized by price competition, capitation, and an emerging emphasis on outcomes.

This book is an empowerment resource for physician leaders and executives as they chart the course of change in health care communities across the country. One overriding principle that must be followed is: *patients first*. Leaders have the responsibility of doing what is principled and ethically right, as well as what is financially viable, in the creation of sustainable, patient-focused health care delivery systems.

Part I

Creating the Physician Infrastructure

Chapter 1

Building Effective Physician Equity Alliances and Organizations

Douglas Goldstein with Hank Fanberg, M.B.A.

INTRODUCTION

How does a multifaceted Physician Organization make the transition from a medical practice to a quality-oriented, risk-managing health care delivery system without sacrificing patient care? The challenge is to develop the mindset of a group practice, which requires a different way of organizing and managing care delivery. Tomorrow's health care delivery systems will go beyond today's fragmented managed care approach because of the integrated web of relationships linked by culture, shared values, and information found in evolving physician organizations. These physician-driven entities will stimulate performance by internal peer motivation and communication rather than external review and discipline. Integrated delivery systems consist of physicians and other providers who are at risk for delivering services along the continuum of care for individuals within defined populations. Quality patient care and financial success clearly depend on physicians and the organizations they lead.

While future Physician Organizations present an appealing vision of a seamless continuum of care, physicians and executive leaders must still grapple with the question of how to merge practices, teach physicians to work in groups, and improve the health status of entire populations of patients. New and evolving health care organizations have a lot of work to do to integrate and organize the fragmented health care system of today to meet patient and purchaser needs of today and tomorrow.

This chapter explores numerous variations on the Physician Equity Alliance that are being implemented across the country. It analyzes Physician Practice Management Companies, a critical component of many of these entities. Next, it profiles the evolution of different physician organizational entities, which are often managed by owned or contracted management service companies.

FROM MEDICAL PRACTICE TO PHYSICIAN EQUITY ALLIANCE

One of the fastest-growing trends in health care is the development of physician group practices and other Physician Organizations. Both the Medical Group Management Association (MGMA) and American Medical Association (AMA) report astronomical growth in group practice formation. Studies have shown that Integrated Group Practices have always been the most efficient practices, with Independent Practice Associations (IPAs) a strong second. FHP of California, one of the largest group practices in the country, has spun off its staff physician network into its own group practice. Consumers demand choice of physician, and the managed health plans are responding by adding more primary care physicians to their panels, even in states without willing provider laws. Some states have enacted laws prohibiting Health Maintenance Organizations (HMOs) from having restricted physician panels. In these states, HMOs must include "any willing provider" in their panels.

Alliances: Strategies for Building Integrated Delivery Systems describes the basic models of integration of health systems and Physician Organizations.[1] It emphasizes that the key to success in building Integrated Delivery Systems rests with clinically effective physicians and integrated Physician Organizations. However, recent events demonstrate that there is more than one strategy or way to develop a system. One specific integrated model or organizational entity is insufficient. Organizations often have to implement group practices, specialty networks, Management Services Organizations (MSOs), and other entities simultaneously to deal with complex market conditions.

The health care system has seen the rapid rise of private and public practice management entities, often referred to as Physician Practice Management Companies (PPMCs) or MSOs. The gross revenue flowing through the practices is accumulated by PPMCs and reflects the total revenues of hundreds of medical practices being managed by a series of regional MSOs. Billions of dollars of capital have poured into these PPMCs from private investors, institutional investors, and public markets. There is even an investor analyst newsletter dedicated to the MSO and PPMC market, *PPMC: Market, Financial and Operating Statistics for Physician Practice Management Companies*, published by Sherlock Company, Gwenedd, Pennsylvania. It reported in August 1995 that the total market capitalization for this emerging industry was $6.2 billion.[2] Chapter 8 provides additional details on the financial aspects of this emerging market.

Over the last several years, there has been a rapid rise in the physician equity model of integration or Physician Equity Alliance. It has been popularized by Mullikin Medical Centers, Ochsner Clinic, Atlantic Health Network, Physician Health Care Alliance, Montana Associated Physicians, Baltimore Medical Group, Sac Sierra Medical Group, and many others. The various forms of Physician Equity Alliance are generally centered around a series of linked structures: a physician-owned, Integrated Group Practice; a practice management services organization; and various affiliated network or IPA entities that provide greater geographic access. It has the ability to merge and link together hundreds of medical practices into a financially, legally, and operationally integrated organization that controls health care expenditures.

Wall Street and other investors never fully supported or capitalized Physician-Hospital Organizations (PHOs) because the revenue stream was small and uncertain; many lacked infrastructure and managed care contracts; and they were usually dominated by hospitals, which created a conflict for investors. The MSOs that are the central management entity within a Physician Equity Alliance are different. They control 100 percent of the revenue and cash flow of merged practices, manage the managed care contracting on an exclusive basis for hundreds of additional practices, and manage a large enough network of primary care physicians and specialists to attract full-risk contracts. Consequently, there has been a rush to fund and capitalize numerous variations on the Physician Equity Alliance and Management Services Organization.

SIX TYPES OF PHYSICIAN EQUITY ALLIANCE

Physicians throughout the country are being approached to sell or merge their medical practice into some type of equity alliance, management company, or Integrated Delivery System. There are numerous variations on the physician equity model. These variations can be organized into six basic types:

1. physician regional network
2. physician health system joint venture
3. Physician Practice Management Company
4. specialty services network
5. venture medical management company
6. PhysicianEquity Alliance

This section profiles each of the types by discussing organizational description, vision and goals, ownership, capital, governance, management, business lines, revenue generation, revenue distribution, and when to use or implement a specific model. In some cases, variations are highlighted. There are significant similarities and differences between the types. One type of equity alliance can, and often does, evolve into another type that is larger and more integrated. There are significant differences between the equity types in the funding source and how capital is accessed. Different investors have different goals in mind, which results in very different strategic objectives for the various types of equity alliances. Most if not all physicians are concerned with maintaining control of the decision-making process regarding patient care. Hospitals and health systems are concerned with maintaining financial viability and maintaining and increasing market share, which in the age of managed care equates to *covered lives* or *member-months*. Venture capitalists have no inherent desire to own physician practices and are seeking above-average rates of return on their investments and significant appreciation of value as a result of the growth of the PPMC. They take organizations public or sell out at an appropriate time to recoup their principal, once they have made a sufficient return. The source of capital results in different strategic goals and objectives for each of the six types of Physician Equity Alliance, which result in different management direction and outcomes.

The rush to consolidate represents a major change in health care delivery from a small cottage industry to an organized, large-scale operation. The underlying purpose of all the Physician Equity Alliance variations is to become the provider of choice for any and all payer groups. The major differences among them are how they are capitalized, who owns them, and who controls their strategic decision-making process. Thirteen years after the publication of *The Transformation of American Medicine*, Paul Starr's observations regarding the corporatization of medicine are becoming a reality.[3] In order to provide care and have access to the revenue necessary to accept risk, a large population is necessary. Large groups require large provider networks. The consolidation that has occurred in Minneapolis and California is the harbinger of things to come. Whether through purchase, acquisition, or contractual affiliation, expect to see the expansion and growth of systems that cover large geographic areas. For physicians to maintain control, or at a minimum have some say in the game, they need an ownership position in the developing organizations. Their ability to maintain control will, in part, be determined by how much ownership they retain.

Physician Regional Network

Description

Individual physicians or small group practices jointly form and capitalize a new corporation whose primary purpose is to represent the individual physicians as a single cohesive contracting network (see Figure 1–1). This structure is not a practice merger. The new corporate entity is similar to an IPA in function. Its purpose is to perform any and all business functions that the network wants it to do. This model does not require financial or legal integration of the individual practices, but it does attempt to unite the practices for managed care contracting. Each practice retains its autonomy and, in essence, forms a joint venture company that is equally owned by all physician members. Because this is a business entity, the form of incorporation is important; the limited liability corporation (LLC) is being used more frequently. This organization can be 100 percent primary care, 100 percent specialty care, or a combination of the two, which results in a true multispecialty representation. The key in a multispecialty network is to attain an adequate ratio of primary care physicians to specialists. This type of organization also has been called a "group practice without walls" or a "clinic without walls." This type is formed for offensive rather than defensive reasons; the physician founders want to have an initial vehicle that will grow and evolve as necessary, based on market competition.

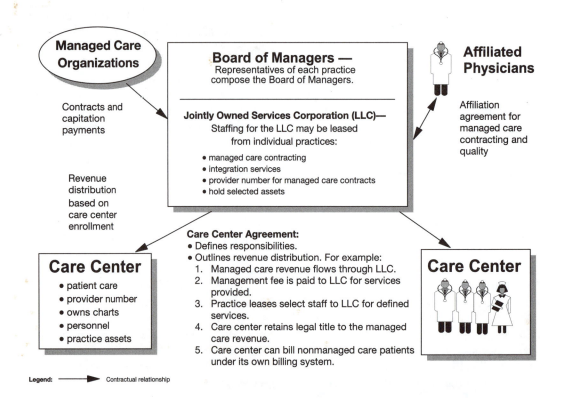

Figure 1–1 Physician regional network. Courtesy of Medical Alliances, Inc., Alexandria, Virginia.

Ownership and Sources of Capital

This network management entity is wholly owned by its physician members, who provide all capital for the start-up and ongoing operating expenses. The physicians must come up with the funds to form the network, establish an identity, provide operating capital for ongoing business tasks, acquire information systems, hire staff, and perform all of the managerial tasks related to the business conducted by the group. The contribution required by each physician can be equal, or different levels may be established by medical specialty. In some instances, the LLC structure is used to bring in an outside capital partner (such as a health system), who acquires an interest in the corporation in exchange for a cash contribution.

Vision and Goals

The primary vision is to create a physician-owned and managed business organization that will allow physicians to maintain their influence while becoming more competitive in the marketplace. Key goals include the following:

- Develop the capability to accept financial and other types of risk.
- Provide outstanding patient care in the most cost-effective manner possible.
- Create a seamless physician referral system that does not place an undue burden on the patient.
- Implement cooperative marketing programs to attract patients.
- Evolve aggressively to meet market and competitive requirements.

Governance

The network entity is governed by its physician owners, who act as a board of managers (the name for the board of directors of a LLC). The makeup of the board reflects the founding physicians and overall membership. In multispecialty networks, the board can have designated slots for specialty representation. The board of managers establishes other committees and is responsible for moving the organization forward. Usually, four committees are set up: (1) network development—focuses on organizational expansion, (2) quality or medical management—emphasizes care guidelines and overall quality issues, (3) managed care—works on all managed care contracting issues, and (4) infrastructure—is responsible for information systems, governance, and related concerns.

Management

Many physician regional networks are physician-managed, especially during the start-up phase. While there are tremendous advantages of having professional staff on hand from the beginning, it may be prudent to wait until activity level or size requires staffing. The board of managers usually functions in the management role in the early stages of the network's life. There is usually a direct relationship between organizational size and executive management team. Possible start-up costs include first-year employment expenses (annual salary and benefits, including leave, health insurance, retirement/pension plan, and other perks offered by the company) of key managers, who likely include an executive director and manager of contracting. Total start-up expenses—including staffing, legal, and business consulting—may well represent an investment of $10,000 per physician for a 20-person equity alliance. Until a critical mass of business activity is reached, many equity organizations rely on sweat equity in the form of time by physician leaders to manage the organization. Most, if not all of these self-managed networks, rely upon the advice and assistance of outside consultants for strategic and operational planning and implementation.

Lines of Business

The purpose of the physician regional network is to ensure its members adequate patients and cash flow through managed care contracts. These contracts, in many markets, can be considered as the basic purpose of the corporation and one of the most important methods by which revenue is driven to the corporation. This network may therefore find itself in competition with other entities, such as Physician-Hospital Organizations, attempting to negotiate global or percent of premium contracts from managed health plans and other payers. There can be two levels of membership in this entity: (1) affiliated physicians, who would only access managed care contracts and agree to conform to quality guidelines; (2) care centers, which would receive managed care contracting plus a host of other services. (These services could be delivered on an individual or bundled basis and could include group purchasing, information systems, medical management, and others.) The physician regional network could also be used for joint marketing efforts to attract more patients from competitive practices. Each care center would be assessed a monthly service fee for services utilized.

Systems

The most important systems include management information, medical and quality management, and financial resource utilization (capitation and its distribution). Other systems to be implemented after a period of operations include human resources and outcomes measurement.

Revenue Generation

Revenue is generated from retaining a portion of the managed care contract revenue from contracts negotiated. The percentage varies from 8 to 15 percent, depending on the specific services included. These contracts should be risk contracts, which allow the network to achieve higher financial rewards for improving outcomes and resource utilization effectiveness. Often there is significant lag time of a year or more from initial organization until patients come into the practice from new managed health plan contracts. Physician leaders must be prepared to subsidize operations during this start-up period and conduct joint marketing efforts to attract more fee-for-service patients.

Distribution of Income

Managed care revenue negotiated by the service corporation flows through the LLC. In some cases, the individual care centers retain the right to bill current patients with their own systems; in other situations, the physicians agree to centralize the billing and collection function. The consolidation of all staff into one system reduces operating costs and offsets the new overhead of the service corporation. In some examples, the compensation system is standardized. One specific measure of work commonly used by many networks is the *relative value unit* (RVU). Many advocate utilizing Health Care Financing Administration's Resource-Based Relative Value Scale (RBRVS), because it is uniform and takes into account the entire universe of physician procedures. Detractors argue that only 1,500 or so of the Current Procedural Terminology (CPT) codes were actually time studied and, therefore, this may not be a good scale to use. Still, an agreed-upon relative value scale methodology is the best way to determine the amount of work performed by all members and can be used for direct compensation by units worked. The difficult part may be defining "work." Most income distribution formulas are reevaluated on a regular and ongoing basis.

When To Use

The physician regional network is most appropriate in level 1 or level 2 markets. Since it does not integrate the underlying financial and operational components of the medical practices, many purchasers do not view this as a single contracting entity. See Chapter 4 to review the five levels of managed care development.

Variations

There are numerous variations of the physician regional network. Every network or group practice merger must go through an evolution, as managers and physician leaders learn to work as a team. In the organizing effort there will be variations on the degree of integration, number of shared services, size of the governance board, and so forth. The key issue is to start somewhere and quickly develop higher levels of competition to achieve greater influence and financial leverage.

Physician Health System Joint Venture (PHSJV)

Description

For the last several years, health systems have been launching management services organizations that will acquire or manage medical practices (see Figure 1–2). These PHSJVs have been organized as either for-profit or nonprofit entities. Many hospital-based health systems have actively acquired physician practices and established wholly owned MSOs to operate these practices. Other health systems have recognized the benefits of equity structures and the need to compete with the well-capitalized, public PPMCs, so they have established jointly owned for-profit management companies with select groups of physicians. A jointly owned venture between a health system and physicians provides practice management services to its physician owners and sells these services to other providers. PHSJVs have been formed when physician leaders take the initiative to form an MSO, develop a business plan, and then invite the health system to invest capital for an equity position. Conversely, they have also been started by health systems who establish the MSO and then outline how physicians can gain equity through the exchange of tangible and intangible assets of their individual practices.

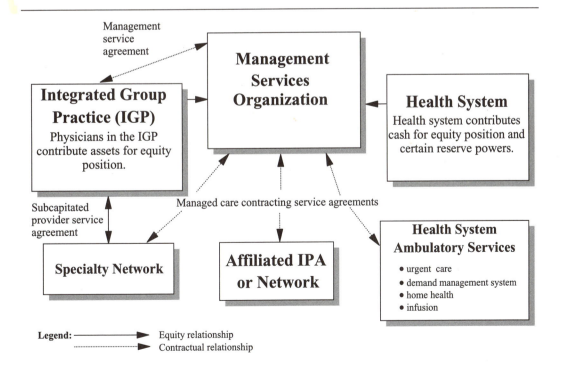

Figure 1–2 Physician health system joint venture. Courtesy of Medical Alliances, Inc., Alexandria, Virginia.

Ownership and Capital

There are two distinct classes of owners—individual physicians and the health system. The hospital or health system holds common and/or preferred stock in the business corporation. The PHSJV is often owned 50/50 by physicians and the health system. Increasingly, the health system is a minority equity partner because of the growing leverage of Physician Organizations resulting from the numerous suitors who are seeking to gain control over the revenue flow of the practices. A major reason for allowing a minority partner into the organization is to get the capital to acquire the systems necessary to perform the basic business functions of the new corporation. C corporation (a standard corporation entity used to conduct commerce and trade) structure is better if the entity has plans to go through several stages of capitalization from different strategic allies and an overall plan to go public at some point. LLCs can work if capital comes from a strategic partner committed to a long-term partnership with no vision of someday taking the entity public.

Visions and Goals

The vision of a PHSJV is to create a community-based, physician-driven ambulatory care system. The primary goal of this new organization is to capture full-risk managed health plan contracts. In geographic areas with competition, the goal may be to prevent other groups or hospitals from obtaining these contracts. Additional goals include the development of new technologies that enhance efficiency and communications, reduced costs, and improved outcomes as measured by the patient. Health systems are increasingly recognizing the need for dedicated MSOs focused on managing a variety of ancillary or ambulatory services.

Governance

The PHSJV is frequently set up as a C corporation, although it can also be set up as a limited liability corporation. Regardless of corporate status, the health system participates as a member of the governing board and may have multiple seats that are often in proportion to the health system's ownership stake. However, depending upon the strategic linkages and the reason for its investment, the health care system may demand certain reserve rights or rights of first refusal. One such right may relate to information systems, with the stipulation that over time, all members will use the same information system. This information system may be provided by the health care system, which may spend a great deal of time and effort to obtain the best system for its market. Other reserve rights generally sought by health systems include control of all risk contracting and ability to veto any sale or dissolution. Four to six operating committees are set up to manage quality, credentialing, network development, infrastructure, managed care, and other issues. Depending on the size of the organization, topics such as quality and credentialing can be handled in one committee. However as the organization grows, a separate credentialing committee should be formed.

Management

Outside consultants are frequently used during the start-up period to accelerate managed care contracting, estimate actuarial risk, support operating committees, and start up information system infrastructure. As internal executives and managers are recruited or assimilated from the medical practices or health system, the use of outside consultants can be reduced. Including a health care system in the joint venture may result in the system's providing guidance for many management functions during the start-up period. This depends on the appropriate outpatient and medical practice operations expertise existing within a health system. Some staff can be pulled on a part-time or full-time basis from the participating medical practices. However, at some point the staff must dedicate 100 percent of their time to the operations of the management company.

Lines of Business

As a complete management company, there will be several primary lines of business: (1) managed care contracting and support (IPA management), (2) comprehensive practice management (practice business operations), and (3) ambulatory service management of related services such as home health, durable medical equipment, urgent care, and demand management systems. Often the management of related ancillary or ambulatory services by the jointly owned management company can mean the difference between an MSO that loses money and one that is profitable. Comprehensive practice management includes performing all of the business and clinical support functions for group practices and all geographical locations. In all endeavors, the management team focuses on revenue generation, efficiency, and controlling costs.

Systems and Functions

The personnel, computer, and communication systems must support the following three functions:

1. **Managed care contracting:**
   - analysis
   - negotiations
   - information services
   - medical director services
   - quality
   - contract management
   - credentialing
2. **Comprehensive practice management:**
   - expense reduction
   - personnel
   - customer service
   - systems development
   - management
   - financial reporting
   - marketing
   - communications
   - billing and collections
   - purchasing
   - capitation management
   - income distribution
3. **Clinical support:**
   - outcomes measures
   - medical management
   - clinical reengineering

Revenue Generation

A management service agreement between the MSO and group practice describes how the revenue is allocated between the two entities. All of the revenue flows through the MSO, which, in turn, receives fees for practice operational activities (such as billing and collections), as well as fees for contract negotiations and management. Depending upon the size of the group, a personnel agency, information system, or telecommunications business may also be developed to create additional revenue by providing these services to the individual practices. Also, revenue and profits can be generated from management of emergency rooms, home health agencies, and other ancillary services by functional and operational management entity.

Distribution of Income

Compensation of the individual physicians, including base salary and benefits, is decided by the compensation committee of the Integrated Group Practice. Various compensation arrangements from salary and performance bonus to modified productivity are used. As the percentage of revenue from capitation contracts increases, the Physician Organization should move toward a salary and bonus structure. Net profits from operations of the MSO are distributed to the individual owners in the form of annual dividends, according to a schedule set by the board of the MSO. The equity interest of the MSO can be held by individual physicians in the group practice or by the Integrated Group Practice as a corporate entity. Likewise, a minority share of the MSO could be owned by an IPA in exchange for a capital investment and a long-term relationship. Distribution of profits can vary. In some cases, profits are retained in the group practice and distributed as year-end bonuses to all members. Other options are to retain profits in the MSO for distribution to equity holders or application to general corporate purposes. To become and remain a strong player in a competitive market, the MSO must retain profits to support the growth of the corporation.

When To Use

This multifaceted MSO business and service company is most appropriate in a level 1 or 2 market. In a level 3 or 4 market, the management company must acquire additional capital to compete, and all physician assets need to be transferred from the group practice or network to the management company. The MSO must show profitability to acquire additional capital for the acquisition of medical practices or other health services.

Variations

There are two variations of the physician health system joint venture. One variation occurs when the health system provides all of the capital to start up the venture. As more doctors buy into the venture, the percentage of the physicians' ownership increases and the percentage of the health system's ownership decreases. A second variation to the scenario occurs when the health system puts up capital equal to the combined assets of the physician practices that are merged into the venture. As with the first scenario, as more physicians join the venture, the percentage of physician ownership increases and the health system's percentage decreases. In both cases, the health system may also offer opportunities to physicians to invest cash, in addition to assets, to increase the physicians' ownership.

Examples

Examples of PHSJVs include: Focus Health Services and Front Range Medical Management, Denver, Colorado; and Integrated Physician Services, Fairfax, Virginia.

Physician Practice Management Company (PPMC)

Description

The public PPMC is a publicly held company that excels in managing medical practices, emergency rooms, group practices, IPAs, and other health care services. The primary focus of most PPMCs is the acquisition of the tangible and intangible assets of group practices for a combination of stock and cash and the long-term management of the revenues and operations of group practices. The PPMC generally should own or manage a certain number of physicians either in a managed group practice or an IPA network in order to attract capitated contracts and benefit from operational economies of scale.

Figure 1–3 illustrates the corporate structure of a holding company and various subsidiaries. In this example, rapid national expansion demands dedicated physician and management teams within wholly owned subsidiaries to focus on different aspects of managing business operations for hundreds of physicians in dozens of group practices and networks. For instance, a number of management consulting firms have been purchased by PPMCs in an effort to obtain a dedicated team of experts in practice acquisition, physician education, and managed care. The PPMC can be characterized as an aggressive consolidator because the corporation will buy a central group practice and then acquire a number of smaller practices in the surrounding geographic area.

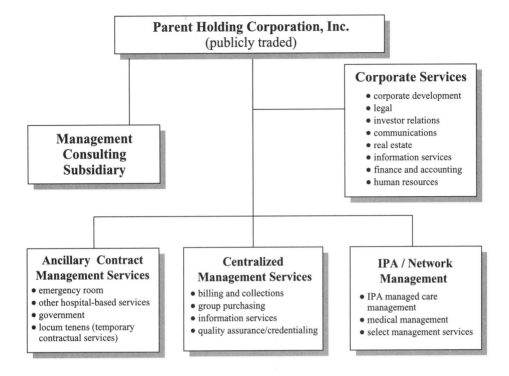

Figure 1–3 Corporate organizational chart for a PPMC. Courtesy of Medical Alliances, Inc., Alexandria, Virginia.

Ownership and Capital

The public holding company, a C corporation, is usually majority owned by the management team and the public markets. Some PPMCs are majority owned by physicians, such as Coastal Health Care Group, Raleigh-Durham, North Carolina (51 percent held by physicians), but it is important to note that a significant portion of the physician ownership could be held by a small group of insider or founder physicians.

Capital is obtained from the public capital markets. Funds for expansion and acquisition are obtained by the sale of stock through public offerings. Institutional and individual investors acquire stock in the entity in this manner. The exchange of paper stock certificates for cash strengthens the balance sheet of the PPMC and allows it to obtain very large short- and long-term lines of credit from major lending institutions, which can further accelerate acquisition of medical practices and national expansion.

When a group practice is acquired, the tangible and intangible assets are moved from the professional corporation to the wholly owned regional management company or the national holding company. Whether there is one or two C corporation entities depends on the number of states served, overall size, and service scope of the PPMC endeavors.

In the acquisition transaction, physicians are given an equity position within the parent company, and the group practice signs a long-term (10- to 30-year) management service agreement with the PPMC. The PPMC develops a regional business plan describing the services and specialties of the group.

It provides all capital for regional expansion, using the anchor group practice as the expansion vehicle. This is an effective development strategy for creating a regional or statewide network and becoming a dominant market force within a particular geographic location. See Chapter 6 for more information on the merger and consolidation process.

Vision and Goals

The vision of the PPMC is to become one of the dominant ambulatory management organizations serving the nation or significant multistate regions. Existing public PPMCs are racing to become billion dollar revenue companies, while newly formed still privately held PPMCs are seeking to break the $100 million mark in the revenue category. The goals of public PPMCs are to: (1) increase revenue and profitability through service expansion and aggressive marketing; (2) grow through merger and acquisition; (3) control at least 25 percent of the medical practice market in operating regions; (4) link together core group practices with networks in a hub-and-spoke pattern to obtain geographic coverage for efficient marketing; (5) position the integrated ambulatory network for full capitation contracting; (6) control the revenue flow of hundreds of medical practices and related health care services; and (7) invest capital necessary for state-of-the-art information systems that will allow revenue maximization under fee-for-service arrangements and efficient operations under capitation.

Governance

There is only one board of directors for the public PPMC. Often, there are regional advisory boards composed of management and physicians who provide advice and counsel relative to regional operations (see Figure 1–4). The regional management companies are supported by an array of com-

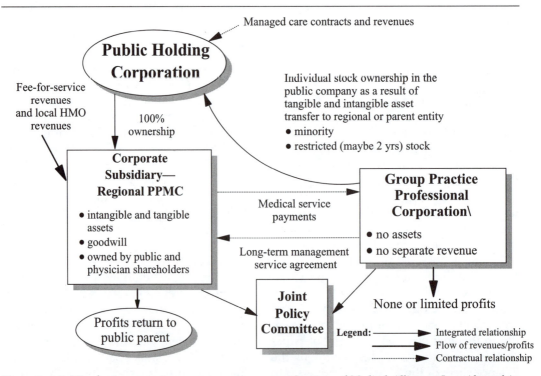

Figure 1–4 Public physician practice management company. Courtesy of Medical Alliances, Inc., Alexandria, Virginia.

mittees, from quality and compensation to managed care contracting and network development. The role of the purchased group practice is spelled out in the management service agreement. Reserve powers related to budget control, agreement modifications, and dissolution are retained by the PPMC. The PPMC sets strategic goals and objectives. Local physician leaders and management develop and implement one- or two-year operating plans. Performance clauses are often built into the management service agreement.

Management

Upon acquisition of the medical practice, some elements of the local management team will be retained if of a suitable caliber. Additional senior executives will be brought in to guide the conversion and expansion of the acquired group practice according to the business plan that is developed.

Lines of Business

The national PPMC includes a number of support services, from owned management consultants to centralized information services. These support services assist regional group practices in upgrading and converting to new systems. All business and clinical support services necessary for the operations of diversified group practices, IPA networks, and related ancillary services are delivered.

Systems and Functions

Comprehensive services are provided in all necessary areas. See the systems and functions list under the physician health system joint venture on page 11 and the function descriptions in the following sections for a discussion of many aspects of management companies.

Revenue Generation

A PPMC generally budgets a percentage of total revenue for operating expenses and shares any benefits from exceeding performance standards with the group practice. The PPMC may offer shares in the corporation to the physicians as additional incentive to practice cost-effective medicine and to share in long-term profits of the corporation.

Distribution of Income

Compensation distribution with the captured group practice is determined by the physicians on the compensation committee of the group. The amount of money available for distribution is based on the terms negotiated in the management service agreement with the management company. In addition, the physician members of the group who have sold their practice assets often receive stock in the PPMC. Over time, depending on the performance of the PPMC, this stock could realize significant appreciation or decline. Periodically, based on the decisions of the board of the public company, profits could be distributed as dividends to all shareholders including physicians. As a shareholder, a physician profits from improved performance and sale of stock back to the company when the physician stops practicing or decides to terminate the relationship. Often individual practice assets are sold to the management company, merging the doctors into the core group practice; this provides a base income while providing incentives to increase profits through productivity and cost reductions.

When To Use

The PPMC can be effective in any stage market, due to its ability to increase fee-for-service revenue while positioning the company for managed care and capitation. This very aggressive corporate organization relies on achieving geographic dominance across a region, state, or multistate area. It can be structured to maximize profitability under fee-for-service in a level 1 or 2 market. In addition, the PPMC can be used to manage group practices, IPAs, and other ambulatory services to allow them to go at risk under capitated contracts with a continuum of owned or managed health care services.

Variations

Variations to PPMCs include public PPMCs and private PPMCs. Public PPMCs have been discussed above. Private PPMCs include numerous privately held management companies that have started from the merger of medical practices or from savvy entrepreneurs who craft business plans, have access to capital, and start acquiring practices. Often, private PPMCs evolve through several stages of capitalization before doing an initial public offering or selling to a larger entity. For instance, Mullikin Medical Centers formed its management company in the late 1980s with approximately $3 million of physicians' money. In 1994, after significant growth, it brought in a minority partner, the Daughters of Charity (a health system), which in turn invested roughly $30 million for a 15 percent equity stake and one seat on the board. In late 1995, Mullikin merged into MedPartners (a public PPMC) and subsequently Pacific Physician Services to create a billion dollar national entity.

Examples

Examples of PPMCs include: PhyCor, Nashville, Tennessee; Coastal Health Care Group, Raleigh-Durham, North Carolina; MedPartners/Mullikin/Pacific Physician Services, Birmingham, Alabama, and Long Beach, California.

Specialty Services Network

Description

Primary care physicians are not the only physicians organizing. In many areas, specialists are developing single-specialty networks in response to market opportunities and the development of primary care dominated group practices. Specialties that are being organized include oncology, cardiology, orthopedics, mental health, and ophthalmology. Many of the regional and national specialty networks involve both a physician network and a management company. The physician network often is a partially integrated structure such as an IPA, LLC, or one or more group practices. The management company is usually a C corporation. If the entity is national, it usually consists of a series of regional management companies that are focused on a state or metropolitan area (see Figure 1–5).

An advantage of a single-specialty network is that the physician component is quicker to organize, because it involves setting up an IPA-like structure rather than merging medical practice assets. The jury is still out on the long-term ability of single-specialty networks to retain hard-won managed care contracts. As integrated, multi-specialty networks form and demonstrate the ability to deliver quality, cost-effective care, purchasers and payers may find the convenience of one-stop shopping and check writing too great to continue working with numerous different single-specialty networks.

Ownership and Capital

The Physician Organization, whether a professional corporation (PC) or limited liability corporation (LLC) group practice, or IPA, is owned 100 percent by the physicians. The critical issue in forming such a group is the functions and services that will be the responsibility of the affiliated Physician Organization. The ownership of the management company varies, depending on the size, scope, and history of the organization. In an aggressive national expansion of a specialty network, the majority of all tangible and intangible assets have been turned over to the management company. If the physician founders take more risk by investing their own capital for the start-up and bringing in an alliance partner after initial operations, then a greater percentage of the management company may be owned by physicians.

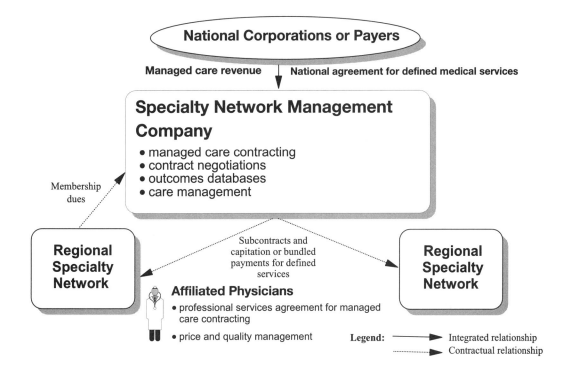

Figure 1–5 Specialty services network. Courtesy of Medical Alliances, Inc., Alexandria, Virginia.

Vision and Goals

The vision of the specialty services network involves creating geographically accessible single-specialty networks with high-quality practices that can go at risk for a defined set of medical and health care services and deliver quality, cost-effective health services related to a particular specialty. Many of these specialty networks are attempting to create a critical mass through the expansion of locations in major markets and the linkages of affiliated practices within the specialty that meets the needs for geographic coverage in a market area. Many of these entities are focused on regional and national development.

Governance

The Physician Organization is governed by a physician board of managers with various physician committees that may include: quality, risk management, and compensation. The election of the physician leaders and committee members is defined in the bylaws of the organization. The management company has a board of directors that is representative of its investors and capital partners. If physicians own 51 percent of the stock, then they may have a majority of the seats on the board, with alliance partners (such as venture capitalists or a health system) holding other seats. The PPMC management also holds one or more seats on the board. The total number of board members, method of election, and committee structure vary—depending on the bylaws of the organization.

Management

A management team on a national and regional basis must be developed to operate the PPMC. Often the regional component of the PPMC would involve an expansion of the existing practice administrative staff of the IPA or group practice. For instance, the National Cardiovascular Network (NCN) has a centralized management function and uses the regional practice management staff of each cardiology member. In this case, because NCN is primarily a membership organization, the local administrative staff remain employees of the local cardiology practice. On the other hand, Physician Reliance Network employs all clinical and management staff of regional practices that merge in or are acquired by the parent.

Lines of Business

The primary services relate to the activities required for managed care contract management. These include contract negotiation, performance tracking, medical management, and selective practice management consulting. More aggressive types of specialty initiatives involve the consolidation of medical practice assets under a private or public management company. In this case, comprehensive practice management services are delivered and involve the employment of all business staff and management of business operations.

Systems and Functions

Many single-specialty networks focus on providing managed care contracting, information systems, capitation management, and medical management services. Some single-specialty networks involve the total merger of practice assets and consequently deliver managed care contracting/medical management services and comprehensive practice management of all business operations of integrated medical practices.

Revenue Generation

The primary source of revenue is the medical practice revenue generated through physician services provided. Depending on the specialty, various ancillary services are integrated into network operations for enhanced patient services and revenues. For instance, a comprehensive ophthalmology network could include a series of optical shops with eyeglasses and optometrists, a statewide obstetrics/gynecology (OB/GYN) network could include an infertility center, and an oncology network could involve comprehensive outpatient cancer treatment centers.

Distribution of Income

Many types of specialty networks do not involve a total consolidation of medical practices, but merely an agreement to be a participant in managed care contracts. In this case, medical practice members would generate revenue from contracts and services delivered under negotiated contracts by the national alliance and from existing patients in the practice.

Variations

There are three approaches to the specialty services network:

1. **Union-like.** The union-like specialty care network can come with numerous business and legal problems. If it is not designed with the right geographic distribution and number of specialists, it begins to resemble a union, with too many physicians of the same specialty. This could raise significant antitrust concerns. While a union-type organization may raise more money, it is not likely to attract purchaser contracts, due to the oversupply of physicians relative to the needs of the patient population.
2. **Selective panel.** The selective panel single-specialty network is appropriately designed and involves a limited number of geographically dispersed specialty practices throughout a region or state. To attract managed care contracts, the specialty network must be in specialties that have high-volume and high-cost procedures. Medical specialties that purchasers are receptive to in-

clude cardiovascular; ophthalmology; OB/GYN; ear, nose, and throat; and orthopedics. Successful versions of these networks have several characteristics in common, including a strong medical director, an effective information system, physicians who are savvy about managed care, and a good management team. Sometimes all of the practices in a geographic area are managed by a common MSO owned by physician members of the network, and other times the practices go through a true merger of assets.

3. **Network of networks.** In several areas of the country, there are efforts to organize a series of specialty networks under a common management company. This can be called a network of single-specialty networks. For instance, an IPA management company may establish five to seven different IPAs, one for each specialty. Then the management company would package the range of services and market to managed care organizations for an entire range of carve-out contracts in the combined specialties. The physicians would maintain ownership of their practices but would access managed care contracting services from the central management entity. To be successful, specialists must not view this as a way to protect income, but as a way to maintain the practice of selected specialties in a fixed-budget, capitated environment.

When To Use

In a level 1 or 2 market, organizing single-specialty networks can be very advantageous. Many managed health plans are just learning how to capitate, and a coordinated network of specialists with a strong medical director has the chance of winning capitation or bundle contracts. Single-specialty networks can also serve as a joint marketing vehicle to stimulate patient flow to member practices in a predominantly fee-for-service environment. In a level 3 or 4 market, as utilization in the specialist market decreases dramatically, the single-specialty network is one option for physicians who are forced to merge to access patients from group practices or integrated delivery systems.

Examples

Examples of specialty services networks include the following:

- Physician Reliance Network is one of the nation's largest oncology practice management companies. It is a Dallas-based national provider of management facilities, administration, technical support, and ancillary services necessary to establish and maintain a fully integrated network of outpatient oncology care. The company is the largest oncology practice management company in the United States, managing the practices of 173 physicians in 59 practice locations. In 1995, several public offerings were completed that raised over $80 million. Its shares are traded in the NASDAQ Stock Market (National Market) under the symbol PHYN. President Michael Reese, M.D., says:

    Physician Reliance Network is a logical choice for oncologists who are increasingly concerned about the impact of managed care and the demands of payors. We help oncologists retain the important responsibility for providing high quality, personalized services to their patients by developing oncology networks which deliver cost-effective care. Our company recognizes the major role of the physician in the cost/quality equation, and we ensure that they will have access to capital, management and business expertise to participate as equals with other providers.[4]

- A leading example of a specialty carve-out network is the National Cardiovascular Network (NCN) based in Atlanta. The founders include physicians involved in the original Health Care Financing Administration (HCFA) cardiovascular charge bundling demonstration projects. It has approximately 700 physicians from 35 cardiovascular group practices across the country and is targeted to grow to 60 practices in major regional markets. It currently holds managed care contracts for inpatient and outpatient invasive cardiac services with an emphasis on coronary artery bypass grafts and angioplasties for over 7 million patients. The network aims to go at risk and accept global bundled fees for a full range of cardiac procedures. It contracts with HMOs, Preferred Provider Organizations (PPOs), and self-insured employers and is creating a national database on resource use, length-of-stay outcomes, and so forth to improve practice guidelines. In late 1995, NCN formed an alliance with Johnson and Johnson, which invested significant capital in exchange for 20 percent or more equity position.
- Additional examples include: Pediatrix, Fort Lauderdale, Florida (specialty pediatrics); Physician Resource Group, Houston, Texas (ophthalmology); Salick and SalickNet, Los Angeles, California (oncology); Omega, Memphis, Tennessee (ophthalmology); Viva and Medical Network Enterprises, North Miami Beach, Florida (multispecialty).

Issues

Should a Physician Organization include specialty physicians as well as primary care physicians? If so, how many and of what type? Should a specialty care network consist of a variety of specialties or a single specialty? Before developing a specialty care network, ask these questions:

- Does the nature of procedures warrant special attention on cost management and bundled pricing?
- Will the Managed Care Organizations buy the service or procedure? How do you know?
- Where has a similar network been developed? What have been the results? What are the critical success factors?
- What is the network's potential in this area?
- What is the appropriate capitation rate for your specialty?
- How much risk are you willing to tolerate?
- What is included and excluded in managed care negotiations?
- How would you rate the quality and cost-effectiveness of physicians and groups in your networks?
- What are the needs of demographic groups that would use your services?

Venture Medical Management Company

Description

In a venture medical management company, a physician group practice teams up with a well-funded capital partner such as a venture capitalist or mezzanine financing firm to (1) rapidly merge and consolidate hundreds of medical practices, (2) show a reasonable profit margin, and (3) take the management company public within one to three years. Mezzanine financing is a second or third stage of capitalization that is acquired after one or two rounds of owner financing, but before a public offering. This type of equity alliance must grow rapidly and expand services through a variety of regions to meet the investment criteria of public markets. Rapid growth demands significant capital for practice acquisitions, mergers, management, and infrastructure development. This fast track to a public offering for the lead management company moves rapidly through several stages of capitalization: founders' contribution, one or two private placements, and eventually a public offering. This is not a sale of a group practice to an existing public PPMC; it is the progressive development of a private management company that hopes to go public on its own at some point in the future (see Figure 1–6).

Ownership and Capital

Physician members typically retain 100 percent ownership of the group practice, but nearly 100 percent of its assets are transferred to the management company. The amount owned by venture investors varies widely from minority to majority status. All financially driven investors are seeking an above-average rate of return (from 25 to 40 percent per annum over time). This return may be in the form of annual dividend distributions, profits from the sale of stock in an initial public offering (IPO), or sale of the company to a larger corporation. In many cases, the greatest financial return for physician owners and investors may be through an IPO.

Vision and Goals

The vision of the venture medical management company is to build a very large regional or national publicly held health care services company. The goals include building a profitable practice management company, improving the delivery of care while lowering its costs, improving operational efficiencies, and practicing cost-efficient medicine that provides acceptable levels of patient quality and satisfaction.

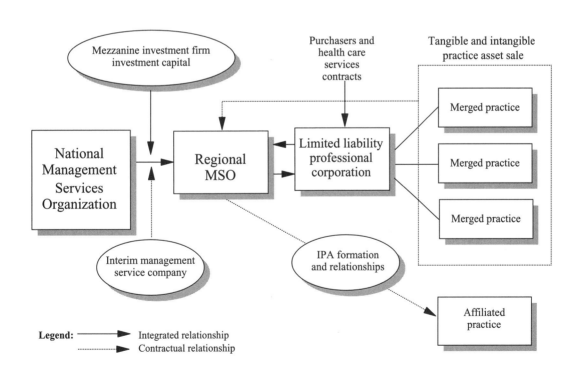

Figure 1–6 Venture medical management company. *Source:* Adapted from American Clinical Management, Sudbury, Massachusetts.

Governance

Governance varies with each situation. Generally, because the capital infusion from outside, nonphysician investors occurs during the organization's early stages of rapid growth, the outside investors own a larger percentage of the management company from the outset. However, an investment entity is critical for introducing other financial or management resources that ensure that the venture is successful and achieves a public offering or profitable sale to an outside corporation. Regardless of minority or majority status, the investor group will insist upon certain rights, which usually include the right to make final financial decisions regarding the acquisition of major capital equipment, dissolution, approval of annual operating budget, and perhaps veto on selection of senior management.

Management

Professional managers are brought in by the investor group to ensure proper development and attainment of group goals. The venture capital firm provides oversight management of business functions related to capitalization and overall growth, but allows the physicians to practice medicine and the management teams to run day-to-day business operations.

Lines of Business

Venture medical management companies focus on managing group practices, including managed care contracting and other practice operations, and managing the managed care contracting for affiliated IPAs or networks. The focus of these organizations is to increase revenue through service expansion while the opportunity exists in many markets and to position for managed care through the development of regional networks. In many markets where fee-for-service is still the dominant form of reimbursement, there is a tremendous opportunity to build additional patient volume for underutilized services through combined regional marketing activity. The major services include comprehensive practice management, which includes all business and clinical support services required in the current market.

Variations

There are numerous spins on the venture medical management company. Some of these companies have two levels of MSO and others only one. The role of the capital partner varies, depending on the firm. It is important to ask for a copy of the venture's business plan, including the five-year financial projections. When practices sell into this sort of arrangement, they are betting on the fact that the management team has a successful track record in developing public companies and has the development expertise to meet expansion goals. Major variations relate to the phases of capitalization and whether there are two, three, or more stages of private financing prior to a public offering.

Examples

Examples of venture medical management companies include: Continuum Care Corporation (PhyChoice), West Palm Beach, Florida; Prime Health, Bloomington, Connecticut; American Clinical Management and TA Associates, Boston, Massachusetts; and Sheridan Healthcare Group, Fort Lauderdale, Florida.

Physician Equity Alliance

Description

These multifaceted Physician Organizations are centered around three linked structures: an Integrated Group Practice (IGP), a practice Management Services Organization (MSO) that is majority-owned by physicians, and an associated Independent Practice Association (IPA). The Physician Equity Alliance focuses on the development of clinically effective multilocation group practices—composed initially of primary care physicians and selected specialists—through a total merger (financial, legal, and operational) of solo and small group practices (see Figure 1–7).

Ownership and Capital

The physician group practice and IPA are owned 100 percent by the physician members. The management company is initially capitalized by founding physicians and their medical practices. During the first year of operations, the management company is owned 100 percent by physicians. Lines of credit may be obtained from health systems or lending institutions to support initial operations. Physicians capitalize the merger and management company with internally generated funds.

Following a merger, the development of managed care contracts, and the integration of operational functions, these multifaceted organizations typically sell a minority interest in the MSO to a strategic ally. After evaluating possible allies (such as a health system, pharmaceutical company, or private investors), the alliance selects a partner who complements community, market, and business objectives. The relationship is based not on making the Physician Equity Alliance a secondary subsidiary of a Physician-Hospital Organization or Medical Foundation, but on making it a leader that can work with purchasers. This approach maintains most of the practice equity and feelings of ownership that exist in private practice but creates a

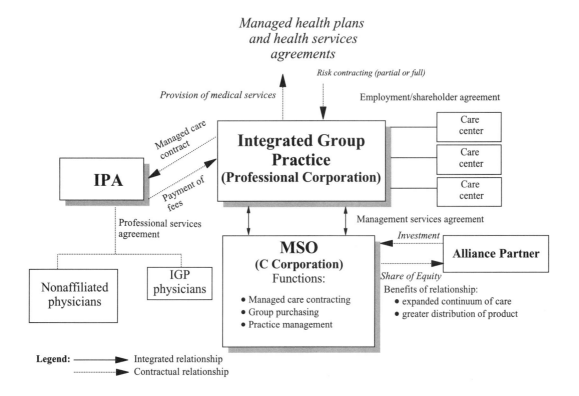

Figure 1–7 Physician Equity Alliance. Courtesy of Medical Alliances, Inc., Alexandria, Virginia.

structure that can compete in today's marketplace.

Vision and Goals

The vision of the Physician Equity Alliance is to create a large, multispecialty ambulatory health care delivery system that is sufficiently capitalized and has majority ownership by physicians. The overall goal is to maintain majority physician ownership for as long as possible during the development and expansion process. Other goals include improvement of practice operational efficiency, aggressive marketing through traditional and new media to attract new patients, enhancement of quality through collaboration, and expansion of geographic access to ambulatory health care services. Revenue growth is a major objective. Because this entity is a complete merger, the development or acquisition of additional ancillary services such as laboratories, imaging services, or surgical centers can occur. Outside management contracts for urgent care centers and other ambulatory care services can also be obtained.

Management

The management team is assembled from the strongest practice managers and staff from the merging group practices. Other management positions will be filled from the outside. Creating a functional management team is absolutely essential. The CEO and president must have a track record in building growth companies that evolve very quickly from business enterprises of $10 million to $100 million or more.

Lines of Business

The major services of the Physician Equity Alliance include comprehensive practice management, which includes all business and clinical support services required in the current market. These include group purchasing, support staff, billing and collections, managed care contracting, marketing, cost management, business development, physician recruitment, and anything else required by a group practice and affiliated IPA network.

Functions and Systems

The management company provides a comprehensive array of services to every location within the core group practice and all of the affiliated IPA members. All practice management and managed care contracting activities are provided to the group practice. For the affiliated IPAs, a limited management service agreement guides the provision of managed care contracting and medical management services for a fee of 10 to 15 percent of the physicians' revenue via contracts negotiated by the PPMC.

Revenue Generation

Revenues are generated from professional fees, ancillary services, management fees for managed care contracting services from affiliated IPAs, and risk and withhold pool distributions.

Variations

The pure Physician Equity Alliance is similar to the venture medical management company, except that the Physician Equity Alliance is majority physician owned throughout its private and public shareholder status. In the venture medical management company, public markets or private, nonphysician investors could be the majority owners from the outset and maintain control throughout the organization's development.

Examples

Examples of Physician Equity Alliances include: American Health Network, Indianapolis, Indiana; Doctors Healthcare, Inc., and Baltimore Medical Group, Baltimore, Maryland; Atlantic Health Network, West Palm Beach, Florida (IPA, MSO, and Group); Physician Health Care Alliance, and CHCPhysicians, New Haven, Connecticut.

Issues

The key principle of success for the Physician Equity Alliance is to be a health care company and not merely a primary care delivery business. When comparing Physician Organizations, Integrated Delivery Systems, and Physician Equity Alliances, use the following questions to analyze the appropriateness of a new health care organization to a specific community:

- Is governance from the top down, or is it from the bottom up and based on physician involvement?
- Are managed care contracting and medical practice management featured in the same organizational structure?
- Who owns the majority interest of the new organizational entity—the community, a Physician Organization, an insurance entity, or a Wall Street-backed health care management company?
- Do the values and goals of the capital source match community values and the goals of physicians and executive leaders?
- What are the entity's sources of capital? Are these sources public or private? Is sufficient capital available to achieve the vision? How will future sources of capital affect the ownership and governance structure?
- How does the governance structure determine who will make strategic and operational decisions?
- What information systems strategy will support integration? How much information systems infrastructure is already in place?
- Does the evolving alliance meet criteria for long-term financial viability and a stable patient care delivery system?

It is the responsibility of clinical physician leaders to ensure that new equity alliances and integrated systems: (1) meet community needs for quality, (2) reorganize the care delivery system to cut costs, (3) address legal issues, and (4) redesign governance and management systems so they are capable of managing the health of entire populations rather than simply treating sick individuals.

PROFILING MANAGEMENT SERVICES ORGANIZATIONS AS A CENTRAL ELEMENT

MSOs or PPMCs are the ubiquitous glue of Physician Organizations, as they bind together the practices and implement standardized practice management systems and operations. An MSO can, in reality, do whatever its owner wants it to do. But its focus is on managing physician practices more effectively than ever before and, therefore, making them more profitable than ever before. And the most effective way to accomplish this is through economies of scale. See Figures 1–8 and 1–9.

MSOs are multiplying rapidly. Every type of business—from electronic data systems, to major pharmaceutical companies, to physician group practices and health systems—sees an opportunity with MSOs. These businesses have determined that negotiating managed care contracts is but one step in an extended process, and that the real challenge comes in managing and coordinating large-scale, primary care medical networks to achieve resource consumption and utilization goals.

Wall Street–backed management companies, health systems, group practices, and other health care organizations have already established PPMCs to acquire and manage group practices and IPA networks. For example, insurance companies such as New York Life have purchased medical practice management companies as vehicles to acquire and manage primary care medical practices. Elsewhere, investors are channeling billions of dollars into for-profit, privately financed companies such as Med Partners/Mullikin/Pacific Physician Services and publicly traded physician practice management companies such as PhyCor and PHP Healthcare.

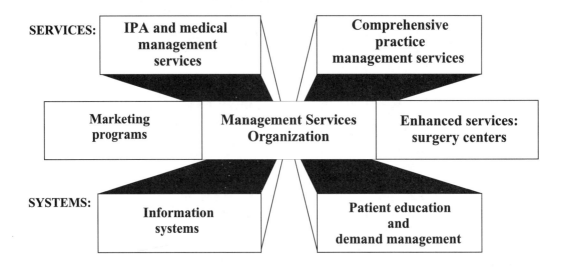

Figure 1–8 Profile of MSO services categories. Courtesy of Medical Alliances, Inc., Alexandria, Virginia.

Other groups—from emergency medical management companies such as Coastal Healthcare to Physician-Hospital Organizations—have launched MSOs to gain control of primary care practices and climb to the top of the managed care contracting pyramid. Their rationale is: the closer an organization is to the top of the pyramid, the easier it can achieve profitable operations under fixed capitation contracts.

The composition of MSOs also varies. Some emphasize primary care and feature internal medicine, family practice, pediatrics, and OB/GYN. Others, such as PhyCor (Nashville, Tennessee), focus on the acquisition of multispecialty group practices with more than 30 physicians. (PhyCor has recently acquired an IPA management company out of Texas and started a second network management company with off-balance-sheet financing.)

MSOs respond to physicians' desire to focus on practicing medicine by allowing other parties to take over the organization's business management. While some MSOs acquire medical practices, others serve exclusively as a comprehensive practice management company, obtaining long-term contracts to deliver such services as facilities management, group purchasing, billing and collections, and managed care contract negotiations. Acting as a separate legal entity, an MSO improves a practice's cost-effectiveness by managing its business operations. Typically, a central medical management company provides comprehensive practice management services to group practices, independent physicians, or perhaps an IPA (see Figure 1–10).

Highly flexible, the MSO offers a variety of services and functions in different configurations. Consider these examples:

- PhyCor signed a 30-year management service agreement with a group practice that gave PhyCor rights to 100 percent of the practice's revenue stream. Contemporaneously, PhyCor signed a provider service agreement stating it would return 40 percent or some other set percentage to the group as physician compensation. Often, profits generated are split between the medical group and management company. Group practices

Building Effective Physician Equity Alliances and Organizations 27

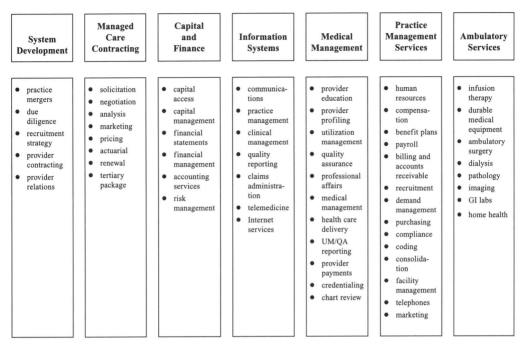

Figure 1–9 Management Services Organization services and functions. Courtesy of Medical Alliances, Inc., Alexandria, Virginia.

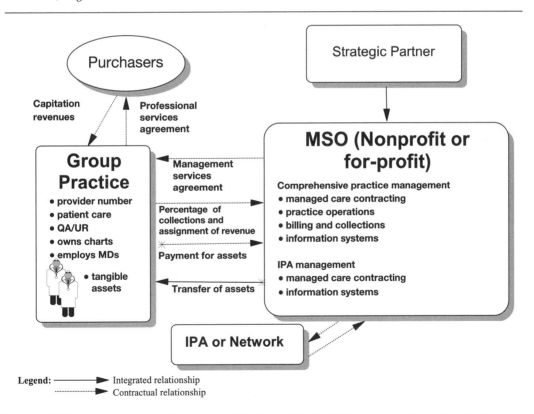

Figure 1–10 Management Services Organization. Courtesy of Medical Alliances, Inc., Alexandria, Virginia.

that enter into these long-term agreements must pay attention to the management company's ability to unilaterally reduce the percentage or change the terms of the compensation agreement after an initial term of three to five years.
- A subsidiary of a major pharmaceutical company is planning to make 10 to 15 minority investments in physician-owned MSOs that provide management services such as operations management, outcomes tracking, and managed care contract negotiations.

Despite the advantages, some experts question the impact of a long-term relationship with a for-profit, publicly traded management company on physician income. In explaining why physicians who sold their practices to Coastal Physician Group, Inc., subsequently sold their stock, Coastal's senior vice president of investor relations said: "Many physicians are selling shares to supplement salaries that were decreased after they sold their practices to Coastal. There are significant decreases in salary. They need access to the liquidity."[5]

Some health care organizations also use MSO management structures to develop one or more group practices, which tend to be composed of primary care physicians. In these cases, the MSO's executive director serves as a skilled practice manager and as senior executive who guides the development of a multilocation, multispecialty group practice. Sometimes the MSO or group practice development team may also turn to outside management consultants to assist physician leaders in organizing new group practices.

The MSO typically contracts with group practices to provide business management services and managed care contract negotiating services, but it stops short of providing clinical services. The group practice retains the provider number as well as patient charts. The MSO acquires the tangible assets of the practice, leaving intangibles such as charts and goodwill with the group practice. Often compensation and quality management remain the responsibility of the group practice. The decision to retain tangible and intangible assets usually depends on the type of MSO and the desires of the group practice physicians.

There are several major variations of the MSO:

- **Service bureau MSO.** In this scenario, physicians remain independent legal entities who purchase services from the MSO at fair market value. These services, which can include practice assessments, billing, collections, group purchasing, negotiating/contracting, physician referral services, personnel services, equipment leasing, practice valuation, and coding review, are arranged in a menu from which any physician or group practice can choose. While similar programs frequently operate through hospital-based physician relations programs, the management company of a service bureau MSO functions as a separate legal entity.
- **Comprehensive practice management MSO.** Typically headed by executives who can manage medical practices effectively and run entrepreneurial businesses, this type of MSO provides comprehensive practice management services to group practices for 35 to 60 percent of net collections. Assuming responsibility for nonphysician expenses and employing all office and business staff, the MSO provides all business services including group purchasing, hiring, training, financial controls, billing, and contracting. However, it stops short of acquiring the practice's tangible or intangible assets.
- **Management and asset acquiring MSO.** This MSO pays fair market value for the hard assets of practices in the process of being consolidated into a multilocation group practice. How-

ever, to steer clear of legal pitfalls, non-profit health systems usually avoid paying for patient charts, ongoing value, or the value associated with inpatient referrals. In most cases, the physician or group practice signs a long-term management contract for which the MSO provides all business and managed care contracting services. Compensation for services arrives in the form of a percentage of the practice's collections, cost plus, or some other fee arrangement.[6]

MSOs seem to have become the most prevalent integration structure in health care markets across the country. Group practices, health systems, Managed Care Organizations, and some pharmaceutical companies are launching practice management initiatives to ally with or acquire medical practices. For instance, pharmaceuticals represent about 7 percent of the health care dollar, so rather than think of themselves as chemical companies, they see themselves as health care companies. Integrated Physician Organizations and group practices can acquire capital from majority or minority investors at significant valuation. According to Thomas Hodapp, Vice President of Robertson Stephens & Company, "Physician practice management companies and the wave to Integrated Delivery Systems . . . [is the] initial stage of a major trend. This is a tremendous untapped investment opportunity—physicians represent over $150 billion or 19 percent of the health care budget; further, physicians control additionally over $500 billion in referral revenue. Meanwhile, publicly traded physician practice management companies represent under $1 billion in market value."[7] This popularity is a function of an MSO's flexibility, the ability to attract capital, and the need to affect the way ambulatory facilities are organized and function. Over the next several years, MSOs will continue to grow in size and influence.

UNDERSTANDING EVOLVING PHYSICIAN ORGANIZATIONS

Successful Integrated Delivery Systems depend on strong, clinically effective Physician Organizations, and these entities must evolve to meet the demands of a restructured health care market. The real priority is not the organization's relationship with a hospital or HMO, but relationships and communications between and among physicians and effective organizational structures for housing Physician Organizations. The second priority is to expand and develop the organization so physician leadership and ownership remain a core characteristic.

Figure 1–11 illustrates a continuum of physician organizational types, moving from less integration to more integration of clinical, financial, and operational functions. This continuum is not straight, which is represented by the curves in the line. The more integrated the Physician Organization, the more bends and curves in the development path. As physicians organize and integrate, it is necessary to evaluate the differences between horizontal and vertical integration. Horizontal tends to represent flatter, more networked organizational structures, while vertical reflects hierarchy and more layers of governance. Information system technology is an enabling technology that allows network arrangements to compete very effectively. Across many industries in the country today, organizations that are structured in flatter, network fashions are demonstrating they can compete better than vertically oriented hierarchies. The keys to integrating physician practices are communications and information systems that allow various network structures to compete effectively to manage care.

Examples of dramatic and rapid evolution in the physician practice management market include the following:

- In 1991, PhyCor acquired long-term management service agreements with

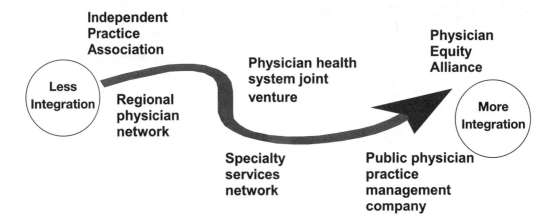

Figure 1–11 Types of Physician Organizations. Courtesy of Medical Alliances, Inc., Alexandria, Virginia.

multispecialty group practices in rural markets and increased fee-for-service revenue. By 1995, PhyCor managed group practices in suburban and metropolitan areas, owned two IPA network management companies, and was positioning aggressively for capitation.

- In 1990, PHP Healthcare was primarily a military contractor operating primary care clinics for various divisions of the military. By 1995, it had successfully shifted to the private sector, operating primary care centers for Blue Cross Blue Shield plans and other health care organizations under long-term management agreements. Its stock price rose from approximately $5 to over $40 per share during this period.
- In 1994, Friendly Hills Medical Group converted to a nonprofit medical foundation and gained IRS approval for tax exemption, following a legal contest that lasted 18 months and cost millions of dollars. At the time, it was being heralded as a sustainable, nonprofit, tax-exempt health system. In 1995, the assets of Friendly Hills were acquired by Caremark International, a diversified health management company that was shifting its strategic focus from home care to the PPMC market.
- In 1993, MedPartners was a privately held management company with no physician practice under management. But, it had access to a high-quality management team and hundreds of millions of dollars of Wall Street capital. In early 1995, it went public with 400 physicians under management. By the end of 1995, it was the largest public PPMC after mergers with Mullikin Medical Centers and Pacific Physician Services. Total revenue at the end of 1995 was expected to reach $1.4 billion.
- From 1993 to 1995, a little over two years, Baltimore Medical Group—a group of 20 primary care physicians—has evolved from 20 physicians in a group practice without walls to a regional health system called Doctors Health System. It grew through physician leadership and collaboration with several alliance partners.
- American Health Network is a joint venture between primary care physicians and The Associated Group (a $4 billion diversified insurance company) that grew from five physicians in 1994

to more than 200 in 18 months. It expanded from its base in Indianapolis to over seven regional markets in the central part of the United States.

The six major types of physician equity models described in this chapter are not hard and fast. One type of organization can often evolve into another through a merger or an acquisition. For instance, a venture medical management company could be sold to an Integrated Delivery System or go public and become a publicly held Physician Practice Management Company. When a PPMC goes public, some key questions for physicians are: (1) How much of the company is still owned by physician shareholders, initial investors, and now the public market? (2) What are the implications for physician owners?

One thing about the future is clear: integrated, multispecialty, multidimensional, multiple-entity health care organizations will play a clear leadership role. Health care is a trillion dollar industry. It is big business, and consumers require a lot of it. The industry mission must be to transform the care delivery model from individual to group practice and to create a vehicle for providing total care to defined populations for fixed fees. The primary goals are: (1) to develop a geographically dispersed ambulatory care network that is attractive to purchasers; (2) to accept and manage risk contracts by spreading risk among more physicians; (3) to provide enhanced revenue and income security to physicians; and (4) to improve the quality of life for physicians by allowing them to focus on practicing medicine and reducing on-call requirements.

As physicians expand and pursue new variations of Physician Organizations and Physician Equity Alliances, they continue to struggle with control issues. To deal effectively with the conflict and politics surrounding these issues, physician leaders need to differentiate between (1) clinical control; (2) business operations control; and (3) financial and cash flow control. Only by dealing with each type of control separately and in the context of an organization's core values can physicians make wise decisions about the kind of Physician Organization to pursue.

As physician leaders guide the merger process, they must identify the functions and services to be centralized and the entity that should hold practice assets. Among the issues that must be addressed are the following:

- Where does the market demand positioning the initiative?
- Will the new group operate ancillary services?
- Is the group serious about accepting risk and capitated contracts?
- Can physicians truly cooperate to manage care?
- What sources of capital will be used to develop the management and information systems?

The answers to these questions are critical. But too frequently the questions remain unasked. Physician and executive leaders tend to forsake a marketplace focus in favor of doing "what will work for the merging physicians."

TODAY'S MARKET COMPETITION DEMANDS ACTION AND MERGER

The many variations of the Physician Equity Alliance recognize that provider organizations need allies. For physician leaders, the results are worth the effort. Developing such organizations requires risk and investment of both sweat equity and practice skills. Still, by moving through progressive rounds of financing and applying lessons from other start-up and emerging growth companies, physicians can build increasingly large organizations with physician influence and clinical control. In this process, it is important to follow the growth principles outlined in Exhibit 1–1.

Exhibit 1–1 Growth Principles

- Nurture strong, visionary physician leaders.
- Establish agreements on goals, values, and guiding principles.
- Invite the best physicians who get along with one another to merge first.
- Recognize that where you start is not where you will finish.
- Do what the market requires, not what physicians want.
- Think multispecialty, but make sure there is a primary base and leadership.
- Consolidate legally and financially.
- Obtain the best executive and management talent.
- Seek capital partners who match your values.
- Avoid consensus decision making and develop a strong governance structure.

The Physician Equity Alliance offers a unique alternative for physicians wooed with buy-out and employment offers from control-oriented hospitals, for-profit management companies, or insurance companies scrambling to build staff model delivery systems. It does not make sense for physicians to sell out at a low valuation when they can produce higher long-term financial returns by investing in a powerful multispecialty group practice and an owned Management Services Organization.

NOTES

1. D. Goldstein, *Alliances: Strategies for Building Integrated Delivery Systems* (Gaithersburg, Md.: Aspen Publishers, Inc., 1995).

2. PPMC: Market, Financial and Operating Statistics for Physician Practice Management Companies, PPMC, August 1995, p. A.

3. P. Starr, *The Transformation of American Medicine* (New York, N.Y.: Basic Books, Inc., 1982).

4. M. Reese, *Business Wire*, 11 September 1995.

5. K. Dennard, Docs Who Invested Spur Coastal Selloff, *Triangle Business Journal* (Durham, N.C.), 25 November 1994, p. 1.

6. Goldstein, *Alliances*, pp. 114–115.

7. T. Hodapp, Physician Practice Management and the Wave to Integrated Delivery Systems (Institutional research, Robertson Stephens & Company, New York, November 23, 1993).

Chapter 2

System Building Blocks To Manage Capitation

Douglas Goldstein

INTRODUCTION

The changing health care environment and the rise of capitated reimbursement are fueling the development of organizational structures that can manage financial risk and compete with other medical organizations in delivering high-quality health care. These new, medically directed, market-driven Integrated Delivery Systems will ultimately replace independent medical practices.

The mergers and consolidation of providers and health plans of the mid-1990s laid the groundwork for risk-bearing, medically coordinated, management-linked organizations that can deliver high-quality, cost-effective health care services along the continuum of care. In the near future, the health care environment will feature local and regional "cradle-to-grave" health care delivery networks formed, defined, and directed by physician leaders.

What do these developments mean for physicians? To survive and flourish in the medical marketplace of the twenty-first century, physician leaders and executives must learn to catalyze, guide, and manage the physician and clinical provider networks that will be the backbone of new Integrated Delivery Systems. But how can physicians make the transition from their traditional roles as independent medical practitioners to leaders and team members of physician organizations that provide a quality-oriented, risk-managing, integrated health care delivery system? What linkages must they forge? And where do they begin?

This chapter explores the basic system building blocks necessary for managing Physician Organizations. These building blocks are nothing less than the essential clinical and business systems of effective health care organizations. Ultimately, these systems are the keys to business cost control, improvement of quality and care delivery, and success in the tough environment of fixed-payment and capitated reimbursement.

Figure 2–1 illustrates the nine clinical and management system building blocks needed to deliver high-quality, cost-effective health care:

1. integrated communications and information systems
2. process measures and outcomes reporting
3. multispecialty physician networks
4. demand management and disease management systems

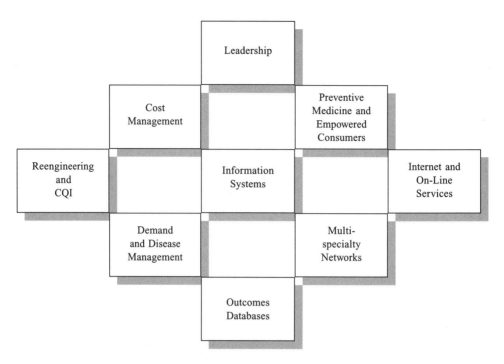

Figure 2–1 System building blocks. Courtesy of Medical Alliances, Inc., Alexandria, Virginia.

---

5. continuous quality improvement (CQI) and clinical reengineering
6. Internet and on-line services
7. cost reduction and cost management
8. preventive medicine and empowered consumers
9. physician and executive leadership

The central building block is the information management system. It is the heart of such critical elements as outcomes databases, multispecialty networks, and disease management techniques. The information management system also affects the ability to deliver clinical reengineering, quality control, and innovative applications of on-line technologies for patient access. These system building blocks interconnect with those dealing with cost management, disease prevention, and consumer empowerment. However, physician and executive leadership remains the most critical building block of all.

INTEGRATED COMMUNICATIONS AND INFORMATION SYSTEMS

The merger, integration, and linkage of small medical practices into larger, physician-driven organizations require advanced information systems. Capturing financial and clinical data is essential to integrating insurance and care delivery and meeting the needs of a market that cries out for real-time, quantitatively based quality measures, exceptional customer service, and value-based purchasing.

Communications and computer technology continue to revolutionize customer service, care delivery, cost management, patient care, and interactions among physicians. If physicians want to maintain control over health care delivery, they must invest in information technology that supports coordinated inpatient and outpatient care.

The benefits of advanced information systems are well documented. Using these systems, Physician Organizations can accomplish the following:

- measure, manage, and reduce costs
- enhance customer services
- retain medical management capabilities
- prepare for risk by analyzing patient demographics
- provide health services under capitation
- track quality and utilization data
- manage referral patterns

Physician Organizations must create organized systems of care that function like electronically and digitally linked virtual networks. These systems must be seamless and designed from the patient's point of view. When a patient contacts a Physician Organization by phone or walks into one of its offices or diagnostic centers, up-to-date patient records should be immediately available. Moreover, the system should be able to quickly perform insurance functions such as immediate verification of eligibility and benefits. To allow seamless access to patient information for patient assessment, the following information technologies are required:

- a telecommunications network
- physicians and office staff trained in the use of computer and network technology
- high-speed (486 or better) computer equipment
- a broad-band network
- computers with graphical-user interfaces
- electronic data interfaces with lab systems
- master patient index
- summary registration information
- electronic medical record (EMR)
- relational database archive

Even more communications and information tools are needed during patient treatment and follow-up:

- a wide-area network
- teleradiography, telepathology, and telemedicine
- systematic measurement
- data entry into relational databases
- standardized patient care information
- standardized outcomes surveys for all patients
- financial and clinical cost accounting systems
- decision support systems, including software for statistics and clinical databases for research

Unprecedented demands for information from employers, patients, and physicians have already led to the creation of medical informatics, a discipline that focuses on the storage, retrieval, and use of biomedical data for clinical or operational decision making. Moreover, a growing number of health care organizations are using advanced information systems to integrate *transaction systems* for scheduling, order entry, results reporting, and laboratory information; *analytical support systems* such as cost accounting, market research, and executive information; and *communication systems* that link providers along the continuum of care.

While many organizations still depend on different computer systems for the laboratory, outpatient surgery center, or outlying primary care centers, a growing number have turned to electronic data interchange (EDI) to address the challenge of exchanging data between different systems. Figure 2–2 illustrates the basic functions of EDI in an ambulatory setting. Typical EDI capabilities include sharing of patient demographics and order/procedure data with practice management and managed care systems; electronic integration with laboratory systems; and sharing of clinical and procedural data with specialists, hospitals and health plans.

Figure 2–3 illustrates the differences between point-to-point EDI and an integrated hub-and-spoke approach. An integrated

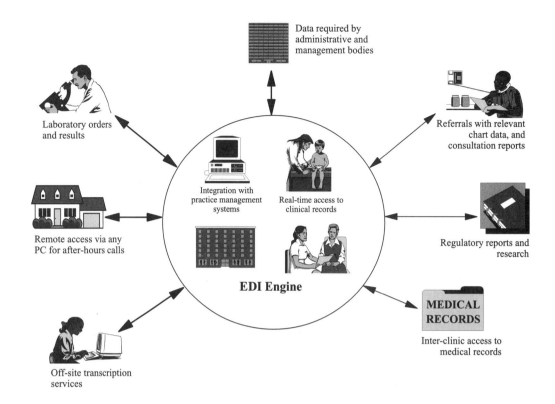

Figure 2–2 Electronic data interchange functions. Courtesy of MedicaLogic, Inc., Beaverton, Oregon.

hub-and-spoke approach to EDI allows organizations to send data from one part of the system for translation and ultimate transmission to another part of the system. By helping computers communicate, EDI helps organizations access information quickly without the ordeal and added expense of data reentry. And EDI is now so fast that it can quickly integrate information systems across physician practices and along the continuum of health care services.

Even though integration hub EDI requires an initial investment of time and money, it is still less expensive than implementing point-to-point connections. Costs usually involve a licensing fee of between $75,000 and $150,000 and incremental payments for connections made after installation of the first set of interfaces. Table 2–1 compares the cost of point-to-point EDI with the integration hub. Organizations that are considering a move to EDI should shop around in a competitive market that is full of new product offerings and a variety of payment arrangements.

Widespread use of EDI would produce dramatic cost savings. Steven Easthaugh, Ph.D., professor of finance and economics at George Washington University and author of *Facing Tough Choices: Balancing Fiscal and Social Deficits*, estimates that automating 11 key transactions through EDI could save $73 billion of the $220 billion spent annually on health care administration, with the greatest savings accruing in the areas of claims submission, enrollments, payment/remittance, and scheduling. Other savings would occur in the areas of eligibility, prescription ordering, claims inquiry, referral authorization, test order/results, material management, and coordination of benefits.[1]

Installing an integrated health care information infrastructure calls for three components:

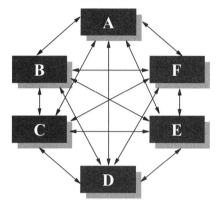 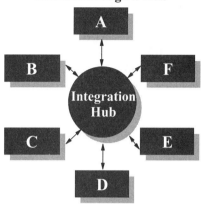

*HubLink Integrator is used as an example.

Figure 2–3 EDI: Integration hub versus point-to-point approach. Simple organization means fewer computer connections and lower development expense. *Source:* Reprinted with permission from *Modern Healthcare*, Copyright Crain Communications, Inc. 740 N. Rush St., Chicago, IL 60611.

Table 2–1 Costs of EDI: Integration Hub versus Point-to-Point Approach

	Point-to-Point	Hub*
Cost of each interface**	$30,000	$6,000
Number of interfaces required	30	12
License fee	None	$100,000
Total cost to construct	$900,000	$172,000

*HubLink Integrator is used as an example.
**Figures are approximate.

Source: Reprinted with permission from *Modern Healthcare*, Copyright Crain Communications, Inc. 740 N. Rush St., Chicago, IL 60611.

1. regional communications networks for moving information along the continuum of care among hundreds of different providers
2. clinical databases and electronic medical records (EMRs) for monitoring outcomes and managing the delivery of cost-effective, high-quality care
3. advanced ambulatory management systems for managing increased numbers of patients under capitation in the outpatient settings

Regional communications systems—which include local and wide-area networks for transferring patient information between the doctor's office, hospital, pharmacy, nursing home, and other providers—are designed to transmit data so that specialists in different locations can read patients' records simultaneously. This transmission of information, which can include everything from radiology images to video images of arthroscopic surgery, is known as telemedicine, a technology that will undoubtedly help experts consult with physicians faster and less expensively than they do today.

The second piece of an integrated information infrastructure involves clinical databases of information about patients and customers. Some organizations depend on large-scale, relational databases to monitor outcomes and compare them to regional or national benchmarks. However, more sophisticated organizations have also incorporated information on patient satisfaction and health status ratings. The payoff comes in the analysis. When cross-functional teams of nurses and physicians review these databases, they typically find ways to improve critical paths and approaches to treatment.

A critical element of clinical databases is the electronic medical record (EMR), which offers one-time data capture and real-time (almost instantaneous) access to data and test results as patients move from one care setting to another. In an ideal scenario, home care workers could access a patient's EMR via phone lines and portable computers, or physicians could dial in to a cardiac intensive care unit and receive an up-to-the-minute status report on a patient. Unfortunately, the EMR is still in the developmental stages, stymied by political issues such as squabbles over software, hardware and communication standards, data definitions, and financial concerns.

The third and last piece of an integrated information system is an advanced practice management system designed for physicians who practice in a variety of integrated network settings. Moving beyond standard practice management systems, these systems tend to feature managed care capabilities such as claims processing, authorization, and referral tracking. Fortunately, systems such as CompuSense, IDX, Databreeze, Reynolds and Reynolds, Medical Manager, and Medic are already helping Physician Organizations manage capitation and risk.

Despite the many reasons for optimism over information systems in Physician Organizations, barriers to system development continue to challenge physician executives. Among the most notable impediments: the health care industry's slow investment in an information system infrastructure; the lack of standard clinical nomenclature for treatment and lack of agreed-upon electronic standards; and the large number of information systems vendors and providers, which makes it difficult for anyone to forge a central communications and information network.

According to many experts, success in information systems over the next five to ten years will depend on agreement on standards and transmittal procedures, investment in integrated communications systems, and support for retraining system personnel. Ultimately, Physician Organizations need far more than "techies" who can establish data processing requirements. They need chief information officers—leaders who can think strategically, guide system development, and oversee the right level of financial investment.

PROCESS MEASURES AND OUTCOMES REPORTING

Because purchasers and patients are demanding that physicians and other providers be held accountable for outcomes, Physician Organizations must implement efficient clinical practices and eliminate unnecessary, ineffective ones. Purchasers and patients want information on anticipated outcomes of care and how one physician's performance compares with the performance of others. And purchasers and patients will continue to question standards of practice and health care prices. Among their questions: Do different approaches yield the same result? How can we get the best result through the least costly process?

Outcomes research and measurement, which focuses on the outcomes of medical interventions, is different than *quality assurance*, which typically focuses on structure and process. Still, health organizations continue to emphasize quality. According to the Washington, D.C., Healthcare Advisory Board's outcomes strategy report, health care organizations use more than 8,000 quality measures for tracking and benchmarking.[2]

In the years ahead, however, the role of quality measures may change. Under capitation, outcomes research and its applications will increasingly serve as the protectors or guardians of quality. The shift to capitation gives physicians the incentive not to provide more care, as under fee-for-service reimbursement, but to provide less care. The challenge for outcomes management is simple: to demonstrate how, where, and when lower levels of care compromise quality of care and patient health status. Physician organizations should track the following dimensions of quality and outcomes:

- **Service quality**—Evaluate patient satisfaction and assess quality.
- **Appropriateness**—Determine what should be done for the patient.
- **Clinical performance**—Compare providers' performance using severity-adjusted systems.
- **Functional status**—Evaluate patients before and after treatment.
- **Access**—Evaluate the number and convenience of care sites available to populations by the network or health plan.

The issue of accountability arises most often in the form of reporting on the Health Plan Employer Data and Information Set (HEDIS), process measures developed for use with Medicaid and other populations by the Washington, D.C.-based National Committee for Quality Assurance (NCQA), a nonprofit organization supported by major employers and purchasers. NCQA has emerged as the accreditation entity for managed health care plans; managed health care plans and Health Maintenance Organizations (HMOs) are increasingly holding contracted providers accountable for reporting against these process measures.

Among the major categories tracked by managed care plans and HMOs using the HEDIS format are quality, access, patient satisfaction, membership, utilization, and finance. Exhibit 2–1 shows elements within these major categories, which includes childhood immunization rates, mammography screening, and global inpatient and ambulatory care numbers and rates.

The evolving HEDIS system lays the groundwork for Physician Organizations to compare quality and performance against 60 process measures or quality indicators. In the future, health plans and physician-driven Managed Care Organizations will convert databases with data such as HEDIS indicators into report cards that allow for uniform data reporting and give purchasers helpful information for selecting providers.

As purchasers and NCQA continue to hold payers accountable for measuring processes, health care providers will increasingly shop for the information systems and trained staff to gather, consolidate, and report the information. The ability of managed care providers and physician networks to meet NCQA's reporting requirements will undoubtedly be an ongoing competitive contracting advantage.

Process measures are only the first step that many organizations are implementing now. In the outcomes field there is an explosion in two major areas: (1) clinical practice guidelines and (2) outcomes research. Most medical specialty societies have established specific practice guidelines for their specialty. During the last several years, a number of Integrated Delivery Systems and leading medical group systems have moved outcomes measurements and practice guidelines to the communities. This trend is driven by physician leadership and the demands of regional payers to hold their contractors accountable for tracking process measures today and outcomes in the near future. Physician Organizations must measure the right things and have an organizational ability to act. This means taking steps to cut costs; to move care into less costly settings; and to

Exhibit 2–1 HMO HEDIS Measurement Components

PREVENTIVE SERVICES

Childhood Immunization

Year	Overall	DPT	OPV	MMR	Hib
1993	85.4%	88.3%	91.2%	95.6%	93.7%

Description: The percentage of continuously enrolled children who have received four DPT and three OPV immunizations in the first two years of life, and one MMR and at least one Hib conjugate vaccine in the second year of life.

PRENATAL CARE

Low Birthweight

Weight in Grams	Percent of Live Births
<1500	1.4%
<2500	8.7%

Description: Two birthweight measures are reported for CHCP's New Haven regional OB/GYN department (enrollees and fee-for-service patients): (1) low birthweight—the percentage of infants whose birthweight was less than 2,500 grams; and (2) very-low birthweight—the percentage of infants whose birthweight was less than 1,500 grams. Enrollment in New Haven region is 77.2% of total membership.

ACUTE CHRONIC ILLNESS

Asthma Inpatient Admission Rate

Year	Age Range	Proportion of Members with 1 or More Admissions	Proportion of Members with 2 or More Admissions	Ratio of Members Admitted More than Once to Members Admitted at Least Once
1993	2–19	0.27%	0.05%	18.52%
1993	20–39	0.07%	0.00%	0.00%

Description: Three asthma measures: (1) asthma admission rate—the proportion of enrollees having at least one admission for asthma; (2) asthma readmission rate—the proportion of enrollees having more than one admission for asthma; and (3) the ratio of enrollees admitted more than once to enrollees admitted at least once. Rates are provided for two age groups because of a difference in the incidence of asthma in pediatric and adult populations.

Courtesy of Physicians Health Care Alliance, New Haven, Connecticut.

---

enhance the quality of care, based on the accumulated and analyzed data throughout the cycle of a chronic or acute disease.

Commercial resources for clinical practice guidelines are widely used. For example, Milliman and Robertson, a leading actuarial firm, publishes extensive practice guidelines and protocols by specialty for the ambulatory setting. Many providers use these guidelines as a starting point and to implement their outcomes research and measurement programs. The process requires accumulating custom databases on specific populations, adapting software, and developing a consensus among physicians on how to reengineer care while improving quality.

The Agency for Health Care Policy and Research (AHCPR), as established by the 101st Congress, promotes research on medical outcomes and develops care guidelines for medical practice. The highest priority has been assigned to outcomes research on medical issues that: (1) affect the most people, (2) cost the most money, or (3) create the greatest misery. Because Medicare accounts for almost 40 percent of all hospital expenditures in the United States, governmental research also reflects the need to increase cost-effectiveness in the illnesses that affect Medicare beneficiaries. The approach used is (1) to search the world's literature on the given condition and (2) to conduct epidemiological research, comparing treatments in various locales. If the above procedures do not provide solid outcomes data, researchers conduct randomized, controlled clinical trials to determine the most effective treatment.

The second major area of research on medical outcomes is focused outcomes research. Commercial companies with outcomes measurement systems such as Iameter and MediQual have focused on selling inpatient performance comparison systems. Recently, however, these companies have developed information and comparison software products focused on benchmarking and comparing ambulatory services.

Unfortunately for these proprietary systems, the Health Care Financing Administration (HCFA) rejected all commercial severity-adjusted systems for the Medicare population in favor of the Uniform Clinical Data Set (UCDS). Developed at HCFA by Henry Krakauer, M.D., the system includes 1,600 data elements, requires 1.5 hours per chart to extract, and is currently being applied to the charts of 10 percent of Medicare patients.

Funding for outcomes research comes from federal grants issued through a variety of agencies, pharmaceutical companies that invest more than $8 billion annually on clinical trials, and integrated managed care Physician Organizations that set aside capitation dollars to spearhead the development of local databases.

One outstanding effort to further the outcomes discipline is the American Group Practice Outcomes Management Project. It was started in 1989 with six leading medical group practices including Cleveland Clinic, Scott and White Clinic, Park Nicollet Medical Centers, and others and has expanded to over 40 leading medical groups nationwide. With the goal of developing a national database, it has focused on eight diagnoses or procedures: (1) total hip replacement, (2) total knee replacement, (3) cataract surgery, (4) diabetes, (5) asthma, (6) low back pain, (7) hypertension, and (8) sleep disorder. The project has identified several key success factors:

- Data quality and integrity must be maintained.
- Valid comparisons require standardized data sets.
- The benefits of outcomes measurements must be explicit and quantifiable.
- Outcomes measurements must be provider driven.

The outcomes management revolution has already begun to achieve cost savings. GTE Corporation retrieved significant cost savings by analyzing cost data on more than 90 health plans using HEDIS 2.0. For example, when employees and their families moved from indemnity plans to HMOs, the company saved $1,000 annually per employee. And when employees moved from lower-quality plans as measured by HEDIS to higher-quality plans, the company saved an additional $500 annually per employee and family.

As the outcomes movement grows, organizations will increasingly compare a variety of approaches to a health care problem or need. Outcomes information will help purchasers decide what services to pay for and what providers to use. At the same time, patients will grow more comfortable with data and make decisions based on numbers, as well as on intuitive, personal preferences. This new and refreshing focus on the patient is probably the most unusual characteristic to emerge from the outcomes movement.

The benefits of outcomes research are broad. Outcomes management provides a systematic approach to improve the quality of health care and reduce variations. It identifies outliers and informs physicians so that they can change their behavior. The outcomes movement addresses why these variations exist and suggests appropriate practice patterns that can be incorporated into critical paths. This new information on outcomes will require health care professionals to communicate at higher levels to ensure the incorporation of findings into patient care.

MULTISPECIALTY PHYSICIAN NETWORKS

The rapidly changing health care environment raises a number of significant issues about how to build and operate new group practices, specialty networks, and other newly emerging Physician Organizations that can manage risk and capitation. Ultimately, success in capitation depends on effective Physician Organizations that can balance cost and quality under capitated reimbursement systems. Physician leaders must catalyze, guide, and manage evolving ambulatory medical practice networks that compose the backbone of Integrated Delivery Systems.

New organizational structures must provide physician leaders and executives with information and knowledge that will guide and empower them in developing Physician Organizations that can meet purchasers needs, react to aggressive network competitors, and meet community needs. Physician Organizations must be market driven and medically directed to meet patient needs and expectations into the year 2000.

During the last several years, primary care physicians have actively organized group practices without walls and more integrated group practices across the country. Primary care physicians, in their role as gatekeeper, have gained new power and prominence in the health care delivery system. In fact, there has been a frenzy in many markets to buy the tangible and intangible assets of primary care practices in an effort to be attractive to managed health plans. Today, primary care physicians function as gatekeepers in managing costs and eliminating unnecessary procedures from the system; however, multispecialty networks will increasingly assume this function in the future.

Several trends reinforce this prediction. With the advent of advanced triage and demand management systems and the rise of midlevel and alternative providers, primary care physician time is too valuable to serve as an enforcement-oriented gatekeeper. Also critical is the movement from small group practices without walls to large, multi-faceted, integrated organizations composed of group practices, Independent Practice Associations (IPAs), nonprofit foundations, and Management Services Organizations (MSOs) that meet market and regulatory requirements for size and integration. Stark II (Omnibus Reconciliation Act of 1993, Public Law No. 103-66, codified at 42 U.S.C. §1395nn.), a new federal statute that governs allowable referral arrangements to avoid antikickback regulations under Medicare, suggests that physicians must become members of true group practices if they want to operate ancillary services such as imaging or home health care. In addition, many purchasers will continue to decline sharing risk with Physician Organizations that are not financially integrated. Finally, true quality care depends on collaboration between physicians across specialties.

The evidence of the clinical and cost benefits of organized multispecialty care versus primary care–driven care is growing. Mayo Clinic research indicates that specialties treat certain illnesses and conditions more cost-effectively than primary care physicians. Depression, asthma, lower back pain, and certain heart conditions all benefit from earlier specialist intervention; specialist intervention results in more efficient diagnosis, avoidance of unnecessary office visits, effective use of emergency department services, and reductions in X-rays and other services.[3]

Successful physician-driven multispecialty organizations maintain physicians' market leverage through merger, contract, or alliance. In many cases, multispecialty group practice and network formation receive support from a progressive health system that wants to develop a partnership with the evolving Physician Organization. The primary goals are: (1) to develop a geographically dispersed medical practice and affiliated network attractive to purchasers; (2) to accept and manage risk contracts by spreading risk among more physicians; (3) to provide enhanced revenue and income security to physicians; and (4) to improve the quality of physicians' lives by allowing them to focus on practicing medicine.

In choosing to pursue an integrated, multispecialty practice, physician leaders should lead by:

- taking responsibility, accountability, and risk
- keeping clinical delivery and management oversight in physicians' hands
- attracting purchasers because physicians have a vested interest in the appropriate use of health care resources, while also upholding patient rights
- preserving physicians' clinical control, thus leading to higher productivity and patient quality
- demanding knowledge about capitation and appropriate medical care, as well as comprehensive care guidelines for inpatient, outpatient, and ambulatory services
- requiring use of advanced information systems for clinical reengineering
- breaking down the operational, legal, financial, and clinical barriers that separate medical practices

The future is integrated multispecialty and multi-entity Physician Organizations. Only provider-based groups can be Managed Care Organizations. HMOs, Preferred Provider Organizations (PPOs), and other health plans are value-added distributors of premium dollars. Rapidly expanding Physician Practice Management Companies are focusing on the management of core multispecialty medical group practices and affiliated IPA networks. Quality, cost-effective care ultimately depends on a cooperative, multi-disciplinary approach—not a primary care only or externally dictated approach to care delivery.

DEMAND MANAGEMENT AND DISEASE MANAGEMENT SYSTEMS

Managing health calls for the application of advanced demand management technologies and disease state management (DSM) techniques. The components of demand management include the synergy of customer and teleservices technology with triage, algorithm-driven care guidelines, and provider services databases. It involves the use of decision and self-management support systems to empower consumers to make appropriate decisions and actions concerning the use of medical services.

At the core of demand management is the integration of knowledge, information systems, and interactive media to promote self-care, wellness, and consumer education. Through consumer counseling and easy-to-access information, demand management blends services ranging from lifestyle management and smoking cessation, to stress management and weight reduction.

As these programs and new technologies expand from the corporate environment to provider-based delivery systems, studies have demonstrated the wisdom and cost-effectiveness of the demand management strategy. For example, a two-year study conducted by the Center for Corporate Health for the 24,000 members of the Wisconsin Insurance Association found that a self-care program with access to phone-based nurse counseling saved $4.75 per dollar invested versus $2.40 per dollar invested for the self-care resources presented through a printed manual and newsletter. Aetna Health Plans also concluded that a nurse counseling hotline reduced ambulatory visits by 1.1 visit per member per year. At an average visit cost of $85, this translated into a $3 savings for every $1 invested in the hotline service.[4]

In 1995, only 58 percent of HMOs offered a nurse or self-care advisory hotline phone service. This statistic identifies an opportunity for Physician Organizations to reduce unnecessary costs and empower consumers by delivering provider-based nurse hotline services and other interactive education opportunities. One example of national demand management leadership is United Health Care Corporation. It recently developed OPTUM Nurseline, which provides 24-hour, toll-free access to counselors and nurses, and Total Care Management, which assigns a primary nurse to integrate medical, behavioral, pharmacy, and disability management for high-risk families.[5] Working with back-up resources, this nurse oversees all benefits, claims, utilization review, and case management concerns before assigned members get sick. The guiding principle is not simply to *deliver* acute care, but to *manage* care.

Industries faced with rising costs and increased competition—such as the financial services and retailing industries—have turned to telemarketing or teleservices technologies to save money, improve customer service, and increase sales. Health care vendors and systems have, in turn, borrowed and adapted these technologies to educate and empower consumers. Among the leaders are the following:

- Access Health Marketing, a publicly traded NASDAQ company, has installed Ask-a-Nurse in hundreds of health systems to improve access and build a foundation for demand management. The company also markets Personal Health Advisor to HMOs, Blue Cross plans, and others on a per-member-per-month basis and promotes the concept of offering one number for members to call and gain access to self-care or wellness information.
- The Tel-Patient Network answers patients' questions on tests ranging from a cardiac stress test to a thyroid scan.
- The Medical Information Line promotes 900-number access to confidential, reliable, up-to-date information on over 300 pre-recorded topics, such as breast cancer, abortion, acne, and heart attacks. Searle Pharmaceuticals acquired the sponsoring company as part of its strategic diversification plan to expand demand and disease management programs.

Yesterday's physician referral function is the foundation for tomorrow's demand management teleservices program. Inbound telephone calls and direct mail inquiries on issues such as physician selection or general hospital information can be handled through a central counseling facility that features stations staffed by highly trained health care specialists or care access counselors. Each station, in turn, can be hooked into a computer-driven database that maintains up-to-date information on thousands of physicians and hundreds of regional programs and services.

Within minutes, consumers can select physicians who match their needs and are located close to homes or workplaces. After consumers make their choice, a care access counselor can provide them with information on other system-sponsored programs and services. Just as important, these care access counselors can initiate calls to promote local health fairs or other special events, or conduct health risk appraisals of high-risk populations identified through clinical database analysis (see Figure 2–4).

Advanced teleservices customer support systems will play a vital role in demand management programs. Higher costs and lower health status in ambulatory care tend to be rooted in failure or reluctance of patients to keep appointments, follow treatment instructions, and use prevention programs.

Other evidence on the effectiveness of demand management abounds. A September 29, 1994, article in the *New England Journal of Medicine* reports on the results of a Connecticut study by Yale University School of Medicine, Yale–New Haven Hospital, and others. The study reported that home visits and other interventions "resulted in a significant reduction in the risk of falling among elderly persons in the community."[6]

In the years ahead, offering patients health-risk assessments, self-care information, and prevention services will no longer be viewed as "do-gooder" public relations or community service strategies. The name and mission of the game are simple: **empowerment**. The goals are to help people evaluate their health care problems, get involved in self-care, move to the most appropriate level of care, and—in the long run—prevent or curtail hospital admissions. Physician Organizations with tens of thousands of members under capitated reimbursement could save millions by developing teleservice centers with the ability to receive and initiate calls to patients and family members.

Fortunately, some Physician Organizations have already instituted advanced teleservices centers to handle inbound and outbound calls from patients, consumers, purchasers, and participants in the network. Teleservices operations tend to be composed of two elements: (1) the call-handling center, which handles thousands of requests from consumers, and (2) the teleservices consulting group, which works with other elements of the delivery system to use telecommunications technology. These teleservices techniques and systems will play an integral

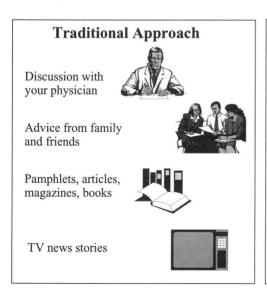

Figure 2–4 Demand management strategies. Courtesy of Ashby Montrose & Company, Denver, Colorado.

role in effective demand management as they do the following:

- Check consumer satisfaction.
- Provide health information over the telephone.
- Promote the efficient, appropriate use of health care resources.
- Enhance access to providers within the Integrated Delivery System.

Another area closely related to demand management is the rapidly evolving discipline of disease state management (DSM), which involves systems designed to improve outcomes through interventions made throughout the life cycle of an acute or chronic disease. Among the users of these programs are pharmaceutical manufacturers, pharmacy benefits management firms, Physician Organizations, and managed health care plans.

Based on the principle of meeting patients' needs before they move to costly hospitalization, DSM programs use health-risk appraisal systems, claims databases, and knowledge systems to predict acute or chronic conditions experienced by people at varying stages of the life cycle. Examining care provided across the continuum, DSM programs work to prevent further problems and manage care in the least expensive, most appropriate setting.

Built around clinical practice guidelines, specific pharmaceutical products, or disease states, DSM programs also integrate patient care with data analysis. Moving beyond case management, DSM programs work to optimize care through systematic measurement and proactive patient intervention. While the focus of many DSM programs has been on chronic conditions such as asthma, diabetes, and ulcers, the programs are increasingly focusing on conditions such as arthritis, heart disease, and depression.

Marching in the vanguard of DSM are pharmaceutical companies that increasingly see themselves not merely as chemical companies, but as health care providers. Aware that pharmaceuticals represent only 8 percent of the health care premium dollar, while services and administration represent 92 percent, many of these companies plan to obtain a greater percentage of the premium dollar distributed through capitation by developing and expanding disease management programs. This goes on, in spite of the fact that some physicians and health plans question the underlying motivation of pharmaceutical companies—the desire to sell more drugs at a lower price.

Among the organizations leading the way through DSM:

- Caremark International has developed DSM programs for a variety of disease states.
- UpJohn Company has created Greenstone Healthcare Solutions to provide services such as prospective health care, clinical practice optimization, therapy management, and data management services for managed health plans, health systems, payers, and business coalitions.
- Eli Lilly has established integrated data management and has allocated $50 million to develop DSM programs.
- Merck/Medco plans to incorporate financial incentives into its pharmacy benefits management services to encourage patients to enter DSM programs.
- Zeneca Pharmaceuticals acquired a 50 percent interest in Salick, a cancer center operator, to expand its provider capabilities and cancer database for a larger DSM initiative.

Never quite buying into the DSM initiatives of pharmaceutical companies, managed care plans and Physician Organizations have also launched programs. John Deere Health Care, a subsidiary of John Deere with more than 300,000 covered lives, takes advantage of a joint ambulatory care venture with Mayo Clinic to pioneer DSM strategies for asthma, hypertension, low back pain, ischemic heart disease, gallstone disease, diabetes, breast cancer, and headache. These strategies consider the progression of a disease from beginning to end, including the appropriate use of primary care physicians and specialists for quality and cost management. And through an asthma management program, Harvard Community Health Plan's hospital admission rate for pediatric asthmatics dropped by 25 percent while adults' admission rate dropped by 10 percent.

The potential for even greater savings and enhanced quality of patients' lives is significant. More than $92 billion is spent annually on diabetes care and treatment, amounting to 15 percent of U.S. health care expenditures incurred by 3 percent of the population. This explains why HMOs such as Group Health of Puget Sound target diseases such as diabetes. Although only 3 percent of plan members are afflicted by the disease, it accounts for 13 percent of the plan's costs.

The consulting firm of Ashby Montrose & Company and Diabetes Treatment Centers of America, Inc., estimate possible cost savings of 15 to 35 percent simply by moving interventions into arenas of self-care and the medical office. Figure 2–5 illustrates early intervention strategies made before costly hospitalizations. Through education and interactive outreach, care can be moved into more cost-effective settings, and serious illness can be prevented through early intervention. DSM programs have incredible potential if physician leaders and health care organizations will commit to developing and testing programs that focus not on treating acute illnesses, but on managing health.

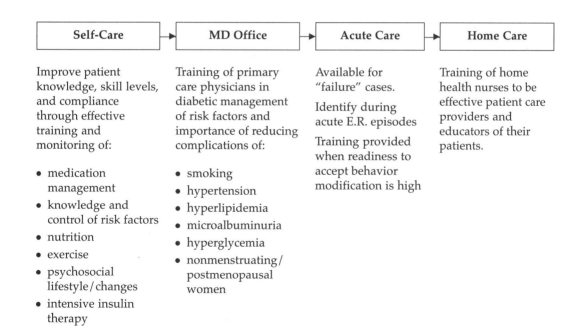

Figure 2–5 Diabetes disease management continuum. Courtesy of Ashby Montrose & Company, Denver, Colorado.

CONTINUOUS QUALITY IMPROVEMENT AND CLINICAL REENGINEERING

Thousands of health care organizations have moved away from quality assurance to continuous quality improvement (CQI) programs. CQI involves defining quality in clinical operations and service processes through projects such as critical pathways, flowcharts depicting the progress of a patient through the hospital, and programs that reduce problems such as the number of needlesticks incurred by nurses. CQI focuses on three major areas for improving quality: administration, clinical performance, and patient service. The four basic steps in the CQI process are:

1. assessing the problems and defining the study
2. benchmarking and collecting internal data
3. taking action and improving
4. analyzing results and improving

After identifying problems, health care professionals gather data, enter it into databases, and compare it against industry standards. The information resulting from this analysis eventually leads to a CQI action plan, which emphasizes processes that reduce waste and enhance productivity. Because health care professionals never stop monitoring CQI action plans or making adjustments, CQI typically produces long-term productivity and quality gains.

In contrast to CQI, reengineering uses advanced information technology to promote the radical process redesign and achieve dramatic leaps in performance. In fact, in *Reengineering the Corporation: A Manifesto for Business Revolution*, authors Michael Hammer and James Champy define *reengineering* as "the fundamental rethinking and radical redesign of business processes to achieve dramatic improvements in critical, contemporary measures of performance, such as cost, quality, service, and speed."[7]

Applying CQI and reengineering principles and techniques to systems within Physician Organizations calls for a closer look at the business and clinical systems needed to deliver care. Because capitation involves fixed prepayments based on the number of enrolled patients, Physician Organizations achieve profitability not by doing more procedures or raising prices, but by reducing operating costs. Physician Organizations can reduce the cost of practice operations by organizing care systems that involve group purchasing of equipment, insurance, and other supplies; streamlining patient flow; and enhancing services through DSM and demand management. The major tools of clinical improvement and health care reengineering include the following:

- **Clinical practice guidelines**—The National Academy of Sciences, Institute of Medicine, Washington, D.C., has coined *clinical practice guidelines*—in favor of the equally popular "clinical protocols" or "practice parameters"—to refer to standards that guide physicians on appropriate care in specific cases. Standards of the AHCPR's clinical practice guidelines include acute pain management, early HIV infection, benign prosthetic hyperplasia, and otitis media with effusion in young children.
- **Practice parameters**—These clinical protocols are educational tools for physicians that provide the advice of recognized clinical experts and report the clinical significance of new and often conflicting findings.
- **Clinical pathways/critical pathways**—These clinical management tools organize the major interventions of physicians, nurses, and other health care staff (e.g., pulmonologists) and chart the sequence and timing of interventions.
- **CareMaps**—More detailed and complex versions of critical pathways, these diagrams use a timeline to show the relationships between sets of interventions and sets of intermediate outcomes.

They combine standards of care with standards of practice in a cause-effect relationship across time.

At the core of clinical reengineering are physician-directed medical management systems. Organizations interested in taking the lead in clinical reengineering must manage internally their medical management functions such as information systems, case management, peer review, DSM, and physician education. The goal is simple: to empower physician clinicians to work with managers to search for the most appropriate, lowest-cost settings for delivering care to patients.

Among the national leaders in medical management systems is MedPartners/Mullikin, an 800-plus physician integrated health care organization, which continues to capitalize on the innovations introduced by Mullikin Medical Centers before its late-1995 merger with MedPartners. MedPartners/Mullikin's physician management approach, which emphasizes the concept that patient care decisions should be made at the level closest to the patient, continues to guide all clinical operations. MedPartners/Mullikin lives the philosophy that the best physician managers are not necessarily those who participate in board room discussions and management meetings, but rather, those who treat patients. For this reason, only practicing MedPartners/Mullikin physicians oversee managed patient care. All physicians in clinical management at MedPartners/Mullikin—including regional, facility, and line managers—are practicing physicians. This keeps full-time physician managers to a manageable minimum.

Even though care delivery remains within the scope of the individual MedPartners/Mullikin physician, each MedPartners/Mulliken physician is organized into a four to five physician facility or care team that provides support and oversight for its members. This small unit or team approach to care delivery establishes two functions simultaneously: resource review and peer review. Although a facility medical director and regional medical director offer an additional layer of peer review and support, each physician assumes responsibility for managing medical resources and delivering care. This makes management and quality training for physician managers and lay administrators one of MedPartners/Mullikin's highest priorities.

By increasing the knowledge and skill level of every care provider and manager within a Physician Organization, physician leaders can achieve higher levels of customer satisfaction and cost-effectiveness and help people understand how and why they must work together to achieve financial and patient care goals (see Figure 2–6).

INTERNET AND ON-LINE SERVICES

News about the Internet is everywhere. But are health care organizations using the Internet? Can the Internet offer providers, vendors, and associations worthwhile business and patient care opportunities? If so, how—and how fast—do physician executives gain access?

With a growing number of resources available to improve quality, enhance access, and increase cost-effectiveness, the Internet has become an important resource and tool for health care executives and physician leaders. The World Wide Web sites presented in Exhibit 2–2 represent the wealth of data related to business and clinical care as well as the abundance of hypertext links to related sites.

The reality is that the Internet is neither a passing fad nor a false alarm. It offers a new way for organizations to disseminate and retrieve information, conduct market research, orchestrate advertising and public relations campaigns, and sell products and services. Health care organizations are using the Internet safely and successfully—from getting connected and creating a presence on the highly touted World Wide Web, to doing business with important constituencies.

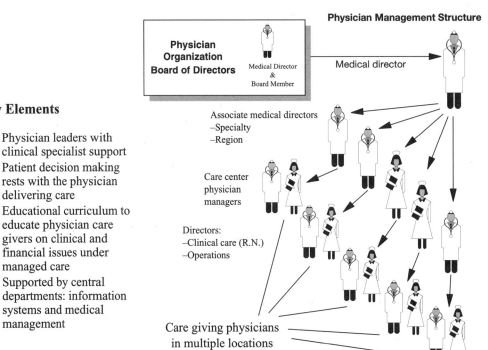

Key Elements

1. Physician leaders with clinical specialist support
2. Patient decision making rests with the physician delivering care
3. Educational curriculum to educate physician care givers on clinical and financial issues under managed care
4. Supported by central departments: information systems and medical management

Figure 2–6 Physician driven medical management.

The three major components of the Internet related to health care include:

1. *Health-focused on-line services*—These services include the health and medical components of major commercial services such as Prodigy, America Online, and Compuserve. Also included in this category are dedicated on-line services such as Health Online, sponsored by Healthcare Forum and Leland Kaiser and Associates, and Physicians Online, an award-winning service focused exclusively on serving physicians.
2. *Clinical professional resources on World Wide Web sites*—These sites are established and supported by a full range of health care organizations, including the National Institutes of Health, which sponsors MedLine and the Grateful Med, as well as academic medical centers, medical schools, group practices, associations, and consulting firms.
3. *Consumer health and wellness resources on the World Wide Web*—A growing number of individuals and groups have developed home pages or sites on specific disease states such as AIDS, heart disease, diabetes, and asthma, as well as new health care products or approaches to treatment.

While investments in computerized databases and information systems may seem extravagant, they yield long-term economic gains. A study published in *Academic Medicine* reported that an on-line database search performed by a medical librarian can save thousands of dollars in health care costs. Conducted by medical librarians at four Detroit-area hospitals, the study verified the

Exhibit 2–2 Best of the Net Ratings of World Wide Web Site

A WORLD WIDE WEB CANCER GUIDE

Name: Steve Dunn's Cancer Guide

Location: http://bcn.boulder.co.us/...cancer/canguide.html

Sponsor: Boulder Community Network

Audience: Cancer patients and their families; physicians who want to communicate better with patients

Purpose: Cancer Guide is dedicated to helping the average health care consumer find answers about cancer and learn how to ask intelligent questions.

Features: Among the features are the pros and cons of researching one's cancer, cancer statistics, cancer types and staging, recommended books on cancer, the Cancer Information Service, clinical trials, medical literature, medical databases, medical library, on-line cancer information sources, information on specific or rare cancers, bone marrow transplants, and alternative therapies.

Most intriguing feature: By far, the most accessible and friendly cancer site around, Cancer Guide offers a Cancer Guide Tour for the panic-stricken patient or family. For example, consumers are guided to a specific reference if they are confronting a tough diagnosis, want to consider an experimental treatment, yearn to dig into the literature for themselves, or have a rare form of cancer. Always candid and direct, Dunn provides an easy-to-understand roundup and commentary on cancer resources, such as Cancer Net and Oncolink, plus listings of popular news groups and mailing lists. And he welcomes interaction from cancer patients and family members.

Cautions and advice: While Dunn acknowledges that Cancer Guide represents significant research, he admits that he is not a medical or health professional, and he advises people to consult with a physician or other health care provider.

Rating: Four stars

Contact for more information: Contact Dunn by E-mail at dunn@bcn.boulder.co.us

Source: Best of the Net Online Guide to Healthcare Management and Medicine, Goldstein, D. and Flory, J., Irwin Professional Publishing, Inc., 1996.

---

assumption that the sooner providers intervene, the more they save. Earlier database searches produced lower costs in 70 percent of the cases, lower charges in 68 percent of the cases, and shorter lengths of stay in 65 percent of the cases. Patients who had lengths of stay of more than 21 days benefited from lower costs if the librarian performed the search in the first two weeks of hospitalization. And for patients with a length of stay of less than two weeks, the earlier the search was completed, the lower the total cost. The average savings for a single case involving a literature search was $7,379.

Developing a presence on the Internet can help an organization stand out as a sophisticated, up-to-the-minute leadership force in a community, region, and even in the nation. But even if an organization decides not to invest in developing its own Web site, the World Wide Web remains a perfect resource for health care professionals who do not have the time or patience to learn confusing UNIX commands or feel their way through difficult software programs but still want access to the vast health care information resources. Through the World Wide Web, organizations can navigate the far reaches of health care cyberspace, using software that acts like similar programs on MacIntosh or Windows systems.

For health care professionals, being on the Web is much like taking a stroll through a large medical campus or visiting a health care trade show. Resources on nutrition, fitness, prevention, wellness, and self-care—or finance, marketing, quality, and banking—can be found with a few clicks of a mouse and some well-conceived search queries. The best news is that the majority of resources are free to those who know the basics of how to move around and access information.

Interest in the Internet will undoubtedly grow in the years ahead. In 1995, experts identified 100,000 Internet sites, a figure projected to mushroom to 500,000 sites by 1998. Experts such as Nicholas Nigroponte of the Massachusetts Institute of Technology's Media Lab go so far as to estimate that the number of World Wide Web sites doubles every 53 days. Exhibit 2–3 outlines some of the leading and most useful sites for health care professionals and clinicians. These sites have demonstrated the ability to deliver valuable content, ease of navigation within the site, efficient links to related health and medical sites, and numerous useful services and features for the Web-browsing professional.

Given this growth and the steadily increasing number of savvy professionals and consumers who will embark on their on-line adventure, it makes sense to view the Internet as a breakthrough vehicle for meet-

---

Exhibit 2–3 Top World Wide Web Sites for Physician Leaders

COMPREHENSIVE SITES AND DIRECTORIES

Cyberspace Hospital
http://ch.nus.sg

Health Resources (Inter-Links)
http://www.nova.edu/Inter-Links/medicine.html

Medical Matrix—Internet Clinical Medicine Resources Guide
http://www.kumc.edu:80/mmatrix/index.html

MedNexus
http://www.mednexus.com/

MedWeb: Biomedical Internet Resources (Emory University)
http://www.emory.edu/WHSCL/medweb.html

National Institutes of Health
http://www.nih.gov

National Library of Medicine—HyperDoc
http://www.nlm.nih.gov/

Virtual Hospital
http://vh.radiology.uiowa.edu/

Virtual Medical Center (Martindale's Health Science Guide)
http://www-sci.lib.uci.edu/~martindale/Medical.html

HEALTH AND MANAGEMENT ORGANIZATIONS

American College of Healthcare Executives (ACHE)
http://www.ache.org

American Health Care Association
http://nhic-nt.health.org/htmlgen/htmlgen.exe/Entry?HRCode= 'HR1573'

American Medical Association (AMA)
http://www.ama-assn.org

Medical Group Management Association (MGMA)
http://www.mercer.peachnet.edu/www/health/mgma.html

National Health Care Skill Standards Project
http://www.fwl.org/nhcssp/health.htm

EMPLOYMENT OPPORTUNITIES

FSG Online Career Services
http://www.gate.net/biotech-jobs/

MedSearch America
http://www.medsearch.com/

GOVERNMENT AGENCIES AND DEPARTMENTS

Agency for Health Policy and Research Guidelines—Consumer Guides
http://text.nlm.nih.gov/ahcpr/ahcprq.html

continues

Exhibit 2–3 continued

Center for Health Law Studies (St. Louis University)
http://lawlib.slu.edu/centers/hlthlaw/hlthlaw.htm

Centers for Disease Control and Prevention (CDC)
http://www.cdc.gov/

Community of Science
http://cos.gdb.org/

Federally Funded Research in the United States
http://medoc.gdb.org/best/fed-fund.html

FedWorld
http://www.fedworld.gov

Health Care Financing Administration (HCFA)
http://www.ssa.gov/hcfa/hcfahp2.html

Health Care Liability Alliance (HCLA)
http://www.wp.com/HCLA/

Intergovernmental Health Policy Project
http://www.gwu.edu/~ihpp

Joint Commission on Accreditation of Healthcare Organizations
http://nhic-nt.health.org/htmlgen/htmlgen.exe/Entry?HRCode= 'HR1458'

National Center for Health Statistics (NCHS)
http://www.cdc.gov/nchswww/nchshome.htm

National Health Information Center (NHIC)
http://nhic-nt.health.org/

National Institute of General Medical Science
http://www.nih.gov:80/nigms/

Occupational Safety and Health Administration (OSHA)
http://www.osha.gov/

Public Health Service
http://phs.os.dhhs.gov/phs/phs.html

THOMAS: Legislative Information on the Internet
http://thomas.loc.gov/

U.S. Department of Health and Human Services
http://www.nttc.edu/gov/departments/hhs.html

U.S. Food and Drug Administration (FDA)
http://www.fda/fdahomepage.html

HEALTH MANAGEMENT AND ADMINISTRATION

Academic Medical Center Consortium
http://www.amcc.rochester.edu/

Administrators in Academic Psychiatry (AAP)
http://www.umdnj.edu/~pulierml/AAP.home.html

American Medical Specialty Organization, Inc. (AMSO)—Managed Care Forum
http://www.amso.com/

European Healthcare Management Association (EHMA)
http://www.iol.ie/~ehma/

Health Administration Resources on the Internet
http://mercer.peachnet.edu/www/health/health.html

Healthcare Financial Management Association (HFMA)
http://www.hfma.org/

Health Guidepost, The (Aspen Publishers)
http://plainfield.bypass.com/~slarose/

Health Information Resources and Services (HIRS)
http://www.hirs.com/

Institute of Management and Administration (General)
http://www.ioma.com/ioma/index.html

Lumina—Decision/Risk Analysis
http://www.lumina.com/DA/

Medical Source
http://www.medsource.com

Quality Resources Online
http://www.quality.org/qc

Quality Wave
http://www.xnet.com/~creacon/Q4Q

Wisconsin's Healthcare Information Network (WHIN)
http://www.fetch.com/whin/net.html

continues

Exhibit 2–3 continued

PRODUCTS AND SERVICES	INFORMATICS AND DECISION ANAYSIS
Avicenna Online Medical Information http://www.avicenna.com	Decision Systems Group—Harvard Medical School and Brigham and Women's Hospital http://dsg.harvard.edu/public/general/DSG.html
Biomet http://www.biomet.com	
FirstMark, Inc. http://www.firstmark.com/	HCIA, Inc. http://www.hcia.com/
Home Health Business Report http://www.sireport.com/hhbr/index.html	Lumina—Decision/Risk Analysis http://www.lumina.com/DA/
MedInstrument Network http://www.welcome.com/~mednet	
MEDMarket Healthcare http://www.medmarket.com	Medical Records Institute http://www.medrecinst.com
MedWeb (Med X Change) http://www.gate.net/~medxxx/cbl.htm	MIT Clinical Decision Making Group http://medg.lcs.mit.edu/

ing patients' needs for self-care information and providing professionals with ready access to a world of valuable clinical and business knowledge.

COST REDUCTION AND COST MANAGEMENT

The transition to capitation demands that physicians change their practices and improve every aspect of their operations: finance, human resources, information systems, compensation, and contracting. Examining, understanding, and eventually controlling costs call for dividing costs into two categories: fixed and variable.

The easiest costs to assign are direct service costs related to general patient care, which tend to be variable costs such as labor, materials, pharmacy, and other ancillary costs. Other costs with a variable component include maintenance, dietary, marketing, and administration, which also have fixed components. In contrast, fixed costs include land, building, equipment, depreciation and amortization, and utilities.

By using a variable-costing income statement format, it is possible to calculate the contribution margin that represents the organization's contribution to fixed costs and profit. The more specific the costing methods, the more accurately organizations can track performance and profit. Successful cost reduction calls for abandoning antiquated accounting systems in favor of cost accounting systems. Instead of relying on the cash method of accounting, Physician Organizations should invest in people and information systems that can handle cost accounting and report on a contemporary accrual basis.

Physician Organizations must be able to track the flow of money, typically paid in advance in capitated systems. Because patients often change health plans, organizations must purchase tracking systems that interface with health plan systems. The alternative is far worse: organizations could provide care to patients who are no longer eligible, which would increase costs and inefficiency and decrease profits under capitated reimbursement.

Even though health plans often pay Physician Organizations in advance for services specified in a capitated managed care contract, the organization must reconcile payments received from the HMO or managed health plan. For example, if a contract pays for members weighted by age, the provider must verify each age group. Only then can the provider ensure that the payment from the health plan is not too low because of inaccurate age information provided by the managed health plan.

Although it is relatively simple to verify the first monthly payment, Physician Organizations may need to make adjustments after the first few months of the contract. In some cases, there may be a time lag between the date of payment and the date a patient enrolls or disenrolls from the health plan. The consequences are obvious. If the provider organization cannot track enrollment, it could receive payment for a patient who has already disenrolled or, even worse, receive no payment for a new enrollee.

Thus, it is critical for Physician Organizations to communicate with the health plan regularly and obtain updated enrollment files on tape or disk. Physician Organizations should make sure their computer systems can integrate with the computer systems of health plans and electronic claims clearinghouses. Among the actions needed by Physician Organizations:

- Match members on the tape (or disk) to those already in the system.
- Identify new members by active date.
- Report members whose enrollment date does not match the current month.
- Pinpoint members who disenrolled in the current month, as well as those who are backdated to a previous month.

After making these comparisons, physician organizations should print out these categories and compare them to the capitated payment.

Another financial item that should be tracked is incurred but not reported (IBNR) costs. For example, a primary care group practice may have a capitated contract for full medical risk, meaning that the medical group is prepaid for all of the ambulatory medical services provided to a defined population. The primary care organization contracts with a network of specialists on a discounted fee-for-service basis. As a result, when a primary care physician refers a patient to a specialist, such as an oncologist, the primary care group incurs a cost and obligation the day the patient consults with that oncologist. Unfortunately, the oncologist might not bill the primary care physician group for the visit until 30 days or more afterward. If the primary care group has not documented the IBNR cost, members of the group are likely to perceive their profit as higher than it actually is. The lesson: Physician Organizations should use information systems to track the IBNR costs that occur in capitated payment systems.

In addition to analyzing the existing operation's cost structure, the Physician Organization must decide whether to own or subcontract health care services such as imaging, home care, or durable medical equipment. Exhibit 2–4 outlines issues to analyze when deciding what services to expand, build, buy, or eliminate.

PREVENTIVE MEDICINE AND EMPOWERED CONSUMERS

Empowered consumers and preventive medicine are critical building blocks of integrated health care delivery. Consumer-oriented patients want to participate in their own care. The nation's largest health care provider is neither the hospital nor the physician but the patient. Self-care embraces all the actions people take to care for their own bodies. Much of the information people seek is aimed at preventing illness, overcoming a disease, or mobilizing the still untapped power of the mind and emotions to enhance the immune system.

Helping consumers make more informed health care decisions goes far beyond the telephone. Even with health care information reported in publications as diverse as *Good Housekeeping* and *Men's Health* maga-

Exhibit 2–4 Cost Reengineering Questions

- Do we have a cost accounting system that can allow us to evaluate our operating costs per service?
- Can we track incurred but not reported costs relative to our capitated patients and service delivered?
- Which services should we continue to offer and which should we discontinue, based on the operating costs of the service compared to the market?
- Should we provide a particular service, acquire it, or contract for it from another organization?
- What is our clinical and business cost structure for delivering a particular service?
- Should we buy or lease the proposed equipment?
- Should we change our service delivery methods to reduce operating costs?
- Should we expand a particular department or service to have an integrated continuum of care?

Source: Adapted from Lourdes Winberry, Capitation Management 1995, Medical Alliances, Inc., Special Report.

zines, and on television shows as varied as *Phil Donahue* and *20/20*, consumers are hungry for guidance on how to prevent disease, confront illness, and mobilize the power of mind over body. Consumers will undoubtedly continue to turn to self-help books such as *The Mayo Clinic Health Book*,[8] as well as health newsletters from Johns Hopkins, the Mayo Clinic, and local health care organizations.

As society continues to barrel down the information highway, consumers are more likely to invest in relatively low-cost ($50) software packages that help them track medical history, diagnose medical conditions, and learn about potential drug interactions. The Harvard Community Health Plan's study on the effects of home-based computers on unnecessary visits reflects the critical future role of computers in prevention, self-care, and wellness.

With the aging of the Baby Boomers, the most educated generation in human history, patients have become increasingly sophisticated about health care. They want to be involved in decisions about their bodies, minds, and spirits—and those of their family members. While they may not expect the bravado of the physicians on the television program *ER*, or the idealized compassion of Marcus Welby, M.D., they want a physician who is willing to engage in a dialogue, explore treatment options, and discuss prevention and lifestyle with the same respect typically given to surgery and medications.

The February 1995 issue of *Consumer Reports* reports that even though most patients are satisfied with their physicians, many complain about physician reluctance to answer and ask questions, take a complete history, and provide lifestyle information. In short, many patients are convinced that physicians cannot communicate.

Consumer empowerment is related to other building blocks such as outcomes databases, demand management, and clinical reengineering. It is also affected by Internet and on-line services, which will emerge as primary communication channels for tomorrow's health care consumer.

Prevention and wellness also will play a significant role in solving the health care crisis. The reality is simple: People who don't get sick or injured don't consume health care resources. Thus, keeping healthy people out of the health care system is one of the best strategies available for addressing the escalating costs of care.

Evidence of consumers' growing interest in prevention is already obvious in the explosion in purchases of organic or health foods, the rise in popularity of reduced and low-fat foods, and the expansion of health food grocery stores. Once prevalent only within a small subculture of society, these products and services have now penetrated the mainstream population. Even the

Exhibit 2–5 Physician Leadership Profile

- takes action to reengineer the health care system
- merges practice into an integrated Physician Organization
- is informed on state-of-the-art medical management
- takes time to educate other physicians
- anticipates the needs of the market
- leads by example; makes personal changes first
- keeps the interests of patients first
- focuses on teamwork
- is knowledgeable about information technology

most traditional grocery stores feature health food sections and stock organic and low-fat foods.

In the short-term, the gospel of prevention will ensure loyalty to a health system. If a health care system decides to run high-quality, cost-efficient fitness programs and centers, it can easily spin off excess revenue and channel it back into the community. If and when community residents do get sick, they will be more likely to use the facilities and physicians of the sponsoring health system. Moreover, health systems that implement this approach will be better prepared for capitation and the accompanying incentives to keep patients out of costlier care settings.

PHYSICIAN AND EXECUTIVE LEADERSHIP

Physicians' decisions drive more than 80 percent of health care expenditures. Because of physicians' central decision-making responsibility, organizations must resist the temptation to coerce physicians into new organizational alliances or force them to contain costs at the expense of patient care. Physicians—not health care purchasers or health plan executives—must lead the way into the future. No one can do a better job of gauging the needs of patients and balancing patient care against economic considerations. Exhibit 2–5 shows how physicians must serve as leaders in merging independent practices into integrated Physician Organizations. This level of leadership involves persistent, hard work; the will to remain informed and up-to-date; and the desire to lead by example.

NOTES

1. S. Easthaugh, Nationwide EDI System Can Trim Administrative Costs, *Healthcare Financial Management* (1995): 45.

2. The Advisory Board, *Outcomes Strategy Measurement of Hospital Quality under Reform* (Washington, D.C.: The Advisory Board, 1993), 45.

3. S. Larrimer, Mayo's Disease Management System Shows Specialists in Better Light, *Report on Physician Trends* 3, no. 5 (1995).

4. M.A. Goldstein, Demand Management Looks Promising, Too, *Modern Healthcare* 25, no. 34 (1995): 144.

5. M. Edlin, Demand Management: Saving Money with Self-Health, *Managed Healthcare* 5, no. 8 (1995): 30.

6. A Multifactorial Intervention To Reduce the Risk of Falling Among Elderly People Living in the Community, *New England Journal of Medicine* 331, no. 13 (September 29, 1994).

7. M. Hammer and J. Champy, *Reengineering the Corporation: A Manifesto for Business Revolution*, Harper & Row, New York, May 1993.

8. *The Mayo Clinic Family Health Book*, Morrow Publishers, New York, 1994.

Chapter 3

Strategies for Communicating with Physicians in the Era of Health Care Restructuring

Matthew J. Lambert III, M.D., M.B.A.

INTRODUCTION

Communication is something we rely on every day yet frequently take for granted. Anyone who travels to a foreign country and is unable to speak the language quickly learns to appreciate the utility of clear and effective communication. Health care professionals may feel like tourists in a strange land as they watch the restructuring of the financing and delivery of medical care in the United States. In order to compete more effectively in this new environment, health systems, physicians, managed health plans, and other alliance partners are coming together to form Integrated Delivery Systems and organized provider networks.

This chapter explores the role of effective communication in achieving such integration and highlights some of the obstacles that must be overcome. It concludes with recommendations to leaders of any organization seeking to achieve greater dialogue with physicians.

MARKET DYNAMICS AND THE ROLE OF COMMUNICATIONS IN INTEGRATION

There can be no doubt that the world of health care is in a state of confusion. There is a pervasive sense of unease in the medical community as the country wrestles with the future of health care delivery and financing. A major source of angst for health systems—and for physicians, in particular—is the erosion of physicians' influence and autonomy as managed health plans, insurers, and the business purchasers seek to control medical costs.

The burgeoning federal deficit and the looming insolvency of the Medicare Trust Fund remain significant concerns. Legislation proposed to address such issues relies on significant reductions in payments to physicians and health systems, which further increases financial pressure on providers. The volume of uncompensated care is expected to rise as states struggle with ballooning Medicaid budgets and declining federal assistance.

Health care providers have sought to restore the balance of control through activities that emphasize relationship building. The current wisdom is that the independent practitioner and the stand-alone hospital are anachronisms and that strength can only be found by entering partnerships with others. These activities are frequently classified as *integration*—certainly a prime candidate for the most overused word in health care in the 1990s. Many of these efforts fall short because they result only in the *mixture* of disparate elements involved in health care delivery rather than true integration of financial, legal, and operational aspects of care delivery along the continuum of care. Such failures can be attributed to the lack of attention paid to the need for mutual understanding among groups of health care providers, a goal only achievable through effective communication.

A period of chaos nearly always accompanies the movement from equilibrium to a new state. At such times, a trustworthy and steady flow of information becomes a requisite element for a successful transition and continued growth and development. Success in the new health care environment requires innovative approaches to the delivery of efficient, cost-effective care and a willingness to collaborate with multiple partners and different disciplines. However, the existing communication processes for many organizations are likely to hobble that effort. Many surveys list poor communication as a major problem confronting organizations. The attention paid to improving communication is one measure of organizational well-being.

The subject of communication is fundamentally about relationships—how individuals interact with one another, with groups or organizations of which they are a part, and with society. Communication is often discussed as if it were a *thing*—something that one does to another—with a one-way feel about it. In actuality, communication is a dynamic process that is circular in nature rather than linear. It is a transaction in which each party participates continuously in the process and affects the other party in an interdependent manner (see Figure 3–1). What is it about the new era of health care that makes an effective communication process both imperative and problematic at the same time?

In the years after the Second World War, hospitals and physicians enjoyed progressive improvement in their prestige and income. Hospitals provided technological resources and personnel, while physicians provided patients and clinical expertise. It was difficult for one to exist without the other, yet communication was primarily unidirectional—from physician to hospital—and focused on physicians' requests for additional technology to ensure state-of-the-art care. Physicians enjoyed the halcyon days of their autonomy, and hospitals were able to grow and develop capabilities in a wide variety of clinical areas.

In essence, physicians and hospitals operated on parallel tracks. Incentives were aligned, and communication appeared adequate and was rarely an issue. In the early 1980s, the advent of diagnosis-related groups (DRGs) exposed the weaknesses in physician-hospital relationships. Incentives were suddenly no longer aligned; hospitals focused on shortened lengths of stay and resource conservation, while physician reimbursement still rewarded resource-intensive care and prolonged hospitalizations. The commensal relationship that the two parties enjoyed was soon rife with conflict, as physicians saw hospitals usurping their authority and dictating medical care. A climate of distrust has developed and persisted, which has complicated efforts at integration.

However, the adoption of a DRG approach by other payers, increasing market penetration by managed care, and a business community concerned about costs have caused physicians and hospitals to take a new look at their relationship and view each other as potential allies to cope with market-based health care restructuring. With the merger

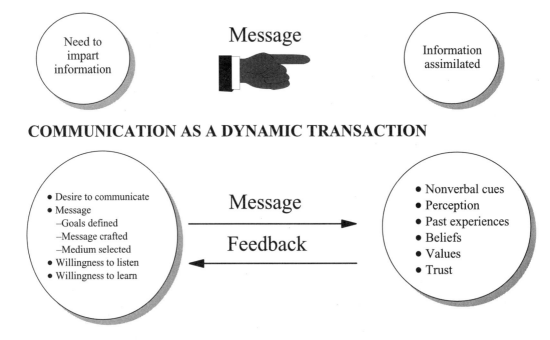

Figure 3–1 Communication process. Communication is not a one-way process, but a dynamic transaction that is capable of refining the message for greatest effect.

---

and consolidation that is leading hospitals to become *health systems* and independent physicians to join large *Physician Organizations*, the need for honest, effective communications is paramount.

Physicians and health systems find themselves in dialogue on a variety of issues. Primary care physicians have climbed to the top of the contracting pyramid and, in highly capitated markets, are in control of the health care dollar. Many health systems and hospitals are primary care–poor and specialist-rich, a professional mix that is unlikely to gain market share and a healthy bottom line. They have sought to strengthen their position by recruiting or purchasing primary care physician practices and their precious inventory of "covered lives."

The ascendancy of the primary care physicians has been more spiritual than financial. Most physicians still see declining reimbursement and increasing overhead as they seek to keep up with the burgeoning administrative demands of managed health care plans. Some have simply opted out of independent practice and sought employment from health systems or other for-profit entities. Others have preferred to exchange a certain portion of their autonomy for a stake in primary care or multispecialty group practices. Certain of these have flourished, especially in areas where managed care penetration is high and capitation is the major form of reimbursement.

Loosely organized Physician Organizations have developed in an attempt to compete for managed care contracts, but many have floundered because of a paucity of business acumen, lack of true integration, and an inability to fund or develop vital information systems. Physician-Hospital Organizations (PHOs) sought to formalize and solidify long-standing relationships with hospitals; they were possible because of hospitals' access to capital, information systems technology, and business expertise. Physicians were able to gain a 50/50 share in governance with little financial investment because they held the trump card—patients. These attempts have been accompanied by problems, primarily due to the clash of bureaucratic and professional cultures and overall control by the hospital and specialists.

The health system, the multispecialty group practice, the PHO, the Physician Organization, and the primary care group are organizations of varying degrees of complexity that are subject to both external and internal pressures and influences. Each is bureaucratic to a varying degree and should pursue actions that further its goals and objectives. Health care executives and physician leaders in charge of such organizations need to put patient and organizational interests above personal goals.

Physicians, on the other hand, value their autonomy and professionalism. Historically they have been the final arbiters of health care decisions, and their stated goal is to provide the highest quality medical care to their patients. For many physicians, this means use of the required resources regardless of cost. Physicians have sought to preserve this autonomy, while integrated organizations have attempted to standardize medical care and optimize the use of scarce resources. The following represents a common example of conflict between these two perspectives:

Example: A newly formed PHO in a market rapidly moving to a managed care standard charged its care management committee with the evaluation of the care provided by its physician members in the intensive care unit (ICU). Lengths of stay were longer than those of comparable institutions, and there were no standards for admission or discharge from the unit. In addition, patients with certain diagnoses, such as acute myocardial infarction, were admitted by numerous physicians, and wide variations in treatment were noted. Although comparable outcomes data were difficult to obtain, the PHO had the impression that its morbidity and mortality statistics were worse than those publicized by other PHOs. The PHO moved to limit the numbers of physicians admitting to the ICU by enforcing strict credentialing standards and selecting those with the best outcomes. In certain cases, mandatory specialty consultations were required. This created an uproar among the physician membership, and several physicians resigned. However, the physician leaders remained focused on their goal; within six months, outcomes and quality standards had improved dramatically, leading to additional managed care contracts for the organization.

In health system organizations, managers are usually responsible for a component of the operation yet remain accountable for the work of varying numbers of subordinates. Physicians see themselves as responsible only for their individual ministrations and not those of their colleagues. The manager's goals are the goals of the organization, but the professional's goals are individual. The evaluation of organizational employees is based on how well their results contribute to the organizational objectives. Physicians are measured by the results of individual patient encounters and how well they uphold the standards of their profession. Take, for instance, the following synopsis of one hospital's efforts to reduce costs and maintain quality:

Example: A merger of two 350-bed community hospitals was consummated in an attempt to gain market share and operational efficiencies. The physicians remained independent. The merged entity embarked on a systemwide reengineering effort in which employees were cross-trained in a variety of clinical areas from phlebotomy to housekeeping and the focus was on a team approach to the delivery of patient care. The transition was difficult for employees; physicians resisted the effort, convinced it would compromise patient care. Orientation sessions for the medical staff on reengineering were poorly attended, and many physicians attributed any problems with patient care to the new program. A number of physicians elected to move their practices to a competing hospital.

Authority in organizations is positional and legitimized by one's place in the hierarchy. In some cases, it may not reflect a person's personal qualities or talents. For physicians and other professionals, the concept of authority is not a central issue. One expects only to defer to an individual on the basis of knowledge and experience. This particular factor is particularly troublesome, because physicians often question the opinions or judgment of any layperson when the issue involves patient care. One might say that the qualities most admired in a physician—such as independence, self-reliance, patient advocacy, and insulation from issues of resource allocation—are antithetical to the smooth working of an organization. Such a conflict has often occurred when organizations have embraced continuous quality improvement and the use of multidisciplinary teams.

Example: A financially successful and progressive community hospital elected to revamp its quality improvement program. Members of the administrative staff and the medical director went to a one-week intensive training course on quality improvement principles. Nurses, administrators, and clinical directors enthusiastically endorsed the quality improvement principles when the group returned and began educational programs. Many physicians refused to participate on multidisciplinary teams dealing with issues of patient care or contributed only rarely. A quality improvement project that was designed to optimize the diagnosis, treatment, and education for breast cancer included four physicians. Two surgeons on the committee refused to entertain suggestions for improvement and resisted plans for institutionally sponsored educational efforts for patients recovering from breast cancer. No changes were made.

Physicians move through a highly competitive premedical and medical curriculum that emphasizes individual accountability and achievement. This orientation is fostered during residency training where, despite the presence of a team of physicians, decision making is not participative but authoritarian. Each person is responsible for a component of patient care, and individual performance—not overall outcome—determines one's evaluation.

Many executives in health care administration are used to a more participative environment. Those who have attended graduate school learn the concept of team study and team project development, in which each person contributes to the end product. Even those with on-the-job training are used to the "group think" form of learning and accomplishment. As a whole, administrators train in a more collaborative environment and understand organizational dynamics.

As health care executives and physicians communicate on more substantive issues, problems with interpretation of messages arise. In some circumstances, it appears as if the two groups speak a different language. Physicians tend to view new initiatives from a clinical rather than a management perspective, and a suggestion that may seem perfectly reasonable from a fiscal vantage point may have clinical consequences not recognized by laypersons. The obverse is also true.

There is a cultural divide that must be bridged by education and communication. Executives must learn about the clinical side of their enterprise in greater detail, and physicians must think more globally about their decisions. Too often, management decisions are made in isolation and handed down for implementation without physician input. Physicians frequently make decisions or requests without regard to their impact on the organization, other patients, and their colleagues.

Physicians work independently and their styles of practice vary. Requests for consultation are formal, as are the replies. Correspondence between physicians is polite, and any criticism of a physician's management or outcomes is verboten, except in the most egregious circumstances. Physicians' communication is most often in the form of a dyad, the one-on-one encounter that is the most basic of human interactions. Both persons simultaneously interact as both source and receiver of a message.

Physicians avoid meetings because they see them as activities that intrude on their clinical practices. The standard quarterly meeting of a medical staff is usually brief and rarely involves any substantive discussion unless it centers on issues of physician autonomy or the erosion of professional stature. Decision making by physicians is generally time-sensitive, and physicians have a low tolerance for ambiguity or delays in implementation.

On the other hand, a health care executive's day tends to be full of meetings—long meetings. Issues are rarely clear-cut, and decisions may not be made for weeks or months. In many cases, the outcome of a specific decision may not be revealed for years. Meetings tend to be multidisciplinary and encourage constructive criticism. These meetings substitute for more formal communication by letter, but phone messages, electronic mail, memos, or direct conversations are useful adjuncts.

COMMUNICATION STRATEGIES FOR INTEGRATION

Such different styles of learning and communication must be understood if physician and executive leaders are to prove effective in organizing and managing Integrated Delivery Systems. Effective communication is one of the most important characteristics of successful organizational-physician interactions. A list of methods to effect an improved communication environment is shown in Exhibit 3–1.

Establish a Climate of Trust

Trust and effective communication are inextricably linked. One cannot have effective communication without trust and vice versa. The last few years have been stressful for all health professionals. At times, organizational decisions are made in haste and the ramifications poorly understood. Those decisions that have negatively affected physicians have contributed to a climate of distrust. Such issues must be acknowledged and a commitment made to move forward honestly and openly on all issues. Trust will develop based on such interactions, but it

---

Exhibit 3–1 Essential Communication Strategies for Integration

- Establish a climate of trust.
- Stabilize relationships with physicians.
- Share good and bad news.
- Seek input and involvement on strategic issues.
- Build physician leadership and expertise in business management.
- Focus on values, not just control.
- Take responsibility for self-education.
- Learn to listen intently.
- Welcome feedback.
- Look for small wins.
- Be very responsive.
- Be flexible and market driven.
- Mine for real solutions rather than fads.
- Make problem solving part of your culture.
- Be willing to admit mistakes and move on.
- Invest your time in people.
- Develop a "guerilla management" style.
- Make any meeting worth the time.
- Be visible.
- Take time to dream and vision.

must be earned and re-earned every day. Relationships are fragile, and lack of attention to them can undermine or destroy the trust that is their foundation.

Stabilize Relationships with Physicians

A major impediment to effective communication is the rapid turnover of health care executives in today's climate. Perhaps only the position of manager of the New York Yankees turns over as rapidly as a hospital's CEO and for the same reason: the team isn't winning. A new CEO often brings a number of new executives and managers to the institution that necessitates a complete rebuilding of the physician communication network. It is in stable and productive health care organizations that effective communication is most often found; in the troubled, marginally successful organization where it is most needed, it is absent or in disrepair. Communication is about relationships; frequent short-term encounters will not engender a sense of security, trust, and a willingness to become involved in the organization's future.

The responsibility for building and maintaining physician relationships should not be left solely to the medical director, the administrator in charge of physician recruitment, or the director of a Managed Services Organization (MSO). Numerous executives and managers in the health systems organization should have this as one of their primary objectives, so that as executives depart, others will continue the relationship-building and follow through on commitments previously made. In this way, the effective communication network will be relatively unaffected by management turnover.

Share Good and Bad News

Too many organizations view their information as proprietary. The strategic plan is often only completely shared with other executives and the board. Financial data are guarded like the secret of eternal youth. Physicians should be part of this information network. They need a context in which to frame efforts at reengineering, cost reduction, and the push toward shorter lengths of stay. Any successful integration effort requires a commitment of the involved parties, and such commitment requires full disclosure. Physicians learn to analyze data and come to reasonable conclusions and outline plans for action. More physicians should serve on key organizational committees. Such information sharing should be an integral part of medical executive committee and quarterly medical staff meetings and informal discussions with physicians.

Seek Input and Involvement on Strategic Issues

Physicians should participate in virtually every major organizational decision that impacts patient care, whether it is a building project, cost-reduction effort, or capital budgeting issue. The Medical Director/Vice-President for Medical Affairs position has assumed a certain prominence as a result of that individual's ability to provide the "physician's perspective" on issues to management and the board. A logical extension of ensuring the physician's perspective is to install a physician as organizational president and CEO, an increasingly frequent occurrence. The broader the consensus of physicians, the easier it will be to implement an initiative. If no input is solicited until late in a project's development, resistance will be maximal and valuable time will be wasted trying to placate physicians who feel disenfranchised.

Build Physician Leadership and Expertise in Business Management

After residency, physicians routinely begin a business that grosses hundreds of thousands of dollars after only a few years. This business requires skills in employee management, recordkeeping, billing, and customer relations—for which physicians have no training. Their day-to-day concern is for individual patient encounters, and not corporate finance or the impact of federal or state policies on health care delivery and finance. However, this information is critical for their survival and should be part of any communication effort.

Physicians often attain leadership positions because of seniority or clinical skill rather than business acumen. Most physicians have little, if any, formal management training, and some are not even able to run an effective meeting. Such physicians should attend seminars on management training such as those sponsored by the American College of Physician Executives. The health system or Physician Organization should fund such educational opportunities or invite management and business gurus to the community for lectures, discussion groups, and workshops. There is also great benefit in visiting Integrated Delivery Systems and physician leaders who are progressive and successful in the current health care climate. Physician Organizations should encourage and support informal and formal physician leaders in gaining critical business management and strategic planning skills from one of the many educational training programs sponsored by leading health systems or graduate schools. Success of any communication strategy rests with educated and motivated leadership.

Focus on Values, Not Just Control

In their recent book, *Built To Last: Successful Habits of Visionary Companies,* James Collins and Jerry Porras of Stanford Graduate Business School identified the characteristics of visionary companies.[1] Interestingly, the most successful companies did not have a charismatic leader. Rather they had a set of core values that transcended any one person. The most valuable CEO or administrative leader is the one that gets the job done—not the one that gets all the credit. Power is useless if it does not effect change and achieve success.

In nonprofit Integrated Delivery Systems, it is imperative that strong consideration be given to augmenting physician participation on the board of directors. Shared governance along with shared management will go a long way to augment the level of trust and solidify these new relationships. Federal guidelines limit formal physician governance to no more than 20 percent of the board in tax-exempt organizations. However, an informal committee composed exclusively of physicians could review proposals and initiatives and make recommendations to the board, ensuring that the physicians' perspective is taken into account. Participation on such a committee could be a fertile training ground for future physician board members.

This shared governance must focus on the vision, values, goals, and objectives of the organization. Physicians should see their leadership role as bringing a clinical perspective to decision making rather than serving as a lobbyist for the medical profession. Nothing is as sure to doom the future of an integrated organization as an adversarial relationship among its leaders. Leaders should adopt the aphorism: Share the power to build a more effective, viable, and committed organization.

Take Responsibility for Self-Education

Integration and effective communication are abetted by the willingness of the parties to learn as much about one another's culture and concerns as possible. CEOs, executives, and physician leaders should become familiar with all areas of the organization. Physician leaders should allocate a portion of their day to visiting nonclinical areas or learning about finance, budgeting, and marketing. Health care executives should visit clinical areas on a regular basis. It has a decidedly positive impact on physicians (and employees) to see a CEO don surgical scrubs and tour the operating rooms, spend time in the emergency department, or visit a physician's office. Attempting to gain such knowledge from one's administrative office is impossible. One needs to walk in another's shoes to the extent that this is possible. This willingness to learn and an openness to new ideas will build a trusting relationship and foster effective communication.

Learn To Listen Intently

Anyone wishing to become an effective communicator must be an extremely good listener. We often become too focused on our message and how we deliver it and neglect to listen to the feedback that informs us as to how the message was received. Remember communication is a circular—not a linear—process, and each oral message is a unique event that cannot be reproduced. Lack of attention or allowing oneself to become distracted is a disservice to others and to ourselves. In a typical day about 75 percent of our communication time is spent in verbal communication—30 percent of the time we are speaking and 45 percent of the time we are listening—so it is critical that we develop active-listening skills.

Welcome Feedback

It is only through feedback that one learns whether the message was interpreted as intended. Feedback also allows one to modify or refine the message, or it may include new information helpful to the process. Feedback highlights the dynamic nature of communication, and its absence saps the potential vitality of the communication process. Colleagues and subordinates learn from experience about a person's attitude toward feedback. If feedback is not solicited, treated with disinterest or disdain, or greeted with a defensive attitude, then it will cease to be offered and communication will be ineffective.

Oral communication allows one to receive instantaneous feedback by observing another person's reaction through facial expression or body language. Written communication lacks immediate feedback and should encourage the individual receiving the message to voice concerns or make suggestions. Written communication must be carefully crafted, edited, and reviewed so that unintended messages are not sent. The unavoidable lag time for feedback in written communication can be disastrous in situations where a communication is controversial or misunderstood.

Look for Small Wins

Health care today offers little opportunity for the "big score." So many elements of health care delivery—from reimbursement to lengths of stay—are profoundly influenced or controlled by outside agencies. The goals and objectives for health care organizations have timelines of several years. Physicians are impatient and used to seeing the results of their efforts over a much shorter time frame. To build the climate of trust essential to effective communication, organizations should look for opportunities to make changes that will immediately affect the quality of physicians' and patients' interactions with the organization. Streamlined registration, billing, scheduling, and results reporting can go a long way to increase customer satisfaction. Education in customer service should be a part of every new employee's orientation and a criterion for year-end evaluations.

Be Very Responsive

One of an organization's primary objectives should be for its constituents to view it as responsive. Physicians often complain that executives take too long to get things done. Even though many of the issues affecting physicians are complicated and take time to resolve, they may become mired in the bureaucracy as projects are started one after another without any one of them coming to conclusion. Leaders must establish a climate of accountability, in which expectations for project development and completion are articulated and adhered to. In particularly complex or difficult projects, updates should be provided to physicians on a regular basis to let them know that the project has not been forgotten and is moving forward. Standards should be established throughout the organization for everything from responding to patient complaints to returning telephone calls.

Be Flexible and Market Driven

For individuals in leadership roles who have access to reams of information and analysis, it is difficult not to sometimes feel that the path is clear and that there is one solution to a problem. Suggestions from outside of management are often treated in a patronizing manner or discarded without much thought. The fact is that no one has all the answers, and creative solutions often come from the most unlikely sources. Physicians know clinical medicine and the highs and lows of delivering care to patients. Because of their day-to-day interaction with patients, physicians are often able to identify impediments to care and offer possible solutions that could make such care more efficient and patient-physician friendly. Leaders should be willing to entertain any suggestion and implement a pilot project to see if it has utility. Such an openness to new ideas is one major way to get physicians more involved in problem solving and to help achieve the type of integrated organization desired.

Mine for Real Solutions Rather Than Fads

It would be embarrassing to determine how much money has been expended on consultant and lawyer fees in health care organizations during the last 10 years. It would be even more revealing to assess how many of the recommendations from such consultants and lawyers bore any fruit whatsoever or were still in effect. In desperate times, people look for the quick fix, the easy answer, that winning lottery ticket that will vault an organization to the top of the industry. There are, however, no stock solutions to the problems facing health care today. Like politics, health care is primarily a local phenomenon that demands solutions that are responsive to the local marketplace.

Physicians and managers have come to expect a "fad of the month" from leadership that often turns an organization upside down for very little long-term gain. There is no question that selective consultations may have value, but with every new trend there arises a group of consultants who are but one chapter or one project ahead of the organization that hires them. If a problem is identified, it is worthwhile to work initially with physicians and internal managers to develop a locally generated solution as opposed to expending additional financial resources on outside "experts." Such an approach will generate additional credibility and mark the administration as serious about finding real solutions.

Make Problem Solving Part of Your Culture

The health care highway was at one time a pleasure to travel. There were few roadblocks to overcome on the way to achieving personal, professional, and organizational goals. Now that same highway is littered with impediments that significantly affect the ability to achieve desired goals and objectives. A good deal of the communication process is now directed at problem solving and requires particular techniques for decision making and implementation. Success in problem solving is predicated on realizing that each individual may view a particular obstacle differently, based upon how it impacts that individual's journey. It is important, therefore, to begin problem solving by attracting a multidisciplinary task force of physician leaders and executives committed to developing a solution geared to the community and market.

The goal of such a task force would be to resolve the cognitive dissonance created by the problem and restore equilibrium. Problem-solving skills must be acquired through experience that necessarily implies both successes and failures. A true problem solver must be capable of patience, reflective thinking, and understanding. Any problem-solving effort will be affected by the individual member's attitudes, motivations, values, beliefs, behaviors, and perceptions.

There are a number of stages in problem-solving communication, beginning with an analysis of the problem. The problem must be identified and stated clearly. One needs to know the history of the problem, its perceived severity, and whether some components might be addressed separately. If there are current efforts underway to solve the problem, they need to be identified and a decision made as to whether additional efforts are needed. To achieve a sense of urgency, it is helpful to envision the consequences if the problem is allowed to persist.

A multidisciplinary task force is valuable when the problem is first analyzed. Brainstorming is a form of communication through which multiple possible solutions are offered free of initial evaluations and judgments. The tendency to reject such offerings out-of-hand must be avoided until the process is complete. The process should then move to define certain parameters within which any solution must fall and then evaluate the proposals in light of such standards. For instance, any proposal must lead to a real solution, not just a superficial improvement or temporary amelioration of the condition. It clearly must be workable in light of any resource constraints and should be as complete as possible. Finally, it must be acceptable to all parties or at least there should be consensus that the proposed alternative is the best available solution.

The implementation must be carefully planned because it often involves other individuals or groups who have not been exposed to the extensive analysis and dialogue that have led to the proposed solution. This may be the most common juncture at which the communication process breaks down. Perhaps it is the enthusiasm of the problem-solving task force to implement the solution that often leads to resistance on the part of those charged with implementation. The communication must be as carefully crafted as any element of the problem-solving process and must include an analysis of the problem, the method of developing proposed solutions, the rationale for settling on one alternative, and the plan for implementation. The feedback process is essential for evaluating the effectiveness of the solution and should involve everyone affected by the problem and its solution.

Be Willing To Admit Mistakes and Move On

Robert MacNamara, the Secretary of Defense for President Lyndon Johnson, published a book in 1995 that acknowledged the many mistakes made by American political leaders and advisors during the prosecution of the war in Vietnam.[2] How useful was this exercise compared to the value of articulating such concerns 30 years earlier? Mistakes should be acknowledged before they become obvious to everyone. Any initiative must be constantly monitored to ensure that it is achieving the organization's goal. There should be mileposts set up beforehand to allow an objective appraisal of the project. Many projects cost a good deal of money, especially in areas such as work redesign or continuous quality improvement. Some of these initiatives will not bear fruit; however, because of the substantial initial investment, many leaders are unwilling to scrap a project lest they be criticized for expending resources unnecessarily. This is the philosophy of the gambler who is on a losing streak—put in more money and perhaps the losses can be regained. There will be good investments and bad investments. The important thing is to be willing to invest but to know when to quit and how to move on to the next challenge.

Invest Your Time in People

People—not projects—make a health care organization great. Leaders who spend their time creating larger edifices or acquiring additional technology at the expense of their relationships with others will have a short tenure. The attitudes of physicians and executives are intimately related. If one group is unhappy, the other is likely to be similarly affected. In many cases, patients will suffer if administration-employee-physician relationships are poor. It is easy for a leader to occupy days with meeting after meeting, often with the same small group of individuals, discussing organizational finance or strategic planning. Some part of every day should be set aside for talking with the people who form the backbone of the organization, listening to their concerns and suggestions. In the long run, these hours will prove more productive and important to the organization than most of the daily meetings.

Develop a "Guerilla Management" Style

Managers and staff will adopt the management style of their leader. If he or she spends the day in meetings or the office, then so will they. Administrative offices located far from the organizations' day-to-day activities can be detrimental by limiting leaders' exposure to physicians, patients, and employees. Every member of the management team should spend a good part of their day "on the road" taking the pulse of the organization by spending time in clinical and nonclinical areas. Many meetings can be held during these visits, even while walking around and discussing the issue at hand with member physicians and staff.

Physicians should be visited in ambulatory care clinics, the hospital, and their offices. Such an office visit should allow some time to be spent with the physician's employees to learn what the health care organization can do to make their job easier. This direct approach is the best way to demonstrate concern for the physician, the practice, and the patients and should be employed with all parties who interact with the hospital, especially third-party payers. Establishing such relationships can position the Integrated Delivery System to be receptive to managed care and can place the physicians in a favorable light as members of an organization that is proactive about cost control.

Make Any Meeting Worth the Time

Meetings are a necessary evil in any organization's day-to-day operations. The reason that meetings have such a bad reputation is that they are poorly organized and poorly run. Physicians have little patience for sitting in a room for an hour or two and then leaving with the sense that little was accomplished and their time was wasted. They frequently opt out of meetings and are reluctant to serve on committees or task forces because of the time involved. However, if someone held a series of meetings that guaranteed to show physicians how to increase their income by 50 percent, attendance would not be a problem. The secret to physician involvement in meetings is twofold: being sensitive to the physician's time and ensuring that the meeting delivers value.

In the majority of instances, physicians attending meetings are volunteers. Their time could be better used seeing patients and earning income. They are willing to give up that remuneration for the greater good of the organization that will hopefully benefit them and their patients. Many participants arrive at meetings unclear about the meeting's purpose because it has not been conveyed beforehand. Many meetings do not even bother with a clear agenda. In addition, a good part of the meeting may be spent developing data that could have been derived ahead of time.

Anyone asked to commit time to a meeting should be clearly informed of the meeting's purpose along with its goals and objectives. Supporting documentation or background material should be submitted ahead of time. Questions that need to be asked and opinions that need to be voted on to allow the meeting to move forward expeditiously should be presented beforehand and the data collected and analyzed for the meeting. An agenda should be distributed, listing all topics to be discussed and the time allotted for each, and the time the meeting will start and adjourn. Meetings should start on time. Many organizations allow a 9:00 meeting to start at 9:30. Persons attending such meetings will rarely arrive on time because they know they will have to sit around for 30 minutes doing nothing. If meetings start on time, people will get the message and begin arriving on time so they do not miss the information.

Meetings should not take more than an hour or 90 minutes at the most. It is important that meetings end on time and that unresolved business be taken care of with a follow-up meeting or by way of "virtual meeting" where the issues can be further analyzed by correspondence or individual meetings. Meetings can be dynamic, informative, and fun if the organizers pay attention to these few simple principles.

Be Visible

Physicians learn early in their careers that one predictor of success is visibility. The consultant no one sees rarely gets a referral. Visibility connotes concern, dedication, and involvement. Physicians view an organization's leader the same way. It matters little if the leader puts in a 12-hour day working behind closed doors or in meetings. The management staff needs to be receptive and accessible. Too often they act like the Wizard of Oz, manipulating the environment but sequestered behind a management curtain unavailable to persons desperate for information and individual contact.

A few minutes in dialogue with physicians can pay significant dividends by alerting the administrator to potential problems before they grow. The time can be used for a straw poll on a particular idea or initiative that is being considered. Visibility is especially important in areas of patient care. An extension of the goal of visibility is to actually work on a patient unit for a few hours. Whether one is a lay or physician administrator, there is work that can be done. That effort—that willingness to be a part of the day-to-day operations of an organization—goes a long way to building credibility, commitment, and effective communication channels.

Take Time To Dream and Vision

Much of the workday is spent on issues that should be relegated to the bottom of the "in basket," but most people feel compelled to deal with them immediately. People answer almost every phone call, even though they may be in the middle of another project. What is not done is to set aside part of the day to think about the future. Quiet time, reflective time, visioning time, creative time—whatever one wishes to call it—is absent from the days of most physicians and health care executives.

A portion of every day should be committed to such reflection, a time when other issues should be put on hold. Such time not only brings some balance into lives filled with stress but also affords one the opportunity to think about how the organization can and should change in response to the evolving health care environment.

In addition, physicians, executives, and board members should take a special time each year to get away and discuss the future of health care and their role in it. If the future is left to the future, organizations will continue to struggle as changes occur and they are unprepared to deal with them. This type of communication with physicians is perhaps the most important, for it allows a sharing of visions and an opportunity to create something new and lasting together.

EMPOWER COMMUNICATION PLAN AND PHYSICIAN LEADERSHIP

Any communication plan should be creative and tailored to meet the needs of the organization and the current environment. It should receive as high a priority as any traditional element of strategic organizational or business planning. Most of all it must be interactive. In this age of virtual organizations, networks, and the Internet, people learn by doing, and interactivity is the key to learning.

Communication, like many routine activities, is taken for granted. The majority of our organizational and personal problems can be attributed to a breakdown in the communication process. In health care today, one cannot afford to disregard such a fundamental skill. Effective communication between physicians and between physicians and executives is possible and necessary for organizational effectiveness and survival. It must not be neglected. But it is the responsibility of both physician and executive leaders to lead by example as they implement the basic and advanced strategies for communications that build trust and lead to clinically effective health care systems.

NOTES

1. J. Collins and J. Porras, *Built To Last: Successful Habits of Visionary Companies* (New York, N.Y.: Harper Business, 1994).

2. R. MacNamara, *In Retrospect: The Tragedy and Lessons of Vietnam* (New York, N.Y.: Times Books, 1995).

SUGGESTED READING

Flower, J. 1995. Built to last. *Healthcare Forum Journal* 38, no. 5: 62–68.

Harlem, O.K. 1977. *Communication in medicine: A challenge to the profession.* Basel, Switzerland: S. Karger.

Hepner, J.O., ed. 1980. *Hospital administrator-physician relationships.* Vol. 2. St. Louis, Mo.: C.V. Mosby Company.

Hershey, N., ed. and author. 1982. *Hospital-physician relationships: Case studies and commentaries on medical staff problems.* Gaithersburg, Md.: Aspen Publishers, Inc.

King, M., et al. 1983. *Irresistible communication: Creative skills for the health professional.* Philadelphia, Pa.: W.B. Saunders.

Munn, H.E., Jr., and N. Metzger. 1981. *Effective communication in health care: A supervisor's handbook.* Gaithersburg, Md.: Aspen Publishers, Inc.

Peitchinis, J.A. 1976. *Staff communication in the health services.* New York, N.Y.: Springer Publishing Company, Inc.

Rubright, R. 1984. *Persuading physicians: A guide for hospital executives.* Gaithersburg, Md.: Aspen Publishers, Inc.

Shortell, S.M. 1991. *Effective hospital-physician relationships.* Ann Arbor, Mich.: Health Administration Press Perspectives.

Smith, V.M., and T.A. Bass. 1979. *Communication for health professionals.* Philadelphia, Pa.: J.B. Lippincott Co.

Stewart, J. 1972. *Bridges not walls: A book about interpersonal communication.* Reading, Mass.: Addison-Wesley Publishing Company.

Wheatley, M.J. 1992. *Leadership and the new science: Learning about organization from an orderly universe.* San Francisco, Calif.: Berrett-Koehler Publishers, Inc.

Yaggy, D., and P. Hodgson, eds. 1985. *Physicians and hospitals: The great partnership at the crossroads.* Durham, N.C.: Duke University Press.

Chapter 4

The Five Stages of Managed Care and Physician Organizations

Russell C. Coile Jr., Ph.D.

We have some idea of where we would like to be in the year 2000. The question is: what do we do in 1995?

Gerald McManis, CEO Summit on Physician-Hospital Integration

INTRODUCTION

America's physicians, hospitals, and Health Maintenance Organizations (HMOs) need transitional strategies to move them through the development of tomorrow's Integrated Delivery Systems (IDSs). Will the integration vehicles of today effectively make the transition to tomorrow? Five years from now, Independent Practice Associations (IPAs), foundations, Management Services Organizations (MSOs), and Physician-Hospital Organizations (PHOs) may be relics.[1]

The last frontier of twenty-first-century medicine is *integration*. In the next five years, America's 600,000 practicing physicians will join groups, develop multisite regional medical networks, and create long-term strategic alliances with hospitals and managed care plans. Even the most skilled practitioners cannot go it alone. Solo practices and small groups are substantially disadvantaged in the industrialization of health care. More than half of practicing physicians will form or join groups before the year 2000. The rush to integration is inevitable, driven by economic threats and managed care contracting opportunities.

Physician Organizations will be centerpieces of regional health care delivery. Multisite medical groups will manage the care and costs of thousands of enrolled HMO members. A consensus is emerging on the characteristics of tomorrow's Integrated Delivery Systems:

- Capitation will be the dominant form of payment.
- IDSs will serve an enrolled population base of at least 250,000.
- Provider networks will organize physicians and hospitals on a regional or statewide basis.
- IDSs will have multiyear, exclusive relationships with insurers and HMOs and may own a captive HMO/insurer.
- Physician Organizations will accept and manage risk under capitation.
- IDSs will provide physicians with shared governance and equity opportunity.
- Systems must manage clinical care to control costs.
- Care managers must have immediate access to clinical and cost data at the point of care.[2]

But for every rule of IDS formation, there will be exceptions. In rural areas, an IDS may serve 25,000 enrollees, not 250,000 to 500,000 people. Nonprofit and for-profit hospitals may become partners in the same Integrated Delivery Systems. Some HMOs and insurers like Aetna, Prudential, and Foundation Health will own their networks through physician practice acquisition. Other HMOs like U.S. Healthcare and FHP will simply "rent" providers at market prices.

Providers are moving aggressively to develop their own integrated systems that can contract on an exclusive basis with HMOs, insurers, and employers. Large multi-hospital systems like Sacramento's Sutter, Los Angeles-based UniHealth, Sisters of Providence in Seattle, and Sentara in Norfolk will own HMOs. Physician groups and multispeciality medical clinics will own and manage large regional systems, such as the Geisinger, Oschner, and Mayo Clinics.

The battle to dominate regional provider networks is just beginning. Physicians have the lead in the West Coast model, where medical megagroups like Mullikin, Friendly Hills, and Hill Medical Group hold global capitation contracts. Elsewhere, hospitals and health systems, with their deep pockets, are purchasing hundreds of primary care physicians and specialists. Provider-sponsored integrated systems assume long-term cooperation between physicians and hospitals. But given the economic and competitive pressures of a managed care market, will physicians and hospitals compete for a "shrinking pie" of health care reimbursement?

PHOs—ARE THEY WORKING AND WILL THEY LAST?

The integration of physicians and hospitals is still in the early stages. More than half of all PHOs (51 percent) have been established less than one year, according to a 1995 study by Ernst & Young's national health care group in Washington, D.C.[3] Fewer than 15 percent of PHOs are more than five years old. Contracting, collaboration, and capitation are the primary reasons that providers are taking these first steps toward integration.

The goal of PHO formation is to improve leverage of physicians and hospitals in managed care contracting, and the concept is working. PHOs are gaining contracts and covered lives rapidly. One in four PHOs is managing more than 75,000 managed care enrollees. Already, PHOs have been formed in more than 40 states, especially in localities with greater than 15 percent managed care penetration. Early feedback from PHO organizers is positive: a majority of PHOs are meeting key objectives in collaborating, improving physician relations, sharing financial risk, and enhancing quality of care (see Figure 4–1).

The PHO is a form of strategic business alliance that links private physicians and medical groups with hospitals and health systems. There is no merger, acquisition, or employment. The PHO is a partnership; it will succeed because it puts hospitals and physicians on an equal footing, as business allies in a contractual agreement. PHOs may be the parent companies of tomorrow's integrated delivery networks. The PHO model of shared governance, typically with 50/50 representation of physicians to health system administrators and lay trustees, may provide a model for future delivery systems and Managed Care Organizations.

Futurist Jeff Goldsmith calls this "virtual integration." The strategy of *virtual integration*, like virtual reality, is a low-investment set of arrangements between hospitals, doctors, and managed care plans to provide services. What holds these *virtual* systems together and makes them profitable are (1) the operating system, which is the framework of agreements and protocols for managing patients; and (2) the framework of incentives that controls how physicians and hospitals are paid. Goldsmith, president of Health

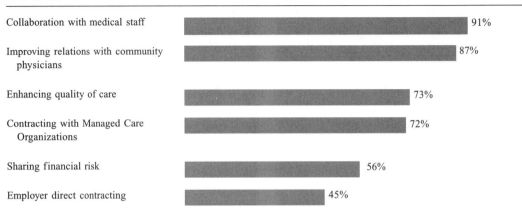

Figure 4–1 Satisfaction levels with PHOs meeting established goals. *Source:* Data from Ernst & Young and *Healthcare Financial Management*, 1995.

Futures in Bannockburn, Illinois, fears that the current frenzy of system restructuring may actually make it more difficult for hospitals and physicians to function under capitation. Goldsmith counsels: Don't put your capital into purchasing hospitals or physicians. The fatal flaw in many integration efforts is the desire to acquire, control, and manage all aspects of a fully comprehensive delivery system.[4]

TWENTY-FIRST-CENTURY HEALTH REFORM WILL BE PHYSICIAN LED

Capitated physician groups and HMOs are leading a market revolution. If Hillary Clinton put the nation's 41 million uninsured out to bid at California HMO prices, health reform would cost only $10 billion dollars, at rates averaging $125 per member per month, or $2,500 per year. In a recent issue of the *Los Angeles Times*, CareAmerica advertised that it was accepting self-employed individuals and families, and in the same issue Foundation Health Plan advertised its HMO plan with age-specific prices.[5] When trendsetting California HMOs market to "groups of one," the rest of the insurance industry is sure to follow.

Chances of achieving sweeping health reform and insurance protection for America's 41 million uninsured are limited between now and the year 2000. But many of the goals of health reform are being achieved by voluntary actions of physicians, hospitals, HMOs, and employers. It is market reform—not policy reform—that is driving the future of America's health industry.

HMO prices in California and the nation have been driven down by employers consolidating their purchasers' clout. When California's Public Employee Retirement System, bargaining on behalf of 900,000 covered lives, declared it would not pay HMO price increases, Fortune 500 employers took notice. The result: in 1995, HMO prices fell by 1.2 percent. Major employers stood up to their insurers and managed care plans, demanding price reductions, and HMO stock prices fell by 10 to 20 percent. This is yet another example of a California wave that crashed on many distant beaches.[6]

What about markets far from California? How can providers and health plans calculate new strategies for integration in other markets that are far down the learning curve? The answer is to follow the example of more advanced markets. The key to market reform is increasing levels of HMO enrollment, which will transform American medicine and the nation's $1 billion industry as it goes through the five stages of managed care.

FIVE STAGES OF MANAGED CARE

There are five stages of managed care, with quite predictable market events and strategic responses. At every stage, a new set of relationships evolves among the major players, including physicians and hospitals, HMOs and insurers, and employers and government. That is, at each level of managed care penetration, providers, payers, and purchasers restructure their relationships, as each party seeks to control its market and its destiny. Pay attention! There are lessons to learn and patterns to predict in each of the five stages.

The key is HMO enrollment. Look for the markets with high levels of HMO penetration. New patterns often arise in response to HMO moves. That has been demonstrated over and over, usually in managed care hot spots like southern California and Minnesota's Twin Cities. But managed care is spreading quickly. As of July 1995, more than 42 million Americans were enrolled in HMOs—some 20 percent of the population.[7] In major metropolitan areas, HMO penetration averages 23 percent. HMOs are now growing in all regions. Midsize cities are the next target for HMO marketing. HMOs grew by 21.4 percent in markets with population between 250,000 and 1 million.

Most Americans live in stage 1 to stage 3 markets. Stage 4 markets are mostly located on the coasts. Baltimore and Boston have recently joined Los Angeles and San Diego with HMO penetration of from 25 to 40 percent. Based on pure HMO enrollment, there are only a handful of stage 5 markets, according to Minnesota-based InterStudy, which maintains a national database on HMO development (see Table 4–1). Where are stage 5 markets? West Coast locations like Sacramento and San Francisco/Oakland are now being joined by Miami; Tucson; and Wheeling, West Virginia—which have more than 40 percent HMO membership. These are the most heavily penetrated markets in the nation.

Stage 1: Can't Spell HMO

Characteristics

Stage 1 markets have little managed care and few pressures to change (see Table 4–2). Preferred Provider Organizations (PPOs) are the most common form of managed care plan in these market regions. Most hospitals organize open-panel Physician Organizations (IPAs), which create a distribution network for discounted patients from health insurers. Physician interest in getting organized is usually low. Medical leadership rarely goes beyond organizing an IPA.

In stage 1 markets, providers should beware of "PHO-itis" in the rush to integration, cautions medical strategist Jonathan Lord, M.D., physician consultant to the American Hospital Association. Frequent mistakes are: (1) the "y'all come" model of Physician Organization with no selection criteria; (2) "$200 in a hat" financing from physicians, which provides little capital or commitment; and (3) the "let's really get an advanced foundation model," an expensive option in states like California with strong corporate-practice-of-medicine laws.[8]

Stage 1 has long ago faded in the rear-view mirror in advanced managed care markets like California, Minneapolis, and Oregon. Today's stage 1 markets are mostly remote and rural. Only two states (Alaska and Wyoming) still had no licensed HMOs in 1995. But managed care is finally arriving in places like Augusta, Georgia, and Bangor, Maine. Managed care penetration is low, but HMO enrollment is

Table 4–1 Top 10 HMO Markets: Large, Medium, Small (July 1994)

Metropolitan Area	Enrollment	Population	Penetration (%)
Large (1 million +)			
Rochester, NY	629,743	1,150,085	54.8
Buffalo, NY	516,093	1,048,336	49.2
San Francisco, CA	804,290	1,735,896	46.3
Miami, FL	925,003	2,096,779	44.1
Dayton-Springfield, OH	415,941	1,029,609	40.4
Los Angeles, CA	3,622,336	9,593,812	37.8
Minneapolis-St. Paul, MN	1,033,788	2,747,970	37.6
Oakland, CA	811,187	2,254,598	36.0
Baltimore, MD	926,704	2,578,462	35.9
Boston, MA	1,282,443	3,624,632	35.4
Medium (250,000–999,999)			
Trenton, NJ	250,158	352,656	70.9
Worcester, MA	442,283	768,202	57.6
Vallejo-Fairfield, CA	241,350	488,393	49.4
Eugene, OR	150,986	306,220	49.3
Salem, OR	145,512	300,916	48.4
Madison, WI	189,087	397,361	47.6
Santa Rosa, CA	174,983	420,200	41.6
Tucson, AZ	292,563	721,874	40.5
Santa Barbara, CA	152,315	400,067	38.1
Albuquerque, NM	249,204	663,422	37.6
Small (less than 250,000)			
Wausau, WI	87,126	124,912	69.7
Medford-Ashland, OR	95,446	158,468	60.2
Vineland-Bridgeton, NJ	81,579	149,484	54.6
Champaign-Urbana, IL	99,700	187,261	53.2
Jacksonville, FL	70,797	162,148	43.7
Kenosha, WI	59,920	138,768	43.2
Jackson, TN	35,944	84,429	42.6
Dubuque, IA	37,863	93,523	40.5
Muskegon, MI	68,456	149,484	39.8
Olympia, WA	62,070	174,487	35.6

Source: Reprinted with permission from *The InterStudy Competitive Edge*, Vol. 5, No. 1, © 1995, Interstudy.

---

rising quickly, the ripple effect of HMO marketing efforts in nearby Atlanta and Boston. Aggressive medical groups like PhyCor, Caremark, and Coastal Physicians are purchasing primary care physician practices throughout the Southeast and Midwest. Local hospitals are being wooed by emerging nonprofit networks, and by expansion-minded for-profit organizations like Columbia/HCA. Few hospitals will stand alone with affiliation by stage 3.

Examples of stage 1 markets include Bangor, Maine; Las Cruces, New Mexico; and Springfield, Massachusetts.

Strategies

The most essential strategic steps that physicians and hospitals can take in stage 1 markets include:

- Educate physician leaders and trustees about managed care.

Table 4-2 Stage 1: "Can't Spell HMO"

Characteristics	Strategies
HMO <5%	Independent HMOs start up
Provider payments	Discounts, prior authorization
Capitation	Bundled prices for specialty care
Indemnity >30%	Insurers ignore HMOs, develop PPOs
Employers	Install first HMO options
Solo/small groups	Form open-panel IPAs
Free-standing hospitals	Prefer to "go it alone"
Ambulatory <15%	Don't compete with physicians
Profits 6–10%	Invest in capital spending
Quality	Respond to Joint Commission on Accreditation of Healthcare Organizations regulations

- Develop open-panel PHO as a joint venture with physicians (50/50), and announce plans to close the panel within two years.
- Inform the hospital board that the hospital will experience declining utilization and revenue shortfalls as managed care grows; present California data from stage 3 markets.
- Undertake hospitalwide cost containment programs to boost financial reserves.
- Seek designation as preferred provider by insurers and newly established HMOs.

Stage 2: Managed Care Gets Aggressive

Characteristics

Stage 2 markets are often jolted into the next stage by an unexpected act that breaks up historic patterns, like the sale of a key medical group to a Physician Practice Management Company. Managed care tactics get rougher. HMOs may switch hospitals in stage 2, sometimes without warning. Now that the ground is shifting, hospitals and physicians finally recognize that managed care's arrival is inevitable, and begin to prepare (see Table 4–3).

Providers in stage 2 markets can expect lower prices and more hassles from HMOs. Worse yet, traditional insurers begin to act just as aggressively as HMOs in denying treatment. Urban HMOs soon arrive in droves, searching for new markets in more thinly populated markets with fewer large employers. Examples are Kaiser's market entry into Bakersfield, California, and U.S. Healthcare's entry into Atlanta. Stage 2 markets are especially vulnerable to a stage 4 move, like Aetna and Prudential purchasing local practices and establishing insurer-owned primary care networks.

In stage 2, busy physicians may ignore the slow spread of managed care, throwing those contracts in the trashcan. Large, successful single-speciality groups may refuse to contract with HMOs completely in stage 2. But younger physicians sign up eagerly. Hospitals in stage 2 markets are often reluctant to purchase physician practices, not wanting to offend their key referral sources. Large out-of-area medical groups take advantage of hospital reticence and begin to acquire primary care physicians (PCPs) in these underdeveloped markets.

Table 4–3 Stage 2: Managed Care Gets Aggressive

Characteristics	Strategies
HMO 5–15%	HMO contracts with PCP groups
Provider payments	Deeper discounts, tougher controls
Capitation	First capitation contracts to PCPs
Indemnity <25%	Insurers convert to PPOs, start HMOs
Employers	Form coalitions, share data
Medical groups	Small groups expand, "without walls"
Hospital systems	Purchase weak hospitals
Ambulatory care <20%	Build MOBs to put physicians on campus
Profits 2–3%	Cost containment (but no layoffs)
Quality	Insurers select "institutes of quality"

Examples of stage 2 markets include Atlanta, Georgia; Dallas and Houston, Texas; Knoxville, Tennessee; and Pittsburgh, Pennsylvania.

Strategies

The most important strategies that physicians and hospitals can pursue in stage 2 are:

- Hire a strong medical director who can develop a real medical organization.
- Physician specialists should begin to develop networks, identify potential merger partners, and recruit young physicians to expand the group.
- Physicians groups must quickly develop capital reserves through retained earnings and self-investment, or they will be dependent upon hospitals and entrepreneurs in stages 3 and 4.
- Encourage the development of primary care–based medical groups.
- Develop a regional network of preferred hospitals.
- Hire managed care vice-president to plan and direct strategy.
- Upgrade information systems and purchase software for HMO contract management.
- Educate physician and trustee leadership with site visits to Los Angeles, Minneapolis-St. Paul, or San Diego.
- Defer all capital investments for facilities. (Note: Save capital for HMO investment and medical organization.)

Stage 3: Managed Care Domination

Characteristics

Stage 3 markets are chaotic. Old patterns are really breaking down now, and networking is very active, with frequent announcements of new alliances among hospitals and physicians. In stage 3, at least one hospital or system is purchasing physician groups, and it may spend $5 to 10 million. Established multispecialty group practices are buying small groups and solo practices. Insurance companies and HMOs compete to purchase physicians and develop their company-owned primary care networks. Provider-sponsored HMOs have an opportunity to be home-grown, especially if they bring in an experienced HMO/health plan partner. Secondary markets like Baton Rouge, Louisiana, begin to be invaded by Medicare HMOs in stage 3 (see Table 4–4).

Table 4-4 Stage 3: Managed Care Domination

Characteristics	Strategies
HMO 15–25%	HMOs aggressively use market power
Provider payment	Fees/per diems drop below cost
Capitation	Widespread capitation of PCPs
Indemnity <15	Insurers convert PPO enrollees to HMO
Employers	Companies start direct contracting
Physician groups	Everyone buys PCP groups
Multihospital systems	Expand regional/state networks
Ambulatory care <35%	Network of satellite ambulatory care centers
Profits 0–1%	Restructuring/layoffs
Quality	Reengineering/patient-focused care

Traditional patterns break down in this stage. Crossing of ownership and religious boundaries can be expected in stage 3 markets, like Columbia/HCA's acquisition of a Catholic health system in Cleveland, Ohio. Multihospital systems grow in Stage 3, adding affiliates and merging with smaller hospitals with weak finances.

Remember those "busy physicians" who would not sign up with HMOs in stages 1 and 2? By stage 3, these physicians are swamped by HMO controls and sinking revenues. Physician specialists feel the economic impact of managed care in stage 3. Depression is widespread, and some physicians leave the market. Physicians begin to recognize that they must organize to compete. To have leverage in the managed care marketplace requires at least 20 physicians in a single-speciality group, 40 to 75 in a multispecialty group, and 200 to 500 in an IPA. Capitation will become widespread for primary care–based medical groups. The groups develop satellite clinics to serve a wider regional market with thousands of capitated covered lives. Specialists merge practices and form local networks, but capitation contracts do not usually come until stage 4.

Hospitals bring in the attorneys to construct PHOs in stage 3. The goal is to integrate managed care contracting and to package physicians for HMO enrollment. PHOs are built in hopes of increasing provider leverage with HMOs, to get capitation contracts. Not all physicians want to put their eggs in the hospital basket. The result is physician-sponsored Independent Physician Organizations (IPOs), which are not owned by any hospital or health system, to cut their own deals with HMOs and insurers. Many IPOs are strategically developed, with first invitations to primary care physicians. Specialists are added slowly and selectively.

Examples of stage 3 markets include Birmingham, Alabama; Hartford, Connecticut; Las Vegas, Nevada; Phoenix, Arizona; and Seattle, Washington.

Strategies

Physicians and hospitals must increase the pace of change as they enter stage 3. Networking and physician strategies must be built now, or providers may be left out. Stage 3 strategies include the following:

- Develop regional PHO network of hospitals and physicians as a managed care joint venture.

- Capitalize network venture with $10 to 15 million, and plan to add $5 to 10 million annually for the next five years.
- Providers should develop a new HMO, purchase a joint interest (50/50) in an existing HMO, or bring in an HMO partner.
- Independent physicians form their own medical network (IPO).
- Close the physician panel and provide performance data on costs and clinical outcomes to all doctors.
- Convert PPOs to HMO point-of-service model.
- Begin to capitate primary care physician groups/networks.
- Initiate development of clinical paths and standardized medical protocols.
- Tell the board and medical staff to expect that patient-days and revenues will fall by 15 to 25 percent in the next three years.
- Reduce staffing levels and costs quickly as utilization declines. (Note: Do not wait to see if utilization will improve—it won't.)

Stage 4: War of the Networks

Characteristics

Aggressive employers provide managed care momentum in stage 4 markets (see Table 4–5). San Francisco Bay Area employers demanded HMO price cuts in 1994. The ripple effect forced HMOs to demand provider payment reductions, setting up the confrontation between managed care plans and providers. Stage 4 is becoming a "war" between HMOs and provider-sponsored networks. John Henderson, president of SMG Marketing in Chicago, predicts that by the year 2000, two-thirds of all Americans will be covered by Integrated Healthcare Networks. SMG estimates that the nation's 70 million HMO and PPO enrollees will continue to increase at an annual rate of 6 to 8 percent per year.[9] The question is: Who will own the networks—HMOs and insurers, or providers?

Stage 4 markets are located in California's urban centers. Provider networking is expanding vigorously, on a regional and statewide basis. One of the most ambitious networking efforts is taking place in California now, with the emergence of two nonprofit networks to challenge Kaiser. These include (1) California Health Network, which will link San Francisco's California Healthcare System, San Diego's Sharp HealthCare, Sacramento's Sutter Health System, and UniHealth, Adventist Health System/West and Loma Linda University Medical Center in the greater Los Angeles area; and (2) a Catholic health care network that will link hospitals affiliated with the Daughters of Charity Health System/West, Catholic Healthcare West, and Scripps in San Diego.

Both of these statewide networks are lining up additional hospitals and physician groups, and may be positioning to develop their own capitated health plans, suggests managed care consultant Peter Boland of Berkeley-based Boland Healthcare.[10] In Los Angeles, some of the region's best-known hospitals have recently linked to form PrimeHealth. Cedars-Sinai and nearly a dozen other hospital members of Volunteer Hospitals of America (VHA) are forming a regional managed care network and have hired an experienced HMO executive to lead the initiative. Will forming provider networks work? A PacifiCare executive commented that the HMO does not contract with networks like PrimeHealth, only with individual hospitals.

Established physician groups will grow and merge in stage 4. Mullikin has moved beyond its Southern California base, seeking opportunities statewide. The Hill Medical Group is managing IPAs across the San Francisco Bay Area and Sacramento. Medical groups in San Diego, San Jose, and the Bay Area are expanding into new territory. Friendly Hills has recently been acquired by Caremark in a $140 million acquisition. The

Table 4–5 Stage 4: War of the Networks

Characteristics	Strategies
HMO 25–40%	Regional networks and competition for control of networks
Provider payments	More payment cuts from HMOs
Capitation	Expanded to specialists, hospitals
Indemnity <5%	Converts to point-of-service plans
Employers	Purchasing coalitions
Multispeciality groups	Acquire groups/partner
Ambulatory care >40%	Physicians in satellite clinics
Regional hospital networks	Consolidate services
Profits 1–2%	Reengineer clinical care
Quality	Clinical paths/outcomes

new capital is likely to spur an expansion move. The largest physician groups may purchase their own hospitals, like PPS in San Bernardino.

In stage 4, physician specialists will build regional medical networks in self-defense. This horizontal integration of physicians will be by specialty (orthopedics, obstetrics, cardiology, and more). In stage 4, IPOs will grow explosively, signing up hundreds of doctors in Burbank, Berkeley, Orange County, San Diego, and the East San Gabriel Valley. Thoroughly pulverized by HMOs, these once-defiant physicians will now willingly submit to self-imposed cost and quality discipline. If HMOs accept IPOs, these doctors will be rewarded with capitation contracts and a new shot at managed care success.

Examples of stage 4 markets include Sacramento, San Diego, and Los Angeles/Orange, California; Baltimore, Maryland; Philadelphia, Pennsylvania; and Portland, Oregon.

Strategies

Sophisticated hospitals and physician groups can now gain major market advantage from the managed care strategies. Key actions in stage 4 include the following:

- Merge PHOs on regional basis.
- Hospitals form super-regional and statewide networks.
- Independent physicians merge IPAs, expand networks.
- Physician panels drop doctors whose clinical and cost performance is below standard.
- Capitate hospitals and specialists.
- Selectively reduce HMO contracts to concentrate on a few key health plans that will contract on partnership terms.
- Expand the scope of patient-centered care reengineering projects and clinical protocols.
- Expand Medicare/Medicaid HMO enrollment.

Stage 5: Integrated Delivery Systems

Characteristics

As the United States moves deeper into managed care, the structure of the ultimate IDS is not completely clear. Competing models are emerging. But one thing is already evident. In this fifth and final phase of transition, providers will be merging with payers in truly integrated arrangements. SMG

Marketing's John Henderson predicts the following:

- Integration and affiliation will concentrate "sellers power" in dealing with purchasers.
- Emphasis on clinical efficiency and demand reduction will limit costly inpatient services and shift treatment emphasis to ambulatory care and prevention.
- Coordination of care will manage patients for efficiency across a comprehensive continuum of care.
- Integrated Delivery Systems will use their purchasing clout to form partnerships with suppliers on very cost-effective terms.[11]

Providers can credit the market—not health reform—for integrating financing and delivery. In California, for example, the San Francisco Bay Area will be the largest urban area in California to reach 40 percent managed care penetration. Providers are moving into three predictable patterns: (1) Kaiser, the staff-model HMO; (2) a Catholic network; and (3) a community nonprofit network organized by VHA members. Physician Organizations are growing, like the Hill Medical Group and Mullikin Medical Centers. They must ultimately choose to align with networks in long-term arrangements—either provider-sponsored or HMO-controlled networks.

HMO consolidation has reduced the number of managed care plans in stage 5, and more mergers are likely in the near future. California's Wellpoint, Foundation Health, FHP/TakeCare, and PacifiCare are poised to acquire additional plans or merge with other large health plans. Independent HMOs like United Healthcare, U.S. Healthcare, and HealthSource are in aggressive growth modes. Smaller, local HMOs can find geographic or Medicaid niches, like Seattle-based Group Health Plan of Puget Sound or San Diego's Community Health Plan.

The last element of stage 5 consolidation is still to come—the integration of financing and delivery. California HMOs do not seem ready for full integration, continuing to exploit the surplus of hospitals and doctors. Unlike Minnesota, there is no merger of HMOs and provider networks in the immediate future for the Golden State. Provider-HMO consolidation may be more likely in markets like Portland, Philadelphia, and Dallas (see Table 4–6).

Examples of stage 5 markets include Minneapolis-St. Paul, Minnesota; Rochester, New York; San Francisco, California; and Tucson, Arizona.

Strategies

Transition to stage 5 will be accelerated when employers demand more price cuts from HMOs, forcing a final confrontation—or collaboration—between health plans and provider networks. Strategies for a stage 5 market include the following:

- Provider networks merge with an HMO or insurance company.
- Multiyear, exclusive contracts are developed between physician groups and hospitals.
- Hospital networks develop joint planning process to begin clinical consolidation on a regional basis.
- Regionalize high-tech, high-overhead clinical services (e.g., emergency/trauma).
- Close unneeded hospitals or convert from acute care to continuum-of-care functions.
- Consolidate Physician Organizations into multispecialty group practices.
- Merge the Physician Organization with the hospital network.
- Eliminate the titles and positions of hospital presidents, and replace with physician/nurse chief operating officers.
- Place all hospitals under regional executives.

Table 4-6 Stage 5: Integrated Delivery Systems

Characteristics	Strategies
HMO >40%	Expand Medicare/Medicaid HMOs
Provider payments	More than 50% capitation
Capitation	Reduce capitation payments
Indemnity 0%	Strengthen point-of-service networks
Employers coalitions	Purchase on quality
Ambulatory care >50%	Develop continuum of care
Integrated health networks	Merge with HMO/insurers
Physician megagroups	Equity/staff models
Profits 2–6%	Managing clinical costs
Quality	Outcomes/patient ratings

- Complete development of a regional network of ambulatory care centers under the network's "brand-name."
- Reconfigure medical office buildings for group practice.
- Complete the development of clinical paths/treatment protocols for all diagnoses and procedures.
- Complete computerization of information system to paperless systems.
- Identify 10 to 15 percent high-risk enrollees for continuous case management.
- Install in-home monitors for chronically ill enrollees.
- Publicly report cost and quality data to enrollees, network providers, purchasers, and the public.
- Develop a new strategic plan for "stage 6."

THREE SCENARIOS FOR INTEGRATION

Every future has possible alternatives. Futurists call them "scenarios." Looking ahead to the next five to ten years, three scenarios of integrated health systems have the greatest potential to bring together purchasers and providers in new structures to discipline and manage care in the twenty-first century:

1. payer-driven networks
2. provider-sponsored systems
3. partnership models[12]

Scenario 1: Payer-Driven Networks

When the insurance company or the HMO chooses the providers, then the payers "own" the network. These health plans do more than simply market to enrollees. Payers are in charge of the key components of network management, including the following:

- developing provider selection criteria
- selecting preferred providers
- defining terms and conditions of network participation
- negotiating payment rates
- authorizing treatments
- controlling utilization
- conducting performance assessment
- monitoring clinical quality
- disciplining providers
- surveying consumer satisfaction with providers

- preparing report cards on provider performance

As long as payers act as if they own the enrollees, providers will not be equals in this model. When the payer rules the relationship, providers are vendors. All parties act in their own interests in such a one-sided business relationship. That is beginning to change. Some insurance companies and HMOs are now moving toward multi-year contracts, volume-based pricing, and performance-based compensation. These are positive steps, but they fall short of a balanced partnership in which payers and providers jointly share risks and rewards.

Scenario 2: Provider-Sponsored Systems

Across the United States, physicians and hospitals are scrambling to develop provider-sponsored integrated systems. There are two dominant models: hospital-led systems and physician-managed networks.

Hospital-Led Systems

Hospital-led systems are pursuing horizontal integration strategies, in which hospitals are the basic building blocks. Each hospital brings its physicians, who are then linked contractually for managed care contracting. Most provider-sponsored systems being formed today are network models, structured as joint ventures between the hospitals and sponsoring systems. Hospital networks are typically formed on a regional or statewide market basis.

Hospital-sponsored networks are emerging almost daily. In Louisville, Kentucky, the Baptist Health Care System recently announced a collaborative venture with Alliant, which will bring the systems' seven hospitals together in a new nonprofit corporation for regional and statewide contracting, guided by a 16-member board that will include 50 percent physician representation.[13] Physician networks in the Kentucky model will be organized at the local and regional levels. Most provider networks are hospital-driven. In Southern California, nine hospitals are forming the PrimeHealth network, together with Physician Organizations representing 3,000 physicians. The medical groups affiliated in the network are specialty oriented, "but we're working to change that," said a network spokesperson.[14]

Physician-Managed Networks

Physician-managed networks take a very different approach, with large, well-organized physicians groups as the core building blocks. Finding hospitals to serve physician-driven organizations is not a problem. Hospitals are always ready to contract out their empty beds, and most facilities are willing to contribute both capacity and capital. In northern California, the Bay Physicians Medical Group has taken the lead in creating a for-profit MSO that serves as the full-risk contractor for the large medical group and the Alta Bates Medical Center in Berkeley, California.[15] This is a "super-IPA" network whose 835 physicians are affiliated in three local IPAs. Its strategic goal is to establish a regional provider network for capitation contracting. The organization already has 65,000 covered lives. Equity stock is shared 50/50 with physicians. To ensure that physicians have the lead role, the doctors hold a majority vote on the network's day-to-day operational decisions. The overall network board includes five physician representatives from the IPAs, with three from the medical center.

Scenario 3: Partnership Models

Fully integrated health systems will combine providers and payers in full at-risk arrangements for regional market dominance. To meet the demand for price-competitive managed care products, insurers are expanding into health care delivery.[16] The goal is to combine the enrollees and managed care marketing expertise of the insurer or HMO with the provider's facilities, caregivers, and cooperation for cost management. Partnership models share equity and governance, to align incentives and reduce the internal costs of "provider versus payer," which have been a major contributor to the estimated 15 to 25 percent administrative cost burden of American health care.

In Cleveland, the Ohio Blues and Meridia Health System recently announced a strategic partnership for the creation of an IDS. The two organizations would jointly offer several new health insurance products, and position Meridia at the center of a new "super-Blue" provider network.[17] Meridia, the region's largest hospital system, is linking with Blue Cross to fight its biggest rival, the University Hospitals Health System. Cleveland is rapidly shaping up as a "3-IDS market," with the third system driven by the Cleveland Clinic in partnership with the Kaiser Health Plan. Payer-provider partnerships who manage their costs through cooperation, not competition, may be the ultimate winners in the coming battle between mega-IDS systems.

ALTERNATIVE PATHS TO INTEGRATION

In the next five years, there is no single best way for physician integration. Physicians will have alternatives in an integrated marketplace. It is clear that the market wants options, and consumers are willing to make tradeoffs between price and choice. The IDS provider networks will range from loose to tight—where one IDS may serve a population of 500,000 with fewer than 500 doctors (50/50 primary care/specialists) and three hospitals, while a competitor may provide access to 1,500 community physicians (20/80 primary care/specialists) and a dozen facilities. How much do consumers and their employers want to pay for access to more specialists and hospitals?

Physicians are concerned that the incentives of managed care and capitation will discourage use of high technology. Under managed care, the question is how much technology are consumers willing to pay for? Health plan A may price its plan low by limiting high-tech care, but provide consumers with ready access to ambulatory services and alternative therapies such as herbal remedies and aroma therapy. A competing HMO B at the high end of the price spectrum may offer gamma knives and PET scanners, "Ritz-level" hospital accommodations, no waiting in doctors' waiting rooms, and valet parking. Low-cost HMO plan C may appeal to buyers who only want basic protection and will pay higher copayments and deductibles for services. There will be choices for consumers, even as physicians struggle to maintain a balance between their roles as patient advocates and resource controllers.

Physicians are understandably concerned about the changes that managed care and integration will bring in the decade ahead. The stage is being set for large-scale competition between very different approaches to health care delivery. Advanced markets like Minneapolis-St. Paul, Albuquerque, Portland, and California will be the "test kitchens" for the new recipes of health reform. Most observers predict there will be only a few competing integrated systems when the millennium comes in the year 2000. Ultimately, the future of American health care will not be the physician's responsibility. *The market will decide which integration scenario and system is "best."*

NOTES

1. G. McManis, Meeting the Future: CEO Summit on the New Health Care Delivery Alliance, *Hospitals and Health Networks* 68, no. 11 (1994): 46.

2. R.C. Coile Jr., The Five Stages of Managed Care, *Hospital Strategy Report* 6, no. 19 (1994): 1–8.

3. F.B. Abbey and K.M. Treash Jr., Reasons Providers Form PHOs, *Healthcare Financial Management* (August 1995): 38–48.

4. J.C. Goldsmith, The Illusive Logic of Integration, *Healthcare Forum Journal* 37, no. 5 (1994): 26–31.

5. *Los Angeles Times*, 23 January 1995.

6. R.C. Coile Jr., Five Stages of Managed Care in California, *Northern California Medicine* (July 1995): 24–27.

7. R. Hamer, Regional Market Analysis, *InterStudy Competitive Edge* 5, no. 1 (1995): 1–111.

8. J.T. Lord, "PHO-Itis": A Disease Affecting the American Healthcare Scene, *Health System Leader* 1, no. 2 (1994): 29–30.

9. J.A. Henderson, Integrated Healthcare Networks: The Future Is Now, *SMG Marketing Letter* 8, no. 4 (1994): 2–3.

10. C. Sardinha and T. Rudd, Integration Trend Spells More Competition for Managed Care, *Managed Care Outlook* 7, no. 11 (1994): 1–3.

11. J.A. Henderson, Integrated Healthcare Networks: The Future Is Now. *SMG Marketing Letter* 8, no. 4 (1994): 2–3.

12. T.M. Droste, PowerPlay: Tracking Who Has It and Who Doesn't As Managed Care Evolves, *Medical Staff Strategy Report*, no. 6 (1994): 5–7.

13. D. Burda, Kentucky Systems Collaborate, *Modern Healthcare* 24, no. 39 (1994): 20.

14. L. Kertesz, Prime Health In Nine Los Angeles Hospitals *Modern Healthcare* 24, no. 30 (1994): 14.

15. T.M. Droste, East Bay Medical Network a Contracting Entity for Physicians and Hospitals, *Medical Staff Strategy Report* 3, no. 7 (1994): 2–4.

16. D. De LaFuente, Group Insurance: Insurers Bypass Hospitals, Join With Medical Groups to Assure Survival, *Modern Health Care* 24, no. 24: 39–44.

17. T. Rudd, Atlanta Not-for-Profits Aren't Circling the Wagons over Columbia/HCA Deal, *Healthcare Systems Strategy Report* 11, no. 12 (1994): 11–12.

Chapter 5

Using Advanced Physician Management Structure To Ensure Clinical Effectiveness

Steven S. Lazarus, Ph.D., F.H.I.M.S.S. and John Lucas, M.D.

EXECUTIVE SUMMARY

Health care delivery organizations in a competitive, managed care environment require an effective physician management structure to develop organizational goals and objectives and the mechanisms to deliver efficient, quality health care. Lovelace Health Systems (LHS), based in Albuquerque, New Mexico, is an example of an integrated health care delivery system with an advanced physician management structure. The management structure has been designed to address episode-of-care and disease management objectives. The program of pre-primary care screening of new enrollees is designed to identify patients at risk and enroll them into the appropriate case management program. The aggressive internal programs that are being used to create change within the organization include adoption of clinical practice improvement (CPI)/continuous quality improvement (CQI) methods, physician education, acknowledgment of physician responsibility for clinical practice improvement, and care management for high-risk patients. Medical group practice data for selected specialties are used to illustrate physician profiling and other performance measures that can be utilized to help physicians understand and improve their clinical practice from a recent resource management perspective. Physicians have a key role in developing and using the next generation of information systems to support a data-driven clinical approach to patient care.

INTRODUCTION

In the past, most physicians have been organized in one- and two-doctor practices. In 1991, there were 184,358 physicians practicing in medical groups of three or more physicians.[1] The 25-year trend of a growing percentage of physicians practicing in medical groups is expected to continue for the foreseeable future.

In 1991, one-third of physicians practicing in medical groups were in groups of 100 or more physicians. Although the percentage of group practice physicians practicing in these large organizations is significant, the 189 medical groups with 100 doctors or more represented only 1.2 percent of all medical groups. It is these relatively few large physician practice organizations that provide the models for advanced physician management structures.

One of the leading health care integrated delivery systems with a large medical group practice is LHS. The state of New Mexico has a population of 1.6 million people. Of these, 250,000 have health insurance through Health Maintenance Organizations (HMOs). Another 180,000 lives are covered under triple-option point-of-service plans, the fastest growing type of health plan in New Mexico.[2]

LHS is comprised of an urban Integrated Delivery System, health plan, and a statewide network. At the center of this physician-driven health system is a 300-physician group practice that interfaces with and supports a growing network of affiliated provider partners. LHS also includes a 200-bed hospital, 20 care delivery sites, 10 pharmacies, a mental health facility, and 141,000 health plan members. The New Mexico marketplace is both highly competitive and highly penetrated by Managed Care Organizations, necessitating an adaptive and flexible approach by the LHS physician leadership. The LHS vision is to create the best value in health care in the state; the plan will be in the lowest tier of price, service levels will exceed the competition's, and the system will demonstrate superior health outcomes. LHS is implementing a highly innovative population health model that will incorporate three components—health risk appraisal, care management, and disease management—to be described in more detail later in this chapter. Proactive pre-primary care screening of new health plan members and clinical disease management are new approaches being implemented to support a population health care model.

As focus changes to a more data-driven patient treatment environment, new measures are needed to evaluate organization and physician performance, and the information systems infrastructure must change to support data access and patient care and to measure performance. Examples of data analysis capabilities include physician profiling and episodes of care. Information systems priorities include the integration of billing, clinical data, and operations management (such as appointment and resource scheduling).

THE LHS IMPLEMENTATION OF ADVANCED PHYSICIAN MANAGEMENT

The Role of Physicians in Governance and Management

The LHS organizational culture has a deeply rooted belief that strong physician leadership results in improved efficiency and effectiveness of health care delivery. Moreover, it is the LHS position that professional autonomy of the organized physician group results in highly innovative approaches to treating patients.

The LHS progressive integration over the past 20 years has successfully preserved the strong influence of physicians over all operations: LHS remains the quintessential physician-driven health care system. This principle is authenticated at the level of the nine-member LHS Board of Directors. Three physicians are selected from the six physician members of the Medical Practice Board. The Medical Practice Board is elected by the physicians of the Lovelace Physician Group as its governing board. Additionally, the chief medical officer is appointed to the LHS Board and the physician CEO serves as chairman.

LHS uses a comprehensive matrix management structure to support its operations. All major divisions of the system are comanaged by a physician and an administrator working together as a team. Physician executives are fully represented on the senior management team and participate in all facets of planning and operational policy development.

The LHS Board of Directors has delegated the responsibility for quality oversight to the Medical Practice Board. The Medical Practice Board fulfills these obligations by receiving monthly reports from specialty department chairpersons and by conducting an intense peer review concerning measured physician performance. A member of the Medical Practice Board reports on quality matters on a routine basis to the Board of Directors at its quarterly meetings.

Changing Management

While LHS has led the marketplace in terms of managed care, its competitors have also become very effective in this arena. Albuquerque has been described as one of the country's most advanced health care markets, characterized by greater than 50 percent managed care penetration and intense competition by three integrated and multiple health plan systems. There are effectively no physician free agents in the market. These developments have required the Lovelace Physician Group to redefine physician performance and commitment requirements. In addition to patient care, the Lovelace Physician Group has stipulated that the role and responsibility of physicians must include a commitment to clinical practice improvement and general health status improvement in the population served.

The LHS vision is that to retain the position as market leader the organization must demonstrate its superior value. Service levels must exceed the competition and LHS must be in the lowest tier of price and deliver superior outcomes. To fulfill these aims, the organization requires that the Lovelace Physician Group accepts full accountability for certain physician performance targets. The scorecard includes measures of patient satisfaction, per member per month (PMPM) costs, and clinical outcomes.

The Medical Practice Board's role is pivotal in enabling the medical group to accept and support the change initiatives brought to the fore by management. Tactics for improving professional performance include renewed support for organizational learning, the adoption of CPI/CQI methods, the development of measurement systems for increased accountability, and the introduction of a variable compensation system that links physician compensation to enterprise success. To successfully roll out these tactics among all of the medical staff members, management has given programmatic oversight to the Medical Practice Board for the activities described below.

Lovelace University

To accelerate the LHS transformation, a significant commitment is being made to new organizational learning for the Lovelace Physician Group. The Medical Practice Board requires that management develop an intensive orientation program for physicians who join the group, and that more senior Lovelace Physician Group physicians are offered a managed care curriculum that includes capitation economics, methods for improving communications with patients, tools for improving communications with patients, and tools for CQI and CPI. LHS specialists are required to teach primary care physicians certain patient management skills so that the roles and responsibilities of primary care physicians can be expanded in the continuum of care. The next generation of topics will include epidemiology, statistics, and decision support tools for physicians. The ultimate goal is for LHS physicians to practice evidence-based medicine.

The Medical Practice Board's Support for CPI

The Medical Practice Board ratifies all professional policies that are developed for the Lovelace Physician Group by management. In late 1992, the Medical Practice Board approved a policy that states: "In order to be a member of the Lovelace Physician Group, a physician must assume responsibility for clinical practice improvement within the LHS." CPI must address two types of processes: (1) improving the way decisions are made by practitioners on behalf of patients, and (2) improving the process of health care delivery. With reference to the clinical decision-making process, the policy states that physicians will be encouraged to improve the ordering of diagnostic procedures and treatment interventions so that high-value services are recommended. Pertaining to care delivery, physicians are to provide leadership to teams that redesign and improve delivery systems that carry out treatment interventions in a consistent error-proof management.

Physicians can demonstrate commitment to CPI in the following ways:

- develop a personal education plan to learn about CPI
- stay informed about new LHS guidelines
- participate on CPI teams
- support outcomes measures

CPI Initiatives in Primary Care

The organization views strengthening primary care as a key strategy for creating a competitive advantage in the market. These primary care initiatives include the following:

- a standard for panel capacity with a goal of 2,000 member equivalents per primary care physician (A weighting system was created to adjust panel size according to age/sex demographics—e.g., one Medicare patient is equivalent to two commercial HMO patients.)
- access standards that are satisfactory to patients/members (A risk-screening program will be developed to determine which patients need enhanced access for the management of chronic conditions.)
- user-friendly demand management systems that promote patient self-care, consumer information, and nurses' triage
- a goal to redirect primary care to primary care physicians (LHS wanted to shift the focus on episodic urgent care from 25 percent of visits to less than 15 percent without compromising patient satisfaction to allow for better primary care coordination and reinforcement of the panel concept.)
- a definition of the expected core competency of primary care physicians for managing common chronic disease states and a plan to address any measurable gaps in ability
- participation with specialists in the creation of practice guidelines as coequal partners in the process
- individual and team accountability for medical costs generated on behalf of patients in one's panel

CPI Initiatives for Specialists

To expand the role of primary care physicians (PCPs), the Lovelace Physician Group has recast the role of specialist care physicians (SCPs) who now will serve in a pure consultant role. SCP departments are encouraged to improve efficiency by designing referral protocols that identify the optimal point of handoff between SCPs and PCPs. LHS has improved PCP access to SCPs for telephone consultation, which enables PCPs to manage certain care problems and improves the appropriateness of referrals. SCPs also assist PCPs in rural areas in managing complex patients via telemedicine. As a result of these efforts, the Lovelace Physician Group has been able to recalibrate the group from a PCP/SCP ratio of 30/70 to 50/50. Referral profiles are now part of the PCP evaluative process, and referral guidelines have been codified and made available to all Lovelace Physician Group PCPs for guidance.

Lovelace Physician Group as an Accountable Physician Organization

Management and the Medical Practice Board have worked closely together to create a data-driven peer review methodology that can be administered at regular intervals with feedback provided to the professional staff. The elements of the physician report card include patient satisfaction scores, resource utilization including pharmacy and referral statistics, and medical costs. The experience of the Lovelace Physician Group has been that physicians rapidly modify behavior when given objective feedback. Physicians are now provided with a biannual profile, which is also reviewed by their physician managers and the Medical Practice Board. The physician managers provide coaching to physicians who wish to improve their scores. Techniques for doing so include participation in the Bayer Institute for Health Care Communications, as well as enrollment in Lovelace University courses that address how to manage chronic disease more efficiently. Physicians are also encouraged to sponsor departmental service improvement initiatives.

Incentives for Lovelace Physician Group

The Lovelace Physician Group has changed its philosophy concerning compensation with a move from straight salary to variable compensation. The motives behind this change are to increase the group's responsiveness in terms of improving LHS's competitive position in the local marketplace. While the financing of the incentive pool is linked to overall enterprise success, bonuses are paid to individual physicians based on certain performance parameters including access, patient satisfaction, cost-effectiveness, and quality improvement activities. It is necessary to place a certain amount of base salary at risk (e.g., 15 percent, with a potential of up to 15 percent bonus).

THE LOVELACE PHYSICIAN GROUP POPULATION HEALTH MODEL OF MEDICAL DELIVERY

To support episodes of care, LHS developed a comprehensive, population-based health service management model with three distinct components: health status management, care management, and disease management. The components embody many features from the traditional public health model of primary, secondary, and tertiary prevention.

Health Status Management

In the first two decades of managed care, health plans have in many ways deemed it unnecessary to incorporate a comprehensive and effective array of preventive services into their medical delivery systems. While a great deal of lip service has been paid to this activity, nearly all plans have focused on event-based cost avoidance, and delivery systems have focused on curative services. In many plans, there has been much skepticism about the value of preventive services. At times preventive services have been viewed as part of the cost/utilization problem, and they have not been leveraged effectively to make a bottom-line contribution in cost reduction or health status improvement.

The thrust behind the health status management component is that plans can be held accountable to enable the LHS to proactively manage the health risks of a population of enrollees. Underpinning this initiative is the belief that health-risk management is necessary to lower the cost of care measured on a PMPM basis in order to accomplish these objectives.

The LHS will pioneer the development of a pre-primary care process that will enable membership services to screen by telephone all of the health plan's membership to determine general health status, high-risk behaviors, and any unmanaged chronic illnesses. As a result of the screening, a database will be created concerning the health status, health risks, and disease prevalences for the entire population. These data will then be segmented for individual employers, so that each can be made aware of the health risks in the population assigned to health plans. The employers will then be in a position to monitor health plan performance in terms of managing the health status of the employees and dependents for whom care is being financed.

There will be distinct opportunities for LHS as a result of the creation of this database. First, LHS will be able to craft a primary prevention and health promotion road map relevant to the measured needs of the enrolled population. LHS will also be able to work closely with employers on health promotion strategies that pertain to the health risk profiles of their employees.

Second, health risk profiling will allow focused intervention on health risks by the Lovelace Physician Group, which now accepts economic responsibility for managing all the medical needs of the enrollees on a capitated basis. New enrollees with high risk or those with unmanaged medical conditions will be detected earlier by LHS case managers who will routinely search the database. These case managers will contact high-risk members to make these individuals aware of their risks and to facilitate access to primary care and specialty services. It is likely that portions of the process will be automated and performed at relatively low cost. Primary care physicians will have incentives and support systems to leverage the opportunities created by the pre-primary care system. Physicians will have risk-adjusted capitation rates and risk-adjusted panel sizes. In addition, early access and speedy evaluations for high-risk enrollees will become a performance objective for the primary care system in order to reduce risk, improve health status, and reduce costs for these patients.

Third, the primary care system will improve the satisfaction level of health care consumers who select LHS by creating an opportunity for shared responsibility between the members with identified high risk and the New Mexico providers. Most of the LHS marketing and health education resources will be directed toward developing consumer health informatics to help the individual consumer access information with a view toward self-management of health status. A system of incentives and special programs will be crafted for member segments where significant barriers exist for entering a therapeutic alliance with the system providers.

Finally, the pre-primary care system will allow the Lovelace Physician Group to move the focus of medical care out of the primary care system into work sites, schools, and—when necessary—homes.

A set of indicators will be developed to monitor the performance of the pre-primary care system, which will undergo the same rigorous evaluation and CQI activities as other components of the medical model.

Care Management

Care management should have the following synergistic goals:

- to develop a methodology for supporting members who have been detected to have high-risk behaviors or unmanaged potentially chronic medical conditions
- to support LHS providers in improving the functional capabilities and health status of members of the service population with chronic disease
- to develop and manage the LHS infrastructure that supports the continuum of care for patients with chronic disease

- to enable LHS to manage resources appropriately and meet its utilization and cost goals

Support Members at Risk for Chronic Disease

The result of active screening for high-risk members will require care management to add a new element to the care continuum: care management services for high-risk populations. These populations will include the frail elderly, the socially disadvantaged, and members with unexplained high utilization of certain services including emergency services, specialty services, and pharmacy services. Leadership for the program will be provided by a doctorate-level behavioral medicine specialist. Ultimately, LHS will grow in its expertise in developing and adopting methods for improving health status and consumption patterns for these groups.

Support LHS Providers

A second objective of care management will be to assume that members with or at risk for chronic disease are able to forge a therapeutic alliance with a physician. Concomitantly, primary care physicians will be supported in proactively managing and improving the health status of their assigned panels. In this evolving structure, care managers will be assigned to support a number of panels by facilitating communication and access between high-risk patients and their providers. The care managers will play an active role in assisting physicians to coordinate care and manage the most challenging patients. With regard to specialty care physicians, LHS will continue to build upon existing specific case management systems.

Develop and Manage the LHS Continuum of Care

The purpose of the care management program is to ensure that all elements of the care continuum are seamlessly integrated to support patients and their families, with a view to slowing the progression of chronic disease and preserving the functionality of the individual. A secondary purpose is to support the system's effectiveness by appropriately maintaining the patient at the least resource-intensive level in the care continuum.

Elements of the care continuum include the following:

- demand management systems
  1. case management of high-risk patients
  2. consumer medical informatics
  3. primary care physician case coordination
  4. self-help groups
- alternative institutional sites of care
  1. acute inpatient
  2. subacute
  3. skilled nursing and custodial care facilities
  4. rehabilitation
  5. hospice
- home health programs
  1. assisted-living arrangements
  2. parenteral therapies
- clinical pharmacy programs

Manage Resources

Care management will participate in the development of medical action plans for reducing costs and utilization. LHS will use the continuous improvement model in terms of setting annual budgets that demonstrate reduced PMPM medical costs and decreased reliance on the more costly points in the care continuum. The ultimate goal will be to provide the most cost-effective care in the community and attain heretofore unseen levels of performance concerning utilization of hospital and ambulatory resources.

Disease Management

Inherent in the concept of managed care is the premise of efficient delivery of integrated health care that fulfills the complex needs of patients while holding down costs.

However, health care delivery in the United States has been oriented to measuring and paying in discreet units of service rather than aggregate units of service encompassing a disease state. Health care systems have been organized around specific departments and divisions related to types of practitioners or organ systems. This organization has contributed to the fragmentation of care to patients with acute and chronic disorders, and its inefficiency has interfered with attempts to control costs. In addition, Integrated Delivery Systems are spending an increasing amount of limited dollars to finance the care of people with chronic diseases for which there is no coordinated program to efficiently manage the disease and the associated financial burden. The rapid implementation of capitation as the primary financing mechanism is forcing systems to change their organizational strategies.

LHS will implement a new approach that effectively engages health care providers to improve clinical performance. As an integrated system providing care across the care continuum, it makes sense for LHS to adopt a more systemic, coordinated approach to clinical practice improvement that incorporates primary and specialty care in both inpatient and outpatient settings. In addition, the highly competitive Albuquerque health care market dictated the development of an effective method of cost containment and quality improvement. Analysis of computerized Lovelace patient data revealed that most of the utilization costs are driven by a small number of complex, chronic diseases. LHS estimates that 30 health conditions account for approximately 80 percent of the costs associated with LHS services. The proper conceptual model for LHS will address these costly, high-volume conditions, which are derived from the episode-of-care (EOC) approach described by Hornbrook and Hurtado in the mid-1980s.[3] In the LHS model, an episode of care is comprised of all of the services provided to a patient with a particular medical problem within a specified period of time across the continuum of care in an integrated system. An episode is intended to incorporate all care components, including prevention, primary care, specialty care, hospital care, and long-term care. The EOC teams will have representatives from all levels of care, including primary care physicians and specialists, and incorporate tools for patient education and self-care. An episode integrates previously isolated quality improvement tools, including practice guidelines, care maps, and key process and outcomes measures. In addition, each episode must assess patients' response to treatment, both subjectively (e.g., patient satisfaction and functional status) and as measured by pathophysiologic and psychosocial outcomes.

Because of its comprehensive nature, the EOC approach appears to be most promising as a model for disease-specific clinical practice improvement programs that use "systems thinking." As the model is perfected, it should be readily transferable to other health systems. At LHS, initial EOC teams covered the following disease entities:

- diabetes
- pediatric asthma
- coronary artery disease
- birth
- breast cancer
- stroke
- low back
- depression

All of these teams are functioning with variable levels of success. New teams have been started at LHS at the rate of two per quarter.

INFORMATION REQUIREMENTS TO SUPPORT ADVANCED PHYSICIAN MANAGEMENT

Performance Measures

To effectively measure the performance of physicians and the overall organization under capitation, new measures are needed. These measures are based on the treatment of the population and the effective management of disease.

Population-Based Measures

A key factor in developing measures for health status and the effectiveness of health care is risk adjustment. Risk is associated with age, sex, and underlying medical conditions—especially chronic conditions in various segments of the population. Many advanced physician group practices adjust their capitated populations from year to year based on age and sex. However, there are no published and readily available standardized adjustment factors for age and sex associated with risk. It will be helpful to utilize standardized risk-adjustment factors in the future for resource planning and performance evaluation. Several of the clinical performance measures presented in the next section should be adjusted for age, sex, and risk.

New Measures and Definitions

Clinician performance measurement is changing. Traditionally, for procedures performed in the hospital, peer review and other mechanisms have been used to evaluate the clinical performance of physicians and the institution. In the physician office, physician performance often has been measured by billed charges as a surrogate for productivity. Both aspects of performance measurement are changing to reflect changes in payment and patient-oriented care.

A significant transition in performance measurement is the shift from the measurement of length of stay and procedure-based success while in the hospital for specific patient cases to the measurement of performance based on population utilization rates, resource utilization, and outcome over an episode of care, and the ongoing management of patients with chronic disease. Successful implementation of these performance measures begins with their identification and definition. In many cases, the measurement involves new recordkeeping concepts and the development of new information system capabilities. The latter are essential for patient case management and to provide feedback to providers.

In the future, the quality of clinical performance will be measured by outcomes in both the inpatient and ambulatory care settings. The significant change for inpatient care is the increasing emphasis on patient recovery and outcomes following discharge from an inpatient stay. Patient satisfaction, quality of life for chronically ill patients, and the disease stage timing of first intervention for patients at known risk will become key components of the measurement of clinical performance.

Management Performance Measures

Management performance measurement is expanding from efficiency and cost management issues to include developing and maintaining winning relationships with key stakeholders and other organizations, managing change, developing and implementing new organizational approaches to health care delivery, and increasing the involvement of physician leadership in organizational management. Managing change and developing and implementing a clear vision for the entire organization are key management challenges. The measurement of management performance will involve evaluating the ability of the organization to implement the right changes successfully in a timely fashion, communicate them effectively, and motivate the organizational components to support new missions and objectives as they are formed. The shift in management performance measures is illustrated in Exhibit 5–1.

In addition, clinical performance will be the responsibility of a team effort managed

Exhibit 5–1 Management Performance Measures

TRADITIONAL MEASURES

- active accounts receivable
- billed charges
- days in accounts receivable
- efficiency
- net income
- number of patients seen
- overhead cost per physician

ADVANCED ORGANIZATION MEASURES

- cost per disease category per capita
- cost per episode of care
- cost per member per month
- efficiencies
- net income
- number of capitated lives
- patient access
- patient retention
- patient satisfaction
- responsiveness of the decision-making process
- subscriber retention rate
- successful implementation of change

Exhibit 5–2 Clinical Performance Measures

TRADITIONAL MEASURES

- charges
- complication rate
- hospital length of stay
- mortality rate

ADVANCED PHYSICIAN ORGANIZATION MEASURES

- appointment wait times
- C-section rate
- emergency department visit rates for specific patient categories
- episode of care based on utilization and outcomes
- for specialists, the percentage of office visits for new patients or consultations
- immunization rate
- mammography rate
- outcomes
- panel size
- patient satisfaction
- performance based on a clinical team
- physician profiles
- population incidence rates for specific conditions

---

by one or more physicians. Many advanced Physician Organizations are implementing team approaches to both routine care and care for high-risk patients. By using combinations of physicians and other health care professionals (e.g., nurses, nurse practitioners, physicians' assistants, etc.), organizations can increase patient access to the system and direct resources toward case management and early intervention for patients at risk. The change in clinical performance measurement is illustrated by the examples in Exhibit 5–2.

Physician Profiling

Physician profiling is a new approach to ambulatory care resource use analysis that can be helpful in understanding whether physicians are utilizing their time effectively. The data presented in Tables 5–1 and 5–2 are compiled from several multi-specialty and single-specialty group practices. While the clusters of procedure codes of interest vary by specialty, for most specialties there is interest in how the physician (or caregiver team) workload is distributed among new patient office visits, established patient office visits, and office consultations. This is of particular interest to specialty physicians implementing the consulting model.

Table 5–1 shows the frequency per month for allergy, family practice, internal medicine, and orthopedic surgery visits. The number of physicians represented varies from a low for 15.2 full-time equivalent

Table 5–1 Frequency (Number of Visits) per Month by Specialty

	Frequency per Month			
Type of Procedure	Allergy (N=15.2)	Family Practice (N=198.9)	Internal Medicine (N=159.9)	Orthopedic Surgery (N=111.5)
New patient	7.3	19.7	27.9	39.6
Established patient	120.3	194.1	253.2	118.6
Office consults	11.8	0.2	2.6	15.6
Total	139.4	214.0	283.7	173.8

Source: Data from C. Cressy et al, "PSPA Comparison Report—January–June, 1994, Center for Research in Ambulatory Health Care Administration, Englewood, Colorado.

(FTE) allergists to a high of 198.9 FTE family practice physicians. The data are from 26 medical groups ranging in size from 5 to 380 physicians. Thirty-two specialties are reported, with at least five medical groups participating in each specialty. The reporting period is January to June 1994. While Tables 5–1 and 5–2 are based on data from physicians in medical group practice, the physician profiles represent a mix of fee-for-service and capitated cases, as well as single-specialty and multispecialty group practice. The LHS strategy of establishing a 50/50 mix of primary care and specialist care, together with the specialists performing a consulting role, should result in very different profiles than those shown in Tables 5–1 and 5–2. For instance, in Table 5–1, the allergists see an average of 11.8 consults per month, compared with 7.3 new patients and 120.3 established patients. The consulting approach would significantly reduce the established patient load, shifting the routine follow-up care to primary care physicians.

As might be expected, family practice and internal medicine physicians have more office visits per month than do allergy and orthopedic surgery physicians, and the frequency of office consultations is higher for allergists and orthopedic surgeons. This strategy will significantly increase the number of consultations and new patient visits and a relatively high proportion of patient visits will be in the more comprehensive relative value level office visit categories.

Table 5–2 Average Relative Value per Procedure by Specialty

	Frequency per Month			
Type of Procedure	Allergy (N=15.2)	Family Practice (N=198.9)	Internal Medicine (N=159.9)	Orthopedic Surgery (N=111.5)
New patient	2.4	1.4	1.8	1.5
Established patient	1.0	0.9	1.0	0.8
Office consults	2.8	2.0	2.8	2.4

Source: Data from C. Cressy et al, "PSPA Comparison Report—January–June, 1994, Center for Research in Ambulatory Health Care Administration, Englewood, Colorado.

A different presentation of the similarities and differences among these specialties is shown in Table 5–2. It presents the average relative value per procedure within each of the three office visit categories by specialty. While the average relative value (or resource utilized) is nearly the same for the established patient office visits, the allergists and internists have more intensive new patient visits and office consultations (the visits take longer and involve more complex issues).

These examples of physician profile presentations illustrate the types of information that can be used to compare individual physicians with their peers to identify best practices, as well as practice patterns that deviate from the norm and require corrections. For instance, in practices where the goal is for allergists to act as consulting specialists—returning patients to the primary care physician for follow-up after the diagnosis is completed and the treatment plan has been developed—the number of office consultations would be significantly higher and the number of established patient office visits would be significantly lower than those illustrated in Table 5–1.

Because the use of these types of data for ambulatory care is in its infancy, physician profile patterns are still under development. Eventually, advanced medical groups will have established physician profiles by specialty (perhaps adjusted for patient age, sex, and risk). Current research efforts are primarily being devoted to develop the appropriate profile measures, identify and learn from best practices, adjust for patient mix differences including comorbidity, and improve the quality of procedure coding to increase data utility.

INFORMATION SYSTEMS

The Growing Importance of Information Systems

Information systems are becoming an increasingly valuable asset to the advanced medical group. The need for significant information system capabilities has progressed beyond the billing and accounting functions. Automated support has become a strategic requirement to handle both the complex administrative aspects and the financial processing of managed care transactions. Moreover, utilization and protocol analyses are required to identify best practices that may be replicable by others, as well as to identify problem areas that require attention. The next generation of advanced information systems applications addresses clinical capability enhancement. The automated medical record, the data warehouse, and decision support are the three fundamental applications that—when interfaced with patient demographic information, managed care administrative requirements, and diagnostic information—automate the current complex paper system and enhance the decision making and clinician management process to improve patient care. Once issues of patient confidentiality and data standards are addressed, there will be extensive sharing of patient data among providers in fragmented delivery systems. In the interim, Integrated Delivery Systems have a distinct advantage in their potential to improve patient care and resource utilization based on their internal information systems structure.

Physician Involvement in Expanding the Information Systems Infrastructure

It is extremely important to involve physician management and physician caregivers in the information systems' design and continued enhancement process in the managed care environment. Historically, physicians have often been involved in the process of information systems replacement/expansion with regard to the capital investment decision. This role continues as the size of the capital investment increases, with expanded functional information systems capabilities required to administer managed care efficiently and to deliver expert clinical care.

The physician's role has expanded in today's managed care environment. Physicians and other clinicians need to be involved in the design specifications of information systems that involve care management, automated medical records, and data repositories that are used for utilization review and resource use analysis.

Exhibit 5–3 summarizes some of the patient care and management activities that can be supported by information systems in an advanced environment. These fall into the three areas:

1. **Clinical database**—supports retrospective studies of patient care outcomes and resource utilization.
2. **Patient care support**—assists the clinician in managing the treatment of the patient by automating patient information.
3. **Clinical team effectiveness**—can be measured by a variety of patient outcome and resource use measures.

It is essential that physicians become involved in the conceptualization and design of systems to support these activities. Only by having physicians significantly involved in the design process can medical group practices be assured that the evolution of these products will be useful to clinicians and have a positive effect on patient care and efficiency.

New Information Systems Functions

In some areas, patient education, including counseling support, will be delivered by future computer networks. The University of Wisconsin has pioneered this concept in the area of breast cancer. For participating patients, this provides immediate increased access to information about their illness, while releasing scarce resources in the medical practice to be redirected toward other patient care needs. Through computer-based, dial-up access, patients with breast cancer and their families can access information about the disease and its treatment, as well as share concerns with a peer group and expert clinicians. This approach complements the traditional clinician counseling role with the patient and family.[4]

It will be a challenge to target appropriate and timely resources to support intervention with patients at above-average risk. Information systems can play a key role in the following areas:

- managing the initial enrollment and the subsequent patient interview screening for risk assessment
- patient monitoring including referral follow-up, prescription refills, and scheduled examinations
- patient education
- patient information including insurance benefits, sources of support in the community, etc.

Exhibit 5–3 Physician Involvement in Information System Design

- **Clinical Database**
  1. episodes of care
  2. utilization review
  3. resource use
  4. outcomes studies, including HEDIS (Health Plan Employer Data and Information Set)
  5. clinician/clinician team effectiveness
- **Patient Care Support**
  1. automated medical record
  2. management tools (e.g., reminders of when all test results are available)
  3. referral and drug-use alerts
  4. tools for information retrieval and presentation
- **Clinical Team Effectiveness**
  1. patient access
  2. resource use
  3. patient satisfaction
  4. outcomes

The Future Importance of Information Systems

In his 1993–1994 study of 10 integrated health care delivery systems, Coddington documented that the majority of the organizations studied were investing significantly in information systems.[5] Undoubtedly, this investment will continue to grow to support provider efficiency, improve management of patient care, and support the research of clinical practice patterns to identify best practices and enhance overall organization performance. In most advanced physician practices, information systems applications will continue to grow over the next five to ten years, enhancing existing capabilities and adding new functions.

CONCLUSION

The following key factors have been identified in this discussion of using advanced physician management structure to ensure clinical effectiveness:

- governance structure that ensures significant physician input and leadership
- physician commitment, education, and support to improve and focus care delivery
- implementation of aggressive patient management programs, designed with physician input (such as pre-primary care screening, case management, specialists as consultants, specialists training of primary care physicians, care management teams, etc.)
- integration of all the significant health care delivery resources so that optimal resource investment and utilization can be managed effectively
- evidenced-based medicine and the information systems to support it
- increased value placed on information systems to promote efficiency, improved patient care, peer review, and identification of best practices
- new performance measures that are consistent with the goals and incentives of the organization
- an incentive reward structure that is consistent with the organization and individual physician goals

An advanced physician management structure provides the environment for implementing progressive change. While some of the change agents exist in the external environment, many new approaches to the delivery of health care can be created, evaluated, and successfully implemented by physician-directed organizations. An effective communication management structure, as well as a significant investment of physician time, is required to implement change successfully in the dynamic health care environment.

NOTES

1. P.L. Havlicek et al., *Medical Groups in the U.S.: A Survey of Practice Characteristics* (Chicago, Ill.: American Medical Association, 1993).

2. Lovelace Health Systems, *New Mexico Marketing Plan* (Albequerque, N.M.: 1995), p. 11.

3. C.E. Hornbrook et al., Health Care Episodes: Definition, Measurement, and Use, *Medical Care Review* 42 (1985): 163–218.

4. D. Gustafson et al., Assessing the Needs of Breast Cancer Patients and Their Families, *Quality Management in Health Care* 2, no. 1 (1993): 6–17.

5. D. Coddington et al., *Integrated Health Care: Reorganizing the Physician, Hospital and Health Plan Relationship* (Englewood, Colo.: Center for Research in Ambulatory Health Care Administration, 1994).

Part II

The Merger and Expansion Process

Chapter 6

Expansion Process for Physician Organizations

Douglas Goldstein

INTRODUCTION

Throughout the country, physician leaders and management executives are organizing and expanding various types of physician equity arrangements into integrated physician networks. This process is being driven by fundamental price pressures from purchasers, the growth of managed care, and expansion of capitation, which are necessitating the use of advanced information systems and mutually aligned incentives to ensure the delivery of high-quality, cost-effective health care.

To be successful in the dynamic managed care marketplace of today and tomorrow, physicians must build and expand Integrated Delivery Systems (IDSs) that are clinically effective in the capitation environment. Often these entities require a combination of organizational types, ranging from staff structures, to group practices, to integrated practice associations and network alliances. Such organizations must be prepared to evolve rapidly, through capital acquisition, strong management, and strategic alliances. Certainly, there are variations in the rate of evolution between urban and rural markets. However, the core issues of control and autonomy in merging practices are the same for physicians nationwide.

This chapter focuses on the progressive steps involved in creating and expanding a multi-entity Physician Organization that serves as the key element of an IDS. Often these entities or Physician Equity Alliances involve several interlinked organizations including a group practice, an integrated Management Services Organization (MSO), and a larger network arrangement such as an Independent Practice Association (IPA). This was illustrated in Figure 1–6, in Chapter 1. This chapter addresses the major considerations and describes the process of building an organized system for the efficient delivery of high-quality patient care. Key points addressed include the following:

- **Conducting action-oriented research**—Physicians must be able to gather information from five key market segments and use the findings to make strategic decisions for a development plan.
- **Pursuing aggressive business development**—Physician leaders must act to

educate, organize, and lead members of the Physician Organization to prepare for the future.
- **Understanding the equity transaction**—Physicians must acquire an in-depth knowledge of the principles and process of business valuation and the fair market value for a medical practice—whether as part of a small one- or two-person entity or as a part of a 200-physician group practice with an owned management company.
- **Using an aggressive business expansion process**—The organization must progress through a five-step process for a legal and financial merger of physicians in an Integrated Group Practice (IGP) and Physician Practice Management Company (PPMC; sometimes referred to as a Management Services Organization). (Note: the terms MSO and PPMC are used interchangeably throughout the chapter as are the terms Physician Equity Alliance and Physician Organization.)
- **Implementing systems**—The management of a clinically effective Physician Equity Alliance involves advanced information, management, cost accounting, and quality systems.

CONDUCTING ACTION-ORIENTED RESEARCH

Developing a viable Physician Equity Alliance through merger, acquisition, or integration requires action-oriented research. Figure 6–1 illustrates how information and findings from five key areas—purchaser research, community research, practice business needs, benchmarking research, and environmental assessment—factor into strategic decisions and, ultimately, into an aggressive business development plan.

The research effort begins with the environmental assessment and continues with the compilation of up-to-date information on three market needs: the health needs of the community, the business needs of the physicians, and the financial needs and strategies of purchasers such as employers and payers (such as insurance companies and managed health plans). In these competitive times, it is essential to put together a market profile of local medical practices, managed health plans serving the area, and regional health system merger and consolidation activities as rapidly as possible—within 60 to 90 days of the anticipated integration start-up.

Researching Managed Health Plans

With managed care and capitation accounting for an ever-growing percentage of a health care organizations' revenue, it is absolutely incumbent upon physician leaders and management executives to evaluate the number, type, and growth of managed care plans and risk-oriented reimbursement approaches in the market area. This information plays a pivotal role in determining how fast to move in the integration process.

In gathering information on the managed care plans serving the area, it is important to document how the various types of plans—Preferred Provider Organization (PPO), point-of-service (POS) plan, staff-model Health Maintenance Organization (HMO-staff), and HMO-network—have contributed to the overall growth of managed care and how they are merging and consolidating. It is advisable to create a matrix that can be used to estimate the market share attributable to managed health plans and capitation reimbursement over a three-to-five-year period. It is also important to note the type of capitation reimbursement. Obtaining the answers to the following questions will help determine the rate of change in each regional market:

- Is primary care capitation the dominant method?

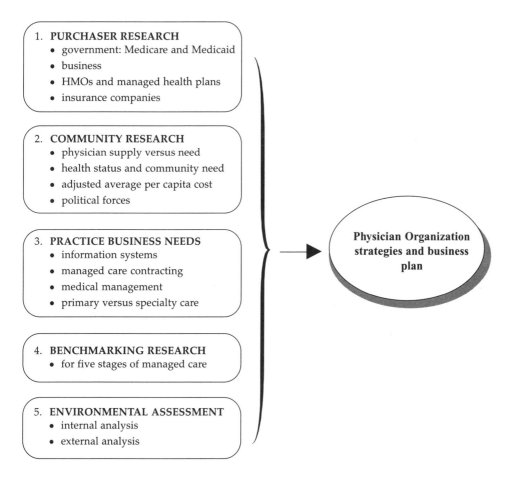

Figure 6–1 Action-oriented market research. Phase I—research, strategy development, and alliance recommendations. Courtesy of Medical Alliances, Inc., Alexandria, Virginia.

- Are any Physician Organizations receiving medical capitation for all professional services?
- Do any IDSs or Physician Equity Alliances have global risk where they manage the inpatient flow of funds?
- How prevalent are single-specialty carve outs for cardiology, orthopedics, ophthalmology, oncology, and other specialties?
- Do any health care providers have a percentage of premium arrangements with managed health plans?

The development of integrated Physician Organizations often stimulates rapid growth of managed care and capitation. Thus, to predict more accurately the course and types of capitation in a specific region, it is useful to know how the market is evolving and compare it to the experiences of other regions and the five stages of managed care evolution as described in Chapter 4.

Other important research issues relate to how fast the market is changing and, even more important, the locality's adjusted average per capita cost (AAPCC) for Medicare expenditures. This is based on a historical average of the expenditures for people aged 65 and over in a specific county. The federal Health Care Financing Administration (HCFA) currently uses AAPCCs to make monthly payments to HMO risk contractors who, in turn, pass the risk on to Physician Organizations in the form of capitation and risk contracts. HCFA approves HMOs and managed health plans on a county-by-county basis to sponsor Medicare HMOs and then pays them 95 percent of a recipient's average expenditure.

Agreeing to assume all of the risk, the Medicare HMOs develop selective panels and shift the risk to providers through capitation and global fees. Then, by marketing the concepts of lower costs and reduced administrative hassles, the HMOs induce a significant number of senior citizens to switch from their current health plans and physicians. If a provider is not on the HMO's panel, this trend, which happens rapidly, can funnel a dramatic number of patients out of the practice. Where the AAPCC is high, like in south Florida, the growth of Medicare HMOs will be rapid.

A concurrent trend, as states seek to contain Medicaid expenditures and reduce budget deficits, is the rising popularity of Medicaid HMOs. The transition of Medicaid from federal to state programs is significantly accelerating the growth of Medicaid HMOs. In addition, to gain experience in risk contracting and capitation, managed health plans are making major inroads into the employer-purchaser market.

Identifying Purchaser Needs

The most critical form of research is identifying purchaser requirements for an accessible, cost-effective health network. Increasingly, health care purchasing coalitions are contracting with lower-cost, provider-based delivery systems, with an eye toward bypassing HMOs managed by national HMO management companies. Federal legislation is also unleashing the ability of Physician Organizations to contract directly with employers under risk and capitated arrangements. Evolving federal legislation is removing some of the antitrust and capital requirements for entities that qualify as provider service networks. The exact nature of these legislative actions will become clearer in 1996, and this legislation will continue to affect Physician Organizations for the foreseeable future.

Research that focuses on the needs, strategies, and decisions of businesses (self-insured and others), managed care and insurance companies, and federal and state government agencies can pinpoint these purchasers' goals for cost containment and health benefit design. This information can then be used to determine the requisite panel composition and marketing message.

A complete understanding of purchaser requirements is critical to successful implementation of Physician Organizations. Several methods for collecting information on purchaser requirements are available. For example, if the targets are business or managed care entities, physician leaders and management executives may want to rely on a combination of personal meetings and telephone interviews. Personal interviews with key representatives of purchaser organizations almost always offer the most extensive and useful information. It is advisable to canvas a broad cross-section of entities: five to ten major employers (self-insured and others), five to ten large managed care plans, five top insurance carriers, and three to five important third-party administrators.

Once the information is gathered, it should be analyzed according to the type and size of organization. For example, developing a profile of large, self-insured employers will generate conclusions about this market segment's needs. In the same way, analyzing panel preferences for a region's largest managed care plans will offer guidance on how to structure the size and location of different health care services within the Integrated Delivery System.

The rapid pace of change within the health care field demands that physicians and executives stay close to the front lines and gather information first-hand. Proactive research is the key to gathering crucial information quickly, making initial strategic decisions efficiently, developing beneficial relationships, and guiding the business development process effectively.

PURSUING AGGRESSIVE BUSINESS DEVELOPMENT

With billions of dollars of capital available from various strategic allies, primary care physicians and specialists must make informed decisions about with whom to form alliances through merger, acquisition, integration, and other relationships. Creating a financially viable Physician Organization with market power requires physicians and executives to take strong, decisive actions. These actions must be patterned on successful rapid-growth companies in various industries from health care and financial services to high-technology and professional services. The essential steps in this process are:

1. Analyze your medical practice and every other major health care player in the target market. Get a fix on your personal and business goals, the competitive environment, and market requirements. Focus on the track records of managed health plans, competitors, and purchasers.
2. Track regional moves. Pinpoint "the urge to merge" among health systems and primary care, multispecialty, and single-specialty Physician Organizations. Identify the strategies and stages of development of the market leaders.
3. Focus on being on top of the contracting pyramid and determining how to split the risk pool. Be certain that the building block systems described in Chapter 2 are in place to allow for effective management and to ensure that the Physician Organization can manage the maximum amount of the premium dollar.
4. Assess, organize, and then ally. Develop a specific alliance strategy. But do so only after examining the leadership strengths, physician quality, access to capital, risk profile, size, composition, and formal business plan of the Physician Organization.
5. Empower physician leaders. Approach the alliance partner selection process by involving physician leaders in a series of discrete decisions, such as the following: Do physicians want to lead or be bought out? To what extent are the physicians willing to invest time, cash, and equity to establish a larger Physician Organization and maintain majority control? Do the physicians understand the benefits of using capital wisely coupled with aggressive management?
6. Understand the varieties of practice valuation and equity arrangements. Only by knowing the available options can physicians make the right decision about with whom to link and how to structure the arrangement.
7. Recognize that timing is critical. In addition to deciding with *whom* to affiliate—pharmaceutical companies, a health system, public PPMC, or an insurer—a pivotal issue is *when* the alliance will take place relative to the stage of managed care development. As part of the merger process, the following steps are essential:
    a. Organize effective management for the ambulatory care sites. Build outstanding service capabilities for the Physician Equity Alliance. Among the services that must function at the highest level are managed care contracting, facilities and equipment management, group purchasing, staff management, billing, practice management information systems, and business development.

b. Develop a fair equity structure. Devise mechanisms whereby physicians can gain a fair equity interest/ownership in the group practice and management company components of the Physician Equity Alliance.
c. Build working clinical relationships. Create an environment whereby physicians have a genuine motivation to manage clinical care to balance cost and quality.
d. Detail the equity exchange terms so it is clearly understood how equity changes. Show physicians how they will take stock/equity in their current practices and exchange it for stock/equity in a larger group and management company according to the principles of valuation and fair market value. Provide written documentation about how the exchange will affect such variables as compensation systems, pensions, and physicians' roles in governance and clinical operations.
e. Develop a long-term governance structure that allows for strong, ongoing leadership. Help physicians understand and appreciate the new and emerging parameters relating to clinical management, quality, compensation, and practice management.
f. Prepare the organization for rapid evolution and continuous growth. As markets and external pressures change, so must the organization. Help physicians accept the need for ongoing, responsive organizational refinement of clinical and management systems. The most important ingredient for success is empowered and enlightened physician leadership knowledgeable enough to obtain professional consulting and management advice that develops a powerful business plan, which in turn attracts capital on favorable terms.

UNDERSTANDING THE EQUITY TRANSACTION

Understanding the equity transaction involves an in-depth knowledge of the principles and process of business valuation and the fair market value of a medical practice as it becomes part of a 200-physician group practice with an associated Physician Practice Management Company. There are numerous variations in the governance and ownership structure of IPAs, group practices, Physician Practice Management Companies, and Physician Organizations. Although virtually all PPMCs or MSOs seek to be viewed as physician-driven or physician-led, the telltale signs of who holds the real reins include the following:

- Who controls the governance of the business entity that controls the revenues?
- If a medical group has sold all of its tangible and intangible assets to a public physician practice management company, what are the options to reverse the transaction?
- What is the role of the group practice in the operations of the regional operating division or parent management company?
- Does a minority investor in the management company hold reserve powers that dilute the ability of the majority to make decisions?
- Who is the majority owner of the business organization?
- Is the physician's role relegated to delivering quality care without much policy, operational, or strategic input?

For example, take the case of an evolving alliance between a primary care Physician Organization and a health care delivery system. If the primary care physicians have acted and formed the management company, developed a five-year business plan, and approached the health system to invest, then the alliance is likely to be on the physicians' terms. However, if the health system has formed a large-scale PPMC to manage risk, the health system will likely approach physicians to buy into its management company or PPMC. Often, a buy-in involves a purchase of the practices in exchange for cash and a minority interest in the management company. In this scenario, physicians let the health system establish the capital structure of the Integrated Delivery System.

An alternative for physicians is to merge into a Physician Organization composed of a large group practice and an interlinked management company. For instance, this transaction could involve merger of 30 or more physicians who then have 100 percent ownership in the management company. The physicians then begin to operate the management company and merged practices in multiple locations. Then the Physician Organization focuses on top clinical and management issues, with special emphasis on training physicians to manage risk under capitation. In this case, with operations of the management company established and a detailed five-year business plan, the health system is given the opportunity to invest in the capital structure of the management company established by the physicians. The health system is likely to be a minority rather than majority partner under this approach.

Numerous professional investors and business executives knowledgeable about the ways of Wall Street are aggressively attempting to buy physician practices. They understand and live by the cardinal rule of investing: "buy low and sell high." They seek to use the revenues of medical practices to take the combined practices under a PPMC umbrella public, realizing a significant appreciation in the investment. If physician leaders invest in their own management companies; take some risk; and expand their Physician Equity Alliances as long as possible with internal cash, debt, and self-financing, they will likely receive a higher appreciation on their equity than if they sell early and low to an outside party.

To understand the equity transactions, physician leaders must be aware of the intentions of all parties, understand the rationale for the mergers, and have access to a detailed business plan that describes the market and business opportunity for the proposed transaction.

Understanding Business and Practice Valuations

An essential component to the merger process is knowledge of the principles and process of valuation. During a merger, the purpose of practice valuations is to place a fair value and price on each merging entity that can then be recouped by the prospective shareholders. It is vital that all parties agree on the methodology of the valuation and believe that the outcome will be equitable. These prerequisites can be achieved by conducting a full valuation, a ballpark valuation, or a hard-asset valuation. Three basic principles or theories of valuation guide the process and evaluation of the business appraiser:

1. **Market approach**—Based on the principle of substitution, whereby a buyer does not pay more for a particular business than it would cost to buy a similar business.
2. **Cost approach**—Also based on the principle of substitution. However, this approach focuses on each individual asset, both tangible and intangible. The buyer does not pay more than it would cost to build a similar practice from the ground up (also called *adjusted net asset value*).
3. **Income approach**—Closest to the "pure financial theory" of valuation. The value of a business is the present value of all future cash flow.

The purpose of the valuation (e.g., merger, divorce, sale, retirement) determines the type of valuation method to use. Thus, it is important that there be consensus as to the rationale behind the valuation. In addition, valuations must conform with all Internal Revenue Service rulings, the Uniform Standards of Professional Appraisal Practice, and applicable regulatory and court decisions. It is also necessary to understand the issues related to the entity that may be purchasing or merging medical practices. If the purchaser is a nonprofit health system, it will require a formal valuation that uses several different methods and quantifies the fair market value. Accurate, quantifiable fair market calculations are necessary because, by law, if a nonprofit organization purchases a medical practice for more than fair market value, it risks losing tax exemption. A for-profit hospital is not bound by such requirements, but it is financially driven and will not want to pay more than can be reasonably expected to recoup through future earnings of the group practice. If physicians are merging their practices, without an outside party, the valuation process may be less formal.

There are several common valuation methods:

- **Discounted future cash flow**—Theoretically, this is the "correct" approach to valuating a business. In this approach, future cash flow is predicted and then discounted back to present value. This approach is used most often in mergers and acquisitions. The advantage of this approach is that it is an all-in-one approach; goodwill and asset values are automatically included into future cash flow streams. The disadvantage is that sometimes it can be very difficult to predict future cash flow. However, as the health care market continues to move toward capitation and long-term management contracts, revenue streams are likely to become more predictable. (Note: Often in a merger situation, a company will use a modified discounted cash flow approach. A common modification is to use just a few years—e.g., five to seven years—of projected cash flow.)
- **Rule of thumb**—These methods of valuation are very popular when discussing a merger, but are seldom used as the sole method of valuation. Some examples of rule-of-thumb methods are: (1) five times the earnings before interest and taxes and (2) three times the free cash flow. In this approach, appropriate financial numbers are plugged into the rule-of-thumb to generate a sales price. This approach is most often used as a check on other valuation methods and is very seldom used as the primary valuation method. The advantage of this approach is that it is very easy to calculate the value of an entity. The disadvantages are that it treats all business earnings or cash flows as identical, and it fails to take into account many other factors that determine the value of a particular business.
- **Excess earnings**—A valuation method based on the discounted cash flow method that modifies historical data to generate a practice value. Earnings are normalized to account for discretionary items often found in financial statements of medical practices. In this approach, the asset value is determined; then earnings are normalized; then excess earnings are capitalized and added to the asset value. This method is often used for medical practices because of its simplicity and accuracy. The advantage of this method is that historical data and normalized earnings are exact, rather than projected figures. The disadvantage is that the capitalization rate is difficult to quantify accurately.

The next piece of the equation is for a physician to understand all of the components that determine the value of a business or, in this case, a medical practice. Exhibit 6–1 provides a detailed list of tangible and intan-

Exhibit 6–1 Medical Practice Assets and Liabilities

TANGIBLES

- assets
    1. cash (revenue predictability and stability)
    2. accounts receivable (aging management)
    3. supplies
    4. equipment—facilities and technology (state-of-the-art/antiquated)
    5. leasehold improvements, etc.
    6. managed care contracts
- liabilities
    1. accounts payable
    2. accrued and deferred liabilities
    3. long-term debt
    4. lease obligations
    5. contingent liabilities, such as malpractice lawsuits, etc.

INTANGIBLES

- goodwill
    1. expected future earnings
    2. location and demographics (urban/rural, market growth, affluent/poor, stability of population)
    3. level of competition and level of managed care (I to IV)
    4. client persistence (stability)
    5. reputation (image)
    6. practitioners' work habits (schedule/productivity)
    7. dependence on referrals versus direct client contact (direct/indirect client base)
    8. proportion of managed care contracts/mix of clients (capitation/Medicare/Medicaid)
    9. vertical potential synergism (propensity to be source of revenue for prospective acquirer)
    10. marketability of the practice

- computer software

- contractual relationships (strength of links with managed care companies/hospitals)

- employees (training and dedication)

- licenses

- noncompete covenants, etc.

---

gible assets of a medical practice. Physicians wearing their business owners' hats must know where the value of the medical practices lies. In most practices it is in owner's discretionary cash, earnings, accounts receivable (to the extent that they represent a small amount and/or fall within 30- to 60-day ranges), and equipment.

Another area of value is goodwill. Whether to pay and how much to pay for goodwill is a highly charged issue. Goodwill is defined as excess earnings, or the amount paid that represents the difference between the average earnings of the type of business involved in the merger and the earnings of the specific business being valued.

Recommendation: Remuneration should be made for intangible assets in cases where these assets will increase the value of the new entity or be retained by the existing company. The amount of goodwill paid should reflect the value added to the new entity.

While it is important to select the right valuation methods for a merger or buyout, it is absolutely essential to use methods that are agreeable to all parties. This concept is captured in the following definition of *fair market value:* The price at which the property would change hands between a willing buyer and a willing seller, neither being under a compulsion to buy or sell, and both having reasonable knowledge of relevant facts.

USING AN AGGRESSIVE BUSINESS EXPANSION PROCESS

This section focuses on the merger of physician practices into the Integrated Group Practice and management company components of a Physician Equity Alliance and outlines the five-step process for achieving a legal and financial merger. The five major steps are: (1) merge medical practice assets; (2) create an organizational infrastructure and enhance operating systems; (3) expand business and clinical systems; (4) identify management talent; and (5) obtain capital under favorable terms to accelerate growth.

The first step in creating a Physician Equity Alliance is finding physician leaders who have the time, energy, and commitment to make the various entities work. Within a task force of 8 to 10 physicians, there usually will be one or two with high leadership potential. These physicians must not only orchestrate a detailed, multiyear plan for developing the organization, but also build support among other physicians by preparing and delivering a strong visual presentation detailing the vision, strategy, structure, and services. Among the key elements of this presentation are guiding principles, goals, governance, equity structure, merger process, development timeline, and business and clinical advantages. This presentation is used for educating and empowering potential physician partners to become part of the Physician Organization and to obtain capital from an appropriate equity partner in the MSO.

Next, physician leaders should identify potential physician partners who will help the organization achieve its clinical care, organizational, and business goals. Using one-on-one sessions and small-group meetings, they should discuss the process and benefits of merging into a large Physician Organization as well as achieving the overarching goal of a clinically effective, cost-efficient managed care contracting organization. It is important to remain flexible. Competitive forces in some markets could cause a core group practice of 30 or more physicians to expand to 75 to 150 physicians, in order to wield negotiating leverage with payers.

As interested physicians are identified, they should be invited to participate in the group practice or MSO task forces or in committees focused on issues related to clinical and business operations, such as managed care contracting, medical management, operations, credentialing, and information systems. It is important to keep motivation high and momentum going by ensuring that each task force is chaired by one of the Physician Organization's founding or highly involved physicians and meets weekly or biweekly. In most cases, task force and committee chairs will report monthly to the lead or core group of physicians, which may have already evolved into a board for the MSO or group practice.

Building the Physician Organization's visibility and credibility among consumers and purchasers calls for powerful public relations, communications, and training. For example, an educational program sponsored by the alliance—possibly titled the "Institute for Quality and Advanced Practice Management"—and offered to all regional physicians and health care executives can build name recognition and add validity to the alliance. The educational program can offer a series of interactive educational programs featuring physicians from such leading-edge organizations as The Carle Clinic and Health Plan. An aggressive publicity program of press releases, direct mail invitations, advertisements in local papers, and broadcast faxes to physicians has produced turnouts of more than 150 physicians and executives per program.

Also critical to Physician Organization success is the education of physician partners in the group practice and potential members of the affiliated IPA network. To supplement the more formal institute program, physician leaders might consider regular distribution of articles from trade journals and the popular business press, site visits to similar organizations located in advanced managed care markets, and distribution of a quarterly or bimonthly newsletter that summarizes regional insurance, capitation, and managed care information and trends.

Recommendation: Assist physicians in communicating with their new partners by taking advantage of wide area computer networks and commercial online information services. Dedicated information networks with an Integrated Delivery System are optimal, but they take time and capital to implement. Commercial options that are easy to implement range from commercial services such as CompuServe, Prodigy, or America Online, to a niche market service such as a "Fax News Update" on managed care, to networking through e-mail on the Internet.

Successful physician leaders have the power to inspire and guide colleagues to take responsibility and action. When leaders empower their colleagues to meet the challenge of change through communication and innovation, the race to create *sustainable* ambulatory delivery systems will be won. Whether the medium is educational seminars, audiotapes, or multimedia presentations, the key to communicating the powerful advantages of a Physician Organization lies in repetition, variety, clarity, and color.

The Merger Process

At the beginning of the merger process, it is advisable not only to define the steps that will be taken, but also to outline the valuation methods that will be used to ensure that they are applied consistently to all the entities involved. Next, leaders should develop a "Merger Partner Screening Checklist" that identifies areas of compatibility between the new merging physicians and the group practice and ensures alignment of principles. This checklist is provided in Exhibit 6–2. After all of the parties have identified common goals, they move through the following steps within the merger process:

1. Sign a confidentiality and exclusivity agreement. This document outlines the agreement of the parties to exchange financial information and maintain confidentiality. It also provides a 6- to 12-month period of nondisclosure and exclusivity, during which no one can initiate mergers with other parties.

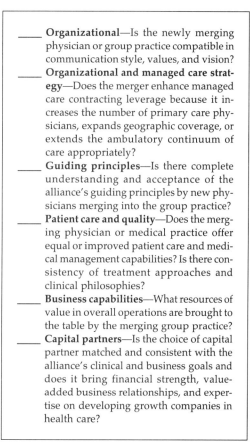

Exhibit 6–2 Merger Partner Screening Checklist

____ **Organizational**—Is the newly merging physician or group practice compatible in communication style, values, and vision?
____ **Organizational and managed care strategy**—Does the merger enhance managed care contracting leverage because it increases the number of primary care physicians, expands geographic coverage, or extends the ambulatory continuum of care appropriately?
____ **Guiding principles**—Is there complete understanding and acceptance of the alliance's guiding principles by new physicians merging into the group practice?
____ **Patient care and quality**—Does the merging physician or medical practice offer equal or improved patient care and medical management capabilities? Is there consistency of treatment approaches and clinical philosophies?
____ **Business capabilities**—What resources of value in overall operations are brought to the table by the merging group practice?
____ **Capital partners**—Is the choice of capital partner matched and consistent with the alliance's clinical and business goals and does it bring financial strength, value-added business relationships, and expertise on developing growth companies in health care?

2. Obtain financial and clinical data on practice operations for valuation and practice assessment. Rely on an outside accounting or practice management firm to verify financial claims made during the disclosure period; estimate the worth of the practice; and evaluate such issues as antitrust concerns, tax liabilities, and Securities and Exchange Commission regulations. An on-site practice assessment often helps to analyze patient flow, financial controls, coding, clinical charting, and other operational issues.
3. Develop a "merger briefing book." Targeted to physicians interested in merging, this manual provides a detailed explanation of the process of asset

transfer to the group practice and MSO and explains the valuation method. Giving physicians a document that they can share with their accountants, attorneys, or other consultants can help accelerate the merger process.
4. Describe the findings of the practice's "history and physical." Provide the merging physicians with the results of the practice assessment and valuation on the individual practices and the network as a whole. Also present a formal offer to merge that includes details on such issues as equity shares and voting rights in the MSO and associated group practice.
5. Sign a "letter of intent to merge." Declaring that the parties agree to the merger pending final acts of due diligence, this agreement authorizes attorneys to finalize all documents and agreements necessary to close the deal. This letter typically precedes a period of legal due diligence that involves verification of legal documents; transfer of all contracts, assets, liabilities, leases, and documents; and drafting of final merger agreements. During this period, the required notices, plans, and documents should be submitted to the appropriate local, state, and federal government agencies.
6. Complete due diligence and finalize the merger. Once the legal and accounting due diligence are completed and all contingencies have been met, set a closing date—typically within 10 to 14 days—when the parties can come together, complete transactions, sign contracts, and exchange money or stock.

Physician leaders must also look inward. A "history and physical" or practice assessment must be conducted on the business and clinical operations of each participating medical practice. If a true merger of financial, legal, and operating systems is to occur in a way that leads to successful postmerger operations, then practices must be evaluated. This assessment usually involves the use of an outside practice consultant who gathers financial and operational information on the operations through an extensive questionnaire. Exhibit 6–3 provides an excerpt from a data request form as an example of information that should be collected. The typical form used by the consulting firm ranges in length from six to eight pages and asks for the following types of information: financial statements, company documents, accounts receivable information, provider information, and legal information. The questions can vary depending on the purpose of the request. A request for data for practice valuation will differ from a request for practice assessment. After some analysis of the data, a site visit is completed.

Finally, a report is provided to the individual medical practices, while a series of comparative diagrams of all the practices is presented to the group of physicians in the merger process. Tables 6–1 and 6–2 provide two comparative charts useful in understanding the operational aspects of the merging practices so there is a basis for resolving differences and finalizing a merger. Table 6–1 is an overview of key operating statistics including productivity, visits per physician, compensation, and other factors that would—at a glance—indicate the similarities and differences among the practices undergoing merger. Table 6–2 is an evaluation of the types of managed health plans and kinds of reimbursement methods for two medical practices merging their assets (see Table 6–1). It also includes the number of lives managed under each contract.

How medical practice assets move from an independent practice to the group practice and management company or MSO during the merger must also be addressed. It is useful to separate and evaluate the three major asset components of a premerger practice:

1. **Practice assets**—tangible and intangible assets of the existing medical practice, such as equipment, medical charts,

Exhibit 6–3 Excerpt From Practice Merger Data Request

Purpose: The purpose of this data request is to gather information necessary for the formation of a group practice merger.

Instructions: Please send all information directly to Medical Alliances at the above address.

Confidentiality: All practice information will be kept confidential and will be used only to conduct due diligence, project financial pro forma statements, and to complete the business plan for the participating entities. No specific referrals will be made as to the particular source of any information.

FINANCIAL STATEMENTS

Please provide the following financial statements for the last three years. This checklist will help your data gathering process.

Item	Gathered	Do not have	Comments
1. Income statements	_____	_____	_____
2. Detail of subsidiaries and/or related financial interests with relevant financial statements or tax returns	_____	_____	_____
3. Copies of all leases including those for equipment and facility. Denote those that are not transferrable	_____	_____	_____

PRACTICE/COMPANY DOCUMENTS

Item	Gathered	Do not have	Comments
1. If incorporated, copy of articles of incorporation, bylaws, and corporate minutes	_____	_____	_____
2. If partnership, articles of partnership	_____	_____	_____

ACCOUNTS RECEIVABLE AND PATIENT DATA

Item	Gathered	Do not have	Comments
1. Accounts receivable aging listed by payer class, run as of the date of assessment (usually the date of the most recent financial information). For example:	_____	_____	_____

Payer	≤30 Days	31–60	61–90	91–120	>120
Medicare					
Blue Shield					
Medicaid					
Commercial					
Total					

continues

Exhibit 6–3 continued

PRACTICE AND PROVIDER INFORMATION

Item	Gathered	Do not have	Comments
1. Provide a brief history of the practice, when established, list previous and current locations, names of providers (with CVs) and specialties (board certification)	_____	_____	_____
2. Provide descriptions of all personnel, including name, position, date of hire, hours worked per week, pay rate or salary, and benefits	_____	_____	_____

LEGAL INFORMATION

Item	Gathered	Do not have	Comments
1. Any loan agreements or guarantees	_____	_____	_____
2. Restrictive share transfer agreements	_____	_____	_____

BUSINESS RELATIONSHIPS

Item	Gathered	Do not have	Comments
1. Accountant (name and telephone)	_____	_____	_____
2. Attorney (name and telephone)	_____	_____	_____
3. Banking (name of institution, type of account, terms of account)	_____	_____	_____

Courtesy of Medical Alliances, Inc., Alexandria, Virginia.

---

supplies, goodwill, and managed care contracts
2. **Ancillary services**—laboratory, imaging center, genetics and infertility services, home health care business, limited or full pharmacy, and after-hours urgent care center
3. **Real estate**—property held within a medical practice's structure

A medical practice's history, corporate structure, and business concerns may raise additional issues that will need to be addressed on a case-by-case basis.

Figure 6–2 illustrates an MSO and group practice asset transaction process for the merger. In this scenario, most practice assets are transferred from the premerger practices to the management company. Assets transferred to the group practice in exchange for group practice stock are likely to include physicians' professional services, goodwill, provider number, and patient charts; assets transferred to the management company (often a C corporation) for stock will probably include managed care contracts, equipment, supplies, practice management information systems, accounts receivable, and leases.

For legal and business reasons, some assets and liabilities of a premerger practice, such as a pension plan or accounts receivable, might not be transferred to the group practice. Instead, they may stay with the

Table 6–1 Highlights of Key Operating Statistics

Key Statistics	Bayside Family Practice	Mariner Family Practice	Surfer Family Practice	North Ocean Family Practice	Great White Family Practice
Number of physicians in group	5	5	6	2	6
Number of office visits per year	36,400	15,000	14,644	12,473	55,575
Number of FTE nurses	8.65	4	2	4	5.725 (1.8 LPNs)
Number of nurse practitioners	0.35	0	1	1	0
Number of physician assistants	0	0	1	1	0
Average physician salary	157,000	108,000	111,763	123,431	113,833
Total practice revenue	2,433,201	1,394,956	1,238,852	1,110,273	1,692,355
Average revenue per physician	486,640	284,995	321,783	234,563	282,059
Salary as percentage of gross revenue	32.3%	38.7%	64.6%	41.6%	40.5%
Compensation structure	Base salary + bonus based on productivity	Base salary + bonus	Base salary + bonus	Base salary + bonus	Base salary + profit sharing

Courtesy of Medical Alliances, Inc., Alexandria, Virginia.

premerger practice for a period of time, determined by the practice's owners. Other liabilities, such as equipment and real estate leases, normally are assumed by the Physician Practice Management Company.

Functions performed by the group practice include clinical management, quality, clinical pathways development, and policy input. Premerger practice functions transferred to the MSO and provided to the group practice pursuant to a management service agreement between the group practice and the management company include billing and collections, human resources and staff management (nonclinical and business), practice development and marketing, managed care contracting, information systems operations, strategic planning, and ancillary service operations.

In addition to the process illustrated in Figure 6–2, it is important to diagram the ancillary service and real estate transfer process. The way these assets are transferred will vary according to state and federal laws and the Physician Organization's business goals. Supplementary ancillary services critical to practice operations are normally transferred from the premerger practices to the group practice, while the MSO obtains a management service agreement from the group practice to operate the ancillary services.

Recommendation: Evaluate each ancillary service or other health care business owned by a premerger practice on a case-by-case basis. Work with the group practice, MSO, and owners of premerger practices to decide whether the Physician Organization should

Table 6-2 Managed Care Contract Summary

Practice	Plan Type	Type of Payment	Number of Covered Lives	Percentage of Practice Population
Bayside Family Practice				
Medicare	25/75 FFS & HMO	FFS/Cap	500	3.35%
Medicaid	60/40 FFS & HMO	FFS/Cap	135	0.73%
Travelers	PPO	Discounted FFS	103	0.69%
Lincoln National	PPO	Discounted FFS	35	0.24%
MetLife	PPO	Discounted FFS	220	1.48%
NCPPO	PPO	Discounted FFS	724	4.88%
PruCare-HMO	HMO	Primary Cap	866	5.83%
Aetna	HMO	Medical Cap	100	0.75%
	PPO	Discounted FFS		
	Managed Choice	Discounted FFS	130	0.88%
	Managed Choice 2	Discounted FFS		
Mariner Family Practice				
Medicare	50/50 FFS & HMO		4000	28.44%
Medicaid	70/30 FFS & HMO		2000	
BC/BS DC	PPO	Discounted FFS	600	2.85%
BC/BS VA	PPO	Discounted FFS	100	0.48%
NCPPO	PPO	Discounted FFS	300	1.43%
MetLife	PPO	Discounted FFS	100	0.48%
PruCare	HMO/PPO	Primary Cap	100	0.48%
Travelers	PPO	Discounted FFS	40	0.19%

Courtesy of Medical Alliances, Inc., Alexandria, Virginia.

acquire the enterprise for cash, stock, or notes. Also make decisions to acquire real estate owned by premerger practices on a case-by-case basis, carefully evaluating the financial strength of the group practice and MSO and capital availability.

Development of Equity and Governance Structure

Guide the development of the equity structure of the group practice and the MSO through established equity principles such as the following:

- The group practice is physician-owned and controlled.
- The MSO is majority-owned and controlled by the physician group practice shareholders with minority interest to be held by an alliance partner compatible with the organization's vision and clinical mission.
- Physicians merging into the group practice and MSO must transfer their tangible and intangible assets in exchange for stock in the group practice and a proportional equity stake in the MSO.

These principles should stay constant throughout the alliances' rapid growth.

Because the majority of an alliance's assets are moved into the management company, this becomes the entity with the greatest financial value. But in structuring the MSO and group practice, it is not necessary for voting rights and governance to be in equal proportion to equity ownership percentages. The degree of governance control

Expansion Process for Physician Organizations 119

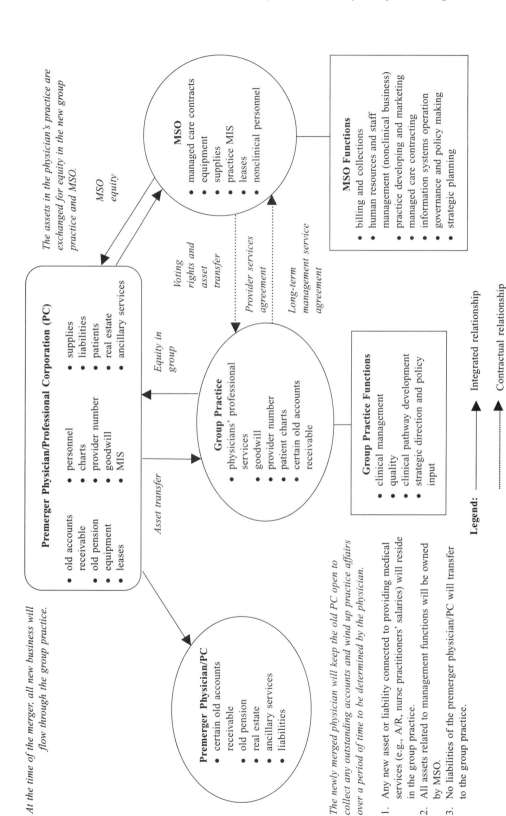

Figure 6–2 Physician Organization asset merger transaction profile. Courtesy of Medical Alliances, Inc., Alexandria, Virginia.

between the MSO and group practice varies, depending upon the organizational bylaws of the two entities. Frequently, a newly merged physician practice will have one share and one vote in the group practice, as well as ownership in the MSO equal to the value of the merging practice. Many Physician Organizations also maintain the "one physician/one vote in the MSO" principle of governance.

Drawing on the expertise of management consultants and lawyers, the parties should choose from among the various methods of distributing equity in the MSO. One approach is to give every fully productive physician an equal equity position in the group practice and MSO, on the basis of the national average for visits for the physician's specialty. Other, more formal valuation methods include discounted cash flow, rule of thumb (such as five times earnings before interest and taxes), or excess earnings. The most appropriate valuation method will vary, depending on whether the transaction is a sale or merger.

The parties involved in a merger can always agree to terms that are different from the formal valuation. In other industries, for example, premiums or discounts are often paid when companies are bought and merged. Notwithstanding, if a practice is being acquired by a nonprofit hospital, then the transaction must take place at fair market value according to approved valuation methods.

To protect all parties and develop structures and equity transfer documents, the parties should obtain legal and financial counsel. For example, stock purchase agreements should provide preset formulas that restrict the transfer of privately held equity and maintain for the group practice the right of repurchase in the event of the retirement, death, or withdrawal of a shareholder from the group practice.

The MSO equity structure can have several different types of stock, each of which has different voting rights and privileges. Among some of the possibilities:

- **Class A common stock.** This is voting stock issued to any physician who merges his or her practice into the MSO and becomes an employee/shareholder of the group practice within the first six months of its operation. The board of the MSO may have five seats dedicated to class A stockholders.
- **Class B common stock.** This stock is issued to physician/shareholders who merge after the first six months of group practice operation. The creation of class B stock may be used to encourage physicians to merge early on. This class may only have three seats on the board.
- **Class C stock.** This stock is offered to outside strategic alliance investors, typically to raise capital to fund acquisition of ancillary services, management information systems, start-up costs, and future expansion. The voting rights and number of seats on the board vary, depending on the investor and the ability of MSO executives to negotiate fair but favorable terms for the founding physicians and MSO.
- **Class D preferred stock.** This is a nonvoting stock issued in connection with the acquisition of ancillary services or health care services owned by existing practices or nonaffiliated organizations. While class D preferred stock allows practices with ancillary services to have a larger equity value in the MSO, it does not permit additional voting power so as not to dilute the principle of one physician/one vote.

Within the MSO equity structure, it is also possible to establish an incentive stock option pool, which is a method to distribute stock to key physician leaders or management at a predetermined price over a set period of time, such as five years. In this way, senior management and physician founders of the MSO who contribute time, incur financial risk, and offer leadership in development are rewarded for their efforts.

The agreement should outline actions that would require an affirmative vote of a super-majority of board members, including mergers with other group practices of more than 30 physicians, changes in the compensation method for physician/shareholders, geographic expansion of activities beyond the initial area, dissolution of the group practice or MSO, and amendments of bylaws. Legal counsel experienced in medical practice mergers and rapidly growing companies can help to structure variations of stock classes and other governance issues.

Long-term success for Physician Organizations and large group practices depends on decisive, experienced, ongoing physician leadership. One rapidly growing Physician Organization has two physicians who will serve as chairman and president of the group practice and MSO for 10 years unless voted out by a 75 percent majority of the boards. Figure 6–3 illustrates another approach to aligning the strategic direction of the group practice and the management company. In this scenario, the group practice and MSO share the same CEO and chairperson, while each board shares three to four physician board members.

Founding primary care physicians should also specify when specialists will be integrated into the group practice. One way to resolve this issue is to ask specialists to apply for membership in the IPA, which would, in turn, ensure future consideration for merger into the group practice and MSO when market conditions demanded it. It is critical to maintain the ratio of group practice primary care physicians to specialists according to market requirements. Across all specialties there must be coordinated care, easy access for patients, and a broad range of services.

The group practice's board of directors can include any number of physicians. Typically, it has between 8 and 15 physician shareholders, and many integrated groups insist on a majority of primary care physicians. The MSO's board of directors, in contrast, usually includes representatives from all classes of issued stock with voting rights. In some cases, outside investors have observer status on the board. The IPA, a not-for-profit

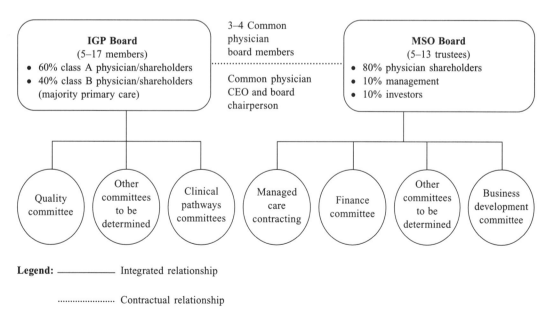

Figure 6–3 Group practice and MSO governance. Courtesy of Medical Alliances, Inc., Alexandria, Virginia.

membership corporation, can have one or more classes of members. For example, a class A member could be a physician/shareholder of the group practice, while class B members might include community physicians who are not yet in the group practice but have passed credentialing standards.

There are many options from which to choose the equity and governance principles of the Physician Organization. Success depends on creating entities that possess the power to coordinate actions, centralize all managed care contracting, and divide decision-making authority between the board and management. If the physician entities abide by the principle that the board sets policies and management executes the day-to-day operations, the organization will acquire the clout necessary to lead, rather than react to, the market.

Development of Agreements Based on Principles and Market Conditions

The Physician Equity Alliance requires numerous legal agreements to guide the governance and operations of its various entities. Among the most important:

- **Management service agreement between the MSO and the group practice.** This 20- to 30-year agreement specifies that the management company will provide comprehensive practice management services, including billing, collection, supplies, nonclinical personnel, managed care contracting, and medical management support, to all the practice locations within the group practice according to a predetermined payment arrangement. This payment serves as the MSO's primary source of income (usually between 50 percent and 65 percent of its revenues).
- **Asset transfer agreement.** This document outlines the terms and conditions of the exchange of physicians' existing practice equity for stock in the group practice and MSO.
- **Physician/shareholder employment agreement.** Physicians merging into the group practice execute physician/shareholder employment agreements that outline the roles and responsibilities of the group practice and individual physician, as well as the compensation plan, benefits, pension, and other key provisions. Ideally, this agreement is as positive and nonrestrictive as possible, while also protecting the group practice's interests. Chapter 9 provides more information on the agreements related to the merger transaction.

It is important to structure the compensation plan to facilitate a smooth transition from productivity to performance-based remuneration over a period of several years. As the group practice's reimbursement shifts from discount fee-for-service to fixed capitation, compensation must turn to salary-based models that slash incentives for excess production and inappropriate utilization. It is advisable to institute a physician compensation committee to manage the change from a productivity-based plan to one that features salary, performance incentives, and payments from withheld pools for hospital-type services.

As a group practice becomes increasingly capitated—approaching 40 percent of total revenues—the compensation plan will typically include two elements: a base salary in line with the market value of specialties, and performance standards or incentives based on objective factors such as patient satisfaction or immunization rates. Credentialing agencies such as the National Committee for Quality Assurance, developers of the Health Plan Employer Data and Information Set (HEDIS) 2.0 and 3.0 measures, are increasingly holding health plans and provider-based Managed Care Organizations accountable for meeting such measures. And the health plans, in turn, are holding their physician contractors to the same performance standards. The group practice should consider the HEDIS measures, along with other nationally recognized performance standards, when developing and revising its compensation plan.

Because physicians own the MSO, they can reinvest profits from operations in the MSO, or use them as dividends or return on equity payments to physician/shareholders. Benefits provided to physicians are a significant component of the physician's compensation. Some benefits are mandatory, such as Social Security retirement, Social Security disability, Medicare Part A, workers' compensation, malpractice insurance, and unemployment insurance. Others, however, are voluntary, such as the traditional benefits of vacation leave; health, life and disability insurance; retirement plans; continuing education; dues and memberships; and monthly allowances for certain expenses.

One of the most difficult issues to address with regard to benefits is the pension and retirement plan. As a first step, consider the physician practice's premerger retirement plan. Is it a qualified plan? Can it be rolled over into the new group practice's plan? What are the pros and cons of rolling over funds in the premerger plan into an IRA, as opposed to the group practice's plan? Is it possible to maintain the premerger plan for a specified period of time, but freeze all future contributions to it? These are just some of the questions that should be answered before merging physicians decide how to treat their existing plans.

Keep in mind that the most successful compensation plans are developed through the active participation of physician/shareholders and a commitment to meet market needs. In developing a compensation plan, work to understand physicians' goals, expectations, and needs, and educate them about their new options. Then, depending on the stage of managed care development, guide them in developing a new compensation plan.

Acquisition of Capital

Developing a functional management company—a multilocation group practice within a Physician Equity Alliance—requires time, resources, and an initial capital investment that can range from $1 million to $10 million or more. Capital requirements will vary according to the size of the group practice, market to be served, information systems to be purchased, management to be hired, health services to be acquired, and the need to renovate facilities or establish new sites for the group practice. Multispeciality Physician Equity Alliances that own operating MSOs can access several sources of capital on favorable terms; specialty group practices in such areas as oncology and cardiology also have attracted the attention of public and private capital markets. Among the investors that have already chosen to invest in combined group practices and MSOs are health care delivery systems, managed health plans, pharmaceutical companies, nursing home companies, home health care organizations, venture capitalists, investment bankers, and other Physician Organizations. Chapter 8 describes these issues in greater detail.

For example, public companies such as PhyCor, PHP Healthcare, and Coastal Health Care obtain favorable reviews and high price/earnings ratios that range from 15 to 50—meaning that $1 of profit is valued at anywhere from $15 to $50. At the same time, investment bankers represented by such firms as Hambrecht and Quist, Soloman Brothers, Bear Stearns, Piper Jaffray, Robertson Stephens & Company, Wertheim Schroder & Company, as well as venture capitalists and several pharmaceutical companies, have become potentially serious investors in Physician Organizations.

Attracting the attention of these investors requires work and a focused investor-oriented business plan. It is crucial that the business plan describes the development and market plan for the group practice and management company and includes detailed five-year financial forecasts of revenue, expenses, and profits. Evaluate any potential investor for financial strength, value-added business relationships, expertise in developing growth companies, and alignment with the clinical and business goals.

IMPLEMENTING AND ENHANCING SYSTEMS FOR GROWTH

Creating functional, operating management companies and associated group practices that do not go bankrupt under capitation requires enhanced systems in the areas of cost accounting, ambulatory management, medical management, and information systems.

Building Advanced Medical Management Systems

Financial viability under capitation depends on leaders who can guide the activities of peers, managers, and executives with the aim of reducing unnecessary procedures and admissions. If a Physician Organization wants to maintain control over risks and costs, it must operate internally managed, physician-directed medical management systems that draw on the power of advanced information systems, case management, peer review, and physician education. The goal is to empower physician clinicians to find the most appropriate, lowest-cost setting for delivering patient services.

Especially critical is obtaining clinical data through advanced information systems that feature clinical databases, with both process and outcomes measures of quality and cost-effectiveness. Organizations already are tapping these large-scale, relational databases to monitor outcomes and compare them to regional or national benchmarks. Advanced versions of these databases, equipped with patient satisfaction and health status information, can deliver objective, reliable, and timely information to clinicians. When used in conjunction with continuous quality improvement (CQI) methods and cross-functional teams, these systems have the potential to improve critical paths and contain costs.

Such clinical databases also lay the groundwork for an electronic medical record (EMR). By offering one-time data capture and electronic distribution of data and test results as patients move from one setting to another, the EMR eliminates redundant testing and allows complete sharing of data along the continuum of care. In the future, home health care workers will access the EMR through phone lines and portable computers, while physicians will be able to dial into cardiac intensive care units from home and receive up-to-the-minute status reports on patients.

Organizing an Effective Ambulatory Management Infrastructure

To establish an outstanding Physician Equity Alliance, it is essential that the practice management capability of the MSO function at the highest level. The staff, policies, and procedures required for managing between 20 and 150 primary care medical practices in numerous locations under integrated information, operations, and financial systems are dramatically different from those needed in the typical two- to five-physician practice. Some key recommendations are presented below.

Use Experienced Executives and Advanced Information Systems to Improve Managed Care Contracting

Capitated managed care contracting is complex because of the risk associated with fixed capitation. As a result of their regional and national experience, managed care plans not only possess the data necessary for managing risk but also tend to hold the upper hand in negotiations. Successful contract negotiation demands that Physician Organizations—many of which are entering risk contracting negotiations for the first time—use legal counsel and managed care experts to protect physicians' interests. In addition, it is advisable to develop information databases that can be used to support negotiations on capitation rates and define the scope of services to be provided under a contract.

Compiling performance data is indispensable to quality assurance, marketing support, negotiation of higher capitation rates, and improved contract terms. For example, the integration of individual physician performance data and credentialing information is essential for effectively marketing a group's performance to managed care purchasers. Also key to managed care marketing and contracting negotiations is the comparison of outcome and performance measures with criteria such as HEDIS 2.0 and 3.0.

Institute Cost Accounting Systems and Abandon Cash Accounting Methods

Instead of using the cash method of accounting, it is worthwhile to invest in an expert system for handling cost accounting and reporting on a contemporary accrual basis. Because profits under capitation are generated as a result of reduced expenses and improved efficiency, it is necessary to know actual operating costs, inasmuch as these will be pivotal in making decisions such as whether to own or subcontract ancillary services (for example, imaging equipment, home care, or durable medical equipment).

It is advisable to purchase or develop a financial system that has the capability to reconcile payments received from managed health plans. For example, if a contract pays for members weighted by age, the system should verify each age group to ensure that the payment from the Managed Care Organization does not fall below the negotiated payment level. Also, make sure that the system can obtain the Managed Care Organization's updated enrollment files and interface with electronic claims clearinghouses. Tracking enrollment will ensure that the organization does not receive payment for a patient who has disenrolled or fail to receive payment for a new enrollee.

To manage global capitated contracts, it is also necessary to track incurred but not reported costs. For example, a primary care group practice may have a capitated contract for full medical risk, which means the medical group is prepaid for all ambulatory medical services delivered to a defined population. Consider what would happen if the Integrated Group Practice contracts with a network of specialists on a discounted fee-for-service basis. When a primary care physician refers a patient to a specialist such as an oncologist, the group practice incurs a cost and obligation the day the patient comes in for the consultation. However, the oncologist might not bill the group practice for the visit until 30 or more days afterward. If the group practice fails to document this incurred but not reported cost, physicians may conclude that they have generated more revenue than is actually the case.

Implement Advanced Practice Management Information Systems

There is almost no resemblance between the information systems needed to managed a Physician Organization in the capitated environment and those required in a fee-for-service environment. In most cases in which organizations fail to manage their capitated contracts, it is because they lack not only adequate practice management and information systems but also the expertise to run them. It is important to invest wisely in information systems to manage capitated contracts for both the group practice and the IPA.

In putting together an advanced practice management system for a mixed fee-for-service and capitated reimbursement environment, it is desirable to have the following capabilities:

- **Covered benefit**—the ability to access a specific managed care benefit and identify such factors as coverage for medication, deductibles, and the need for preauthorization
- **Referral tracking**—the ability to track the clinical response to referrals generated by primary care physicians who monitor the care of patients under their capitation
- **Claims handling**—the ability to conduct traditional claims processing to track accounts payable, accounts receivable, bad debt, and collections
- **Utilization review**—the ability to access a Managed Care Organization's protocols before making contact by telephone

All of the systems highlighted in this chapter are discussed in greater detail in different chapters of this book. These systems will be an essential element of Physician Organizations' ability to effectively expand their scope of services and geographic reach to managed care. Without systems in place, the rapid growth could crumble into disarray.

Focusing on Execution

The ability to complete a large number of mergers and acquisitions in a relatively short period of time is a key capability for Physician Organizations. This is a challenge within rapid-growth organizations. In the process of building new information and business systems, physician leaders and management executives often forget to invest in the retraining and education of their most important resource: people. Make sure that the group practice and MSO have enough financial strength to hire managers and executives with the ability to manage the risks of capitation and the demands of a rapidly growing, multilocation medical group practice, as well as the capability to nurture and lead a management company through the stresses of rapid merger and consolidation. It is absolutely necessary to be competitive, as managed care and capitation reimbursement become the dominant form of health care service delivery in the country.

Chapter 7

Structuring a Physician Compensation Plan That Rewards Performance in the Managed Care Environment

Mark Buchanan, M.D.

INTRODUCTION

Physician compensation has traditionally been one of the most contentious issues in a group practice. Fortunately, many books and journal articles have been written to help groups with their compensation plans. Unfortunately, most of them are of little use, because they solve yesterday's problems. Groups have tried equal shares, straight salary, salary plus productivity bonus, or straight productivity, with most groups going for the last two. These arrangements are only possible when the definition of *productivity* is simple, as is the case under fee-for-service arrangements; here there is little occasion for disagreement, except over how to allocate overhead.

Old compensation schemes are showing signs of strain, and the reasons for this are obvious. More physicians are employed, practices are growing and merging, reimbursement is increasingly prospective, groups are taking risks for services they do not provide, insurers are demanding measurable quality, patients are insisting on better access and service, and supply and demand changes are causing certain specialties to become more or less valued.

Some groups have revised their compensation plan in response to a drop in physician income caused by inadequate revenues or uncontrolled expenses; each doctor hopes that reshuffling the deck will improve his or her own income. This is the wrong reason to change a plan. The compensation scheme's role is to maintain physician morale, encourage growth of the group, and give doctors incentives to behave in certain ways. As reporting and quality demands rise and payment contracts become more complex, groups can no longer be simply collections of individual practitioners working under the same roof. Physicians will increasingly depend on their group colleagues and administrators. Compensation plans must reflect this new reality. This was well put in a recent issue of *The Physician's Advisory*:

- The group is more important than any one (or few) of its members.
- No member deserves an income except as he or she serves the group's purposes and goals.
- No system known to man will be perfect, but compensation is too important a motivator to be ignored.[1]

GETTING STARTED

Before entertaining any suggestions for specific methods of income division, a group must define the structure and guiding philosophy for designing the plan. The group's managing body will need to appoint a compensation committee, which may be part of the finance committee. The group's administrator or chief financial officer (CFO) will naturally be an *ex officio* member. Although this committee will develop and implement the plan, it will need guidance from the governing body, which must clearly state the group's overall goals. For example: Does the group want to grow? How rapidly does it want to change from fee-for-service to capitation? How much risk does it want to take? Does it want to add new services? Is it ready to start measuring quality of care? Answering these questions will determine what sort of physician behavior the plan should encourage. The governing body and administrator should also give the committee a realistic estimate of available resources, indicating what sort of data on utilization and customer satisfaction can be collected and made available for a compensation formula, and whether there is money available for consultants.

Compensation consultants, although ubiquitous in corporate America and frequently used by staff-model Health Maintenance Organizations (HMOs) and hospitals, are often overlooked by free-standing medical groups. The expense is considerable: a comprehensive plan for a multispecialty group of 50 doctors could approach six figures. How can this be justified? The consultant generally interviews physicians, trying to understand their expectations; reviews practice finances, defining the money available for distribution; compares current income against several comparative databases; and establishes a usable plan. The fact that the consultant brings extensive comparative material and has no vested interest in the plan may help sell the plan internally. Using the consultant also relieves the committee members and the group administrator of much of the work, and their time can be spent on other matters to benefit the group. Despite all this, convincing doctors to reduce their current compensation to pay the consultant is not easy.

Whether or not the group uses outside resources, its compensation strategy will be an ongoing effort. Groups should expect to refine their plan annually, and probably will need a major revision or two while making the transition from fee-for-service to extensive global capitation.

CRITERIA FOR A COMPENSATION PLAN

There are three goals for a compensation plan: (1) to maintain morale, (2) to encourage group growth, and (3) to give physicians incentive to achieve desired behaviors. Criteria for choosing a plan flow naturally from these goals.

Maintain Physician Morale

A compensation plan that maintains physician morale should have three features:

1. The plan should be easily understood. One should be able to describe it in simple terms, like "60 percent market-based salary, 20 percent productivity, 20 percent shared bonus." (Unfortunately, plans that sound simple can look very complicated once the actual numbers are put down on paper. But the simplicity is appealing.)
2. The plan should be perceived as fair. It must show internal equity and external competitiveness.
3. The plan should be flexible. As the group's size and specialty makeup change, as its revenue sources change, or as group members identify problems with the plan, the plan must adapt.

As with all criteria, these are the ideal, and reality may fall short. A dose of realism is offered by a reviewer who concluded: "The best you can hope for is to find one compensation plan that is equally unfair to all physicians."[2]

Encourage Group Growth and Discourage Turnover

The compensation committee will want to address the following issues:

- Longevity with the group should be rewarded. A seniority factor encourages retention, which saves the group the expense of recruiting replacements and spares patients the nuisance of establishing a new relationship.
- The compensation should offer parity with the external market. This is a major issue for groups with some high-paid and some lower-paid specialists. For a fuller discussion, see "Building Blocks for a Compensation Plan" below.

Incent Physicians Toward Desired Behaviors

Encouraging doctors to practice in ways that benefit the group has been the focus of most recent innovation in compensation plans. There are two major principles:

1. The plan should resemble the group's own reimbursement patterns. Groups that accept capitation but pay their own doctors on fee-for-service are at risk for excess utilization.
2. The plan should reward behaviors that benefit the group:
   - hard work and accessibility
   - quality outcomes and patient satisfaction
   - internal citizenship
   - efficient utilization

Each of these behaviors is discussed in the next section.

BUILDING BLOCKS FOR A COMPENSATION PLAN

It is easy to say that a compensation plan allocates 5 percent of income on the basis of quality of care, or that a salary is based on marketplace levels. Hidden beneath these statements are major problems with defining the terms and measuring what they describe. Obviously, the group must come to some agreement on what is meant, or the compensation formula will lack meaningful inputs. Sometimes everyone can agree on what a term means, only to learn that the group has no way to measure and report it. This section describes ways of defining and measuring the critical inputs.

Market-Based Salaries

What is a competitive salary? In theory, compensation surveys should answer this question. After all, they are conducted by prominent organizations and include data provided by thousands of physicians, adjusted for group size, specialty, age of the physician, managed care penetration, and area of the country. Examining the results, though, is disillusioning. A recent *Modern Healthcare* article showed median compensation for 14 specialties, as measured by 10 surveys.[3] The difference between the highest and the lowest survey was $35,000 for pediatrics, and up to $100,000 for high-paying specialists such as cardiology. Close examination of the data shows major differences in sampling methods and in definitions of compensation.

How can a group deal with this uncertainty? Consultants are often able to provide their own database to supplement the published material, and they attempt to adjust published material to standardize definitions of compensation and tailor numbers for the local marketplace. The resultant market norms appear more realistic, and therefore, easier to accept at face value than numbers taken from published surveys. Larger groups, of course, do their own market research regularly, just by observing their own success in hiring and retaining physicians at a given income level.

Should the practice offer a salary at all? A salary is a guarantee of income. Groups that pay their shareholders on a pure productivity basis essentially guarantee them nothing. So a salary is only meaningful to their non-shareholder physicians, who are willing to take a guaranteed but reduced reimbursement until they are allowed to participate fully in profits. In theory, a group operating under capitation could likewise omit any mention of salary, and simply offer enough sources of compensation (e.g., productivity, quality, efficiency, etc.) that the typical physician could earn a market-level income. One heavily capitated group, described later, has discarded all salaries and uses the incentive program to control 100 percent of compensation.

There is a contrary view, held by some groups, that a straight salary with performance evaluations is the only proper way to pay physicians, because it frees them from perverse incentives to either do too much or do too little. Unfortunately, this compensation method does not discourage physicians from going fishing at five o'clock sharp if there is no good financial incentive to stay late at the office. A health services researcher at one very large practice reported that the average primary care physician in his system is excused so often for vacations, continuing education, and committee work that he or she only spends 1,700 hours in direct patient care each year. This translates into only 3,800 visits a year—fewer than the group's midlevel practitioners provide. If a salary-based program is to encourage hard work, the organization must set clear expectations, give physicians feedback on their own productivity, and foster a corporate culture that stresses teamwork.

Productivity

Once upon a time, productivity meant *billings*. With Medicare payment cuts and contractual discounts, it came to mean *collections*. Some groups have realized that defining productivity as collections, even under fee-for-service, can distort incentives. It may lead physicians to compete against their colleagues for the better-insured, and it penalizes those with large Medicare panels. As a reaction, a group may decide simply to count visits. While this might satisfy a pure family practice group, it will not work for a group that is mixed between office-based cognitive specialists and hospital-oriented proceduralists. Thus, a variety of relative value-based systems have been developed. These may be based on the McGraw-Hill Relative Value Set, the Medicare Resource-Based Relative Value Scale (RBRVS), or some other publicly available system. Alternatively, the group can design its own. For instance, the Fallon Clinic decided that traditional billing standards compensated procedures too well, and cognitive services too poorly. Fallon therefore drew up its own relative value unit (RVU) scale, rewarding evaluation and management services, and devaluing procedures.[4]

With prepaid care, of course, the practice is not paid for each unit of work. The physician may assign some service code to a visit, but the code does not produce reimbursement. Thus, an RVU-based system is just counting "funny money." The group does not benefit financially when its physicians see prepaid patients in the office. A physician may be ideally productive on behalf of these patients by talking to them on the phone, or teaching them to monitor their own illness, or authorizing a nonphysician professional to see them. The group will want to reward such activity. It will also want to discourage physicians from bringing their patients into the office too frequently. In a productivity-based plan, some physicians may try to shift income to themselves by *churning* their patients. Peer pressure may not be enough to control this. One large West Coast group that depends primarily on managed care and has strong productivity incentives based on the simple measurement of office visits is finding that annual visits per patient are substantially above norms provided by the Unified Medical Group Association (UMGA).

A final issue concerns ancillary services. Traditionally, a physician who orders a test or X-ray done within the group receives extra pay for doing so. This is obviously counterproductive under a prepayment system.

Panel Size

Under prepayment, a physician is not so much responsible for delivering services to people who come into the office as for comprehensively managing the health needs of a defined population. Therefore, using panel size is an appealing replacement for traditional productivity measures. While this method is fairly straightforward, it may need minor adjustments. For instance, no one physician can meet all the primary care needs of his or her patients. The physician may be on vacation, or off call, or swamped with work. So colleagues see the patient. To some extent, this is controllable by the physician, and the physician who persistently "dumps" visits onto others should be penalized for it. This is easily done by transferring some of the credit for an impaneled patient from the designated physician to the one who sees the patient.

Utilization

Building utilization statistics into the compensation plan is vital for a group that assumes risk. Unfortunately, most groups have limited information on their referral, hospital, and pharmacy utilization. Data supplied by the HMO is usually late and crude, and occasionally unintelligible. The group that assumes responsibility for paying its own claims, of course, need not depend on the HMO.

So what can we do while waiting for the perfect information system? Outpatient referrals are easily tracked, even manually, working from the provider's copy of the referral authorization request. The group can track each physician's volume of referrals, by specialty, and compare it to the appropriate denominator, which might be the number of capitated patients, some other proxy for practice size, or the number of office visits. Utilization of services provided within the group can usually be captured from the practice's billing system, providing both volume and cost statistics, and subjected to the same analysis as the outside referrals. Hospital usage may be tracked by average length of stay, by bed-days per 1,000 panel patients, or by adherence to a best-practices guideline. Whatever measures the group uses, it must have a detailed plan for what forms must be developed, who will enter information on them, and how this will be analyzed and reported. Table 7–1 shows the advantages and disadvantages of using different measures of utilization efficiency in calculating physician compensation.

An important criterion for the compensation plan is that it must be perceived as fair. Many physicians are convinced that their patients are sicker than average, and that this explains their higher utilization. Some of these physicians, of course, are correct. Some of the adverse selection is based on specialty; the physician who does a combination of internal medical and diabetology will attract patients who need more resources. Comparison of like specialties, if possible, will lessen unavoidable differences. One large Northeast group uses a crude system that adjusts for age and sex and the presence of a handful of conditions, but is considering incorporating Ambulatory Care Groups (ACGs). These analyze billing data to calculate expected costs, which can be compared to actual costs as a measure of practice efficiency.[5] The Harvard Community Health Plan recently published its own experience in adjusting specialty referrals according to characteristics of each physician's panel, and concluded that this adjustment moves many physicians from outlier to inlier status.[6] Faced with these difficulties, a group may

Table 7-1 Measures of Utilization Efficiency: Pros and Cons

Measure	Reporting Format	Advantages	Disadvantages
Average length of stay	Could be global or broken down by type of admission	Easy to measure. Comparative data are available	May penalize the conservative doctor who uses office or home care instead of a brief hospital stay for the less ill
Bed-days/1,000 patients	Needs to show all admissions for the population, regardless of who actually admits	Comparative data are available	May be hard to identify all admissions. Primary care physician does not have full control over admissions
Adherence to "best practices" for hospital care	Actual versus "optimal" days. Percent of admissions reaching goal LOS	Tends to correct for differences in health status across different panels	Depends on correct assignment of each admission to a given guideline
Volume of outpatient referrals	Could be global or by specialty. For the denominator, could use panel size or number of primary care physician office visits	Fairly easy to identify	Overemphasizes low-cost referrals
Cost of outpatient referrals	Same as above	More relevant than volume to group success	Data difficult to get from insurers
Use of in-house ancillaries	Volume or cost. For denominator, could use panel size or number of primary care physician office visits	Easy to track through the billing system	— —

decide that its utilization incentives should be based on quarterly improvement rather than on absolute levels of resource use.

Regardless of which aspects of utilization the practice wants to review, encourage, and thus alter, it will have to combine them into some "score" that translates into dollars and cents. Before doing so, it must decide what level of utilization is desirable. In the absence of firm data, most groups decide, like the HMOs before them, that "less is more." Prudent groups, of course, balance this with incentives for quality outcomes and patient satisfaction.

Patient Satisfaction

Employers and HMOs are very interested in measuring patient satisfaction. Not surprisingly, a small industry has sprung up to meet this need. Some companies design a custom survey, help administer it, and tabulate and report the results. Others provide the group with input devices (such as touch-screen devices or optical character recognition readers) and software to monitor their own results. Survey instruments may be proprietary to the survey vendor, designed by the medical group, or adopted from published surveys like the Group Health Association of America (GHAA) long or short form.[7]

Surveys should make up most of any patient satisfaction score, since spontaneous expressions of satisfaction or dissatisfaction are unusual and not necessarily representative. But the survey results should be supplemented with complaints or unusual compliments received by the group. There can also be an adjustment to reflect those patients who voted with their feet by changing primary care providers.

Group Citizenship

For any physician behavior to be translated into dollars, it must be converted into a number that can be put on a spreadsheet. Group citizenship is one of the most difficult items to express numerically, because it is based on several subjective measures—such as evaluations by peers, subordinates, and department chiefs. The quality and reproducibility of these evaluations will improve if all evaluators work from a grid that assigns semiquantitative scores for defined behaviors. These evaluations are supplemented by objective measurements of group participation, such as governance activities. Some groups also assign a value to outside activities such as hospital leadership, medical society participation, or publishing.

Quality of Care

In 1990, the Institute of Medicine proposed the following definition of *quality of care:* "Quality of care is the degree to which health services for individuals and populations increase the likelihood of desired health outcomes and are consistent with current professional knowledge."[8] Although it has been widely quoted, usually with approval, it illustrates the limitations of current measures of quality of care. Quality is not defined as actually increasing desired health outcomes; it only "increase[s] the likelihood of . . . [these] outcomes . . . consistent with current professional knowledge." In other words, quality is doing those things that we think work. The emphasis is on the process of care, not the outcome.

Can outcomes really be measured? Yes, but it requires either a lot of work or a lot of data. Several companies (including Value Health Sciences, GMIS, and The Codman Group) analyze enormous amounts of claims data, attempting to reconstruct episodes of care and infer efficiency and quality outcomes. Whatever the validity of such programs, they cannot help a physician group unless it has many months of claims data for all services provided to its patients. Other approaches need less data but more labor. Total quality management projects can show practitioners the results of their work and lead to improvement in results. But this is extremely laborious, and only suitable for interventions whose payoff is rapid. Evaluation of chronic conditions will probably be confined to proxies for outcome. For instance, blood pressure control can be measured to judge quickly the quality of treatment for hypertension, but it would be necessary to wait five years to see whether the treatment effectively prevented strokes. Finally, patient-centered outcomes can be measured by serial application of instruments like the Health Status Questionnaire (HSQ-36). Several large groups are experimenting with these instruments, but few, if any, have reported incorporating quality of care into compensation.

Thus, most quality of care measures—at least until electronic records are used—will stress process, such as success in meeting immunization and screening recommendations. Numerous care processes and outcomes can be tracked. The compensation committee, in conjunction with the governing body and the quality improvement committee, must choose a manageable number. The group need not feel bound to use the same indicators every year. If it thinks a given task is being done consistently and well, it may wish to focus the group's attention on some other aspect of care. Likewise, it makes no sense to put the same quality indicators in each department's reimbursement scheme; a group that contains both surgeons and pediatricians will have to develop a variety of quality measures.

Building Wealth for the Future

In a traditional medical group, there is little opportunity for a physician's equity in the group to grow; the group retains no revenues, and shares in the professional corporation can only be sold to other physicians in the group. However, evolving joint-equity organizations are addressing this problem. In the joint-equity model, the medical group places its assets into a Management Services Organization (MSO) and receives stock in this MSO. Other investors put cash into the MSO, and this cash infusion allows the group to grow through mergers and acquisitions, to market itself to payers and patients, to hire highly skilled managers, and to install sophisticated information systems. If adding these resources dramatically increases the group's revenues, each physician's shares in the MSO will appreciate. Furthermore, these shares are more liquid than shares in a medical group, because nonphysicians can buy them.

If the MSO attracts investment from a practice management firm that is or will be publicly traded, the firm may allow the physicians to trade MSO stock for its own. This indirectly gives the medical group access to the public financial markets, and may yield an impressive return—especially if the physicians join the management company before its initial public offering. This stock swap further increases the liquidity of the physician's ownership in the practice.

Some equity/management firms acquire all the practice's assets. Physicians who sell their practices to these firms will enjoy the liquidity of owning some of the company's stock and receive an initial lump sum from the practice buyout, but they will lose the opportunity to profit directly from growth in the value of their own practice and its affiliated MSO. An alternative model leaves the physicians as majority owners of the MSO; the outside partner invests only as much cash as is needed to meet the practice's business plan. Compared to the buyout, this shared-ownership model gives the physician-owner a chance to build much greater wealth.

STORIES FROM THE FRONT LINES

Harriman Jones Medical Group

Harriman Jones Medical Group is a 75-physician multispecialty group in Long Beach, California. Its efforts to reform its compensation plan, as reported in *Modern Healthcare*, began in 1990.[9] The group had used the traditional, production-based formula typical of other groups that grew up in the fee-for-service setting. In 1990, Harriman Jones's leaders realized that its method of paying its physicians was seriously at odds with its own revenue sources, which were 85 percent capitated. The first approach was very simple: Harriman Jones put everyone on a straight salary. Unfortunately, but not surprisingly, the physician work ethic suffered, and the group had to hire extra physicians to meet its obligations to prepaid care. By late 1993, the group implemented Plan B, which did away with salaries entirely. Rather, physicians are given an opportunity to earn more or less money, based on five inputs:

1. **Productivity** (number of patients seen)—50 percent
2. **Utilization management** (costs per patient for lab, X-ray, pharmacy; average length of hospital stay)—20 percent
3. **Patient satisfaction** (based on surveys)—12.5 percent

4. **Citizenship** (meeting participation)—10 percent
5. **Practice efficiency** (punctuality, efficient use of staff)—7.5 percent

The group estimates its revenue after expenses, then allocates it to the departments based on historical division of income. Each department thus has a fixed amount of money. It can send some of that money outside the group if it wishes, such as by purchasing night call. It can also redistribute that money within the group; for instance, one physician might volunteer to take others' night calls or vacation coverage. Twice a year, the group meets and applies the above formula and associated subformulas to measured behavior and outcomes, and this determines each physician's compensation.

The attractive part about giving each department a budget is that the pediatrician is not compared to the cardiologist in utilization of hospital days; neurosurgery visits, which might include some expensive procedures, are not compared to family practice visits. The drawback is that historical divisions of income may not remain valid. Suppose a practice loses 10,000 Medicare capitated lives, but gains 20,000 commercial lives. It will need more internists and pediatricians and fewer cardiologists. The old division of income between departments will have to be altered. Likewise, if market forces start to markedly devalue some specialty, such as anesthesiology, yet the group continues to fund its anesthesia department at prior levels, it may have trouble competing with groups that are buying anesthesia services at the lower level.

The Fallon Clinic

The Fallon Clinic is a multispecialty group of 300 doctors at 30 sites in central Massachusetts. It owns its own HMO, which covers 150,000 lives and accounts for 85 percent of the clinic's revenues. Its treasurer and income distribution committee chairman, Dr. Robert Yood, recounted the history of the Fallon compensation plan at the 1994 Medical Group Management Association meeting.[10] When Yood joined the clinic in 1979, it paid its doctors based on their billings. By 1985, its HMO business had grown dramatically, and the old billings-based system was replaced by a salary system. Doctors could move up through a seven-level system, with salary appropriate for their specialty. Explicit expectations for workload were provided, and the salary was supplemented by bonuses based on productivity and performance.

Even in 1985, Fallon realized that encouraging procedures would not help a practice thrive under capitation; the organization started to measure "productivity" by its own relative value system, which was weighted toward evaluation and management rather than procedures. No credit was given for ordering ancillary services. Fallon's "performance" measure was a mixture of utilization, quality of care, and group citizenship. Although a lot of effort went into measuring these inputs, the dollars at stake for performance have turned out to be rather small—less than $2,000 per physician. The productivity bonus was worth more, but not nearly as much as in the Harriman Jones model.

As with all compensation plans, Fallon's required frequent adjustments. For instance, in 1992 the clinic decided to recognize the importance of primary care in the capitated environment by making salary schedules for medical subspecialists identical to those of general internists. They also instituted a small annual penalty for physicians who failed to achieve board certification before reaching salary level four.

By the early 1990s, this system was showing signs of age. The productivity bonus encouraged "churning" patients; it discouraged using the telephone, training patients to care for themselves, and delegating some care to other professionals. Fallon decided to pay its primary care physicians the same way the clinic gets paid: by the covered life. After some complicated adjustments to convert fee-for-service care into capitated equivalents, to ensure accurate assignment of patients to each physician, and to adjust for age and sex of the panel, the clinic started to measure productivity by the size of each physician's panel. Salary is adjusted upward or downward, according to how the physician's panel exceeds or falls short of specialty-specific norms.

Although long-term results of this change remain to be seen, the introduction of this plan to family practice and pediatrics was received well enough to extend the plan to general internists. Medical subspecialists still get a volume-related bonus, but are moving toward measures of access and utilization. Surgical specialty groups have been allotted departmental bonuses, to be apportioned by the department chairmen.

Fallon's plan is not perfect. Like almost anything devised and operated by human beings, it is subject to "gaming," and can lead to unexpected consequences that require further revisions in the formula. Its inputs need refinement and continue to keep the compensation committee very busy. But Fallon has made a qualitative leap forward from its previous system, in that physician incentives are now closely aligned with those of the group.

FOUR SCENARIOS FOR INCOME DISTRIBUTION

This chapter has discussed the inputs or building blocks that can go into an income distribution plan. The above examples of two clinics that have used some of these inputs in their own plans illustrate that a compensation plan is never finished. A plan might serve a group for a couple of years, but minor repairs are needed every year and major overhauls every few years. With this in mind, four compensation plans for a hypothetical group are presented below. For convenience and simplicity, the group has only five physicians, all in the same department.

Scenario 1

In Scenario 1, the group is functioning almost exclusively under fee-for-service (see Table 7–2). Capped revenue is low enough that it does not figure into the compensation plan. The funds available for distribution represent revenues minus nonphysician expenses. (Compensation refers to the total package, including salary, pension, and fringe benefits.) The group has decided to recognize the capitated revenue as coming into the entire group rather than to any individual, and this is part of the reason it has allotted 20 percent of its distributable funds to be shared equally. There is no salary as such.

The cash available for distribution is $1,000,000 (line 1). Of this amount, 80 percent is based on productivity, which means that $800,000 will be distributed on this basis (line 2). Each physician's share of productivity is shown on line 8; line 7 translates this into dollars. For equal shares, $200,000 is available, as shown on lines 3 and 11. Total compensation is now a simple addition.

Scenario 2

In Scenario 2, the group has higher capitated revenues and has decided it wants to get away from a heavy emphasis on productivity (see Table 7–3). It wants to make compensation fairly predictable but still allow performance bonuses, so it has set up a salary schedule based on its knowledge of market forces and the group's own history. But only half of the total funds available for distribution go into the salary pool (line 2). Of the total funds, 30 percent goes to productivity (line 3), which is defined as fee-for-service collections plus capitation payment dollars, adjusted for expenses. The group has allotted 5 percent each to increase in managed care lives, managed care efficiency, group citizenship, and equal shares of profitability (lines 4 through 7). The

Table 7-2 Physician Compensation—Scenario 1

1	Entire group:	$1,000,000	100% Total funds available for distribution					
2		$800,000	80% Productivity: FFS + capped revenue (minus expenses)					
3		$200,000	20% Equal share of group profitability					
4								
5			Total	Doc 1	Doc 2	Doc 3	Doc 4	Doc 5
6								
7	Productivity		$800,000	$160,000	$120,000	$200,000	$136,000	$184,000
8	Proportion of total		1	0.2	0.15	0.25	0.17	0.23
9								
10	80% Productivity		$800,000	$160,000	$120,000	$200,000	$136,000	$184,000
11	20% Equal share		$200,000	$40,000	$40,000	$40,000	$40,000	$40,000
12								
13	**Total compensation**		**$1,000,000**	**$200,000**	**$160,000**	**$240,000**	**$176,000**	**$224,000**

salaries in line 11 differ largely due to longevity.

The group has gotten 2,000 new managed care lives. Each physician's growth in lives is shown in line 16, and the proportion of growth on line 17. For managed care efficiency, patient satisfaction, and quality outcomes, a rank order is used. Each place in the rank is awarded some proportion. The value of each rank order can be selected by the group, as long as the proportions total 1.0. In practice, using rank orders rarely makes sense, because if several physicians are very close in their true performance, forcing them into a rank order exaggerates the difference between them.

Table 7-3 Physician Compensation—Scenario 2

1	Entire group:	$1,000,000	100% Total funds available for distribution					
2		$500,000	50% Salary (includes longevity)					
3		$300,000	30% Productivity: FFS + capped revenue (minus expenses)					
4		$50,000	5% Increase in managed care lives					
5		$50,000	5% Managed care efficiency					
6		$50,000	5% Equal share of group profitability					
7		$50,000	5% Discretionary based on group citizenship					
8								
9			Total	Doc 1	Doc 2	Doc 3	Doc 4	Doc 5
10								
11	Salary		$500,000	$100,000	$90,000	$110,000	$105,000	$95,000
12								
13	Productivity		$300,000	$60,000	$45,000	$75,000	$51,000	$69,000
14	Proportion of total		1	0.2	0.15	0.25	0.17	0.23
15								
16	Increase in managed care lives		2000	250	600	150	550	450
17	Proportion of total		1	0.125	0.3	0.075	0.275	0.225
18								
19	Managed care efficiency, rank			1	2	3	4	5
20	Efficiency weighting factor		1	0.4	0.3	0.2	0.1	0
21								
22	50% Salary		$500,000	$100,000	$90,000	$110,000	$105,000	$95,000
23	30% Productivity		$300,000	$60,000	$45,000	$75,000	$51,000	$69,000
24	5% Increase in lives		$50,000	$6,250	$15,000	$3,750	$13,750	$11,250
25	5% Managed care efficiency		$50,000	$20,000	$15,000	$10,000	$5,000	$0
26	5% Equal share		$50,000	$10,000	$10,000	$10,000	$10,000	$10,000
27	5% Discretionary		$50,000	$10,000	$15,000	$5,000	$15,000	$5,000
28								
29	**Total compensation**		**$1,000,000**	**$206,250**	**$190,000**	**$213,750**	**$199,750**	**$190,250**

Comparing the bottom line from Scenario 2 (Table 7–3) to that in Scenario 1 (Table 7–2), one is struck by how much the change in compensation plan redistributes income. This is in part due to the use of dummy numbers. Real numbers are less likely to fluctuate this severely. However, when a group makes any dramatic change in its compensation plan, it may wish to lessen the shock by phasing the new plan in slowly. For instance, in the first year the group would calculate income based on both the old and the new method, then average the results.

Scenario 3

In Scenario 3 (see Table 7–4), the group has over half its revenue from capitation and wants to further downplay fee-for-service productivity, which is reduced from 30 percent to 25 percent (line 3). It also wants to be sure that the set salary does not encourage anyone to be less busy, so it decreases the salary portion to 40 percent. These moves free up 15 percent of income, which is split between equal shares, quality outcomes, and patient satisfaction (lines 6 through 8). This decision reflects the group's growing confi-

Table 7–4 Physician Compensation—Scenario 3

					Total	Doc 1	Doc 2	Doc 3	Doc 4	Doc 5
1	Entire group:	$1,000,000	100% Total funds available for distribution							
2		$400,000	40% Salary (includes longevity)							
3		$250,000	25% Productivity: FFS + capped revenue (minus expenses)							
4		$50,000	5% Increase in managed care lives							
5		$50,000	5% Managed care efficiency							
6		$50,000	5% Patient satisfaction							
7		$50,000	5% Quality outcomes							
8		$100,000	10% Equal share of group profitability							
9		$50,000	5% Discretionary based on group citizenship							
10										
11					Total	Doc 1	Doc 2	Doc 3	Doc 4	Doc 5
12										
13	Salary				$400,000	$80,000	$72,000	$88,000	$84,000	$76,000
14										
15	Productivity				$250,000	$50,000	$37,500	$62,500	$42,500	$57,500
16	Proportion of total				1	0.2	0.15	0.25	0.17	0.23
17										
18	Increase in managed care lives				2000	250	600	150	550	450
19	Proportion of total				1	0.125	0.3	0.075	0.275	0.225
20										
21	Managed care efficiency, rank					1	2	3	4	5
22	Efficiency weighting factor				1	0.4	0.3	0.2	0.1	0
23										
24	Patient satisfaction, rank					5	4	3	2	1
25	Satisfaction weighting factor				1	0	0.1	0.2	0.3	0.4
26										
27	Quality outcomes, rank					2	1	5	4	3
28	Quality weighting factor				1	0.3	0.4	0	0.1	0.2
29										
30	40% Salary				$400,000	$80,000	$72,000	$88,000	$84,000	$76,000
31	25% Productivity				$250,000	$50,000	$37,500	$62,500	$42,500	$57,500
32	5% Increase in lives				$50,000	$6,250	$15,000	$3,750	$13,750	$11,250
33	5% Managed care efficiency				$50,000	$20,000	$15,000	$10,000	$5,000	$0
34	5% Patient satisfaction				$50,000	$0	$5,000	$10,000	$15,000	$20,000
35	5% Quality outcomes				$50,000	$15,000	$20,000	$0	$5,000	$10,000
36	10% Equal share				$100,000	$20,000	$20,000	$20,000	$20,000	$20,000
37	5% Discretionary				$50,000	$10,000	$15,000	$5,000	$15,000	$5,000
38										
39	**Total compensation**				**$1,000,000**	**$201,250**	**$199,500**	**$199,250**	**$200,250**	**$199,750**

dence in its ability to measure quality and satisfaction, and its desire to make all physicians think about what actions benefit the group, rather than individuals.

Patient satisfaction and quality outcomes are assigned weighting factors based on rank order (lines 24 through 28).

Scenario 4

In Scenario 4, the group not only has a majority of its revenue from managed care, but has assumed risk for services it cannot provide. Hence efficiency in managing care has become critically important, and this is rewarded with 10 percent of total compensation. Productivity rewards drop further, and patient satisfaction and quality outcomes are emphasized (see Table 7–5).

Because the practice's business has largely converted to capitation, and physicians are as busy as they think they can be, the bonus for increase in managed care lives has disappeared. The group might want to replace this bonus with incentives based on panel size, much the way the Fallon Clinic has done. This incentive discourages physicians from letting their panel shrink, and offers them strong incentives to keep their current patients happy.

GENERAL COMMENTS ON THE FOUR PLANS

It is intriguing to watch how each plan apportions the dollars in a different way. As mentioned previously, the shifts are exagger-

Table 7–5 Physician Compensation—Scenario 4

Line					Total	Doc 1	Doc 2	Doc 3	Doc 4	Doc 5
1	Entire group:	$1,000,000	100%	Total funds available for distribution						
2		$400,000	40%	Salary (includes longevity)						
3		$150,000	15%	Productivity: FFS + capped revenue (minus expenses)						
4		$100,000	10%	Managed care efficiency						
5		$100,000	10%	Patient satisfaction						
6		$100,000	10%	Quality outcomes						
7		$100,000	10%	Equal share of group profitability						
8		$50,000	5%	Discretionary based on group citizenship						
9										
10					Total	Doc 1	Doc 2	Doc 3	Doc 4	Doc 5
11										
12	Salary				$400,000	$80,000	$72,000	$88,000	$84,000	$76,000
13										
14	Productivity				$150,000	$30,000	$22,500	$37,500	$25,500	$34,500
15	Proportion of total				1	0.2	0.15	0.25	0.17	0.23
16										
17	Managed care efficiency, rank					1	2	3	4	5
18	Efficiency weighting factor				1	0.4	0.3	0.2	0.1	0
19										
20	Patient satisfaction, rank					5	4	3	2	1
21	Satisfaction weighting factor				1	0	0.1	0.2	0.3	0.4
22										
23	Quality outcomes, rank					2	1	5	4	3
24	Quality weighting factor				1	0.3	0.4	0	0.1	0.2
25										
26	40% Salary				$400,000	$80,000	$72,000	$88,000	$84,000	$76,000
27	15% Productivity				$150,000	$30,000	$22,500	$37,500	$25,500	$34,500
28	10% Managed care efficiency				$100,000	$40,000	$30,000	$20,000	$10,000	$0
29	10% Patient satisfaction				$100,000	$0	$10,000	$20,000	$30,000	$40,000
30	10% Quality outcomes				$100,000	$30,000	$40,000	$0	$10,000	$20,000
31	10% Equal share				$100,000	$20,000	$20,000	$20,000	$20,000	$20,000
32	5% Discretionary				$50,000	$10,000	$15,000	$5,000	$15,000	$5,000
33										
34	**Total compensation**				**$1,000,000**	**$210,000**	**$209,500**	**$190,500**	**$194,500**	**$195,500**

ated by using arbitrary numbers. It is important to remember that the purpose of this exercise is not to shuffle and reshuffle the deck in a zero-sum game. The purpose of the compensation scheme is to give physicians incentives to behave in ways that attract patients and conserve resources. If physicians can do this successfully, their net revenues will increase and the average compensation will rise.

The simplified plan just presented does not account for multiple specialties. Groups with sizable specialty departments will need to assign some proportion of their capitation revenue to cover each specialty within the group. Groups with a long history of providing capitated care, such as the Harriman Jones group, can use their own data to estimate how much this should be. Newly forming groups, or groups that add a new department, may have to depend on community-wide actuarial data. Such data will assign a per-member-per-month figure to each specialty and use this figure to convert an enrollment figure into dollars for that department. (Expenses will have to be backed out of this figure, of course, since available figures reflect the costs that insurers have paid for these services.) If a group's own specialty department does not cover all services commonly covered by the appropriate capitated rate (such as a cardiology department that does not provide electrophysiologic studies), the costs to purchase this care will also need to be subtracted from the subcapitated amount.

What of those doctors who function as both specialists and primary care physicians? Many specialists have responded to managed care by turning into primary care wannabees, announcing that they are primary care physicians for patients of a certain sex and age (obstetrician-gynecologists) or with certain illnesses (dermatologists, oncologists). Some of these claims are plausible and some are not, but the group does not have to agonize over who the compensation plan should consider a primary care physician. The HMOs largely decide this. If the HMO allows a physician to accept primary care capitation, that physician's capitation and patient panel can be counted like that of a categorical primary care physician. Assuming that this physician devotes time to both primary and secondary care, the group will have to make his or her compensation a hybrid of the primary and specialty reimbursement plans.

Finally, the scenarios presented do not tell a group when it can cut the checks. The group's financial performance will not become perfectly clear until the end of the fiscal year, but physicians quite reasonably expect to be paid throughout the year. The administrator must project revenue and expenses, and pay out some portion of the expected distributable income as a regular draw. Reconciliation with actual performance can be made quarterly. This is no different than current practice, based on productivity or on equal shares, when bonuses are taken out quarterly or at the end of the fiscal year.

WHEN IS CHANGE APPROPRIATE?

No practice goes from pure fee-for-service to pure capitation overnight. Even if it did, it would not want to change its compensation plan overnight. Physicians need some time to learn the new rules and adapt their practice styles to managed care. This is why this chapter presents a staged approach rather than a simple before-and-after plan. But this begs the question: At what percentage of managed care (or more precisely, at which percentage of capitation) should a practice move through these stages?

A 1993 survey of Integrated Delivery Systems and group practices, conducted by The Leadership Institute, revealed that a change from traditional productivity incentives to salaries with profit sharing typically occurs when capitated revenue reached 25 percent to 35 percent of total.[11] However, this is much too late to start making changes.

Consider a group that gets only 5 percent of its revenue from capitation and has used a production-based compensation plan. Although 5 percent of revenue is not enough to spend a lot of time on, the group must understand that this 5 percent will probably grow to 10 or 15 percent next year, and 25 percent the year after that. If the group does not change its compensation plan now, it will fall behind by next year, and the plan will reward behaviors that made sense for last year's situation. Changing the plan now gives the group time to fine-tune the plan, and gives individual physicians time to adapt to change.

There is another reason for moving expeditiously through the four stages. Consider the group that provides primary care and perhaps a little specialty care, but assumes risk for all professional and institutional care. The work that the physicians do in managing outside resources is a highly leveraged activity. A family practitioner might take an extra 30 minutes to carefully evaluate, educate, and follow a patient with uncomplicated low back pain, and possibly speak by phone with consultants involved in the case. This extra work might eliminate an unnecessary magnetic resonance imaging (MRI) procedure, which would result in savings somewhere between $500 and $1,000. The same physician could simply order the MRI, which takes 30 seconds, and spend the rest of the 30 minutes seeing two additional fee-for-service patients, netting under $100. The group's compensation plan should encourage the former behavior, not the latter.

Scenarios 3 and 4 incorporate items that are more difficult to define and measure than collections and expenses. Defining and measuring will take some practice. Thus, a practice should start measuring and tracking items such as patient satisfaction and quality outcomes well before these are translated into financial incentives. For instance, the medical group could have added these items under Scenario 2, without assigning a dollar value to them.

INCOME DIVISION AND THE PATIENT

In the midst of counting all the beans and apportioning all the dollars, it is easy to lose sight of why physicians are in business in the first place. A physician practice is entitled to payment only to the extent that it meets the needs and desires of its patients. The compensation plan should encourage physicians to do so.

Consider the classic productivity-based formula. This gave physicians the incentive to do as much as possible, consistent with any remote chance of helping the patient, or at least of not harming the patient. Physicians might have been concerned about personal hardship to the patient if the bill ran up too high, but insurance generally quieted such concerns. Of course, no physician could sustain his or her volume if patients were not satisfied with the convenience, manner, and outcomes of care, but there was never a systematic attempt to measure and improve these aspects.

Compare this to the compensation plan proposed in Scenario 4. It rewards efficiency in care, which some fear because they claim it will discourage appropriate care. Countering this risk are professional acculturation and ethics, and regular review of patient satisfaction and quality outcomes. In time, of course, patients will share the benefits of greater efficiency through slower premium rate inflation. The Scenario 4 plan demands an infrastructure that regularly measures patient satisfaction; physicians earn more if they stay accessible by telephone, see scheduled patients on schedule, minimize waiting times for appointments, explain treatment options, and treat the patient with courtesy and respect. As part of group citizenship, the compensation plan rewards participation in quality improvement initiatives. The plan rewards the physicians who can achieve quality outcome goals, whether adherence to accepted treatment guidelines or achievement of targeted levels of physiologic control or symptom reduction. All of these activities improve patient care.

The ideal compensation plan benefits not only the physicians, but the practice's patients and payers. The only losers are the practice's competitors.

CONCLUSION

Traditional income distribution schemes worked well for traditional fee-for-service medical practices, but they are guaranteed to cause serious damage to a group that depends on managed care for its livelihood. The ideal compensation plan is based on the group's current revenue patterns, its specialty composition, and its goals for the future. Since no two groups are alike in these respects, each group will need to find its own way. The following principles will prove helpful:

- Any compensation plan will be an ongoing effort. Major revisions will call for a large input of staff time and possibly outside consultants' fees, and may cause anxiety and dissension within the group. Between these major revisions there will be many minor adjustments, probably occurring once or twice a year.
- As with so much in medicine, certainty about the best approach to compensation is lacking, but this uncertainty should not lead to paralysis.
- Before changing its compensation scheme, a group should write a business plan that defines where the group hopes to be in two and in five years. Based on this plan, the group's governing body should give the compensation committee clear direction about what sort of behavior the plan must encourage.

The plan should be based on inputs that can be measured. If a group thinks an input is important, but cannot measure it, the group should write a compensation plan without this input, but begin now to define a measurement that can serve the plan in two or three years. See Exhibit 7–1 for a list of resources on physician compensation plans.

The ultimate purpose of the compensation plan is not to take dollars away from Dr. X and give them to Dr. Y, but to help the entire group increase its profits and improve the care it gives to patients.

Exhibit 7–1 Resources on Physician Compensation Plans

Compensation plans that work under capitation are being developed by innovative groups across the country. Because the subject is changing rapidly, published materials are of limited usefulness. Nuggets of wisdom are scattered widely throughout journals and newsletters, or are presented at conferences (see the end notes for examples). Three compensation surveys are listed below, and several others are available. Medical Group Management Association's packet of published and unpublished articles is an excellent introduction to income plans under fee-for-service, and it contains a few articles relevant to groups working under capitation.

- *Income Distribution.* Medical Group Management Association Library Resource Center, Search Summary No. 1007, 1994. Medical Group Management Association, 104 Inverness Terrace East, Englewood, CO 80112-5306.
- *Physician Compensation and Production Survey.* Published annually by the Medical Group Management Association, 104 Inverness Terrace East, Englewood, CO 80112-5306.
- *Group Practice Compensation Trends and Productivity Correlations.* Published annually by the American Group Practice Association, 1422 Duke Street, Alexandria, VA 22314-3430.
- *1994 Physicians Compensation Survey.* Ernst & Young LLP, 515 South Flower Street, Suite 1700, Los Angeles, CA 90071.

NOTES

1. L.C. Beck, ed., Does Productivity Income Division Still Make Sense? *The Physician's Advisory* 94, no. 1 (1994): 1–3.

2. D.J. Tenenbaum, Concocting a Palatable Compensation Formula, *Family Practice Management* 1, no. 9 (1994): 48–56.

3. *Modern Healthcare*'s 1995 Physician Compensation Report, *Modern Healthcare* 25, no. 28 (1995): 42–45.

4. A. Podbielski et al., Future Concepts in Physician Compensation (Paper presented at the Medical Group Management Association Annual Meeting, Boston, October 2–5, 1994).

5. J.P. Weiner et al., Development and Application of a Population-Oriented Measure of Ambulatory Care Case-Mix, *Medical Care* 29 (1991): 452–472.

6. S. Salem-Schatz et al., The Case for Case-Mix Adjustment in Practice Profiling, *Journal of the American Medical Association* 272 (1994): 871–874.

7. Reprinted in The National Committee for Quality Assurance, Health Plan Employer Data and Information Set (HEDIS) 2.0, 1993.

8. Institute of Medicine, *Medicare: A Strategy for Quality Assurance*, vol. 1, ed. K.N. Lohr (Washington, D.C.: National Academy Press, 1990).

9. M.C. Jaklevic, Groups Experiment To Find Best Formula for Doc Compensation, *Modern Healthcare* 25, no. 29 (1995): 41.

10. Podbielski et al., Future Concepts in Physician Compensation.

11. R.A. Dickinson, Balance of Payments, *American Medical News* (December 5, 1994): 27–30.

Chapter 8

Capital and Equity Issues in Physician Organizations and Practice Management Industry

Douglas Goldstein and E. James Streator III

INTRODUCTION

The process of merging and expanding medical practices that is changing the landscape of the health care field is creating exciting and risky investment opportunities for physician leaders. Those who are willing and able to take the initiative *now* to organize their practices into larger, integrated health care organizations can look forward to the rewards of participating in creating successful Physician Organizations and Physician Practice Management Companies (PPMCs) that deliver cost-effective, quality health care services.

This chapter discusses several major issues that physician leaders need to understand regarding capital and equity issues for Physician Organizations and related management companies. First, what are the market realities behind the rapid growth industry called *Physician Practice Management* that is being fueled with billions of dollars of capital from various investment markets? Second, what are the sources of capital, valuation components, and financial issues during the growth of a PPMC and large ambulatory medical services network? Finally, how are assets and control of financial issues altered as PPMCs grow through several stages of capitalization?

MARKET REALITIES OF THE PHYSICIAN PRACTICE MANAGEMENT INDUSTRY

Physicians by training and nature are individualists, which helps to explain why many practitioners have been caught unaware, startled, and somewhat unnerved by the incredibly rapid emergence of large, publicly traded PPMCs such as Coastal Healthcare Group, PhyCor, and MedPartners/Mullikin/Pacific Physician Services. Until recently, physicians have not been proactive about joining with their colleagues to form large group practices, even those physicians who have managed to band together are likely to have done so for defensive rather than proactive, market-based reasons, with the result that their organizations are only loosely integrated, if at all. Consequently, the entrance of professional, well-funded entrepreneurs into the health care market during the late 1980s, and the acceleration of merger and consolidation activities during the first half of the 1990s, has caused physicians in many markets across the country to become proactive in organizing and integrating their practices. The influence of physician leaders in the new health care marketplace will largely depend on how effectively they tap into and manage new and distinctly riskier sources of capital and relationships with professional, experienced business development experts.

Growth should not happen for growth's sake, but it should be a response to underlying trends or market demands. Physician Organizations must focus on the needs of the market. Today, patients and businesses are the true *purchasers*, and managed health plans are *payers with clout*. Many purchasers recognize the value of a multilocation, Integrated Group Practice or primary care network as a cost-effective, quality provider. With the consolidation of managed health plans and the trend toward capitation reimbursement, providers are being positioned to accept risk. The pressure to build Integrated Delivery Systems is leading hospitals, for-profit management companies, and managed health plans to acquire or obtain long-term management agreements with medical practices in order to control access to care and the revenue flow of group practices.

Purchasers and businesses are demanding predictable health care costs, aggressively moving patients into managed care plans, and forming regional purchasing cooperatives. If the purchasers of health care are growing larger, then the providers of health care must grow larger and offer a continuum of care or one-stop shopping in a geographic area.

EXPANSION OF THE PHYSICIAN PRACTICE MANAGEMENT INDUSTRY

With capitated payments accounting for an ever-higher percentage of health care revenue, individual patients no longer represent the most important source of income for physician practices. Instead, revenues are derived from blocs of patients, whose health care needs are aggregated and paid for on the basis of an average per capita rate. These blocs of patients are being formed and controlled by private and public sector employers—the true purchasers of health care services. Moreover, by creating local and regional alliances with other employers—and thereby enlarging their patient blocs—these purchasers are able to negotiate, if not actually dictate, the dollar value of each individual patient.

From the perspective of the physician-patient relationship, this trend makes little difference. That is, regardless of whether the payment mechanism for the delivery of health care is fee-for-service or capitated reimbursement, physicians still represent the patient's gateway into the health care system. As such, physicians directly receive about one out of every five dollars spent on health care—nearly 20 percent of the nation's health care expenditures—for a total of more than $150 billion in annual revenues. Physicians also influence the additional expenditure of more than $500 billion annually, through referrals to hospitals, laboratories, ambulatory clinics, and specialty practices.

Thus, once those dollars enter the health care delivery system, physicians are in the seat of power, in terms of control over cash flow. And it is for this reason that hospitals, for-profit management companies, managed health plans, and others are vigorously investing in, buying, and forming alliances with medical practices: they wish to gain access to the health care dollars over which physicians have total control.

These factors have led to the rapid emergence of an industry surrounding the consolidation, merger, and management of medical practices and related health services. Figure 8–1 illustrates the recent evolution of the Physician Practice Management industry as it has evolved from a new, fragmented industry through a number of stages and into the future. In the early 1990s, the industry infrastructure was created; around 1993 credibility was established; and then

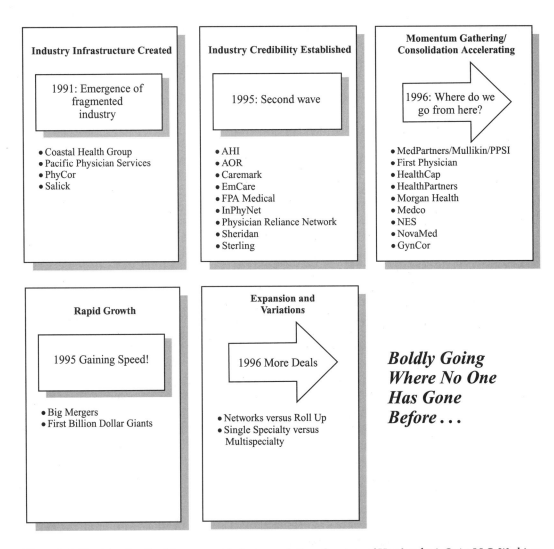

Figure 8–1 Physician Practice Management industry evolution. Courtesy of Hambrecht & Quist LLC, Washington, D.C.

the health care scene experienced an explosion of primary care, specialty, and multispecialty practice management companies. In 1995, the first billion dollar PPMC giants, such as Caremark and MedPartners/Mullikin, emerged. In 1996, the market has seen an increase in single specialty public offerings. And, there is a new type of PPMC that focuses on the management of networks such as Independent Practice Associations (IPAs). The exact future is unpredictable, but what is a certainty is that the PPMC industry will continue to grow rapidly.

Wall Street is bullish on the emerging Physician Organizations—particularly, physicians' initiatives in organizing larger group practices, Management Services Organizations (MSOs), IPAs, and other Physician Organizations—for several reasons:

- Group practice management companies, or PPMCs—including professional corporation partnerships, group- and staff-model Health Maintenance Organizations (HMOs), Physician-Hospital Organizations (PHOs), and investor-owned groups—command annual revenues of $24 billion and have been growing at a compounded annual rate of 15 percent.
- Today, combined revenues of investor-owned companies represent only about 2 percent of the market.
- Rapid growth is expected, because market forces favor consolidation of medical practices and the health care industry in general.
- Shares of stock in PPMCs, in general, have traded at high premiums, varying from 14 to 50 times earnings.
- It is expected that during the next three to five years, the equity and investment value of group practices will accelerate, if properly managed.

Table 8-1 lists several publicly traded PPMCs; describes their share price as of August 12, 1995; highlights their equity market value; and summarizes their current and projected price/earnings ratio.

In 1995, most major investment banking firms, from Hambrecht and Quist and Smith Barney to Solomon Brothers and Piper Jaffray, sponsored major investment forums for institutional investors on this emerging industry. In addition, hundreds of physician groups and entrepreneurs are building private PPMCs in the hopes of taking a company public or selling out to a major national PPMC at a very favorable valuation. In 1995, according to *Physician Practice Management Companies Newsletter*, the industry had total public market capitalization of $6.4 billion with a projected increase to over $50 billion during the next five years.[1]

This level of interest is a result of a very high premium being paid by the market on earnings of these entities. One of the reasons for Wall Street's attention to this growing market is the performance of PPMCs compared to industry standards, as reflected in Figure 8-2. This figure illustrates that public PPMCs performed above NASDAQ and Dow Jones market averages over the last couple of years. Like most markets, the valuation excitement will experience several stages of ups and downs during the next 10 years, but the fundamental economics of health care today point to a long-term growth. In many ways, the Physician Practice Management industry in the mid-1990s is where the HMO industry was in the early 1980s.

The largest public PPMC firms—Coastal Healthcare Group, PhyCor, and MedPartners/Mullikin/Pacific Physician Services—have rapidly been able to accrue annual earnings of greater than 30 percent. How? *Rapidly!* Coastal started as a contractor delivering emergency services for hospitals. Now, an $800 million corporation in terms of sales, it is one of the largest physician management companies. Coastal is also moving up the food chain. It has purchased an HMO and numerous primary care groups, creating, in effect, a company that will be able to contract directly with employer groups and less aggressive payers to provide a capitated product.

PhyCor, one of the oldest, most mature companies, is also rapidly expanding in many states. In addition to its core business of buying the assets and revenue streams of multispecialty group practices, it owns two network management companies focused on managing the capitation and managed care contracting of IPA networks. As of December 1995, the largest PPMC entity—with more than $1.3 billion in revenue and over 1,000 physicians—is MedPartners/Mullikin/Pacific

Table 8-1 Practice Management Comparable Companies Analysis

Company	Ticker	Price on 4/29/96	Market Value ($mils)	P/E Multiples CY96E	P/E Multiples CY97E
Emergency/Primary Care					
Coastal Physician Group	DR	$8.25	$195.5	91.7 x	14.5 x
Emcare Holdings	EMCR	28.00	233.2	22.4	18.4
InPhyNet Medical Mgmt.	IMMI	19.00	296.7	17.8	14.4
Sheridan Healthcare	SHCR	7.50	60.7	14.2	13.6
Sterling Healthcare Group	STER	18.50	116.6	22.8	18.3
		Average:	$180.5	33.8 x	15.8 x
Primary Care/Multispecialty					
AHI Healthcare	AHIS	$6.13	$88.5	34.0 x	9.4 x
Caremark	CK	27.50	2,128.5	22.4	17.9
FPA Medical Mgmt.	FPAM	16.34	118.1	41.9	27.2
Medpartners/Mullikin/PPSI	MDM	28.75	1,440.4	36.9	27.6
PhyCor	PHYC	50.50	2,030.1	59.4	43.2
		Average:	$943.9	33.8 x	20.5 x
Specialty/Disease Specific					
American Oncology Resource	AORI	$49.50	$1,161.3	53.8 x	38.7 x
MedCath	MCTH	37.75	335.7	55.5	43.4
OccuSystems	OSYS	29.00	591.6	48.3	35.4
Pediatrix Medical Group	PEDX	44.25	610.4	53.8	40.8
Physician Reliance Network	PHYN	44.00	1,020.8	41.8	31.7
Physician's Resource Group	PRG	30.00	297.0	36.6	26.8
		Average:	$669.5	48.3 x	36.1 x

Courtesy of Hambrecht & Quist L.L.C., Washington, D.C.

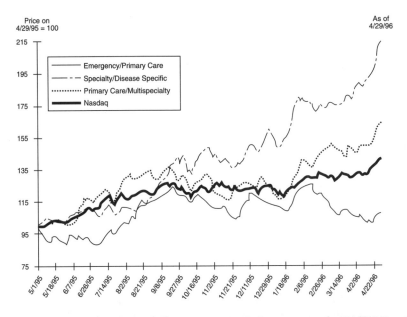

Figure 8-2 Relative stock price performance: Physician practice industry versus the NASDAQ and Dow Jones Industrial Averages. Courtesy of Hambrecht & Quist L.L.C., Washington, D.C.

Physicians Services, an organization created in 1995 through the merger of three of the leading public and private PPMCs in the country. It is likely that this and other organizations such as Caremark International will continue to evolve rapidly—both horizontally and vertically—into the twenty-first century.

PHYSICIANS TAKE LEADERSHIP

Physicians have always served as decision makers and, therefore, have always been a significant force with regard to directing cash flow within the health care system. So, their particular role in the health care system does not, in itself, explain the sudden vigor with which investors in recent years have been targeting medical practices. Rather, the catalyst for this activity has been the change in how those health care dollars are entering the marketplace: as negotiated capitated payments for large patient blocs.

The impact of this change can be seen most vividly in the geographic areas where health care purchasers have had the highest success in moving patients into managed care plans: California, southern Florida, and Minneapolis. In these three areas, the purchasers of health care services have gained control over huge blocs of patients and, thus, tremendous clout in negotiating fixed-price contracts with Managed Care Organizations. In fact, the leverage that these purchasers wield has been so great that not only have per capita health care rates in these areas declined but also the rate of change in the consumer price index for health care nationwide has slowed to roughly one-half of what it was in 1993.

The implications for physicians are numerous and are discussed in greater detail elsewhere in this book. The bottom line, however, is that whichever health care provider gains access to, and control over, the greatest number of patients in a given market will achieve a competitive edge over all of the other health care providers in that market. Thus, it is not merely because of physicians' access to patients but also because of physicians' control over referral revenues associated with those patients that medical practices and the companies that manage them have suddenly become hot investment properties.

As the number of patients (members) covered by managed care plans has grown, payer organizations have taken the upper hand in negotiations with physicians, regarding not only per-member-per-month payments to physicians but also the volume and demographics of patients that physicians will see; the amount of risk, in terms of high-cost disease management, that physicians will bear; the types of cost control incentives and efficiency goals that will be instituted; and the size of any rewards to be given for the efficient delivery of high-quality health care within the established cost constraints.

Consequently, there has been a rush throughout the country to buy medical practices and employ physicians. Health systems across the country have purchased medical practices and employed physicians in outpatient divisions or through closely controlled medical foundations. Some insurance companies have sought to recreate the staff model organizations through the employment of physicians in primary care clinics. Aetna Healthways Health Centers and Blue Cross & Blue Shield of New Jersey's primary care centers are two good examples of the staff approach. However, it is becoming increasingly evident that physicians need to have a stake in the overall equity and governance of the evolving health care organizations; otherwise, productivity can decrease significantly. When this happens, the parent organization employing the physicians can experience operating losses.

In the future, it will be very difficult for vertically integrated health systems with staff physicians to compete against the flatter, market-driven, physician-led PPMCs. These organizations have higher levels of motivation and responsiveness due to their combined centralized/decentralized organizational structures.

Throughout the country, physician leaders are saying "no" to straight buyout offers and instead are linking with one of the numerous variations of the physician equity model that has a public or private PPMC at its center. Physicians are doing the following:

- taking the initiative to organize larger group practices, PPMCs, IPAs, and other Physician Organizations
- building larger group practices of 30 to 250 physicians before taking a minority capital partner
- hiring talented managed care executives to guide the transition of the Physician Organization to the top of the managed contracting pyramid
- assuming the risks of developing large primary care-based, multispecialty group practices, so they can retain the rewards of ownership and equity at higher levels

The importance of critical mass, however, goes beyond the ability to negotiate fairly with payers. The new competitive requirements of the health care marketplace dictate that health care providers be able to deliver high-quality care in an environment characterized by price competition and overall deflation. Profitability under such circumstances depends upon delivering large volumes of high-quality, low-cost care, and this requires advanced information systems and economies of scale that come through consolidation of small medical practices. In order to meet these conditions, Physician Organizations with an integrated PPMC must be large enough to (1) maintain physician decision making with regard to treatment protocols, (2) achieve organizational economies of scale that will reduce the direct and indirect costs of delivering health care, and (3) offer a continuum of care, or one-stop shopping, that can effectively capture a high volume of patients and keep them largely, if not entirely, within the organization's health care delivery system.

To achieve the necessary size for accomplishing those goals, physician practices must have access to capital. And capital must be accessed in ways that fuel the aggressive growth necessary to meet purchaser requirements, economic realities, and competitive forces.

FINANCIAL ISSUES AND CAPITAL SOURCES RELATED TO GROWTH

Rapid growth of organizations depends on understanding the dynamics of progressive capitalization, the role of management, and the creative use of equity in the form of stock and options. To compete in today's marketplace requires Physician Organizations and their PPMCs to grow rapidly. Capital is essential. Access to capital from private or public investors enables the organization to: (1) develop management and information systems infrastructure; (2) integrate with or acquire other physician groups; (3) extend its geographic market; (4) fund the development of new products and services; and (5) create value and wealth for its employees and shareholders. In effect, capital is the currency of the new health care marketplace.

Most growth companies go through predictable stages of growth that can be described in terms of available source of funds, revenue, and earnings. Figure 8–3 illustrates the generalized evolution of capital financing sources and options in an organization's growth and development from a start-up company to a mature operating organization. Many growth companies across a number of industries go from a self-funding status to a public company using a carefully timed combination of debt and equity capital sources to fuel progressive growth.

Capital and Equity Issues   151

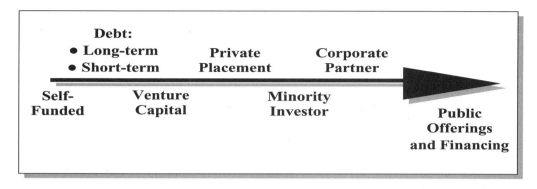

Figure 8–3 Continuum of capital financing options. Courtesy of Medical Alliances, Inc., Alexandria, Virginia.

Start-up endeavors generally have little or no revenue; they are unprofitable with few securing assets. The sources of funds for this stage company include founders, limited partnerships, grants, and charitable contributions. Profits are usually small, or the company operates at a loss. Early-growth companies with sales of up to $10 million have a short operating history with low reserves and are in the process of generating a credit history. The sources of funds for these companies include founders, private equity, and private or guaranteed debt. Emerging growth companies have an operating history of one to ten years, and their operating margins have often been low or running at a loss due to the demands on capital from rapid growth. These organizations have established a credit history and have accumulated some security for debt. The sources of capital for these organizations include founders capital, debt, mezzanine equity, and secured debt. Revenues for these companies range from $10 million to $100 million, with significant profitability likely to occur in the next year or two.

Established companies with revenue from $100 to $500 million have robust revenue and profit growth, a strong historical debt service coverage, some institutional research coverage, possible credit ratings, and a significant track record of retained earnings and assets. The primary sources of capital for these entities include publicly traded stocks and bonds, retained earnings, and a variety of lines of credit from major banking institutions. As organizations mature, they have a history of profitability and debt repayment, strong historical debt service coverage, broad institutional research coverage, investment-grade credit ratings, and significant retained earnings and assets. Again publicly traded stocks, options, and bonds, along with lines of credit, play a role in furthering the corporate growth through acquisitions and product development.

Debt and equity are the two major categories of capital for rapid-growth companies. There are several different types of debt that can be used to acquire cash for growth, and several variations on the equity markets. Of course, there are combinations of debt and equity. The following list summarizes the key types of debt and equity:

- **Debt:**
  1. borrowed money
     (a) long- and short-term
     (b) fixed and variable rate
     (c) taxable and tax-exempt
     (d) publicly offered and privately placed
  2. financing leases

- **Equity Investments:**
  1. limited partnerships
  2. stock—common and preferred
     (a) public offerings—SEC registered
     (b) private placements—Registration D offerings
     (c) intrastate public offerings—restricted stock
  3. retained earnings

A group of physician practices does not truly qualify as a start-up entity due to the substantial amounts of cash flow and operating history. A newly formed group practice from the merger of more than 75 medical practices could have revenue in excess of $40 million, depending on the specialties and services involved in the merger. However, if, at the time of merger, these physicians are also forming a wholly owned PPMC, then in some ways this entity is a start-up entity because it does not have management or infrastructure. Thus, the typical pattern is to look first to the members of the group practice for seed money; then to enter into private joint ventures to develop additional security for debt; and, finally, to issue publicly traded stock to fuel additional services, geographic expansion, and additional acquisitions.

At each step along the way for growth companies, and particularly PPMCs or Physician Organizations, numerous investors and strategic partners want to have influence over revenues and the leverage that comes from alliance or integration with large group practices or physician networks. Table 8–2 outlines the broad range of organizations currently investing in PPMCs and group practices under a variety of minority or majority ownership structures. There are three major classes of investors: (1) strategic partners (either minority or majority) such as health systems or HMOs; (2) institutional investors such as venture capitalists, pension funds, or mutual funds; and (3) individuals who are qualified, accredited investors or people with high net worth. Because of the favorable price/earnings ratios and other factors, billions of dollars of capital are flowing into the PPMC market that promise to further fuel additional practice mergers, acquisitions, and consolidations.

It is important to recognize that there are advantages and disadvantages to every type of investor, whether it is a health system acting as a minority partner or a corporate partner that is essentially buying out the medical practices or group through a long-term management service agreement. For instance, the advantage of taking on debt to grow is that the founding physicians can maintain 100 percent ownership. The disadvantage is that the debt burdens the organization with debt payments that ultimately have to be repaid. An equity investment, which is an exchange of paper stock for cash, increases the strength of the overall balance

Table 8–2 Types of Investors

Strategic Partners	Institutional Investors	Individuals
Health systems	Mezzanine funds	Accredited investors
HMOs	Insurance companies	High net worth individuals
Insurance companies	Pension and mutual funds	
Other physicians	Venture capitalists	
Pharmaceutical companies	Real estate investment trusts (REITs)	
Other corporations		

Courtesy of Medical Alliances, Inc., Alexandria, Virginia.

sheet without burdening the corporation with principle and interest payments.

It is always important to investigate the motivations and goals of a capital partner. For instance, venture capitalists seek to achieve a 25 percent to 40 percent per annum return on their investment, while a health system is less concerned about the financial return and more concerned about the kinds of reserve powers it may hold over a physician majority-owned PPMC. Remember that institutional investors live by the golden rule of Wall Street: "Buy low, sell high."

FINANCIAL IMPLICATIONS OF STRATEGIC ALLIANCE OPTIONS

During the transition from a single entity such as a professional corporation to an integrated, multiorganizational structure such as a PPMC with a dedicated physician network, it is important to assess the control of the revenue stream from the delivery of patient care services. It is also necessary to evaluate the ownership of the Physician Organization and the management company. PPMCs and MSOs were created when leading medical groups such as Mullikin spun off the management components of their group practices into separate C corporations. This provided the vehicle to attract outside capital, because nonphysicians are able to own equity and stock in C corporation management companies but not in physicians' professional corporations.

As Physician Organizations and PPMCs go through stages of progressive growth, the ownership and financial control of the medical practice will shift dramatically. The general rule of thumb in building properly capitalized and managed growth companies is that the greater the risk taken by the founders, the longer the founders will retain control and influence over the company and accrue appropriate rewards in the form of increased equity value.

Aggressive growth in competitive environments requires capital. In PPMCs, capital is needed for the following:

1. **working capital**—preoperational planning and development, start-up operating losses, reserves, and product development
2. **capital expenditures**—building, expanding, or renovating health centers and purchasing information systems equipment and software
3. **acquisitions**—HMOs, IPAs, and other physician practices

Converting small, fee-for-service medical practices into integrated regional networks that can bear risk demands progressive growth through various stages—from the use of debt and private investment to the use of public capital.

In seeking capital sources and potential alliance partners, physician leaders must carefully weigh the pros and cons of each option. The following three options—self-reliance and debt, Physician Equity Alliance, and corporate subsidiary—have advantages and disadvantages.

Option 1—Self-Reliance and Debt

Many growth companies choose to use internally generated cash from operations (equity) and a combination of short- and long-term debt for investments in the equipment, locations, and services that are necessary to secure future growth. Equity ownership, when properly managed, is a dynamic way of building value through the appreciation of company assets. Basically, by financing an organization through self-reliance and debt, each of the physicians in the group practice agrees to forgo a percentage of current cash compensation in exchange for a proportionate share of equity (stock) in a wholly owned practice management company (PPMC or MSO). The carrot, of course, is the expectation that the dollar value of the cash retained in the management company will increase at a rate that is far in excess of the return the physicians might have received by putting the money in the bank or investing it in, say, real estate. Indeed, based on the current industry average, that expectation is well justified, inasmuch as each dollar retained as earnings a few years ago is now worth about $20 if the organization was publicly traded. For example, a physician who initially invested $250,000 in practice value or equity in a PPMC would now have $5 million in equity if the PPMC traded on the public market at a price/earnings ratio of 20.

Figure 8–4 shows the structure of equity and profitability in a medical group that has spun off its business management into a separate C corporation and used debt and retained earnings to support start-up operations. Often, the retained cash is used to form or expand the PPMC. The PPMC, under contract with the physician practice, manages the business functions of the group practice and provides expertise in negotiating with HMOs. The length of the management service agreement is relatively short, often from three to five years. Note that the physician group retains intangible assets such as managed care contracts. The flow of funds is through the group practice who, in turn, pays the PPMC an administrative fee—usually only what is necessary to provide billing, purchasing, office staffing, and other needed services. Any profits generated are paid out to the physicians as year-end bonuses to avoid double taxation.

The consolidation of medical practices and creation of PPMCs also have made more and more bankers willing to extend substantial lines of credit and long-term debt arrangements. Frequently, lines of credit and long-term debt can be secured through real estate or by obtaining a strategic ally, such as a health system, to cosign a note, thereby minimizing the exposure of the group practice.

There are several advantages of using internally generated cash and a combination of long- and short-term debt:

- It allows physicians to maintain 100 percent control and ownership.
- Substantial equity appreciation can accrue to the physician owners.
- Physicians lead and can adjust their business strategies on the basis of market conditions.
- Control over equity rests with physicians who have the ability to sell part or all of the wholly owned PPMC in the future, when the valuation of the combined entity increases and market conditions warrant.

Disadvantages of this strategy include the requirement that physician owners take personal risk related to the guarantees that frequently are needed to secure debt and the capital expenditures necessary to support an experienced management team and information systems to guide the growth of the organization. The addition of debt also depresses the earnings of the medical practice and can restrict the amount of money available for physician compensation. With thinly capitalized medical practices, it is often difficult to obtain enough debt financing to compete aggressively in a highly competitive and rapidly consolidating market.

Option 2—Strategic Alliance Partners and Physician Equity Alliances

In deciding how to phase in capital to support growth, the Physician Organization should objectively evaluate its own resources, as well as those of potential partners, in terms of the likelihood of long-term success. In this regard, it is worthwhile to reexamine the characteristics of successful Physician Equity Alliances as profiled in Chapter 1. These tend to be Physician Organizations with a primary care base, in excess of 50 physicians, with the following characteristics:

Capital and Equity Issues 155

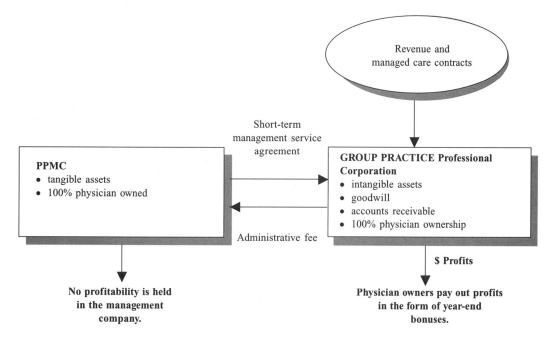

Figure 8–4 Self-reliance and debt ownership and flow of funds. Courtesy of Medical Alliances, Inc., Alexandria, Virginia.

- Have a linked PPMC and group practice structure.
- Are directed by physicians and managed by talented business development and operations executives.
- Provide and arrange the entire spectrum of health care services, using demand management systems for appropriate care facilitation.
- Do risk contracting directly with HMOs, employers, or third-party payers such as Medicare and Medicaid rather than assigning this right to a PHO.
- Develop infrastructure systems to improve quality while reducing cost.
- Deliver superior, high-quality health care at less cost than traditional fee-for-service practices, Preferred Provider Organizations (PPOs), and even some HMOs.

Figure 8–5 represents a number of significant transitions that have occurred in creating the Physician Equity Alliance. All tangible and intangible assets have been shifted from the group practice to the PPMC. This shift is necessary to attract an outside minority investor who will be looking for the management company's ability to generate profitability. In this case, the majority of the PPMC is owned either by the professional corporation as a whole or by the individual physician members of the group practice. The management service agreement between the group and management company becomes long term. The group practice may hold legal right to any managed care contracts signed; however, 100 percent of the revenue initially flows through the PPMC. Then the PPMC pays the group a negotiated percentage of overall revenue as defined in the management service agreement. Any profitability will be either retained by the

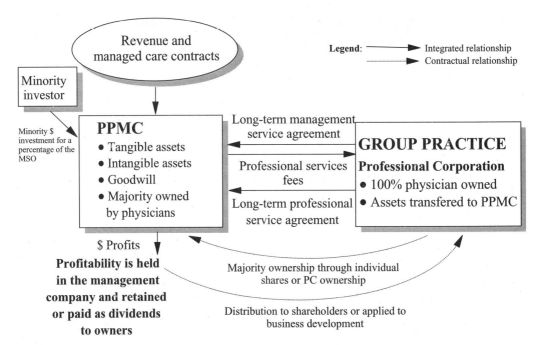

Figure 8–5 Physician Equity Alliance ownership and flow of funds. Courtesy of Medical Alliances, Inc., Alexandria, Virginia.

PPMC or paid out to the physician shareholders. One important factor about the Physician Equity Alliance is that physicians make the decisions on how to use profits from operations—not outside investors, business executives, or public shareholders. However, if one of the objectives of the alliance is to become a public company, then it must demonstrate profitability of the management company.

Accordingly, in making capital investment decisions, physician leaders should determine whether a given option strengthens the factors that are essential for long-term success including physician leadership, vision, and creation of an effective management team. Leaders must have the ability to manage and be at risk for a full range of ambulatory, institutional, and preventive health services, while using advanced medical management systems with active utilization review, case management, and cost management. There also must be a critical mass of primary care providers, good geographic distribution, specialty and acute care support, centralized marketing and administration, and sufficient balance sheet strength.

For Integrated Physician Organizations with strong physician leadership and business management, there are numerous capital and investment opportunities from which to choose. Organizations that help physician-owned group practices and PPMCs to access capital through minority or majority investments range from investment banking firms, such as Robertson Stephens, Piper Jaffray, Solomon Brothers, and Hambrecht and Quist, to strategic allies, such as pharmaceutical companies.

In structuring the physician equity transaction with a minority investor, physicians should examine whether to pursue a pooling transaction or a purchase transaction. In a pooling transaction, the allying companies essentially swap stock in each other. At the end of the day, the companies' shareholders own a respective portion of each other's company. The earnings and balance sheets are combined, and it is a very clean kind of transaction. In contrast, a purchase transaction involves acquiring the stock, usually at a premium to asset value, and transaction costs and other costs are accrued. The decision as to whether to pursue a pooling or a purchase transaction will also have tax and estate planning considerations.

The advantages of forming a Physician Equity Alliance with a minority investor are as follows:

- The relationship maintains physician control and ownership.
- Physician owners are able to retain the increases in value of their PPMC and group practice rather than selling too early at too low of a price in merger and consolidation cycle.
- The relationship does not interfere with physicians' capability to modify or adjust strategies on the basis of market conditions.
- The physician group retains the ability to sell additional minority interests in the PPMC, when its valuation increases.
- It is the closest thing to private practice that will remain viable during the next five years.

Some of the disadvantages of this option are that substantial capital is needed to develop an investor business plan and create the new PPMC so that a minority investor can be brought in on terms that are favorable to the Physician Organization. Management expertise is crucial in order to maximize the physicians' position. It is also much harder not to sell the entire practice today to a health system in a corporate subsidiary transaction because the valuations of medical practices are so favorable. Another old saying states: "Cash is king and if you can make it cash, take it to the bank." Building growth companies involves a high level of risk and requires guts, determination, and belief in the physicians' ability to build a business. It will likely be necessary to hire experienced consultants, lawyers, and accountants to assist during various parts of the business development and capital acquisition process.

Option 3—Corporate Subsidiary and Strategic Partner

Since about 1990, there has been a significant growth in private and publicly traded Physician Practice Management Companies. Examples include PhyCor, MedPartners/Mullikin/Pacific Physician Services, and PHP Healthcare. The majority of group practices acquired by or merged into these entities have been long-standing multispecialty group practices.

In this type of transaction, a national for-profit practice management company buys the tangible assets of the group for a combination of cash and stock. Figure 8–6 illustrates the key aspects of this structure. All of the business functions of the group practice are taken over by the national organization and often delivered through a regional PPMC. The national company obtains ownership of 100 percent of the revenue of the group practice and works aggressively to reduce operating expenses to ensure that bottom-line profits meet the expectations of public shareholders. A long-term management service agreement, often in excess of 30 years, is signed that outlines the responsibilities of each party and defines the revenue that flows back to the group practice for physician compensation.

The revenue flows through the publicly held PPMC with a distribution to the group practice that is defined by the long-term management agreement. Profits of the regional PPMC are returned to the public corporation and distributed according to the decisions of the board of directors, which is usually predominated by laypersons. The structure illustrated in Figure 8–6 is a basic model. Many of the arrangements established by leading public PPMCs today are more complex and have detailed incentive arrangements to ensure motivation of the regional group practices that are under man-

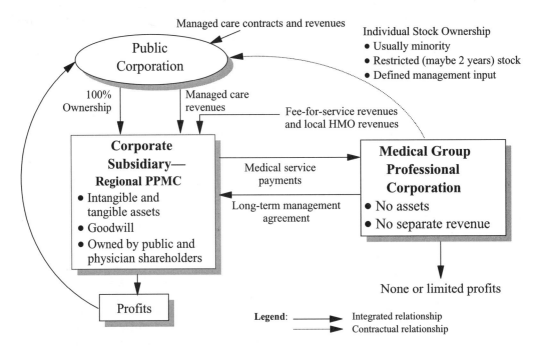

Figure 8–6 Corporate subsidiary ownership and flow of funds. Courtesy of Medical Alliances, Inc., Alexandria, Virginia.

agement. Physicians who exchange their equity in a medical practice or PPMC to a public company generally receive payment in the form of cash and stock in the public companies. This stock is held by an individual physician and could be a form of restricted stock that may not be traded for a defined period of time.

The advantages of becoming a subsidiary of a public national PPMC organization are numerous:

- The physician may get a higher value in cash and stock for being an early mover.
- It is a relatively easy transaction to take part in, because the other organization has the expertise to handle the legal, financial, and personnel matters involved.
- Availability of capital is good, because the partner typically has deep pockets from public capital markets.
- Such an alliance generally is part of an overall strategy to acquire managed care contracts nationwide.
- Physicians gain access to clinical expertise on how to manage risk and capitation.
- The physician leader usually retains a leadership position, participating on national committees.
- The corporate parent develops a business plan for the group practice.
- This type of arrangement generally keeps the existing components of the practice's management staff in place.

However, there also are numerous disadvantages to the corporate subsidiary route. These include the following:

- The parent corporation controls the revenue and money.
- The parent corporation has the ability to alter management agreements after an initial period (usually two years).
- The corporation has the ability to reduce physician compensation over time.
- Physicians lose business and financial control.
- The physicians become, essentially, employees of a corporation that must be responsive to the needs of public shareholders.
- The physician might be selling at too low of a price, given that it is still relatively early in the long-term merge and consolidation cycle.
- The decision to become a corporate subsidiary is irreversible.

How do investors value an emerging private Physician Equity Alliance or PPMC? First and foremost, Wall Street looks at how comparable, public companies are trading; how those companies are traded over time; and how their stocks are performing. Comparable transactions usually are a critical element. However, given the early stages of integration and consolidation in this industry, Wall Street does not have a statistically meaningful subset of transactions from which to devise a standard formula. Unfortunately, the information is not there yet for publicly traded companies.

The private company valuation process usually involves looking at the number of member lives; the payer agreements that exist; the capitated payments that are coming in; revenue growth and profitability; and, probably the most important elements of all, market dynamics and competition—the company's market position and the strength of the competition. Last but not least, the rule of thumb is that a private company is worth between 30 and 60 percent of a comparable public company's overall market value.

Physician Organizations on an aggressive growth path must consider numerous elements to evaluate possible stock value. These include four major categories: (1) market capitalization and total market valuation; (2) earnings ratios (e.g., earnings per share, price earnings ratio, or earnings growth rate); (3) earnings before depreciation, interest, and taxes (EBDIT); and (4) other ratios such as value per member, profit margin, and return on equity and capital. The process of choosing a capital partner starts with a detailed business plan that outlines the goals, objectives, and financial projections for the Physician Organization over the next five years. Physician Organizations who invest the time and money to develop their own business plans will achieve higher valuations, greater influence, and more control, regardless of the exact source of capital. A good business plan is a sign of leadership.

STRATEGIC ALLIANCE DECISIONS

Physician leaders must educate themselves and their shareholding physician members about the financial issues surrounding the decision to take risk, expand a regional PPMC with minority partners, incur additional debt, or sell essentially all of the group practice assets to a public company. These are critical decisions with long-term implications. With a structured process in place to define goals, evaluate market conditions, and weigh various partners, the right decisions will be made to meet the needs of patients and to meet the market challenges.

The market forces that favor consolidation are leading to both vertical and horizontal integration. The purchase of Friendly Hills Healthcare Network, a primary care practice network, by Caremark, a diversified health care management company, is an example of vertical integration. The merger of Pacific Presbyterian Medical Center, a tertiary care and teaching hospital, with the primary care–oriented Children's Hospital to form California's Pacific is an example of horizontal integration. Regardless of the difference in approach, both types of integration have the same goal: to gain access to more patients and achieve economies of scale.

Physicians have received a large number of buyout offers from HMOs and health systems, which are seeking vertical integration. The HMOs want to acquire and employ physicians in order to create a captive delivery network and minimize costs, while the health systems want the physicians to fill beds in the short run and perhaps launch their own HMOs in the long run. These strategies are not necessarily appropriate, however, in light of marketplace trends. For example, the Business Healthcare Action Network, which is a group of 22 companies in the Minneapolis area, has reduced per employee health care costs to 33 percent below the national average and is now bypassing HMOs to negotiate directly with provider-based Integrated Delivery Systems. The network's rationale is that HMOs are spending too much on mergers and passing the expenses along in employers' premiums. Likewise, the overall trend of cutting health care costs would militate against physicians aligning themselves too closely with the hospitals' objective of filling beds. Thus, for good reason, physicians are beginning to say "no" to these types of buyout offers. Indeed, physicians are better off remaining independent and controlling their own destiny.

In selecting a source of capital and a potential alliance partner, physician leaders must compare their practice's internal criteria, values, and goals with those of the external source or partner. For long-term success, it is vitally important that these elements are similar. Factors to be aligned include the following:

- Culture and Values
- Clinical Standards
- Vision and Growth Strategy
- Patient Care Principles

The creation of a regional, physician-driven health care delivery system—whether private or publicly owned—is not achieved overnight. True integration depends on the merger of more than financial assets. It requires clinical, operational, and cultural integration. In summary, development of a successful Physician Organization and ambulatory delivery system depends on strong physician and executive leadership, a market-based vision, excellent business plan, and access to capital. The window of opportunity is open—and smart physician leaders will act now in a thoughtful and progressive manner.

NOTE

1. PPMC: Market, Financial and Operating Statistics for Physician Practice Management Companies, PPMC, August 1995, p. A.

Chapter 9

Legal Issues in Organizing and Expanding Physician Organizations

Philip B. Belcher, J.D., and S. Rogers Warner Jr., J.D.

INTRODUCTION

This chapter describes the legal documentation and the legal processes involved in developing various forms of Physician Organizations, such as Integrated Group Practices, Independent Practice Associations (IPAs), Management Services Organizations (MSOs), and physician-hospital joint ventures. It also describes the legal issues that are likely to arise during the planning and development of each form of organization. Each section describes the development and documentation process and the legal issues involved in the context of that process. This chapter is not intended to be an exhaustive analysis of the processes and issues discussed but, rather, a general description to prepare the reader to understand the methods and issues involved. This chapter does not constitute legal advice for any particular transaction. Parties planning transactions are encouraged to retain their own legal counsel to analyze the specific circumstances of the transaction.

INTEGRATED GROUP PRACTICE— MERGER OF MEDICAL GROUPS

The Integrated Group Practice is on the high end of the integration scale (see Figure 9–1). As such, it is one of the most desirable forms of Physician Organizations, because third-party payers generally prefer dealing with physician practices that can demonstrate the ability to implement quality assurance, utilization management, and administrative effectiveness. These measures often require the tight governance and financial and administrative capabilities only found in Integrated Group Practices. Note, however, that physician autonomy generally decreases as integration increases. Therefore, merging practices should not lose sight of governance and autonomy issues when planning and implementing any practice combination.

One way in which physician practices are formed and expanded is through a merger with one or more other physician practices. A merger of two practices may occur by one

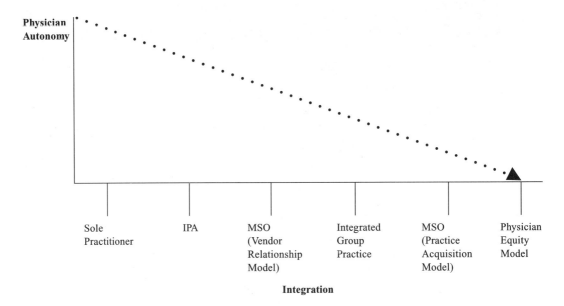

Figure 9–1 Integration and physician autonomy scale

practice merging into another existing practice or by two existing practices merging into a new entity formed by the two merging groups. In either scenario, in a true merger (as opposed to a purchase by one group of the assets of another), the merging corporation is completely subsumed into the surviving entity. At the effective time of the merger, the surviving entity owns all of the assets—as well as all of the liabilities—of the merging group or groups. The merging parties will encounter a variety of legal issues during the merger process, several of which are analyzed after the following brief discussion of the merger process itself.

Merger Documentation

Letter of Intent

A letter of intent is often signed at the outset of the merger process to indicate the parties' intent to negotiate a merger. The letter is a statement of the good faith intent of the parties to negotiate and consummate a merger, providing a foundation for additional negotiation. It sets forth the parties' general understanding of the terms of a proposed transaction and the constraints under which the parties are willing to negotiate. In addition to documenting the nature of the proposed transaction, the letter of intent often includes an agreement by the parties to maintain the confidentiality of information that may be shared by the parties as they determine whether to proceed with the merger. The letter of intent may also include provisions setting time limits on consummating the merger or for signing definitive agreements. Letters of intent often contain *lock-up* language. Lock-up provisions limit the ability of one or both parties to negotiate mergers or other significant transactions with third parties during a specific period of time.

Due Diligence Review

Prior to consummating a merger, it is essential that each party learn as much about the other as possible. The process by which the parties to a merger request and review information about each other is called *due diligence*. The importance of this review cannot be overstated, because the surviving entity in a merger will be responsible for all of the assets and liabilities of the merging entities. If, for example, one merging group does not disclose in the due diligence process that it has a significant unsatisfied professional malpractice judgment outstanding against it, and that its professional liability insurance coverage is inadequate to satisfy that judgment, the surviving entity in the merger could be liable for satisfying the judgment. The due diligence process usually begins when the parties exchange lists of information and documents that they and their attorneys or other advisors would like to review. The information provided in response to these inquiries often leads to additional questions and further requests for information. The information supplied ultimately will be used in the merger agreement itself, being incorporated into the disclosure schedules that supplement (and often contain the details of) the representations and warranties made by the merging parties in the merger agreement.

Organizational Documents

For purposes of this discussion, it is assumed that the parties intend to form a new organization into which two existing corporations will merge. (This course of action is often the most politically expedient and effective means of structuring a merger, because the aura of an "acquisition" may surround a transaction in which one group merges into another currently existing practice.) Several documents are required in order to establish the new entity (which will be referred to as *the medical group* for the remainder of this discussion). Also, a variety of structural forms may be used for this entity, each with its own documentation. For this discussion, a professional corporation will serve as the example. The same general principles apply in the organization and merger of other legal entities.

Articles of Incorporation. The principal organizational document for a corporation is the articles of incorporation. The articles set forth basic information about the corporation and are filed with the secretary of state or similar government body of the state in which the medical group is incorporated. The articles specify the number of shares that the corporation is authorized to issue. They may also list the initial directors of the new corporation and may include certain limits on the liability of directors. In circumstances in which the new corporation has more than one class of stock, the articles of incorporation may specify the rights and preferences of the holders of each class of stock. Each state has its own statutory requirements for the information required or permitted to be contained in the articles of incorporation.

Bylaws. The bylaws of the medical group contain the governance provisions of the new corporation. The bylaws provide, among other things, information concerning the size of the board of directors, the method of electing directors, and the matters upon which shareholders are required to vote. Bylaws may also contain provisions by which the corporation agrees to indemnify directors, officers, employees, or agents of the corporation against costs and expenses incurred in connection with litigation or other proceedings brought against such persons acting in their capacities as representatives of the corporation. Some states require some of this same information to be included in the articles of incorporation.

Shareholders' Agreement. The shareholders' agreement governs the relationship among the shareholders of the medical group and the medical group itself. In medical practices, the shareholders' agreement usually restricts the transfer of medical group stock so that the owners of the practice can maintain some measure of control over ownership of the practice. The nature and extent of such transfer restraints depends upon state law. The shareholders' agreement also discusses the specific events upon the occurrence of which a shareholder may be required to sell his or her stock back to the corporation and the method for determining the value of the stock. The price may be specified but is often described in a formula that is applied upon the occurrence of the event triggering the stock purchase by the medical group.

Physician Employment Agreement

The agreement used to govern the employment relationship between the medical group and a physician employee is often the most heavily negotiated agreement in the merger process. Physicians previously employed by the merging parties will have their own traditions and professional cultures—cultures that are not always easy to combine. Therefore, the parties should communicate their basic assumptions about the terms of physician employment early in the merger discussions. In addition to compensation—which is always important and has its own legal issues—covenants not to compete usually generate the most—and the most heated—discussion among the physicians to be employed by the medical group. Laws relating to the enforcement of such "noncompetes" vary from state to state. The employment agreement also may contain restrictions relating to confidentiality of information and solicitation of former patients.

Reorganization of Benefit Plans

One of the most complex parts of a merger is the reorganization of benefit plans that must occur when two or more entities merge. Decisions regarding the appropriate steps with respect to retirement plans are particularly crucial and require the advice of competent legal counsel with specific experience in medical group retirement benefits.

Merger Agreement

The merger agreement itself describes the transaction and those events that must occur prior to its consummation. The merger agreement explains the method for exchanging existing stock for stock in the new medical group. The merger agreement also contains the parties' representations and warranties concerning a broad spectrum of matters regarding the existing state of affairs of each merging group, including outstanding litigation, outstanding debt, benefit plans currently in existence, and compliance of those plans with relevant laws. The representations and warranties constitute the bulk of the merger agreement and are supplemented and further explained by the disclosure schedules attached to the agreement. As discussed above, the information contained in the disclosure schedules is derived from the due diligence investigation performed by each party to the merger. State law usually requires the parties to a merger to file with the secretary of state (or similar body) articles of merger containing a description of the basic merger terms. Significantly, articles of merger, like many other documents filed with the secretary of state, are available for public inspection.

Legal Issues

Tax

General Principles of Tax-Free Reorganizations. When two or more medical practices reorganize into a single integrated medical practice, the structure of the reorganization is likely to be dictated by tax considerations. The reorganization generally will be effected by transferring the stock or assets of the existing medical groups to an existing or a new medical group in exchange for stock in the existing or new group. The parties to the reorganization generally desire tax-free treatment of the reorganization. If the reorganization is not tax-free, the parties will be taxed as if they sold their stock or assets in their existing practices for cash. A fundamental principle of tax law is that unrealized (or not yet received) gain in property should be taxed only when the property is sold or otherwise disposed of. A corollary to this principle is that if a shareholder of a corporation exchanges his or her stock for stock in another corporation in connection with a merger of the corporations, the exchange should not be taxable because the shareholder is continuing the investment. These principles provide insight into the often intricate tax laws that guide the tax-free reorganizations described below.

Section 368(a)(1) of the Internal Revenue Code *(the Code)* describes a number of different structures for reorganizations that will receive tax-free treatment under the Code. Since in many states professional corporations cannot own stock in other professional corporations, and since physicians generally want equal ownership in their practices, only two of the tax-free structures are generally feasible for medical practice reorganizations: the Section 368(a)(1)(A) statutory merger (known as an *A reorganization*) and the Section 368(a)(1)(C) assets for stock reorganization (known as a *C reorganization*).

A Reorganizations. In an *A* reorganization, one group (the target) merges into another group (the acquirer) in a statutory merger (which is a merger accomplished according to the merger laws of the state in which the transaction takes place).[1] Target shareholders receive either acquirer stock or a combination of acquirer stock and other assets or cash in exchange for their target stock (see Figure 9–2). Pursuant to the merger, the target ceases to exist, and the acquirer succeeds to all rights and liabilities of the target, by operation of law.

In an *A* reorganization, target shareholders will not be taxed on the exchange of their stock for acquirer stock unless they receive nonstock assets, known as *boot*, in addition to the acquirer stock. If target shareholders do receive boot in addition to acquirer stock, they will be taxed only to the extent of the value of the boot. The only requirement for this tax-free treatment of the merger is that target shareholders have a "continuity of interest" in the acquirer. This requirement generally is not a problem in medical practice reorganizations where all target physicians will become equal shareholders in the acquirer and will continue as employees of the acquirer. The following is an example of the effects of an *A* reorganization:

> Practice *A* and Practice *B* decide to reorganize into a single corporation. Each practice has two shareholders, and the shareholders agree that Practice *A* will be merged into Practice *B*. The value of Practice *A*'s accounts receivable, furniture, fixtures, machinery, equipment, and other assets is $120,000, or $60,000 per shareholder. The value of Practice *B*'s accounts receivable, furniture, fixtures, machinery, equipment, and other assets is $100,000, or $50,000 per shareholder. Practice *A*'s shareholders own 100 shares of stock each, and Practice *B*'s shareholders own 200 shares of stock each.
>
> The parties effect a merger of the corporations under state law, and the merger provides that each shareholder of Practice *A* will receive, in exchange for each share of Practice *A* stock, two shares of Practice *B* stock and $100. So after the merger, each of the four shareholders of Practice *B* owns 200 shares of stock in Practice *B*. The former Practice *A* shareholders also received $10,000 in cash each. If the merger complies with the *A* reorganization rules, the merger is tax-free, except to the extent of cash received by the former Practice *A* shareholders.

Of course, more than one corporation can merge into the acquirer in a single transaction. If two or more practices decide to merge but cannot agree on which practice is to survive the merger, they can form a new corporation solely for the purpose of having each existing corporation merge into the new corporation. This option also may provide the additional benefit of avoiding the internal political turmoil that can arise when one group feels that it is being acquired by another group.

C Reorganizations. In a *C* reorganization, the target transfers its assets to the acquirer in exchange for stock in the acquirer. The tar-

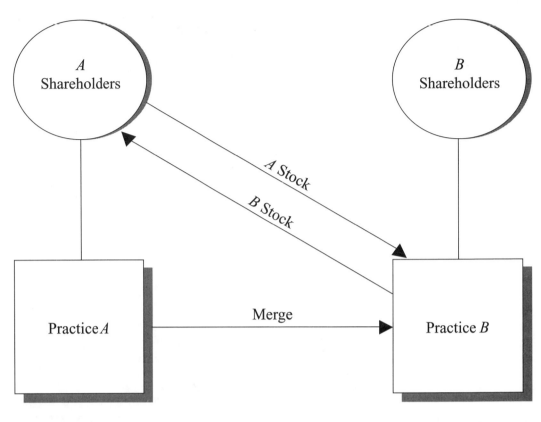

Figure 9–2 A reorganization

get then distributes the acquirer stock to its shareholders (see Figure 9–3). C reorganizations have more complicated rules in order to qualify for tax-free treatment. In a C reorganization, the target must transfer "substantially all" of its assets "solely in exchange for voting stock" of the acquirer.[2] The "solely for voting stock" rule is not, however, a literal requirement. The acquirer may transfer up to 20 percent nonstock assets, or boot, to target for its assets. Assumption of target liabilities by acquirer will not be treated as boot unless other boot is transferred by acquirer, but if any nonliability boot is transferred by acquirer then all assumed liabilities will be treated as boot.

The primary advantage of the C reorganization is that the acquirer will not necessarily assume the target's liabilities, as is the case in the A reorganization. Only specifically listed assets and liabilities of the target are transferred to the acquirer. This is important where an established medical practice desires to acquire a smaller practice but prefers not to assume the potential malpractice claims that may arise from events occurring prior to the transaction. On the other hand, the stricter requirements of the C reorganization make it difficult to effect in the medical practice context. The physicians who are parties to a reorganization generally desire to receive an equal amount of stock in the new medical practice formed in the reorganization. The value per shareholder of the different medical practices participating in a reorganization will, however, almost always differ; thus, it is difficult to issue the same amount of stock to all physicians participating in the reorganization without transferring boot to the physicians whose

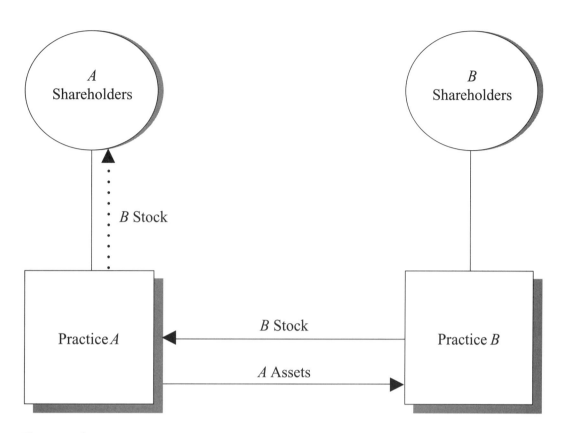

Figure 9–3 C reorganization

former practice is the most valuable. The following example illustrates this problem:

> Practice A and Practice B desire to reorganize into a single corporation. Each practice has two shareholders. The value of Practice A's accounts receivable, furniture, fixtures, machinery, equipment, and other assets is $150,000, or $75,000 per shareholder. The value of Practice B's accounts receivable, furniture, fixtures, machinery, equipment, and other assets is $100,000, or $50,000 per shareholder. Practice A's shareholders own 100 shares of stock each, and Practice B's shareholders own 100 shares of stock each. The parties decide to effect a C reorganization, in which Practice A transfers its assets to Practice B in exchange for Practice B stock.
>
> It would be unfair to the shareholders of Practice A if Practice A transferred its assets in exchange for 200 shares of Practice B's stock, because the result would be four equal shareholders of Practice B even though the former shareholders of Practice B would have invested less in the practice. On the other hand, if Practice B transfers $25,000 in cash to each of the Practice A shareholders as part of the transaction, the transaction will not qualify as a C reorganization because the transfer was not "solely in exchange for stock."

Medical practices are often creative in their attempt to satisfy the "solely in exchange for stock" requirement. For example, a practice might declare bonus compensation to each of its shareholders as an accrued compensation liability prior to a reorganization, and then transfer its assets and the compensation liability to the new corporation pursuant to the reorganization. The new corporation would then pay the accrued compensation liability as compensation over the next year after the transaction. It is uncertain, however, whether the Internal Revenue Service (IRS) would allow the characterization of the accrued liability as an assumed compensation liability to physicians rather than as boot to the shareholders.

Reorganization of Benefit Plans. Parties to a reorganization must determine the retirement and other benefit plans they wish to offer through the new organization, and then must determine how they will shift their existing plans, particularly pension plans with accrued assets, into the new plans. This transition will be affected, of course, by detailed and complex IRS rules relating to retirement plans, particularly in the area of nondiscrimination and the affiliated service group and controlled group rules. The following are three of the various options available for transition of retirement plans of the respective practices. The determination of which of the options is best for a particular reorganization will depend on many factors including the types of retirement plans involved (e.g., defined benefit or defined contribution), the types of assets in which the plans are invested, and whether the plans have been operated in accordance with applicable laws.

1. **Merger of existing plans.** One option is to merge the existing plans into a designated existing plan. The designated plan is adopted as the plan for the new group. Amendments to the plan are made in the course of the consolidation, as desired. This method is relatively easy to accomplish, but the new group takes on the risk that the new plan will be tainted if one of the former plans has not complied with relevant law.
2. **Termination of plans.** A second option is to terminate all of the old plans. The assets of the plans are distributed to employees, and the employees are given the option of rolling their assets into a new plan to be adopted by the new group. This eliminates the potential tainting problem described above, but it can be expensive (a new plan must be drafted and the administrative fee may be high) and will probably require IRS filings. Also, plan assets may not be liquid or may be subject to early termination penalties.
3. **Freezing existing plans.** A third option is to freeze existing plans (keep them in existence but make no further contributions) and draft a new plan for the new group. This option also eliminates problems with tainting the new plan with assets of existing plans. In addition, the illiquidity of assets of existing plans will not be a factor. On the other hand, either the old entities must remain in place in order for the plans to be frozen, so only a C reorganization is feasible or the new company would have to take over sponsorship and liability of the frozen plans. In the event the old entities remain to sponsor the frozen plans, the IRS may find that the old entities are not employers that can sponsor a plan, since they will have no employees. In this event, the new entity is left responsible for the frozen plans anyway. Finally, the old plans will still have to be amended periodically to comply with changing laws and will have to comply with all reporting and disclosure rules even though the plans are not receiving contributions, so this option can be cumbersome.

Antitrust

One of the most significant legal issues involved in the development of an Integrated Group Practice through a merger of medical groups is compliance with antitrust law. This discussion focuses on federal antitrust law, which is generally the blueprint for state antitrust law. Notwithstanding this focus, parties to any form of group combination should be aware that state attorneys general will enforce state antitrust laws and that health care transactions are not immune from scrutiny under state law.

The two federal agencies responsible for enforcement of federal antitrust law, the Antitrust Division of the U.S. Department of Justice and the Federal Trade Commission (together, the *agencies*), have become increasingly active in the health care arena as consolidation of the health care industry has quickened. Historically, most antitrust enforcement activity in health care has involved hospitals, but the same analysis used by the agencies to evaluate hospital transactions can be applied to physician group practice mergers.

Two federal antitrust statutes provide the statutory framework for this discussion. Mergers (and other transfers of ownership and control) may be challenged under Section 7 of the Clayton Act. This statute prohibits acquisitions where "the effect of such acquisition may be substantially to lessen competition, or to tend to create a monopoly."[3] Health care mergers may also be challenged under Section 1 of the Sherman Act, which prohibits joint action (including—but not limited to—mergers) that unreasonably restrain trade.[4]

A proposed merger, therefore, must be evaluated to determine whether it will substantially lessen competition within the meaning of Section 7 of the Clayton Act or unreasonably restrain trade within the meaning of Section 1 of the Sherman Act. The factors that influence these concepts are the product market, the geographic market, barriers to entry by other providers, efficiencies that might result from a proposed merger, and other market characteristics.

The product market and geographic market factors together determine the potential market power of the continued entity resulting from the merger. Determining market power is part law, part economics, and part creativity. The larger the product and geographic markets, the less power will be concentrated through a medical practice merger. For example, an antitrust issue is likely to exist where 60 percent of the orthopedists in a small geographic area combine their separate practices into a single, integrated orthopedic practice. Market analysis may include use of ZIP code lists from patient records, yellow pages advertising information, as well as numerical indices such as the Herfindahl-Hirschmann Index used in the agencies' merger guidelines.

In mergers of a sufficient size, premerger notification of the agencies may be required under Section 7A of the Clayton Act, also known as the Hart-Scott-Rodino Act.[5] The Hart-Scott-Rodino premerger notification program requires the parties contemplating a merger to notify the agencies. The Hart-Scott-Rodino Act specifies a waiting period prior to consummation of the merger and sets forth a system in which the agencies may inquire about the details of the merger. This statutory system, however, is not invoked for all mergers, only for those of a specified financial magnitude. Although most group practice mergers will not meet the relatively high financial thresholds triggering a Hart-Scott-Rodino filing, counsel should check the statute to ensure that a filing is not required, because the penalties for noncompliance are severe.

The Sherman Act forbids any agreement among competitors that has the effect of fixing prices. The price-fixing concern raised in the merger context is that competitive information may be shared in the due diligence process. Practically speaking, by virtue of the nature of a merger transaction, it is necessary for the parties to understand the way in which their future partner has operated its business, and financial projections for the new group may be based on assumptions concerning fees that will be charged for providing services. If the merger is consummated, the new group will set its fees at the amounts determined in accordance with its internal governance procedures. The problem occurs when parties have shared fee information, the merger is not consummated, and the postbreakup fees begin looking more similar than they did prior to the merger negotiations. Parties to a medical group merger should consider the following steps to help protect against an antitrust violation in the merger process:

- If the merger will combine a significant number of providers in a given market area, legal counsel should be consulted about the possible antitrust impact on the proposed transaction.
- At the initial stages of merger discussions—before the letter of intent is negotiated and before any due diligence information is exchanged—the parties should enter into a confidentiality agreement specifying, among other things, that in the event the transaction is not consummated, the parties will return all information received from the other parties during the merger negotiations.
- During the period between the initial conversations about the possibility of a merger and at least three months following the termination of merger discussions, no party should institute significant price changes, if any.

Securities

Securities laws are significant in many health care transactions, but they are frequently overlooked because their application to health care mergers is often not readily apparent. The definition of a *security* has been litigated frequently. In addition to stock and debt instruments, other types of investments and instruments may qualify as securities. For example, partnership interests, membership interests in limited liability companies, and stock in professional corporations, generally speaking, are all securities. Also qualifying as securities are other contracts or transactions in which a person invests money in a common enterprise and is led to expect profits from the efforts of others.[6]

Generally, any offer or sale of a security must either be registered with federal and state securities regulators or an exemption from state and federal registration must be found. Many practitioners will be surprised to learn that a practice merger involves the sale of a security. In a merger, the holders of the equity interests in a merging entity usually receive an equity interest in the entity that survives the merger. This exchange of one security for another constitutes a sale and must, therefore, be registered unless an exemption is found.

A variety of exemptions from registration may apply to mergers. At the federal level, the so-called intrastate exemption generally applies to offers or sales of securities made only to bona fide residents of a single state. Other federal exemptions requiring only notice filings with the Securities and Exchange Commission may apply, depending upon the value of the securities being issued.

On the state level, a variety of exemptions also exists. These exemptions vary, sometimes significantly, from state to state. For example, some states allow exemptions from registration of stock in professional corporations. Also, state securities laws (often called *blue sky laws*) often contain a small offering exemption, exempting from registration offerings to a specified maximum number of offerees. (Note that the critical number under this exemption usually is the number of offers made rather than the number of offers accepted, and that the number of allowable offers varies from state to state). A determination of whether the merger will require securities registration should always be made early in the process of determining the structure of the transaction.

Anti-Referral (Stark Law)

General Prohibitions on Self-Referrals. Effective January 1, 1992, Congress passed a law prohibiting referrals by physicians for Medicare-reimbursable clinical laboratory services to labs with which the physician has a financial relationship. The law defines a financial relationship as either an ownership (or investment) interest or a compensation arrangement. This law, commonly referred to as the Stark law, was expanded effective January 1, 1995 to include Medicaid-reimbursable services and to prohibit such referrals for the following "designated health services":

- clinical laboratory services
- physical therapy services
- occupational therapy services
- radiology or other diagnostic services
- radiation therapy services
- durable medical equipment
- parenteral and enteral nutrients, equipment, and supplies
- prosthetics, orthotics, and prosthetic devices
- home health services
- outpatient prescription drugs
- inpatient and outpatient hospital services[7]

The broad proscriptions of the Stark law are tempered by a number of exceptions. Unlike the fraud and abuse safe harbors, however, proscribed activity that fails to fit within an exception is automatically deemed illegal.

Stark Concerns in the Reorganization Context. In the medical practice reorganization context, the primary Stark law concerns are (1) that the other parties to the reorganization are in compliance with the Stark law, and (2) that the surviving entity will meet the same Stark exceptions as those on which the former practices relied to allow certain referrals. The first concern should be allayed by a thorough due diligence review of each participant in the reorganization. If any noncompliance with the Stark law is discovered, it should be remedied prior to the reorganization, and the other parties should be indemnified against any Stark-related liabilities. The second concern requires structural planning for the new practice. An Integrated Group Practice will generally have income from "designated health services," and so will need to meet one of the exceptions to the Stark law so that the physicians in the practice can maintain that income source. Although the law includes a number of exceptions, only a few apply in the Integrated Group Practice context.

Stark Law Exceptions. With respect to medical practice reorganizations, the primary exceptions to the Stark law prohibitions are the "physician services" exception and the "in-office ancillary services" exception, each of which applies to both ownership and compensation arrangements. The "physician services" exception provides that the Stark proscriptions will not apply in the case of referrals for physician services that are provided personally by or under the personal supervision of another physician in the same "group practice" as the referring physician.[8] This exception allows the group to bill for physicians' services provided in conjunction with ancillary services, so long as the group qualifies as a group practice (see discussion below).

The "in-office ancillary services" exception applies to referrals for services provided personally by the referring physician or another physician in the group practice, or directly supervised by the referring physician or another physician in the group practice, if the services are (1) furnished either in a building in which physicians in the group furnish physicians' services unrelated to designated health services, or in another building used by the group practice for the provision of some or all of the group's clinical lab services or for the centralized provision of the group's designated health services other than clinical lab services, and (2) billed by the physician performing or supervising the services, by a group practice of which the physician is a member under a billing number assigned to the group practice, or by an entity that is wholly owned by such physician or group practice.[9]

The two exceptions described above will generally be necessary for the newly reorganized medical practice to provide "designated health services" without violating the Stark law. Consequently, the new group must meet the definition of "group practice" under the law. The Stark law defines a "group practice" as a group of two or more physicians legally organized as a partnership, professional corporation, foundation, not-for-profit corporation, faculty practice plan, or similar association in which (1) each member physician provides substantially the full range of services that the physician routinely provides through the joint use of shared office space, facilities, equipment, and personnel; (2) substantially all of the services of the physician members are provided through the group, billed in the name of the group, and treated as receipts of the group; (3) overhead and income of the group are distributed in accordance with methods previously determined; (4) no less than 75 percent of physician-patient encounters of the group are personally conducted by group members; and (5) no physician member receives compensation directly or indirectly based on the volume or value of referrals by the physician.[10]

Two aspects of this definition are likely to become important in the reorganization context. First, the definition requires that physicians in the new group provide their services through the joint use of shared office space, facilities, equipment, and personnel. This language dictates that, for Stark law purposes, a reorganization must truly integrate the constituent medical practices. The parties must be careful if they intend merely to organize as a "group practice without walls"; if they do not share their facilities and overhead expenses in some combined entity, they may not qualify as a group practice for Stark purposes.

Second, physician compensation in the new group cannot be based on the volume or value of referrals, either directly or indirectly. The new group must understand that it will not be able to divide ancillary income pools based on referrals and will have to structure its compensation system accordingly. This can be difficult where a practice participating in the reorganization offers certain ancillary services that it will continue to offer—and expects to retain the income—in the new group. The Stark law does allow groups to divide ancillary income based on predetermined methods. One method that can be used effectively is to divide ancillary income according to productivity based on services personally provided by the physicians. This method is specifically allowed by the law.[11] Another method is to distribute ancillary income based on a predetermined formula. Of course, the more the predetermined formula resembles actual ordering patterns, the more likely it will be found to be related to volume or value of referrals and, therefore, not qualify for the exception.

INDEPENDENT PRACTICE ASSOCIATION

Description of Process/Legal Documents

Form of Entity

An Independent Practice Association, or IPA, is a group of separate medical practices or individual physicians that have organized a new entity through which they can offer their services to managed care entities under one contract. IPA participants do not merge their respective medical practices into one entity; rather, their medical practices remain separate, and participants are bound contractually to provide medical services through the IPA. Initially, the parties must decide on the legal structure for the IPA. The IPA generally will be structured as a professional corporation, a limited liability company, or a nonprofit corporation, depending on relevant state laws and regulations and personal preferences of the parties.

Professional Corporation. The professional corporation form of organization is generally familiar to IPA participants because it is often the form of organization of their own practices (see Figure 9–4). The professional corporation structure offers limited liability to shareholders, but may also involve certain restrictions with respect to ownership rights. Most states require that a professional corporation can only engage in the activity for which its shareholders are licensed. Also, all shareholders of the professional corporation generally must be licensed in the activity for which the corporation is formed. For instance, in most states a medical professional corporation can only engage in the practice of medicine and in activities related to the practice of medicine, and the shareholders of the corporation must be licensed to practice medicine. In those states, only individual physicians can participate in an IPA organized as a professional corporation. Also, state law should be reviewed to determine whether the activities of the IPA would be authorized activities of a medical professional corporation, because the function of the IPA is to arrange for services to be provided by its participating providers under managed care agreements (not necessarily to provide those services itself). On the other hand, the professional corporation structure may be advantageous due to state securities registration exemptions for professional corporations (see securities discussion below).

Limited Liability Company. The limited liability company (LLC) is a relatively new entity that has become a popular form of organization for certain types of businesses. Members of the LLC receive limited liabil-

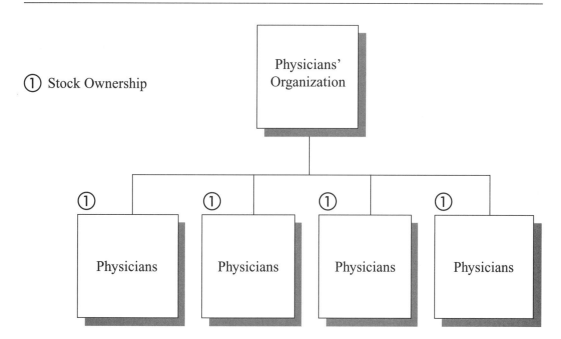

Basic organizational details:
- IPA is a professional corporation.
- Shareholders are physicians licensed to practice medicine in the state of organization.
- Individual physicians in a medical group may have the option, or may be required, to become shareholders of the IPA.
- Stock is sold pursuant to a registration statement or an exemption from registration.
- Shareholders execute a shareholders' agreement restricting transfer of shares and allowing IPA to repurchase shares upon the occurrence of certain events.

Figure 9–4 Independent Practice Association (IPA) ownership (professional corporation)

ity like shareholders of a corporation, and the profits of a properly organized LLC are not taxed at the entity level but only at the member level, like a partnership. It is important to remember, however, that an IPA is generally not intended to be a profit-making entity but rather a means for physicians to maintain their patients and position themselves for new patients by participating in managed care arrangements. Often, fees earned through participation in the IPA network are paid by the managed care entity directly to the physician, so there is no income and no profit at the IPA entity level to be taxed.

If the LLC does not provide any benefits from a tax perspective, then there is no reason to choose the LLC form of organization over the corporate form. The corporate form is often more familiar to the participants, less complicated to operate, and less expensive to organize than an LLC. On the other hand, if the IPA intends to engage in more sophisticated arrangements such that the IPA could earn a profit and build equity value, the LLC may be the preferable form of organization.

Nonprofit Corporation. Nonprofit corporations are generally organized much like general business corporations, but they are usually restricted under state law from distributing profits to owners. The organizers of nonprofit corporations are referred to as members rather than shareholders, since the organizers cannot receive profits in the form of dividends. Because the IPA generally is not a profit-making entity, the nonprofit corporation offers a feasible alternative form of organization. A nonprofit corporation operates much the same as a general business corporation, with a board of directors and with bylaws setting forth the governance provisions of the organization, so often it is familiar to physicians. The nonprofit organization may be beneficial from a securities registration standpoint, because the nonprofit membership may not be considered a security (which, if offered, must be registered under state law).

Organization of the IPA

After the parties choose the appropriate structure, they organize the entity and offer physicians the opportunity to participate. Organization of either an LLC or a corporation is effected by filing organizational documents with the secretary of state. The next step is adopting a governance structure for the organization. In the case of an LLC, the members of the LLC sign an operating agreement providing terms of governance and rights of members. In the case of a corporation, the organizers adopt bylaws to control governance. The entity generally should have a small governing board that makes decisions on behalf of the IPA. The cost of joining the IPA should be based on the projected budget for the IPA and the number of expected IPA participants.

IPAs generally offer physicians an opportunity to participate in the IPA by sending an application packet to interested physicians. The application packet should contain (1) an application, which can resemble the application for medical staff privileges at a hospital; (2) the organizational documents of the IPA (for an LLC, the operating agreement and articles of organization; for a corporation, the bylaws and articles of incorporation); (3) a subscription agreement or similar document in which the participant makes certain representations and warranties to ensure compliance with securities laws; and (4) the network participation agreement (discussed below).

The IPA should require that the application packet be returned with a signed subscription agreement and network participation agreement and a completed application, together with a check for the purchase price of stock or for the membership fee, if any. The organizers of the IPA can review the applications and apply objective membership criteria to determine who will be accepted into the network, or it can accept all applications. Once the IPA organization is completed, the IPA can begin negotiating managed care contracts on behalf of its members. Such negotiations, however, are subject to the antitrust laws discussed below.

Network Participation Agreement

The physicians participating in an IPA commit themselves to provide medical services under contracts negotiated by the IPA. This commitment is accomplished by having each physician sign a network participation agreement. The network participation agreement is the agreement of each participating physician to provide his or her services pursuant to the terms of an agreement negotiated by the IPA (often referred to as a payer agreement because it is negotiated between the IPA and the payer for medical services, such as an insurance company). The strength of an IPA lies in its ability to promise a certain number of physicians to provide services to enrollees in a payer's health plan. The IPA, therefore, will be more attractive to payers if the network participation agreement requires all physicians to provide their services under payer agreements negotiated by the IPA, rather than allowing physicians to opt-in or opt-out of particular payer agreements on a case-by-case basis. Payers will be much less interested in negotiating with an IPA if they cannot determine at the time they sign the contract with the IPA which network physicians will be bound by the contract.

The network participation agreement should require each participating physician to comply with utilization management programs, quality assurance programs, and rules and regulations adopted by the IPA. This requirement will allow the IPA flexibility in developing such programs and in working with managed care entities to implement them. The board of directors of the IPA can appoint committees of physicians to assist in development and implementation of such programs intended to manage the care provided by network providers. Two other important provisions of the network participation agreement are the pricing provisions, which describe the method of negotiating prices by the IPA with payers, and the exclusivity clause, if any, which determines whether and the extent to which participants can participate in other managed care contracting networks. These provisions have antitrust implications and are subject to the following antitrust discussion.

Legal Issues

Antitrust

Analysis of antitrust issues in the IPA context is set forth in the 1994 Statements of Enforcement Policy and Analytical Principles Relating to Health Care and Antitrust issued by the U.S. Department of Justice and the Federal Trade Commission (the Antitrust Statements). The Antitrust Statements expand upon earlier guidance published in 1993 and address, among other topics, physician network joint ventures (the Physician Network Statement). The Physician Network Statement defines a physician network joint venture as a "physician-controlled venture in which the member physicians collectively agree on prices or other significant terms of competition and jointly market their services."

The Antitrust Statements set forth antitrust safety zones for certain described activities. The U.S. Department of Justice and the Federal Trade Commission (*the agencies*) will not challenge, in the absence of extraordinary circumstances, activity that falls within the safety zone. The Physician Network Statement contains two safety zones, one for exclusive physician network joint ventures and one for nonexclusive physician network joint ventures.

The exclusive physician network joint venture safety zone applies to exclusive physician network joint ventures "comprising 20 percent or less of the physicians in each physician specialty with active hospital staff privileges who practice in the relevant geographic market and share substantial financial risk." Additional flexibility is afforded exclusive physician network joint ventures in markets with fewer than five physicians in a particular specialty.

The nonexclusive physician network joint venture safety zone applies to nonexclusive physician network joint ventures "comprising 30 percent or less of the physicians in each physician specialty with active hospital staff privileges who practice in the relevant geographic market and share substantial financial risk." The agencies allow additional flexibility in this nonexclusive category to physician network joint ventures in markets with fewer than four physicians in a particular specialty.

The Physician Network Statement cautions that, because of the different thresholds in exclusive and nonexclusive networks, the parties to the network must ensure that the network is nonexclusive in fact, and not just in name. In other words, if the IPA documents proclaim that the network is nonexclusive but the participants agree by a wink and a nod that the IPA will be the only avenue for access to managed care contracts for the participating physicians, the agencies will pierce the veil of nonexclusivity and analyze the IPA under the safety zone for exclusive physician network joint ventures. The agencies consider the following characteristics to be indications of nonexclusivity:

- Viable competing networks or plans with adequate provider participation currently exist in the market.
- Providers in the network actually participate in other networks or contract individually with health benefit plans, or there is other evidence of their willingness and incentive to do so.
- Providers in the network earn substantial revenue outside the network.
- There is an absence of any indications of significant departicipation from other networks in the market.
- There is an absence of any indications of coordination among the providers in the network regarding price or other competitively significant terms of participation in other networks or plans.

The more difficult issue in satisfying either safety zone is the requirement that the network physicians share substantial financial risk. What constitutes sufficient risk is a matter of significant discussion among lawyers who participate in developing IPAs and other physician network joint ventures. The Physician Network Statement lists two examples of physicians' sharing financial risk sufficient to satisfy the physician network joint venture safety zones:

1. when the venture agrees to provide services to a health benefits plan at a capitated rate (defined as a fixed, predetermined payment per covered life from a health benefits plan to the joint venture in exchange for the joint venture's providing and guaranteeing provision of a defined set of covered services to covered individuals for a specified period of time, regardless of the amount of services actually provided)
2. when the venture creates significant financial incentives for its members as a group to achieve specified cost containment goals, such as withholding from all members a substantial amount of the compensation due to them, with distribution of that amount to the members only if the cost containment goals are met

The Physician Network Statement, however, leaves the door open for other unspecified forms of "economic integration that amount to the sharing of substantial financial risk; the enumeration of the two examples above is not meant to foreclose the possibility that substantial financial risk can be shared in other ways."[12]

One additional point should be made concerning the required financial risk. IPA participants and their counsel must determine whether the risk incorporated into the IPA structure to satisfy the agencies might also constitute insurance risk under the laws of the state governing the transaction. For example, in some states, it is deemed insurance risk to accept capitation directly from an employer. Acceptance of insurance risk may implicate state insurance regulations. See the discussion below concerning the impact of insurance regulation on IPA formation.

If the safety zone requirements seem daunting, it is important to remember that IPAs that do not satisfy the safety zone criteria are not necessarily illegal. Rather, the agencies will examine them under a "rule of reason" analysis either if the physicians share substantial financial risk or if the joint venture offers a new product with substantial efficiencies. A rule of reason analysis "determines whether the joint venture may have a substantial anticompetitive effect and, if so, whether that potential effect is outweighed by any procompetitive efficiencies resulting from the joint venture . . . [It] takes into account all characteristics of the particular physician network joint venture that bear on its likely effect on competition.[13] The rule of reason analysis entails a determination of the relevant market, an evaluation of the competitive effects of the physician joint venture, an evaluation of the impact of procompetitive efficiencies, and an examination of any collateral agreements or conditions that unreasonably restrict competition and are unlikely to contribute significantly to the legitimate purposes of the network.

Securities Regulation

IPA formation often involves issuing an equity interest in the IPA to a significant number of providers, often exceeding the number of investors allowed under the limited offering exemption described earlier in the chapter. At the federal level, the intrastate exemption or an exemption based on certain maximum financial limits may still apply, but finding a state exemption may prove difficult. Some states, as mentioned above in the merger discussion, are exempt from registration offerings of stock of professional corporations. That is not the case, however, in all states. In some states, registration may be required unless the IPA can convince the state regulators that, in light of the particular characteristics of the IPA interests, the IPA interests are not securities. Although this strategy is not always successful, it may be worthwhile to consider it when compared to the costs of registering an offering.

Registration requires, among other things, filing a registration statement with the relevant regulatory body. Because federal exemptions are usually available, state registration is generally the larger concern. A registration statement contains detailed information about the security to be offered and contains a prospectus, or an offering document, which contains a variety of information about the issuer, its business plan, the risks involved in investing in the IPA, and other pertinent information relevant to potential purchasers. The legal and accounting expenses and the time involved in preparing a registration statement make it important at the early stages of IPA development to determine whether registration is going to be required. A registration may significantly impact the development of the IPA, by affecting choices concerning the cost of the buy-in among other things—which may be used to finance the registration costs—and the timing of the offering.

Registration requirements vary from state to state. Some states provide simplified filing procedures for small offerings. Others require compliance with a more detailed and more onerous registration process.

Insurance Regulation

As a result of the antitrust laws regarding joint price negotiation, described above, IPAs often want to contract with self-insured employers or other payers on a risk basis under which network physicians provide services for a capitated fee, or on a fee-for-service basis with a significant withholding of the fees. IPAs are often caught in a legal whipsaw, however, because although the antitrust laws encourage such shared risk arrangements in order to allow joint price negotiation, state insurance laws often prohibit shifting of risk to physicians unless a "regulated entity" is involved in the arrangement. A regulated entity is an entity that has been authorized by a state department of insurance to engage in transactions involving insurance risk, such as an HMO. Insurance risk in the health care context is the risk associated with the cost of health care coverage for a given population. State departments of insurance want to regulate such insurance risk to prevent innocent consumers from being left unable to receive services because of the inability of a plan to pay for the services. For this reason, state laws generally require HMOs to maintain certain financial reserves and to meet minimum net worth requirements (for example, in North Carolina the HMO statutes require a minimum net worth of $1 million and a deposit of $500,000, in addition to other financial requirements[14].) Most IPAs are unable to meet these requirements, do not wish to operate as HMOs, and are therefore unable to accept risk. However, state departments of insurance generally allow IPAs to contract with regulated entities (such as HMOs) to accept risk, because in such a situation the department of insurance regulates at least one of the entities involved in the arrangement. This situation can be frustrating because it can have the effect of driving up the cost of health care by requiring a third party to participate as an intermediary in the enrollee-physician-payer relationship.

Even if the IPA is not an HMO, it may be subject to regulation by the state's department of insurance. Many states regulate IPAs as Preferred Provider Organizations (PPOs). In some states, PPOs are merely required to register with the department of insurance.[15] In other states, registration may require the filing of network participation agreements and organizational documents for insurance department review.[16]

At their 1995 annual meeting, the State Commissioners of Insurance discussed state regulation of IPAs and Physician-Hospital Organizations (PHOs), especially with respect to risk arrangements proposed to be entered into by such entities. The purpose of the discussions was to determine whether some form of regulation is desirable to meet the needs of the health care industry in response to the new forms of provider organizations being developed across the country. No standard form of regulation exists at this time, but proposals for uniform state insurance regulation of IPAs and PHOs may come about in the near future.

Other State Regulatory Restrictions

IPA organizers must be careful to determine whether any other specific state laws regulate their proposed organization. As managed care has become more prevalent, state legislatures have become more involved in regulating managed care relationships. Regulation may take the form of mere registration requirements, as described above, or may actually restrict the functions of the IPA. For example, New York IPAs must first file their certificates of incorporation for approval with the Education Department before they are filed with the Department of State, and New York regulations prohibit any IPA from contracting with more than one HMO.[17] Since such statutory or regulatory restrictions may significantly affect the operations of the IPA, the IPA organizers must be aware of such restrictions prior to beginning operations.

OTHER AFFILIATIONS

Management Services Organization

Description of Process/Legal Documents

Introduction. Many medical groups considering how best to participate in the transformation of the health care delivery system enter into a relationship with a Management Services Organization (MSO). MSO relationships fall within a broad range on the integration spectrum, from a simple vendor relationship (see Figure 9-5), in which the medical group purchases discrete management services from the MSO, to a more integrated approach involving the sale of medical group assets and the purchase by the medical group of comprehensive management services from the MSO. The MSO relationship is often attractive to physicians because it keeps the medical group intact, does not require the physicians to be employed by the MSO, and puts the MSO in a management relationship, rather than an ownership position, with the medical practice. The level of integration in a management services relationship is not as comprehensive as some other hospital joint venture models and, for this reason, it satisfies physician autonomy needs; it allows physicians to retain control over medical group ownership, governance, and employment relationships. MSOs can provide access to a managed care

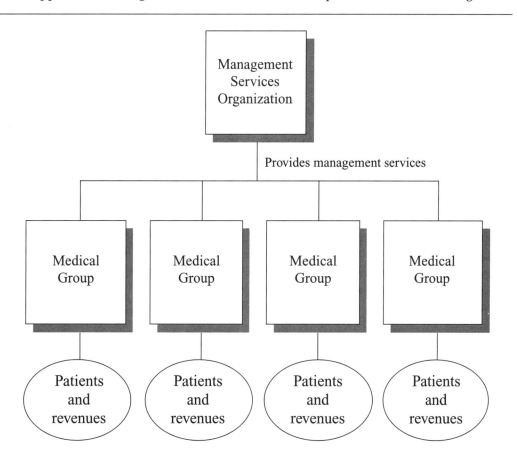

Figure 9-5 Management Services Organization

network, managed care negotiating expertise, and access to capital for future growth and operations, thereby meeting the common capital needs of medical groups without having to obtain funds by reducing physician income.

MSO affiliations involving the sale by a group practice to the MSO of all or substantially all of the group's assets afford a convenient method for purchasing much of the physicians' equity in the practice, thereby reducing the amount of the buy-in for new physicians. The MSO asset purchase also may provide an opportunity for physicians to unload substantial debt incurred in building their practice and to shift to experienced business people the responsibility for managing the assets and finances of the medical group, freeing the physicians to focus on the clinical aspects of the medical practice.

Documentation. Consummating an MSO relationship often consists of three separate but related events. First, the MSO must be organized. Second, the MSO may purchase the assets of a medical group and assume certain of its liabilities. Third, the medical group and the MSO will enter into a management agreement governing the management of the medical group by the MSO.

1. **MSO organization.** The basic organizational documents are similar to those described above in connection with the merger discussion.
2. **Asset purchase agreement.** If the MSO purchases the assets of the medical group, the parties negotiate and execute an asset purchase agreement. An asset purchase agreement is similar in many respects to a merger agreement entered into by parties merging into a new group practice, as described above. The primary difference between a merger and an asset purchase is that, in a merger, all of the assets and liabilities of the merging corporation are merged into the surviving corporation by operation of law. In an asset purchase, the purchaser seeks to protect itself from unknown liabilities by specifying in the asset purchase agreement the particular assets and liabilities that it is willing to purchase and assume, respectively. The reliability of this protection varies from state to state, however, as courts in some states are willing to invoke the doctrine of successor liability where a buyer purchases a going business concern. In that situation, the purchaser may find itself saddled with the acquired party's liabilities, much like the surviving entity in a medical group merger. In any event, the asset purchase agreement includes representations and warranties concerning the assets and liabilities purchased and assumed, the purchase price and how it will be paid, and indemnification provisions protecting the parties in the event the other party's representations and warranties are untrue.
3. **Management agreement.** The management agreement specifies how the MSO relates to the medical group, the services the MSO provides, and the governance mechanism by which a business partnership is created between the medical group and the MSO. It describes the duties of each party to the management relationship and how the MSO will be compensated for its services. In essence, the medical group generates revenues and pays a management fee to the MSO for its services. The method for determining the management fee is often the most complex part of negotiating the management agreement. Fee arrangements usually include some variation of either a set fee or a fee based on a percentage of revenues or net income, in each case based on the fair market value of services by the MSO.

Legal Issues

Fraud and Abuse. A legal issue that inevitably must be examined in an MSO affiliation is the applicability of federal and state antikickback statutes. Although the discussion in this section focuses on the federal regulatory scheme, parties to MSO relationships should also examine with care state law and regulations addressing the same subject. To highlight the potential fraud and abuse concerns that may arise in an MSO relationship, the following discussion assumes that the MSO is funded or owned, at least in part, by a hospital (which is often the case).

The federal antikickback statute states that:

1. whoever knowingly and willing solicits or receives any remuneration (including any kickback, bribe, or rebate) directly or indirectly, overtly or covertly, in cash or in kind—
    A. in return for referring an individual to a person for the furnishing or arranging for the furnishing of any item or service for which payment may be made in whole or in part under subchapter XVIII of this chapter or a State health care program, or
    B. in return for purchasing, leasing, ordering, or arranging for or recommending purchasing, leasing, or ordering any good, facility, service, or item for which payment may be made in whole or in part under subchapter XVIII of this chapter or a State health care program,

   shall be guilty of a felony and upon conviction thereof, shall be fined not more than $25,000 or imprisoned for not more than five years, or both.[18]

The statute also prohibits offers to pay for referrals.

Parties to an MSO relationship should think critically when analyzing the terms of the relationship and attempt to view the transaction in the same way as would a government representative attempting to find a violation of the antikickback laws in the relationship between the medical group and the MSO. They should ask themselves whether any part of the relationship appears as though the hospital is paying, in any manner, directly or indirectly, for referrals by the physicians in the medical group.

The parties should make sure that the asset purchase price is at fair market value. If the MSO purchases the physicians' practice for greater than fair market value, a regulator may be prompted to ask what was purchased by the excess payment. One answer is that the excess payment was for referrals by the physicians to the hospital. Therefore, an independent valuation of the practice is essential.

The other situation in which the antikickback laws are implicated is in the determination of the management fee to be paid to the MSO. If the MSO charges too little for the services provided, including management services and use of equipment and space, the physicians get a better financial deal than they would under a fair market approach to setting the management fee. Again the question is whether the hospital, through the MSO, is paying for referrals from the physicians.

In conjunction with the Medicare and Medicaid Patient and Program Protection Act of 1987, Congress requires that regulations be issued that specify various payment practices that would not be considered a violation of the Fraud and Abuse Act. Final regulations, since revised, were issued in

1991, setting out a series of safe harbors. To the extent that a health care provider or business falls within one of the enumerated safe harbors, the compensation involved in the activity in question will not be deemed "remuneration" under the Fraud and Abuse Act. It is important to remember that activity falling outside of the safe harbors is not necessarily illegal; it simply does not enjoy the protection afforded by the safe harbors.

The safe harbor most relevant in the MSO context is the safe harbor for personal services and management contracts. Under this safe harbor, remuneration does not include any payment made by the medical group to the MSO as long as all of the following criteria are met:

- The management agreement is set out in writing and signed by the parties.
- The management agreement specifies the services to be provided by the MSO.
- If the management agreement is intended to provide for the services of the MSO on a periodic, sporadic, or part-time basis, rather than on a full-time basis for the term of the agreement, the agreement specifies exactly the schedule of such intervals, their precise length, and the exact charge for such intervals.
- The term of the agreement is for not less than one year.
- The aggregate compensation paid to the agent over the term of the agreement is set in advance, is consistent with fair market value in arms-length transactions, and is not determined in a manner that takes into account the volume or value of any referrals or business otherwise generated between the parties for which payment may be made in whole or in part under Medicare or a state health care program.
- The services performed under the agreement do not involve the counseling or promotion of a business arrangement or other activity that violates any state or federal law.[19]

Anti-Referral (Stark Law). The Stark law, described above, may be implicated in the MSO context because the structure of the group practice changes under the MSO model. The parties must structure the MSO so that the medical group can continue to meet the "in-office ancillaries" exception for its provision of designated health services.

As described above, the in-office ancillaries exception requires that services be furnished "personally by the referring physician, personally by a physician who is a member of the same group practice as the referring physician, or personally by individuals who are directly supervised by the physician or by another physician in the group practice."[20] The services must be performed in a building in which the referring physician (or another physician who is a member of the same group practice) furnishes physicians' services unrelated to the furnishing of designated health services, or in another building that is used by the group practice for (1) the provision of some or all of the group's clinical lab services or (2) for the centralized provision of the group's designated health services other than clinical lab services.[21] Based on this language, the MSO cannot operate ancillaries by employing technical personnel who will not be supervised by the group practice physicians in an office of the group practice. The MSO management agreement must provide that the medical group will maintain responsibility for supervising technical personnel and must not segregate the ancillaries away from the physicians.

Joint Ownership of Medical Group by Physicians and Hospital

Description of Process/Legal Documents

Introduction. Although fully integrated health care delivery systems in which hospitals own the medical practices and employ the physicians have become more common in response to market-driven reform in the health care industry, many physicians are reluctant to part completely with the autonomy they enjoy as owners of their practices. Physicians often prefer to maintain an ownership interest in the health care system of which their services are a key component. As a result, some joint venture organizations are being developed in which both the hospital and the physicians maintain an ownership interest.

Choice of Entity. Because physicians often want to maintain a stake in the equity of the joint venture organization, with the intent of sharing in the profitability of the entity, it is often desirable to use a tax-advantaged form of organization. The LLC is generally preferable because it is a flexible vehicle that will allow profits of the entity to be passed through to owners without an entity-level tax. The existing medical practice may want to transfer its assets into a physician-owned LLC (*the physicians' LLC*), which will be the physician ownership vehicle in the LLC owned jointly with the hospital (*the joint venture LLC*). This LLC ownership structure will provide flexibility and tax advantages to physicians who join the LLC in the future (see Figure 9–6).

Physician Contribution. The physicians' LLC acquires the hard assets of the medical group pursuant to an asset purchase agreement. In addition, the physicians each execute an employment agreement with the physicians' LLC, which includes a restrictive covenant limiting the physicians' ability to compete with the physicians' LLC or its successor, in the event of termination of employment. The physicians' LLC will then transfer its assets and assign its employment agreements to the joint venture LLC pursuant to an asset purchase agreement, in exchange for a membership interest in the joint venture LLC.

Hospital Contribution. The hospital pays cash or an obligation in the form of a note in exchange for a membership interest in the joint venture LLC. The contribution of the hospital is based on the value of the assets and employment agreements contributed by the physicians' LLC. This hospital contribution funds operating expenses and capital expenditures, if desired, by the joint venture LLC.

Joint Venture LLC Operating Agreement. The hospital and physicians' LLC execute an operating agreement that specifies the terms of governance and ownership in the joint venture LLC. The joint venture LLC is governed by a board of managers, on which the hospital and the physicians generally have equal representation and an equal vote (assuming they contribute an equal amount of value to the LLC). The board of managers has authority over day-to-day governance of the LLC, including decisions relating to compensation and capital expenditures.

Although the process for creation of a physician-hospital joint venture has similarities to the acquisition of a physician practice by a hospital, the legal issues are even more complex due to the physicians' participation in the ownership and governance of the new entity. These issues are summarized below.

Legal Issues

Tax-Exempt Status

1. *General background.* If the hospital participating in the transaction is tax-exempt under federal law, one of the hospital's primary concerns in a joint venture with physicians is that the transaction not jeopardize its tax-exempt status. Under federal tax laws applicable to tax-exempt organizations, no part of the income of a tax-exempt hospital may inure to the benefit of private individuals.[22] For this reason, the hospital must be careful that amounts contributed by the hospital to the joint venture are not considered to benefit private interests. The contribution of the hospital must therefore be equivalent to the value in the venture that the

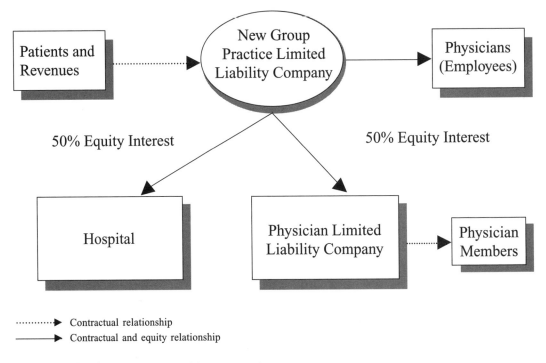

Figure 9–6 The physician equity model group practice

hospital receives in return. The value of the venture will depend on the value of the physicians' LLC contribution to the venture. For instance, if the physician practice is valued at $5 million and each party will have a 50 percent interest in the entity, then the hospital must not contribute more than $5 million to the venture. If the hospital contributes $6 million in those circumstances, the excess contribution likely would be construed as inuring to the benefit of private individuals in contravention of the hospital's tax-exempt status. For the same reason, the system for distributing income of the entity, and the compensation system for physicians employed by the entity, must not allow excess income to inure to the physicians participating in the venture. If distributed to the members, profits of the entity must be distributed based on the ownership interests of the parties. Physician compensation must be reasonable under IRS rules—generally based on compensation figures for physicians practicing in similar practice areas in similar regions of the country.

2. *Valuation of medical group.* Since the hospital's contribution is limited based on the value of the physician's contribution, the method of valuation of the physicians' practice will be important to the hospital and must comply with IRS guidelines. The IRS has indicated appropriate methods for valuation of a closely held business.[23] The parties to a physician-hospital joint venture should have the medical practice valued by an independent third-party appraiser in a manner that complies with these IRS guidelines.

Among the factors cited by the IRS as important in the valuation are:

- nature of the business

- economic outlook of the industry
- book value of the stock and the financial condition of the business
- earnings capacity of the company
- dividend paying capacity of the company
- whether or not the enterprise has goodwill or other intangible value

Corporate Practice of Medicine. In the nineteenth century, large industries such as the railroad industry began entering into arrangements under which physicians were hired to provide medical care to large numbers of employees for predetermined wages. In some situations, laypersons in these corporations made decisions relating to services provided by the physicians employed by the corporation. The corporate practice of medicine doctrine originated from the desire of the American Medical Association to prevent corporations controlled by laypersons from interfering with the physician-patient relationship. This doctrine has been made into law in a number of states as described below. Generally, professional corporations, which are owned by physicians, have been excepted from the doctrine since physicians maintain control over such corporations.

In many states, statutes or case law developed over time specifically to prohibit corporations from employing physicians to practice medicine, with the exception of professional corporations as stated above. In some of these states, the doctrine has not been enforced at all or has been allowed to erode in the face of changes in the health care industry.[24] The doctrine is not currently enforced in most states, but it continues to be followed in a few. For instance, in Texas, the doctrine has been affirmed as recently as 1986.[25]

Based on the disparity in enforcement of the doctrine from state to state, the laws of the state in which the physician-hospital joint venture will be formed must be thoroughly reviewed to determine whether the entity can employ physicians. If it cannot, the structure of the entity must be reconfigured, and a true integrated venture employing physicians will not be possible.

Securities. The transactions involved in forming a group medical practice jointly owned by physicians and a hospital will likely involve the offer or sale of securities. The analysis of the applicability of state and federal securities laws in this context, however, is generally the same as the analysis described above in connection with mergers and IPA development. Note, however, that combinations of physicians and hospitals often involve a series of transactions. The parties to the formation of the jointly owned medical practice must examine each step in the process to determine whether the securities laws are satisfied or whether some affirmative action is required in order to comply with the applicable securities laws.

Fraud and Abuse. The development of a jointly owned group practice will involve, in some fashion, the contribution or sale of medical group assets to the new jointly owned group practice. The principal fraud and abuse concern in that context is found in the price paid for the existing group practice assets. Consider the following example:

> Hospital and ABC Medical Group decide to form a new limited liability corporation (LLC) that will operate as a new provider organization, employing the physicians currently employed by ABC and providing the medical services formerly provided by ABC. After the transaction is completed, Hospital and ABC will each own one membership interest in LLC and will have an equal voice in management. The parties commission an appraisal of ABC, which establishes the value of ABC at $3.5 million. Based on that appraised amount, ABC contributes its assets to LLC in exchange for one membership interest; Hospital, also in exchange for a single membership interest, contributes cash in the amount of $6.5 million.

Under this example, since the parties have equal ownership and an equal governance role, the hospital arguably has indirectly paid to ABC—and through ABC, the ABC physicians—$1.5 million for something other than the ABC practice assets. Parties to such a transaction need to be aware that they may be called upon to justify that arrangement in the context of a fraud and abuse investigation, raising the question of whether the payment of the $1.5 million was a payment for referrals by the ABC physicians to the hospital. Note also that there does not appear to be an applicable safe harbor in this situation.

Therefore, parties to a jointly owned medical group must be aware of the critical importance of the valuation of the medical practice and must be willing to find creative solutions that satisfy the requirements of the antikickback laws and regulations.

Anti-Referral (Stark Law). The physician-hospital joint venture will most likely provide both physicians' services and ancillary services, including the designated health services described in the Stark law. The physicians making the referrals will have both an ownership and a compensation arrangement with the entity. The parties must therefore be certain that referrals for those designated health services will be allowed pursuant to one or more of the Stark law exceptions.

The exceptions on which the parties will need to rely are again the "physicians' services" exception and the "in-office ancillaries" exception, each of which applies to both ownership and compensation arrangements (see Stark discussion earlier in this chapter). In order to meet these exceptions, the new entity must meet the definition of "group practice" under the Stark law, so the entity must meet the same parameters described above. In addition, however, the entity must meet the preliminary portion of the definition of "group practice"; it must be "a group of two or more physicians legally organized as a partnership, professional corporation, foundation, not-for-profit corporation, faculty practice plan, or similar association."[26] So the question is whether an entity that is owned partially by a hospital can be considered a group practice that is a group of *two or more physicians*. The statute does not provide any specific guidance on this issue, and no regulations have been issued that would clarify this issue. Since the list of entities in the definition includes foundations and not-for-profit corporations, it can be argued that the drafters intended to include relationships with hospitals. Also, the intent of the exception is to allow physicians who are legitimately organized in integrated entities to refer within their integrated practice; the physician-hospital joint venture is an integrated practice arrangement, so it should qualify as a group practice. Nevertheless, this area is still uncertain and entails some risk because no official guidance has been given.

NOTES

1. I.R.C., sec. 368(a)(1)(A) (1993).
2. I.R.C., sec. 368(a)(1)(C) (1993).
3. 15 U.S.C., sec. 18.
4. 15 U.S.C., sec. 1.
5. 15 U.S.C., sec. 18a.
6. *Securities and Exchange Commission v. W.J. Howey Company*, 328 U.S. 293, 298–299 (1946).
7. 42 U.S.C., sec. 1395nn (1994).
8. 42 U.S.C., sec. 1395nn(b)(1).
9. 42 U.S.C., sec. 1395nn(b)(2).
10. 42 U.S.C., sec. 1395nn(h)(4).
11. 42 U.S.C., sec. 1395nn(h)(4)(B).
12. Statement of Enforcement Policy and Analytical Principle Relating to Healthcare and Antitrust, 67 Antitrust & Trade Reg. Rep. (BNA) 1682 (September 27, 1994).
13. Statement of Enforcement Policy and Analytical Principle Relating to Healthcare and Antitrust, 67 Antitrust & Trade Reg. Rep. (BNA) 1682 (September 27, 1994), pp. S-16–S-21.
14. North Carolina General Statutes, secs. 58-67-25; 58-67-110 (1994).
15. See North Carolina General Statute, sec. 58-51-55 (1994).
16. See 31 Pennsylvania Code, sec. 152.1 et seq. (1993).

17. New York Comp. Codes R. & Reg., Tit. 10, sec. 98.2 et seq. (1993).

18. 42 U.S.C., sec. 1320a-7b(b).

19. 42 C.F.R., sec. 1001.952 (1992).

20. 42 U.S.C., sec. 1395nn(b)(2) (1994).

21. 42 U.S.C., sec. 1395nn(b)(2) (1994).

22. I.R.C., sec. 501(c)(3) (1994) and Reg. sec. 1.501(6)(3)1 (1994).

23. Rev. Rul. 59-60 (1959).

24. See *Hardy v. Brantley*, 471 So. 2d 358 (Miss. 1985), which expressly allowed employment of physicians by a hospital; 33 N.C. Atty. Gen. Rep. 43 (1955), which found that nonprofit corporations can employ physicians.

25. *Flynn Bros. v. First Medical Assoc.*, 715 S.W.2d 782 (Tex. Ct. App. 1986).

26. 42 U.S.C., sec. 1395nn(h)(4) (1994).

*Part III*

Advanced Information Systems Issues

Chapter 10

Selecting Information Systems for Managing MSOs and Large-Scale, Integrated Ambulatory Networks

Mary de Lourdes Winberry, M.P.H.

INTRODUCTION

The market pressures that are leading to the creation of large-scale, integrated ambulatory networks are also fueling new investments in advanced information systems. In fact, a recent survey of health care executives indicates that nearly one in six health care organizations intends to boost its capital expense budget by more than 20 percent during the next three years, in order to build the basic information infrastructure for providing a continuum of complementary, coordinated care.[1]

This trend is necessitated by the fact that many medical providers have information systems that cannot even share information between their business and clinical departments, let alone with other members of an integrated health care delivery system. Indeed, if an organization's information system was installed 10 or more years ago, it is likely that the technology was selected on the basis of how well it served a given department's needs, not on how well the computer system could interact with other computers. Now, however, Physician Organizations must have the ability to collect, monitor, update, and analyze financial and clinical data to keep abreast of the competition in delivering cost-effective, high-quality care; managing capitation contracts; and sustaining effective, daily interactions among physicians. Indeed, in market areas where health care competition is strongest, expenditures for advanced information systems tend to be the highest.[2]

The most pressing needs are the implementation of user-friendly system interfaces, the ability to access information remotely from all locations, and the acquisition of specialized managed care software.[3] Longer-term needs include development of software to track the use of resources utilized in the delivery of treatment and to link that information with financial information as well as clinical outcomes, and implementation of systemwide resource and patient scheduling. This kind of tracking software will most likely come from a longitudinal patient record—an information system with enough capacity to compile all tests results and observations over time and organize data so entries can be isolated for comparison and analysis.[4]

A LOOK AT THE BIG PICTURE

From Stand-Alone Computers to Information Hubs

In many physician practices, the computer programs used to collect, retrieve, and compile patient data are based on charges, not managed care or capitated rates. Although most health care executives recognize the need to use clinical data, many of their organizations are not technologically oriented to pass this information into a system that can track patient care. Instead, disparate records—many of which are not even computerized—contain different bits of information relating to accounting, pharmacy, clinical services, accounts receivable/payable, laboratory, radiology, billing, office records, inventory, instrumentation, clinical outcomes, and so forth. Just being able to coordinate and share data within the organization's existing information base is a challenge. Technological needs include the capability to access information regardless of location; a comprehensive, integrated database that maintains all clinical and financial data; query tools that can access and manipulate data; and on-line, real-time information processing and distribution.

But that is just the first step. In an integrated ambulatory network, each unit is likely to have a different computer system. For true integration to exist—that is, for every health care setting in the network to have access to a given patient's medical information—the disparate computer systems must be able to communicate and contribute to a systemwide pooling of information. But information cannot be traded or pooled unless it can be converted into something that is understandable to incompatible computer systems.

In the past, this integration would have required point-to-point connections between computers, with a translation mechanism, called an interface, converting the data sent from one computer into a format compatible for the receiving computer. That process was slow, expensive, and not particularly easy to use. Today, however, electronic data interchanges (EDIs) are making this task possible at much less expense and with greater ease and increased speed. In what is basically a hub-and-spoke system, EDI is doing the translating and switching all in one place. From the user's perspective, it is simply a matter of using a mouse to point and click the appropriate icon on the computer screen. See Figure 2–2, Chapter 2 for a diagram of the structure.

Other automated functions that are now available from a variety of vendors allow for electronic billing and filing of claims, automatic distribution of capitated fees, contract management, cost control, utilization measurement, monitoring patient satisfaction, and outcomes analysis. There will probably never be a single system that can do it all, but vendors are under pressure to make their systems compatible and expandable.

Moving toward Regional and National Systems

During the 1990s, health care organizations have been developing community health information networks (CHINs) to allow for the electronic interchange of clinical and financial data between hospitals, physicians, insurers, and other providers. A CHIN is essentially an overriding information highway to which the various integrated health care delivery systems will be able to connect. Eventually, these regional networks will provide seamless connectivity among all the components of health care delivery systems nationwide.

A crucial element of such a network is the electronic medical record, standardization of which is still under development. Eventually, advanced information technology will make it possible to schedule and track patients through the entire continuum of care.

It is against the backdrop of the health care industry moving toward universal managed care that individual medical practices must update their information systems. Physician success will not be measured by how skillfully episodic illnesses and injuries are managed but by how efficient collaborating physicians are in establishing cost-effective, proven standards that keep people well and out of the hospital.

INFRASTRUCTURE NEEDS

Enhanced Software Capabilities

The movement toward capitation and managed care is applying pressure on physicians to demonstrate "product lines" that are effective, high in quality, and reasonably priced. New types of statistical data are required for dealing with competitive pricing, lowered profit margins, administration of integrated health care delivery, and outcomes-based management. To meet these needs, Physician Organizations must acquire software modules, features, and capabilities described below.[5] These features combine practice management capabilities with managed care contract capabilities and often include insurance benefit plan capabilities.

Eligibility and Enrollment

The health care provider must have the ability to determine what services are covered in a contract, whether a patient is eligible for the care being sought, and the amount of applicable deductibles and cost sharing. It is important that this capability be available in an on-line, real-time format, and available to any physician in the system who treats patients, regardless of location.

Case-Mix Management

The provider must have access to a database of claims history and the ability to report on volumes, net revenues, and costs by procedure, diagnosis-related group (DRG), payer, and ambulatory service type.

Utilization and Cost Management

Health care providers must have the ability to develop and report variable and fixed costs at the department, procedure, provider, and case level. These costs must then be meshed with resource utilization data in order for the Physician Organization to be able to measure profitability, establish pricing, and manage productivity. The organization must be able to track and identify costs that are unusually high and warrant close examination. It must also be able to measure and compare resources used by each physician for each case or episode of treatment, and link the resource utilization data directly with outcomes. It should be able to track current utilization with the historical and targeted amount for both utilized and associated costs.

Contract Management

The provider must have the ability to maintain contract databases, calculate reimbursement, monitor contract performance, implement financial terms, and forecast the profitability of new contracts. A system should help the provider competitively price a managed care contract. An understanding of costs is critical when negotiating capitations. When a payer offers capitation, the Physician Organization must be able to analyze its utilization based upon the existing patient population and associated charges by inpatient and outpatient procedure, and calculate the net effect of accepting capitated payments in place of fee-for-service payments. If the organization does not have these data available, it is likely to enter the negotiations blindly. Once contracts are negotiated, it is important to automate terms for withholds, risk-sharing surplus deficit reporting, and incurred-but-not-reported (IBNR) data reporting, to manage the overall profitability for each contract.

Treatment Profiles/Protocols

The health care provider must have the ability to extract data from clinical records and build profiles of resource consumption and clinical protocols/outcomes. The profiles can then provide a performance benchmark and a tool for substantiating prices when negotiating managed care contracts. The clinical protocols are useful as a quality and utilization management tool, in that they demonstrate proven clinical efficacy under certain conditions. Internally, they can serve as a monitoring tool, particularly in multidisciplinary offices.

Capitation Management

Capitation management involves managing referrals and authorizations, tracking and paying out-of-network claims, reimbursing subcontractors, and distributing capitation and risk pools. The Physician Organization should have the ability to track practice and referral patterns of physicians so that it can identify why there is an unusually high number of tests and procedures for which it is financially responsible under capitation. The goal of primary care physicians is to identify cost-effective specialty physicians, while the goal of specialty physicians is to position themselves as the preferred referral for the primary care physicians. Equally important, the organization must be able to protect its interests by monitoring risk associated with age, gender, or industry adjustments and verifying stop-loss agreements.

Case Management and Patient Satisfaction

The provider must be able track patients within the system, triage patients, and make sure that patients receive the right level of care at the right time. While experienced clinicians need to make these decisions, on-line clinical information as well as level-of-care treatment protocols are important for expedient case management.

Patient satisfaction, once previously overlooked in the quality equation, is now an indicator used by accreditating agencies. Certain barometers of patient satisfaction include ease in obtaining an appointment, office hours, waiting time, helpfulness of office staff, time spent with physician, and perceived quality of care. A good report card not only raises the chances that a payer will want to contract with the physician group but also could lead to greater volume as additional payers and employer groups seek to contract with providers that can demonstrate quality, cost-effective care.

Other Provider Information

It makes sense to track information about entities that might be potential partners in business ventures. For example, the Physician Organization should track information about the hospitals at which its physicians practice, as well as information about other physician groups. This information can be useful when negotiating exclusive provider arrangements, analyzing possible mergers or acquisitions, and identifying entities to avoid associating with under risk-based contracting.

New Technologies for Quality Care

For many providers, new technologies for quality care means that information currently captured on paper must be automated in a way that allows for sophisticated diagnostic research, cost analysis, outcomes review, and so forth. Advances in technology are making this feasible.

Previously, the only kind of computer that could handle the amount of data that medical practices needed to collect and analyze was a large, expensive mainframe or minicomputer. These computers were limited in flexibility, in terms of the types of software programs that could be run, and were generally intimidating to use. Software tended to be written on highly technical programs, exclusively understood by programmers. Fortunately, the rapid development of personal computers (PCs), along with advances in local-area networks (LANs) and wide-area networks (WANs), has changed the entire face of computer and communications technology into one that is user-friendly, affordable, and flexible. Some of the technologies that health care executives should be aware of and understand are discussed below.

Open Systems

In contrast with older proprietary systems, where the hardware and software had to come from the same manufacturer in order to work together, today's open architecture allows users to combine hardware and software produced by a variety of vendors. It also makes it possible to add new capabilities to the computer and to integrate the computer with other systems, as needed. This gives users more control over capital outlays, and lets them pick and choose the most appropriate applications to meet current needs. As those needs change, the computer system can be altered or upgraded, without having to start from scratch.

Desktop Computers

Computers have become smaller and more powerful. They are equipped with sufficient memory and secondary storage to perform a wide variety of tasks that used to be done by mainframe and minicomputers, yet they are designed to fit on a standard-size office desk.

Local-Area Network (LAN)

Desktop computers and other personal computers can be linked together by high-performance cables so that users can exchange information, share expensive peripherals (such as laser printers, tape drives, and optical scanners), and draw upon the resources of a massive secondary storage unit, called a file server. LANs offer the advantages of a distributed computing system, in which the computing power is distributed among users, without sacrificing their ability to communicate. When set up as a client-server system, the users (clients) can communicate with one another via electronic mail to share multiuser programs and to access shared databases that are stored in the server. The basic components of a LAN are cables, a network interface card, a file server (which includes the central mass storage), a network operating system, and personal computers or workstations linked by the system.

Wide-Area Network (WAN)

A WAN differs from a LAN in that the computer network is linked by high-speed, long-distance communications networks (such as modems), rather than by cable. Thus, for example, a physician using a laptop computer and modem could, while aboard an airplane flying over Chicago, access a file server in Denver to check on the status of a patient in the intensive care unit.

Application Program Interface

Application program interface refers to system software that provides resources that programmers can use to create user interface features, such as pull-down menus and windows, as well as to route programs or data to LANs. This means that the user does not need to learn complex programming languages to work on the computer. The *graphical user interface* (GUI), in particular, uses on-screen graphics (pictorial representations of computer resources and functions), as well as a variety of visually attractive on-screen typefaces to make computers easier to use. The on-screen graphics, or *icons*, are pictures that closely resemble or remind the viewer of the concept it represents. For example, a trash can would be used to represent the place to discard unwanted files. Likewise, a mortar and pestle might represent a prescription-ordering function.

Object-Oriented Programming

Object-oriented programming languages have natural affinities with GUIs. For example, an electronic medical record might be displayed on screen as an icon—say as a file folder—which could be opened, closed, or moved simply by pointing and clicking a mouse on the icon. Objects created in object-oriented programming are excellent tools, because their internal complexity is hidden from the user. The objects themselves are self-sufficient and susceptible to copying and can even be moved into another object (icon).

Relational Database Management System (RDBMS)

A relational database management system refers to a program for storing and retrieving data to obtain the information needed. Basically, data are stored in tables, which define the relationship between the items listed in the rows (data records) and columns (data fields). A query asking, for example, the names of patients seen by an individual physician on a particular date would, in essence, create a third table to provide the answer.

Structured Query Language (SQL)

A query language developed by IBM, SQL is widely used in client-server networks as a way of enabling personal computers to access the resources of the file server database. An advantage of SQL is that the user does not have to worry about the particulars of how the data are physically accessed. In theory, SQL is hardware independent: it can be used to access databases on mainframes, minicomputers, and PCs. It also has the advantage of being quite concise, with four basic commands (30 commands altogether) that approximate the structure of an English-language query.

Optical Storage Technology

Optical storage technology, such as CD-ROM disks, offers an increasingly economical medium for read-only data and programs. Write-once, read-many (WORM) drives enable organizations to create their own huge, in-house databases. Just as microfiche represents an advance over paper as a storage medium, optical storage disks are a significant advance over microfiche.

Multimedia Capabilities

This refers to the ability of a PC or workstation to display and process not only alphanumeric characters but also full-motion video, graphical images, and sound. The obvious application in the health care sector is the management and display of the computerized patient record, incorporating results from sonograms, X-rays, electrocardiograms, and so forth.

Point-of-Care Devices

Computer technology has advanced to the stage where it is possible to enter data directly in the health delivery setting, rather than pecking the information into the computer at a later time. Thus, instead of writing down a patient's history, a provider could use a palm-top or laptop computer to enter the data directly. Software modules have been developed, for example, that allow home health care providers to enter diagnostic data directly into an electronic patient record that has been downloaded from a file server to a laptop computer.

Internet and the World Wide Web

The explosion of the Internet in 1995 has tremendous ramifications for the health care industry. Advanced Physician Organizations are using the Internet for telemedicine, patient education, and clinical communication with colleagues.

Understanding the current and potential uses of new technology to reduce costs or increase quality can give health care organizations a critical competitive advantage. Given the newness of many of these technologies, it is incumbent on leaders to create new approaches to solving current clinical or business problems.

SELECTING AN INFORMATION SYSTEM

Rapidly expanding Physician Organizations and associated management companies have an entirely new set of requirements for the ambulatory information systems that support operations in a complex fee-for-service and capitation environment. A number of critical steps in selecting the information systems, both software and hardware, are needed to support the expansion efforts for many integrated health systems. Exhibit 10–1 provides an overview of the activities associated with selecting an information system.

Because today's open architecture allows for the selection of hardware and software from different vendors to satisfy specific needs, it is highly unlikely and probably undesirable to commit all needs to a single vendor. However, there should be a central platform that can meet the needs of the newly formed 50-physician group practice or the Physician Equity Alliance that has grown from 100 to over 500 physicians in linked group practice and affiliated Independent Practice Association (IPA) structure.

Also, because of the nature of open systems, it makes sense to establish key short-term strategic goals, to be followed by longer-term information system objects. Chapter 11 provides an excellent overview of goal setting, the budgeting process, and information on setting up an information system task force or committee. One of the most important steps in selecting a Management Services Organization (MSO) information system is to understand the typical management information systems functions of an MSO. Exhibit 10–2 lists major functions within the categories of registration, billing/accounts receivable, marketing, scheduling, general accounting, managed care, reporting, collections, human resources, and case management.

The physician leaders and the task force charged with selecting an information system must also understand the priority of those features relative to one another. This task force should have a thorough understanding of the functions needed to manage in an environment characterized by a complex mixture of fee-for-service and capitated reimbursement system, in order to prepare and evaluate vendor responses to a request for information (RFI).

There are over 5,000 vendors of practice management software and systems in the country, but many of these software products are simply billing and collections programs. These limited programs do not meet the needs of the advanced Physician Organization and MSO in the twenty-first century. With a little research and attendance at key trade shows, the leading one to two dozen vendors of multifaceted systems can be identified. From this list, a short list of five or eight should be identified and sent an RFI, based on

---

Exhibit 10–1 Practice Management Information Systems Selection Process—Key Activities

1. Create information systems task force.
2. Review requirements definition.
   - Define requirements for health system.
   - Review existing systems review.
   - Establish applications required.
   - Establish/review selection criteria.
3. Prepare budget.
4. Draft request for information (RFI).
5. Review RFI with user group.
   - Finalize vendor list.
6. Finalize and release RFI.
   - Receive responses.
   - Prepare matrix outline of responses.
7. Review responses with user group.
8. Select finalists.
9. Conduct on-site visits.
   - Visit vendor offices.
   - Visit installation sites.
10. Evaluate vendor finalists and select vendor(s).
11. Negotiate and finalize contract.

Exhibit 10–2 Summary of the Management Information System Functions of a Management Services Organization

Registration

- insurance verification
- demographics
- patient history
- precertification
- authorization number

Billing/Accounts Receivable

- charge entry
- paper/electronic claim submissions
- patient statements
- automated collections
- rebilling parameters
- payment posting
- aging/credit balance reporting
- cash application

Marketing

- patient origin
- customer/patient referrals
- resource utilization
- payer mix
- current procedural terminology utilization
- demographics

Scheduling

- referral management (fee-for-service and capitated)
- resource scheduling
- serial/follow-up appointments
- recall programs
- part of automatic data transfer within large system

General Accounting

- accounts payable
- general ledger

Managed Care

- enrollment
- eligibility/authorization
- precertification/concurrent review
- claims/billing
- claims/processing
- pricing/repricing
- coordination of benefits
- restricted referral
- tracking
- billing

Management Reporting

- standard/ad hoc reporting
- forecasting/modeling
- on-line inquiry

Collections

- rebilling
- aging analysis of receivables
- collections follow-up (mail/telephone)
- collections benchmarks

Human Resources

- payroll
- benefits
- training
- recruitment
- policies and procedures

Case Management

- precertification
- authorization
- case rate and length-of-stay tracking
- restricted referrals
- utilization reporting

reputation, location, and experience. An RFI often consists of a detailed list of questions that must be answered in the areas of vendor capability, services, and cost, along with many questions about the functions available on a given system. Exhibit 10–3 illustrates some of the questions that must be asked of qualified vendors in the area of managed care contracting and practice management.

A sample timeline for selecting a system is as follows:

Exhibit 10–3 Sample RFI Questions

1.0 Business and clinical system specifications:

___ 1.0.1 Inpatients
___ 1.0.2 Outpatients
___ 1.0.3 Skilled nursing facility (SNF) patients
___ 1.0.4 Hospice patients
___ 1.0.5 Institutional patients, for whom some other facility is providing the health care but our institution is providing a special diagnostic test, or other portion of the total care

1.1 Comprehensive patient identification eligibility authorization, and other screening:

___ 1.1.1.1 Individual's name
___ 1.1.1.2 Aliases
___ 1.1.1.3 Date of birth
___ 1.1.1.4 Social Security number
___ 1.1.1.5 Payer/sponsor name
___ 1.1.1.6 Payer/sponsor address and phone
___ 1.1.2 On-line eligibility checking: ability to connect on-line to another entity's database to identify the patient; verify eligibility; check benefits, deductibles, copayments, and all other data items listed above
___ 1.1.2.1 Balance of available benefit days (for Medicare and other insurers), with emphasis on psychiatric, rehabilitation, and SNF patients
___ 1.1.2.2 Balance of available benefit dollars (for Medicare and other insurers), with emphasis on psychiatric, rehabilitation and SNF patients
___ 1.1.4.1 Precertification requirements (outpatients and inpatients)
___ 1.1.4.1.1 How many days in advance
___ 1.1.4.1.2 CPT and/or ICD-9-DM specific
___ 1.1.4.1.3 Precertification agency name and phone

___ 1.1.4.1.4 Payer specific
___ 1.1.5 Preauthorization: ability to interface automatically via the hospital's computer system directly with an outside authorizing agency to gain preauthorization
___ 1.1.8 Automated on-line connection to insurers' databases to identify patient insurance plan certification and authorization requirements (as in credit card authorization)

1.2 Accommodating multiple providers:

___ 1.2.1 Cross-reference index for multiple hospitals, geographically dispersed physicians' offices, home health agencies, and physician organizations to identify patients (demonstrate MIS's capability)
___ 1.2.2 Visit history: basic patient tracking, prior history, and patient encounters at this and other providers (to avoid duplication of testing and other diagnostic procedures)

1.4 Additional quality/utilization management requirements:

___ 1.4.1.1 Anticipated length of stay
___ 1.4.1.2 Actual length of stay
___ 1.4.1.3 Outlier day(s)
___ 1.4.1.4 Managed care contract type (POS, PPO, HMO, etc.)
___ 1.4.1.5 Admitting MD code and service
___ 1.4.1.6 Attending MD code and service
___ 1.4.1.7 PCP code (for capitated patients)
___ 1.4.1.8 ICD-9 codes for diagnoses and procedures
___ 1.4.1.9 CPT codes for procedures and tests
___ 1.4.1.10 MSO grouper

- **Months 1–2:** Develop list of needs, identify physician and management leaders, form information system task force, conduct education, develop wish lists, prepare sequence for replacing current systems.
- **Months 3–4:** Prepare request for information and forward to qualified vendors. Set deadlines and obtain responses. Do not choose a software vendor on the basis of existing hardware. Issues to address include:
  1. What hardware will the new information system run on?
  2. Will the new system replace software or interface with existing software?
  3. How does the system interface?
  4. Is there an interface engine?

5. How will the system deal with functions related to practice management?
6. What are the system's contract management capabilities?
7. How will the benefit plan be administered?
8. How will the system measure clinical outcomes?
9. How will the system deal with resource/utilization management?

Ask for demonstrations and actual reports. Request copies of screens (the different displays on a computer monitor). Check references. Talk to and visit current users—and remember that "beta sites" are not finished products. (Beta sites are locations where the software has been installed for testing the program in a real environment, as opposed to a laboratory simulated environment.) Identify multiple turnkey (turnkey systems are computer products that include all of the information system's hardware and software components; theoretically, following installation, users need only "turn the key" to gain access to all of the information system capabilities) and remote competitors. Ensure that vendor candidates meet user department needs. Find out how long the installation process will take. Learn whether the vendor is involved in research and development of cutting-edge technologies.

- **Months 5–6:** Analyze responses, narrow the field, have demonstrations by the finalists, and negotiate contracts with vendors. Maximize discounts, remedies, and protections. Obtain guarantees on time periods for installations and start-up dates. Finalize agreements.
- **Months 7–15:** Implement primary applications. Follow user priorities. Install initial hardware. Replace existing software modules.
- **Months 15–24:** Implement secondary applications.

It is important to involve all members of the organization in the system selection process. Probably the best way to do that is to establish a task force that includes managers or other representatives of all the departments or units that will be affected by the new system (e.g., nursing, laboratory, pharmacy, admitting, medical records, patient accounting, materials management, and finance). The task force should also include board members. All other staff should receive copies of the long-term goals and short-term steps that will be taken to achieve those goals.

The task force should meet at least monthly throughout the selection process. At each meeting, it should review progress on short-term goals, determine whether target dates are being met, and review what steps remain. The task force should have responsibility for all key decisions in the process (e.g., which vendors to eliminate from consideration).

The purpose of the request for proposal is to find the vendors that offer the most requested features. But, because many vendor responses to RFIs are written by their marketing departments, it is important for the task force to determine for itself not only what features each vendor's system actually offers but also the quality and adaptability of those features. For this reason, it is important for task force members to observe system demonstrations, talk to system users, read technical documentation about the systems, and visit users of the vendor's system. A pure cost-comparison analysis is not possible, because of all the different systems available. However, it is worthwhile to look at the cost of ownership over a period of 5, 7, and 10 years of operation. Be aware of hidden cost factors too. A low-cost system might require increased user time because of poorly designed software and inability to manipulate data easily.

Analyzing the responses carefully from the RFI will save time and money. It is critical to compare vendors regarding company services and costs, and system functional capabilities. Exhibit 10–4 lists key vendor data—from background, training, and support to system costs, set up expenses, and payment schedule—to be analyzed for each of the top vendors being reviewed. The three to five vendors should be compared in a matrix for hardware, service agreements, costs, and administrative components.

Task force members may have different wish lists of features that can serve as checklists for scoring each vendor's system. This process allows for the ranking of each system. However, before evaluating the systems, task force members should establish and agree upon the criteria for evaluation and the method for weighting each criteria for critical and noncritical functions.

During the selection process, the task force should continue studying literature on information systems for ideas to help evaluate systems. Such literature would include the concepts discussed in this chapter, such as computer-based patient records, community health information networks, bedside computing, statistical techniques in performance improvement, and procedure cost data. Additional educational material would include information obtained by other users that have had experience with each vendor, including the quality of each vendor's initial and ongoing training for users.

In addition to analyzing vendors' services and costs, the task force must compare functional capabilities of each vendor. In Exhibit 10–5 four vendors are compared against one another for the different functions delivered. The functional requirements include the categories of practice management, medical management, medical records, electronic data interchange, financial/business, ancillaries, interfaces, reporting, and managed care. The final version of the matrix may be longer and different, depending on the specific situation and the scope of health services that must be managed. The scoring system for this matrix is a simple ranking system: 5 represents the highest value, 1 represents the lowest value, and 0 indicates that the vendor is unable to deliver the service.

There are numerous pitfalls in the process of selecting an information system. Exhibit 10–6 delivers straightforward advice on the selection process. Selecting a software vendor is essentially selecting a business partner. The success of a new health care system is very much dependent upon its ability to track utilization against target amounts and properly adjudicate claims. A good vendor will solicit the input of its customers and dedicate resources for research and development in order to stay competitive in this fast-growing market. A good system might be the single most important investment that the organization can make, and the organization should allocate the time and resources necessary to make that decision wisely.

STAYING COMPETITIVE

Ultimately, the success of the information system will be judged by how well the users accept and rely on the applications and information available on the network. To help ensure a high level of acceptance, the information system should be available on a 24-hour basis, have short and consistent terminal response time, be easy to learn and use, and produce high-quality information products. The applications also must be easy to maintain and not dependent upon the particular hardware platform on which they operate.

In the next 5 to 10 years, exciting new technologies will allow even more seamless integration of patient information and enable Physician Organizations to be more responsive to the needs of the marketplace. Information technology has been rushing to meet the needs of health care delivery systems, and it is crucial that health care executives ride the wave into the future.

Exhibit 10–4 Vendor Analysis of Service and Cost

Vendor Background

- year founded
- annual revenue (for past two years)
- history of the company
- client references
- geographic scope of services

Implementation Plan

- description of process
- summary of implementation process

Training and Education

- description of program
- recommendation for training staff

Acceptance Testing

- example and plans/procedures
- examples of standard

Pre/Post Implementation

- description of site preparation services

Hardware Maintenance Schedule

- technical support
- hours of service
- response time to system failure

Software Support

- toll-free telephone support
- hours of support
- response time
- user groups

Contract

- copy of contract

Costs

- itemized listing
- initial license purchase
- yearly license renewal/upgrades
- one-time implementation fee
- one-time installation fee
- user training
- monthly/yearly maintenance
- other software conversion costs
- telecommunications fees
- total cost

Hardware and Networking Costs

- initial purchase
- yearly renewal/upgrades
- installation
- monthly/yearly maintenance
- user training
- other hardware costs
- total cost
- first-year operating expense
- other initial start-up costs
- other ongoing costs
- documentation and manuals
- cost of implementation support
- travel, freight, insurance, etc.
- cost of future expansion
- implementation services
- vendors or subcontractors

Payment Schedule

- contract signing
- completion of installation
- completion of acceptance testing
- other time frames

Architecture

- open
- language/operating system

Platform Type

- platform preferred
- memory requirements

Exhibit 10–5 Health System MIS Selection

Function	Vendor 1	Vendor 2	Vendor 3	Vendor 4
Practice management				
Appointment scheduling	5	4	5	5
Automated preregistration	5	4	4	5
Patient registration	5	5	5	5
Master patient index	5	3	4	5
Patient recall system	5	5	4	5
No-show list	5	5	5	5
Materials management	0	0	1	1
Order entry/results reporting	5	3	3	2
Billing	5	5	4	5
Collection	5	4	3	5
Performance/productivity tracking	5	2	4	5
Transcription/word processing	Third-Party	Third-Party	Third-Party	Third-Party
Instructional handouts	5	5	5	5
Medical management				
Concurrent review	5	4	3	5
Utilization review	5	3	3	5
Discharge planning	5	4	5	5
Membership review	5	5	5	5
Provider credentialing	0	1	3	0
Quality improvement	1	0	0	1
Case management	0	0	1	0
Managed care				
Membership eligibility	5	5	4	5
Benefits management	4	4	3	5
Precertification/authorization	4	5	4	5
Referral tracking	4	5	3	5
Copay deductible	0	0	0	0
Claim status	4	5	3	5
Adjudication auditing	3	3	1	4
Other	3	0	0	1
Total score	103	89	85	104

Key: 5 = High
      1 = Low
      0 = Nonexistent

Exhibit 10–6 10 Tips for Selecting an Ambulatory Information System

1. Avoid selecting new software based upon existing hardware.
2. Know what functions the health system will require to operate an Integrated Delivery System.
3. Negotiate price and payment for new systems.
4. Find out how much importance the company places on research and development.
5. Ask about how easily the system can integrate new and additional software programs.
6. Develop a realistic implementation schedule and stick to it.
7. Always request a copy of a report or screen for specific function.
8. Always ask *how* a system performs a function, as well as how quickly.
9. Know the system's capacity for volume and growth.
10. Obtain information on the financial status of the company.

Chapter 11

Managing the Planning and Start-Up Operations for Advanced Practice Management Information Systems

Steven S. Lazarus, Ph.D., F.H.I.M.S.S.

EXECUTIVE SUMMARY

An expanded information system has been identified as a key strategic investment that advanced Physician Organizations must make to be successful in a competitive, managed care environment. Marginal incremental add-ons to existing computer systems will not support the organization's needs. The approach to developing and operating advanced information systems in Physician Organizations consists of strategic planning, expanding the number and scope of information systems applications, responsible financial management through budget preparation and financing, and managing change. Maximum added value will be obtained from expanded information systems only if current work processes are studied and improved, based upon the capabilities offered with information systems support. Electronic communications capabilities throughout the enterprise is a key component of the information systems strategy, in order to provide access for clinical and administrative operations throughout the organization. Several principles are introduced to guide the planning of information systems applications and communications in an environment characterized by changing technological capabilities and expanding application requirements.

INTRODUCTION

Physician practices have used computer information systems for several years, primarily for billing, collections, and word processing. In the late 1970s, computer system vendors began to introduce appointment scheduling applications that increased physician productivity. Electronic claims submission to major insurance companies was introduced in the early 1980s. The computer-based applications of patient registration, billing, collections, appointment scheduling, word processing, and limited electronic claims submission comprised the maximum scope of computerized functions in most physician practices in 1995. However, in the larger medical groups, particularly those consisting of 100 or more physicians, advanced information systems applications are being used to increase productivity and/or improve the quality of care.

In their 1993 study of successful physician-based integrated health care delivery systems, Coddington, Moore, and Fischer identified significant investment in information systems as one of the 10 key factors contributing to the success of the organizations.[1] In addition to increasing the scope of functional capability, advanced physician practices are aggressively converting their computer systems into management information systems. The legacy computer systems in most physician offices process data but have not been designed to store that data for subsequent business analysis. In contrast, the more advanced physician practices, including most large medical groups, are aggressively investing in information systems that expand functional capability and allow retrieval of data to provide information for other business operations or decision making. There are two incentives for this change: (1) to increase operating efficiency (lower cost), and (2) to provide the information resources to improve patient care through best practice studies, provider and patient profiling, and other database analysis methodologies.

In addition, advanced Physician Organizations usually have multiple locations and close working relationships with a few business partners (hospitals, insurance companies, other Physician Organizations, etc.). Electronic communication among the internal locations and with outside organizations is a key strategy to increase competitive position and improve the ability to care for patients.

The transition from computer systems to information systems is complex and expensive. In many cases, existing legacy systems must be totally abandoned in the process of implementing an enterprise information system. Also, there is a dearth of seasoned information system executives with extensive ambulatory care experience who understand both the technical and the organization management issues—the skill sets needed to provide leadership. The need to expand information system capabilities in advanced Physician Organizations is occurring in an environment where technology is changing rapidly and market pressures resulting from the expansion of managed care are encouraging acceleration of the transition process.

Thus, it is strategically important that the approach to information systems be revolutionary rather than incremental. The resulting information system resources should evolve through a process that provides for growth and change.

PLANNING THE INFORMATION SYSTEMS

Purpose of the Information Systems Strategic Plan

Managing the start-up and ongoing operations of the information systems for advanced practices begins with the corporate vision, mission, and strategic plan. The information system investment is likely to be significant because of the communication investment to link all facilities, the need to replace or expand current legacy information systems, and the need to expand staff/contractor capacity to support new missions. Many of the functional capabilities of the information systems will be driven by the strategic needs of the organization. Furthermore, it is essential to link the information systems strategic plan to the organizational strategic plan to gain access to the necessary financial resources and to ensure consistency.

Just as the corporate strategic plan should be updated at least annually to reflect the changing health care industry environment, the information systems strategic plan should be updated annually in conjunction with, or subsequent to, the annual corporate strategic plan update.

Role of the Steering Committee

The information systems strategic plan should be developed and maintained by a steering committee representing multiple functions. Because of the significant capital involved in information systems and the strategic importance of many of the advanced information systems applications, it is appropriate that the chief information officer (CIO) be a member of the corporate strategic planning committee. The information systems steering committee should include the CIO; department directors representing information systems and communications; the chief financial officer; clinical representation from physicians and nurses responsible for quality of care and technology implementation; and managers responsible for managed care, clinical operations, medical records, planning, and marketing. Information systems consultants and/or senior information systems managers from strategic partners may be included on the committee. In some cases, the information systems steering committee is called a strategic planning committee, a task force, or team. The title can be modified to reflect the management style of the organization. The important issue is that the committee function as a combination of technology and user leadership, with significant representation from the user community.

Because of the growing importance of mergers and strategic alliances in the health care industry, the need to coordinate information systems activities with strategic business partners, and the need to develop an information systems environment that is conducive to acquisitions and strategic alliances, the information systems' current environment and the strategic plans of the key strategic partners should be considered in the information systems strategic plan. Among the significant issues to be addressed with outside organizations are common data element definitions, use of standard electronic data interchange (EDI) transaction definitions, compatible security/external access capabilities, and appropriate patient confidentiality policies.

Requirements Analysis

Early in the strategic planning process, it is important to conduct a requirements analysis (also referred to as a needs assessment) to obtain organizationwide input on the information systems capability needs and their priority. All key elements of the organization should be included in this process. The requirements analysis survey can be conducted through structured interviews, structured written questionnaires, or a combination of both. It is best if an outside consultant conducts the requirements analysis, because end-users of information systems tend to be more open in their discussions of present information systems capabilities, future needs, and current and future job functions than they would be with internal staff. This openness can be encouraged by ensuring anonymity. The outsider is often in a better position to challenge obsolete internal policies and bring a future industry perspective to the process. This perspective is important when structuring the interviews and questionnaires so that the results are not automatically restricted to projecting a need for small incremental changes.

Two aspects of the requirements analysis are essential to developing an information systems strategic plan that will be helpful to the organization. (1) It is necessary to provide a broad range of input so that respondents have an opportunity to express their priority needs. (2) Both the questions and the analysis should focus on future needs of the organization rather than on present or historical needs. The future priorities should be derived from the corporate strategic plan and vision statement.

Strategic Plan Maintenance

The process of developing an initial information systems strategic plan usually takes about six months but can take up to a year in new, multicomponent organizations. Annual updates to the plan can normally be accomplished in one to three months, unless the corporate strategic plan or the external environment has changed significantly.

Once the plan has been developed and approved by the appropriate committees and boards, it provides the guidelines for specific information systems functional capabilities, staffing, budget, and timing. If the information system strategic plan contains strategic information concerning the organization's competitive strategy, then the plan should remain an internal, confidential report.

Information Systems Principles

The health care industry environment has changed significantly in the last five years in both the information systems functional capabilities and the technology available to support organizational needs. The physician practice management information systems that support billing and collections under the management of the financial/business office have been replaced in the advanced physician practice with a corporatewide information system that supports billing and collections, patient demographics, managed care administration, cost accounting, marketing, electronic medical records, and ancillary services including laboratory and X-rays. Exhibit 11–1 presents principles for implementing this change. Involving all significant stakeholders in the process of planning an enterprisewide information system is essential. In advanced physician practices, this planning process should include physician leadership and a representation of clinicians.

MAJOR INFORMATION SYSTEMS APPLICATIONS

A number of information systems applications are needed to support the advanced physician practice. The discussion that follows could be expanded to include systems for pharmacies, inpatient hospitals, home health care agencies, and other providers if these entities are owned by or fully integrated with the physician practice. The principles presented in Exhibit 11–1 should be followed in selecting and combining various system applications to support the entire enterprise. Since a single vendor is not likely to offer all of the information system applications for the advanced physician medical practice, open systems with relational databases that are structured query language (SQL; an information system tool used to accomplish queries to one or more databases by entering a word, phrase, date, or other searchable information) compatible allow data sharing, report generation, and data linkages without incurring significant time and expense of customized interfaces and translators to link each functional application.

Examples of the major information systems functional capabilities are presented in Exhibit 11–2. A brief review of each capability is given in the sections that follow.

Exhibit 11–1 Principles for Information Systems Planning

- Involve all stakeholders.
- Involve physicians.
- Add new systems, when available, that are:
  1. open systems
  2. windows environment
  3. relational database
  4. structured query language (SQL) compatible
- Require health care industry data and communications standards.
- Build voice and data communication systems for current needs and future growth.
- Implement security to protect patient privacy and business data.
- Build for the future.

INFORMATION SYSTEMS BUDGET AND FINANCIAL CONSIDERATIONS

Budget Development

An important part of the information system strategic plan is the development and

Exhibit 11–2 Examples of Information Systems Functional Capabilities

- **Patient finances and demographics**
  1. billing
  2. collections management
  3. registration—patient demographics and insurance
  4. eligibility
- **Operations**
  1. appointment and resource scheduling
  2. order processing for laboratory, X-ray, prescriptions, etc.
  3. results reporting (e.g., laboratory, prescriptions, testing, etc.)
  4. referral management
  5. electronic clinical information systems (advanced electronic medical record)
- **Managed care**
  1. premium billing and collection
  2. PPO and HMO pricing
  3. withhold management
  4. claims adjudication
  5. participating provider roster
  6. patient status
- **Performance management**
  1. information warehouse
  2. provider management tools (e.g., case management)
  3. administration management tools (e.g., cost accounting)
  4. external performance measures (e.g., HEDIS)
  5. population-based analysis

Exhibit 11–3 Sample Information Systems Budget Categories

- **Initial capital investment**
  1. computer hardware
     (a) PC, portable notepad, and terminal workstations
     (b) printers
     (c) servers
     (d) backup, uninterrupted power supply, modems, etc.
  2. communications hardware
  3. new software applications
     (a) medical practice applications
     (b) office automation applications (word processing, e-mail, database, etc.)
     (c) special applications (network management, security, backup, virus protection, user support—technical and management)
  4. conversion support from current systems
  5. expert consulting
     (a) communications
     (b) software applications
     (c) planning process
     (d) project management
- **Maintenance and upgrades**
  1. hardware
  2. software
- **Replacement**
  1. software replacement
  2. hardware replacement
- **Ongoing support**
  1. staff
  2. external contractors
  3. supplies
  4. communications use

maintenance of a multiyear budget. A three-year budget is recommended. This provides the capability of budgeting for multiyear projects and early in the process identifies significant budget changes as the organization grows or as information systems capabilities and requirements change. Planning budgets beyond five years tends to be highly speculative because of changing health care information needs, changing technology, and the uncertainty of related costs. Therefore, it is recommended that the information systems strategic plan include a three- to five-year budget with categories similar to those suggested in Exhibit 11–3. Some useful hints in preparing the budget include:

- Include sales taxes on all applicable hardware and software.
- Include fringe benefits and overhead for internal staff.
- Include the cost of training, particularly for transitions to all major system applications and for new employees. Training can be conducted through a combination of internal staff and outside services.
- If the advanced medical practice strategic plan calls for implementing new applications or technologies that do not

have an established track record in similar medical practices, then a contingency of up to 10 percent of the information systems plan budget should be added to cover unforeseen needs.
- Computer hardware, communications hardware, and contractor services should be competitively bid to obtain the best technical skills, service, and cost combination to meet the needs of the advanced medical practice. Cost should not be the only consideration.
- Sufficient resources should be allocated to security, hardware redundancy, and data backup to minimize system downtime, particularly if applications critical to the organization's mission (such as an electronic clinical information system) are used to replace the paper medical record.

Financing Capital Expenses and Ongoing Expenses

Some advanced physician practices have a sponsoring partner (e.g., hospital or insurance company) that has the capital to finance the information systems investment. Advanced physician practices of 50 to 100 physicians or more usually generate sufficient cash flow to obtain favorable financing, unless there is a poor track record of repaying debt or current debt is unusually large. A three- to five-year period is recommended to pay back the capital investment

This short time period is preferred because, in many cases, technology advances and new software functional requirements will result in replacement of information system components within three years. This trend will likely continue for the foreseeable future in the health care industry. Because the industry is currently largely paper based, the potential for gains from automation are significant. In addition, computer and communication technologies are advancing to support current and future applications.

Outsourcing (subcontracting) is an alternative used by some health care organizations to implement advanced information systems. Outsourcing provides a mechanism for spreading the initial system's cost over several years of a contract; usually includes management and operational staff, which may be in short supply or difficult to retain in some markets; and provides a mechanism for addressing the uncertainty of transaction volume and future application needs. Outsourcing can be viewed as either a temporary, bridging strategy for an evolving advanced physician practice, or as a long-term strategy. If this approach is used, there should be sufficient flexibility in the arrangement to expand information system capabilities as new functions are needed.

CONVERSION TO A NEW INFORMATION SYSTEM

Managing the Conversion Process

Converting to a new information system usually presents a formidable challenge to a physician group practice. The project usually requires support from the current information systems vendor (who is being abandoned) and the new vendor, as well as the administrative staff and clinical staff. Technical support for implementing the new system is usually provided by the software vendor. If computer hardware is being supplied from a source other than the software vendor, then the hardware vendor also will provide technical support. In addition, the vendor who supplies the current software, systems integration specialists, and consultants are frequently involved in supporting the implementation of a new information system in larger physician organizations.

Several of the major implementation issues are summarized in Exhibit 11–4. Converting to a new information system is a significant project that involves several complex management and technology issues.

Exhibit 11–4 Major Implementation Issues

- **Support**
  1. staff
  2. vendor(s)
  3. consultants
- **Policy**
  1. uniform definition
  2. pricing structure
  3. managed care participation
  4. account sharing
  5. centralized or decentralized database(s)
  6. centralized or decentralized operations
- **Training**
  1. technical staff
  2. clinical and administrative users
- **Conversion**
  1. design
  2. testing
  3. audit
  4. error correction
- **Work plan**
  1. schedule
  2. responsibility
  3. reporting
  4. project management
  5. benchmarking

Managing the Implementation Challenge

Several significant project management issues must be addressed in implementing a new information system successfully. The challenge is substantially greater when several current information systems, being used by individuals or small groups of physicians, are being converted into one new information system for the larger, integrated physician practice organization. The issues include the following:

- In many cases, the vendors whose systems are being abandoned are required to perform data conversion services with the existing data for an automated conversion to the next system. There is a fee involved in this process, each conversion must be tested, and the current vendor may not be anxious to provide the required support.

- The new system vendor may have limited personnel available to support the conversion and may have limited experience with conversions from the current vendor to the new vendor system.

- Uniform definitions must be developed for the new organization (e.g., account number system, payer categorization).

- The development of a uniform fee schedule for all physicians, or all physicians of the same specialty, may be required.

- The organization must make a strategic decision whether to centralize or decentralize the database(s) of the medical practice. This decision has cost and other implications.

- The organization must decide whether the billing and information systems operations will be centralized or decentralized. This decision has staffing, cost, and risk-sharing implications.

- In some cases, unrealistically short implementation schedules are demanded because of a vendor going out of business, rapid growth that overwhelms the present system, termination of a billing service contract, or problems with an existing system that cannot be fixed.

The Conversion

The process of shutting down the old system, transferring the existing data, and bringing up the operation status is the operational part of the conversion process. The information systems conversion process usually takes several days, but it can take several weeks. If things go poorly, the conversion can take several months. There are cases where physician groups have not been able to send out statements for more than 90 days because of information system conversion delays. Because the risks of failure to convert successfully or significant delays in completing the conversion process are substantial, it is important to plan the process well and to take prudent steps to minimize the risk of delay or failure. Several key decisions can directly affect the complexity and length of the conversion process. However, shortcuts taken to minimize the conversion effort can often result in less information transferred to the new system, with the consequence that information has to be obtained later or important business information is not available for future use. Defining the balance among these factors is an important management decision that will vary, based on circumstances. Shortcuts taken to reduce conversion time or cost usually are paid for later (lost revenue due to lost charges, lost patients, the need to recapture and reenter data, the need to redo the entire conversion, etc.). Alternative approaches that can be considered include the following:

- Simplify the conversion by converting only minimal patient demographics and balance forward, omitting the detail and minimizing the edits on the data.
- Do not merge accounts together for the same patient from multiple practices that are being joined in the new group.
- Make the individual physicians responsible for their historic accounts receivable; therefore, do not convert any of the accounts receivable history.
- Take the time and resources to plan the conversion; merge accounts for the same patient and capture sufficient detail history to manage the practice.
- Test the conversion program on a sample of data prior to conducting the full-scale conversion.
- Train staff on the new information system using the test conversion data. This allows staff to become thoroughly familiar with the system and identify errors that occurred in the conversion in the practice's own data.
- Be prepared to pay a premium for staff time and consultant/vendor support over a weekend to minimize downtime associated with the conversion process.
- Withhold a substantial payment on the purchase of the new software until the conversion has been completed successfully and accepted by the practice.
- Rent or buy a very fast computer processor that could be used in the conversion, which can save days if the databases are large and the conversion logic is complex.
- Utilize vendor staff and/or consultants who have successful experience in systems conversions.
- Be prepared to go back to the old system if the conversion is going poorly.

Training for the New System(s)

Often a significant investment in training is required to obtain a modest level of user expertise in new systems. In most cases, advanced Physician Organizations implement new information systems with either (1) new applications or (2) modification of previous functions to operate in a more user-friendly environment. In either case, end-user staff need to be trained with new skills and technical staff need to become familiar with new technology and its maintenance. Further complicating the staff training issue is that a state-of-the-art physician information system usually involves multiple vendor software and hardware products. In this environment, technical staff need to be trained in troubleshooting and resolving issues related to inconsistency among products selected, because the suppliers may not be able to provide the technical solutions.

There should be a provision in the budget to train both technical and end-user staff. Sufficient time should be allowed to provide that training prior to implementing the new system. Training is best conducted close to the time of implementation. It is very effective to train end-user personnel on the organization's converted data prior to implementation. It is easier for the personnel to relate to the organization's own data than to test "dummy" data. Report capabilities can be tested with the test data results matching the current system, and errors in the conversion programs can frequently be identified when personnel carefully examine the converted data.

Training is often provided by a combination of external and internal resources. A frequent strategy is to use more external sources during the initial conversion and implementation, when staff resources are limited and training needs are greatest.

Work Plan

A good work plan is essential for successful implementation of a new, comprehensive information system in a large Physician Organization. The work plan includes a schedule, assigned responsibilities for major tasks, specific reporting obligations to management and the governing board, project management responsibilities, and benchmarks that can be used to evaluate performance at major milestones during conversion and implementation.

Schedules for implementing a new information system vary considerably. The schedule depends on the urgency, resources allocated, complexity of conversion and implementation, scope of applications, ability of the organization to make timely decisions, and equipment ordering and delivery issues. From the time that the decision is made to plan for a new major information system to completion of the basic conversion effort and initial operation, normally 1 year to 18 months should be allowed. In contrast, urgent implementation of billing functions, where the converted data are minimized, can be accomplished in 120 to 180 days. However, the shorter time frame is not sufficient for full system implementation and often results in the need to reengineer and do additional work later.

Because information systems for advanced Physician Organizations are complex, strategically important, and have significant financial implications for the organization, skilled management of the implementation and ongoing operation is important. The project management team or task force should be vested with the responsibility to oversee the information systems acquisition and implementation projects. The team should establish and be accountable for several benchmarks that occur during the implementation process. Benchmarks can be tied to acceptance testing, budget versus expense performance, evaluation of training, successful installation of equipment, and other quantifiable performance. Failure to meet the benchmarks on time and within budget requires action by the project management team to revise the work plan or redirect resources to correct the deficiencies.

The requirement for project management and work plan development for information systems management and activities does not end with the initial system implementation. Because of today's changing needs for information, advanced Physician Organizations will continually be faced with reengineering existing information systems and selecting and implementing new functions. The ability to understand and support organizational needs, provide technical management, and use communication skills are important characteristics required of the information systems leadership, information systems staff, and project management team.

MANAGING CHANGE

Managing change is a key function of top management at all advanced physician practices. With enhanced information systems, the payoff of the capital and ongoing resource investment will only be realized if significant work flow changes occur to improve efficiency and patient care. This requires significant change beyond information systems expansion and replacement.

Communication throughout the organization, from the top down, is essential to prepare staff for the changes and to motivate them to accomplish them. Perhaps the information systems application that requires the most radical work process change is the electronic clinical information system. Because this functional application is not widely implemented in physician practices, it requires a certain amount of study and adaptation to accommodate the specific practice environment. One of the best ways to accomplish this in an advanced physician practice is to implement the application initially as a pilot project to test the technology, to experiment with the physician and other provider interfaces to the information system, and to make improvements in the work flow based on the capabilities of the system and provider-patient needs.

It is particularly difficult to manage enterprisewide change when there are multiple locations involved. Specific proactive programs should be developed and implemented to reach every location. For instance, in a paper chart environment, telephone inquiries regarding prescription refills are handled either by putting the pharmacy on hold for a significant period of time while the chart is being pulled, or having the pharmacy leave a message and calling back later. With an automated electronic information management system, all of the clinical, demographic, and current medication information about the patient is available from the desktop within seconds, so that the prescription refill inquiry can be processed with one short telephone conversation from any location. If an e-mail connection is available, then both the inquiry and response can be communicated within this mode. The authorization of the refill can be documented in the record at the same time. This process frees up nursing and medical records time, which can be converted to proactive management of patients at risk. For instance, staff members could investigate the clinical database to find hypertensive patients who have not been refilling their maintenance medications and then contact them to encourage compliance with the treatment plan.

In summary, the changes supported by the implementation of comprehensive information systems in advanced physician practices affect the entire enterprise. Support for successful change management involves more than the information systems staff, because the changes involve new approaches to treating patients and organizing work. Thorough planning, identification and implementation of best practices, and testing various feasible alternatives to achieve a shift in work flow are important components to improving efficiency and patient care.

VALUE ADDED

The value added to the practice by enhanced information systems falls into two areas: they make current paper-based processes more efficient, and they support a more effective use of resources to deliver care and maintain the health status of the patient population. There are potential efficiency gains from improved operations and/or improved patient care. In many cases, the most valuable contributions of enhanced information systems result from changes in work roles. A good analogy is found in the transition of merchant payment from largely cash and checks to bank credit cards, which has occurred in the last 10 years. In the previous paper currency and check environment, significant clerical effort was involved in examining picture identifications and writing down driver's license numbers on checks, verifying that large denomination currency was not counterfeit, correctly counting out change, and balancing cash drawers at the end of each work shift. Many merchants also experienced cash losses through embezzlement. In the credit card environment, these manual procedures are significantly reduced; the clerical time is replaced by serving more customers (with increased related sales) because the credit card allows the transactions to occur more efficiently, eliminates the reconciliation and identification activities, and promotes increased purchasing because the limitations of available cash and checking account balances are not an issue.

In the future, a similar transition is likely to occur in health care. Advanced information systems will allow proactive identification and treatment of the population at risk before these individuals become acutely ill. The databases, management tools, and personnel resources made available through increased automation can place more emphasis on prevention and early detection/ management of patient problems. The primary customer will not be the acutely ill patient, but rather the enrolled subscriber. Advanced practice management information systems provide the information resource capabilities to conduct business in this changing environment.

The U.S. health care delivery system is becoming more administratively complex. Although industry leadership and politicians frequently speak of administrative simplification as a key to lowering health care costs, the operating rules continue to become increasingly complex, particularly for managed care. This applies to providers, who normally are not consulted by payers as they design their various managed care offerings. As long as this approach persists, enhancing the information systems capability to automate decision rules and maintain databases with eligible providers, benefits, and enrollment dates is the only approach that can support the administration of large volumes of managed care patients.

ANTICIPATING FUTURE NEEDS

It is difficult to project future information systems needs in an environment where the business practices of health care are changing, technology is changing, and business relationships are changing. However, common themes are likely to occur in most advanced physician practices. These include the following:

- Internal and external relationships will change.
- Resources needed to support information system conversions and training will increase.
- The volume of electronic transactions will increase. In some cases electronic transactions will replace paper or telephone transactions; in other cases, they will support new information needs.
- In many cases, Physician Organization growth will occur through physician practice acquisition or recruitment of more physicians to form larger organizations.
- More patient data will be obtained and stored in order to better manage patient care.
- There will be an increasing need to identify, implement, and maintain best practices, which often will involve information systems support.
- Information systems will be used to support reporting requirements to meet external market needs, as well as to identify best practices and monitor their implementation on an enterprisewide basis.

As the information systems capabilities of advanced physician practices become more technologically complex and the number of vendor products increases, the information systems leadership will become more directed toward contract negotiation, supplier selection and management, strategic planning, and change management. This role will often be filled by a CIO working in collaboration with the physician practice leadership. In some cases, there will be significantly greater reliance on the use of outside expertise to address specific technology or application areas.

CONCLUSION

Several issues have been identified that are important to the successful start-up and continuing operations of management information systems for the advanced physician practice. The scope of functional capabilities of a comprehensive, enterprisewide information system is best determined through the development of a strategic information systems plan based on the organization's strategic plan. For advanced physician practices, information systems include an electronic communications infrastructure and relational databases that can be used for both operations and performance analysis. Significant challenges facing an organization implementing advanced practice management systems include new technology, an expansion of the scope of applications supported by the information systems, information systems based on a foundation that will support uncertain growth, and the scarcity of experienced information systems leadership that understands the future directions of ambulatory care and managed care. Although the combination of specific information systems planned and implemented for each advanced physician practice is unique, several principles have been developed to guide the process of planning the information and communication systems. Perhaps the greatest challenge is to revise the day-to-day work flow in physician practices to take advantage of the expanded information systems capabilities to support the delivery of more efficient and higher-quality patient care.

NOTE

1. D. Coddington et al., *Integrated Health Care: Reorganizing the Physician, Hospital and Health Plan Relationship* (Englewood, Colo.: Center for Research in Ambulatory Health Care Administration, 1994).

Chapter 12

Applying Outcomes Research To Increase Quality

Sanford R. Hoffman, M.D., and Mary de Lourdes Winberry, M.P.H.

INTRODUCTION

A recent editorial by Schoenbaum noted, "It should be disturbing to us as a profession that we have so few outcomes data and use so few in our practices. Most of us [physicians] do not learn enough in our training to collect or analyze our own data."[1] This observation applies to the entire medical delivery system. It is estimated that there is good information on the outcomes of only about 15 to 20 percent of all medical treatment.

The recognition that outcomes data are central to the mission and management of performance in health care organizations has become a critical element in the quality improvement issues affecting all medical care. The measurement of quality improvement and medical treatment outcomes by necessity encompasses the measurement and management of processes. Process measures monitor the tasks and activities that lead to outcomes. The measures are developed by mapping all the steps in a process, identifying the critical tasks and capabilities required to complete the process successfully, and then designing measures that track these tasks and capabilities.

This chapter addresses a major paradigm shift in medical care, as purchasers and payers increasingly demand accountability. Outcomes measurements and practice guidelines are discussed on a historical and philosophical basis, along with specific details regarding the type of outcomes measures that are currently in use. The economic effects of this movement are discussed, along with the newer concept of disease state management. And, finally, steps for starting an outcomes research project are outlined.

HISTORY OF OUTCOMES RESEARCH

Outcomes research (the basis for both measuring and managing outcomes) can be defined as the scientific study of the outcomes (results) for patients receiving different treatments for a single disease or illness.[2]

The beginning of modern outcomes research is attributed to pioneering work by Wennberg and Associates who noticed and reported the so-called small area variations.[3] Wennberg's studies revealed significant inconsistencies in the rate with which specific procedures were performed by physicians in different geographic areas coupled with wide variations in medical practice across disease states. Patients with similar medical conditions received wide variations in medical care with no clarity as to what extent the variations were due to differences in the population, resource availability, or patient preferences.[4] These studies led to the questions, or at least the perception, that there was excessive use of procedures by physicians in different areas of the country.

Other studies, built upon Wennberg's work, questioned the actual appropriateness of the medical care received by patients within many disease states. Using a methodology of appropriateness developed by the RAND Corporation—with extensive pertinent literature review, expert panel review, and structured clinical scenarios derived from the literature review—ratings for the indications for disease treatment were drawn up. These ratings, based upon a scale of 1 to 9, were performed by a panel of nine experts to judge whether procedures or treatments are inappropriate, equivocal, or appropriate.[5] In some instances, the panels judged up to one-third of medical care as inappropriate or equivocal.[6] This is illustrated in Table 12–1, which contains the results from a review of 5,000 medical records as to the appropriateness of three procedures: coronary angiography, carotid endarterectomy, and upper intestinal endoscopy.[7]

OUTCOMES RESEARCH TODAY

Sparked by the concerns stemming from the RAND study and other similar studies, and because of increasing concern over burgeoning health care costs, outcomes management and research has come to occupy center stage in all health care delivery.

Treatment effectiveness has become the focus of providers, patients, and purchasers of health care.[8] (Treatment *effectiveness* refers to the strength of a treatment as used in average conditions; treatment *efficacy* refers to the strength of a treatment in ideal conditions, i.e., clinical trials.) As we come to understand and evaluate desirable outcomes, good practice guidelines and clinical road maps can be created to help all players in the medical decision-making process select the most beneficial and effective therapies.

Enhancing outcomes and quality has taken on even greater urgency as the medical care industry adjusts to rationalize all health care delivery, to measure the cost and benefits of treatments, and to compare the outcomes of different providers (so-called report cards, profiles, and instrument panels). This rationalization is very understandable when a trillion dollars is being spent (15 percent of the nation's gross national product) on annual health care expenditures. Also fueling the "industrialization of medicine" is the increasing availability of tools and methods for measuring and managing

Table 12–1 Results of RAND Health Services Utilization Study: Appropriateness of Medical Procedures

	Appropriateness Category (%)		
Procedure	Appropriate	Equivocal	Inappropriate
Coronary angiography	74.0	8.5	17.4
Carotid endarterectomy	35.3	32.3	32.4
Upper-gastrointestinal tract endoscopy	72.0	10.8	17.2

Source: M. Chassin, R. Park, et al. Does inappropriate use explain geographic variations in the use of health care services? JAMA: 258:2533–7, 1987.

all aspects of health care delivery.[9] Industrialization of medicine refers to the transition of health care services from a charitable activity involving art and science to the business of health care delivery. Health care services, once delivered by small, local providers, are delivered by major corporate entities.

These measurements and quality initiatives derive from the fact that medicine has changed from a patient-based healing art to a fragmented, depersonalized system driven by the pressures of medical economics and an even more cost comparative insurance system.[10] Standardization of care, with more emphasis on data and quality, will benefit the ultimate customer—the patient.

It has become apparent that certain medical therapies are not worth the money.[11] It is hoped that outcomes research will allow documentation of treatment effectiveness to eliminate these variations and become the final goal of developing clinical pathways, practice guidelines, and disease management strategies. The inherent complexity of medical decision making, with each step along a clinical pathway open to numerous competing therapies, makes it imperative that physicians no longer practice in a vacuum.[12] Providers are obligated to look at the processes and the system of health care delivery with a mindset that emphasizes cost and quality and to compare all these components with their competition.

If embraced without bias by the medical community, outcomes reporting and all its adjunctive activities will lead to better health for everyone. Outcomes reporting can help to shed light on the stark truth: in most clinical situations, there is one best approach to a patient's problems.

OUTCOMES DATA—WHAT ARE THEY?

Outcomes research has led to the use of health care "informatics" to draw together disparate information, collate the data, and feed it back to providers. This allows all the players in health care to track the effectiveness of different therapies.

What are the outcomes that should be measured? A broadened description of desirable health outcomes or outcomes of patient care has evolved, which includes the following:

- physical outcomes
- well-being and functional status
- satisfaction of caregiver
- cost of treatment

Outcomes measurements encompass the desired outcomes for a specific disease state or the physical outcomes including the possible complications and therapeutic goals. Coupled with physical outcomes are the effect of the treatment on the patient's general well-being and functional status. There are also service outcomes, which include satisfaction of the caregiver, and cost outcomes, which include the cost of the burden of the disease.[13] It should be clearly understood that the physical outcomes of a treatment are intermediate outcomes; these are true clinical outcomes that patients directly experience that are observable on an individual level. When treating a patient with heart disease, for example, the patient does not really care about his or her serum lactate levels, heart size, or ejection fractions, but the patient does care how these intermediate outcome therapies affect morbidity (functionally and symptomatologically) and the patient's ultimate mortality.

In 1988, Ellwood introduced the concept of an outcomes management system as a "technology of patient experience."[14] This was a pioneering effort in defining the term *outcomes management*. Ellwood described a system of interval measurement of the functioning and well-being of patients coupled with the measurement of disease-specific clinical outcomes. Thus, the two key measurements in any outcomes measurement system are (1) a general health and functional status measure and (2) a disease-specific measure.

GATHERING THE DATA—THE SURVEY

Several general health and functional assessment surveys are being used to gather data. The two surveys that presently represent the gold standard are the SF-36 and the HSQ-39. The items in these two surveys were selected from instruments used in the RAND Health Insurance Experiment and the Medical Outcomes Study (MOS) and from the Diagnostic Interview Schedule. These short surveys are useful in the clinical arena and have the capability of capturing a wide variety of measurements of health studies. The psychometric properties of these instruments have been vigorously tested and have been found to be valid and reliable.[15]

The instruments are divided into eight subscales:

1. **Physical functioning (PF)** is the extent to which health limits physical activity.
2. **Role functioning—physical (RP)** is the degree to which physical health interferes with work or other activities.
3. **Bodily pain (BP)** is an intensity of pain measure.
4. **General health (GH)** is the patient's perception of his or her current health and health outlook.
5. **Vitality (VT)** measures the level of energy.
6. **Social functioning (SF)** is the extent to which health interferes with usual social activities.
7. **Role functioning—emotional (RE)** is the extent to which emotional problems affect functions.
8. **Mental health (MH)** assesses general mental health.[16]

These eight specific health attributes are then grouped under three major health dimensions: (1) overall evaluation of health or general health perception; (2) functional status (physical functioning, social functioning, role limitations attributed to physical problems, role limitations attributed to emotional problems, and bodily pain); and (3) well-being (pain, mental health, and energy/fatigue). In addition, the HSQ measures change in health and risk of depression.[17]

UTILITY ASSESSMENT—PATIENT PREFERENCES

Patient preferences or values play an important role in decision making for specific treatments. Utility assessment is a methodology that elicits patients' values for particular states of health that is often used as an overall measure of health-related quality of life. Utility measures assess the value that individuals assign to different states. It is important to understand this, because utility measures may reflect factors other than health states—such as the value patients place on life, their risk aversion, or their attitudes toward certain medical interventions.[18]

A study of patients with prostrate problems provides an explicit example of the role of patient preferences in the choice of medical care. Studies show that members of the older male population have considerable variability with regard to their symptoms and disturbance of daily activities, despite having similar prostate pathology. Wennberg and Associates have developed interactive videodisks at the Foundation for Informed Medical Decision Making. A hallmark of these disks is the thorough discussion of the applicable disease process and alternative treatment modalities, along with possible benefits and complications of each mode of treatment. Upon viewing the disk on prostate problems, men undergoing therapy for benign prostate hypertrophy have opted for medical therapy over surgical therapy to a significant degree. These findings, and newer capabilities of measuring patient preferences, have important implications for the future of all medical therapies.[19]

ACCOUNTABILITY—ITS IMPACT ON PRACTICE GUIDELINES

In addition to the movement to emphasize outcomes measurement, a number of submovements that affect health care and its delivery have evolved directly from the outcomes movement or in response to the rapidly changing medical marketplace. The common thread connecting all the other movements or measurement modalities is accountability.

The initial thrust for measurement resulted in clinical indicators, served up primarily by specialty societies in an attempt either to cooperate with or to stave off insurers' and regulatory agencies' questions about the indications in medical and surgical treatment. These indicators (because they were weak, self-serving, and usually not evidence based) were quickly supplanted by the movement to develop practice guidelines or practical parameters and policies. Recent surveys indicate that there are more than 1,800 practice guidelines, which in itself is a problem from the standpoints of validity and ease of use. The expanding role of practice guidelines that specify for physicians and other health care providers the proper indications for performing medical procedures and treatments, along with the proper management of specific clinical problems, has widespread implications.

Practice guidelines differ from information in medical textbooks or review articles in that the latter are frequently based on either the author's opinion or weakly gathered scientific evidence. Practice guidelines are usually developed by a group of medical experts in one of four methods: (1) the informal consensus method, (2) the formal consensus method (both with little linkage of consensus to evidence), (3) the evidence-based guideline method, and (4) the explicit approach.[20] Guidelines, in any form or method of formation, can have an educational role in clinical decision making; but there is not yet definitive proof that they will improve the outcomes of health care. Of great concern to all physicians and patients is that the restrictive applications of guidelines by third-party payers, regulators, utilization reviewers, and others may block the access of physicians and patients to necessary services mislabeled as "inappropriate." These concerns have helped focus the debate about guidelines on their clinical and scientific validity, the process of their development (e.g., consensus development, decision analysis, metanalysis), who develops them, and the motives of the developers.

The Institute of Medicine has developed criteria for well-written practice guidelines,[21] and these have been amplified by the American Medical Association.[22] These criteria are outlined in Exhibits 12–1 and 12–2.

ONCE YOU HAVE OUTCOMES MEASUREMENTS, WHAT DO YOU DO WITH THEM?

Practice guidelines and outcomes measurements will help physicians answer the

---

Exhibit 12–1 Institute of Medicine Practice Guidelines Criteria

- validity
- reliability/reproducibility
- clinical applicability
- clinical flexibility
- clarity
- multidisciplinary process
- scheduled review
- documentation

Source: Institute of Medicine Committee to advise the Public Health Service on Clinical Practice Guidelines, M. Field, K. Lohr, eds., *Clinical Practice Guidelines: Direction for a New Program,* Washington, D.C., National Academy Press, 1990.

Exhibit 12–2 American Medical Association Practice Guidelines Criteria

> **Attribute 1**—Practice guidelines should be developed by or in conjunction with physician organizations.
> **Attribute 2**—Reliable methods that integrate relevant record findings and appropriate clinical expertise should be used to develop practice guidelines.
> **Attribute 3**—Practice guidelines should be as comprehensive and specific as possible.
> **Attribute 4**—Practice guidelines should be based on current information.
> **Attribute 5**—Practice guidelines should be widely disseminated.
>
> *Source:* American Medical Association, Office of Quality Assurance, *Attributes to Guide the Development of Practice Parameters*, Chicago, Illinois, 1990.

following questions: How good are you? Can you prove it?

As the health care market changes over the next five years, local conditions will be the driving forces of these changes.[23] The "prove it" portion of the equation will become increasingly relevant and will take such forms as physician profiling and/or physician report cards (depending on the health plan, the governmental agency, or the provider group that employs them). These systems will be able to outline specific portions of a physician's work, such as cost and utilization of ancillary services (e.g., radiology, laboratory), or they will provide a cross-sectional view of the physician's entire practice pattern vis-à-vis his or her peers.

Profiling

Profiling can be used either punitively or educationally. Punitive actions can range from disqualifying physicians from a health plan to limiting their patient panel within the health plan. Educational efforts range from showing physicians how their treatments of similar patient populations with similar disease states differ from their peers, to helping physicians work to improve their performance.

Managing Revenues and Expenses

The medical paradigm shift includes new payment strategies for providers. Fee-for-service is being replaced in many managed care markets by capitation. Capitation pays the provider a fixed dollar amount to care for a defined or fixed population. This amount is usually calculated by the number of patients or members seen by the physician each month (per member per month). Under capitation, it is imperative that providers know their practice costs; they must develop effective patient education programs to help their patients stay healthy, so as to reduce demand on the medical practice.[24]

Developing Treatment Protocols and Referral Guidelines

In capitated arrangements it is very important, perhaps critical, that specialists work with primary care physicians in developing appropriate referral guidelines to help prevent under- and overutilization of specialty services and to ensure the appropriate use of specialty and ancillary services. It is also important for specialists to analyze their own internal treatment protocols to streamline their practices and decrease the variances of disease management. The goal of these strategies is to control excess utilization of services and costs.

Managing Risk

Capitation has evolved primarily because the older managed care arrangements could not sufficiently reduce care or increase profits—especially using fee-for-service, quality assurance, and utilization strategies. So capitation ties providers' incomes to the curtailment of medical services. In the final analysis, the financial risk is shifted to physicians. The newer financial incentives cause concern in many quarters. According to Woolhandler and Himmelstein: "The new risk-sharing arrangements are not simply the inverse of fee-for-service. Instead, they are the inverse of fee splitting."[25] Doctors under the new arrangements can profit from *not* referring patients. Some preliminary reports indicate that these types of inverse incentives will compromise the quality of patient care.

The end game of this shift in risk could be the avoidance of sick patients by physicians, hospitals, and Health Maintenance Organizations (HMOs). Among the consequences of capitation could be unemployed physicians; overextension of the care mandate of primary care physicians; withholding specialty referral; shifting sick, chronically ill patients to overworked, inadequately staffed public health clinics or hospitals; and distorting the clinical and ethical judgment of health care providers.

Many of these problems with capitation could be avoided by applying true cost-effectiveness analysis to medical therapy as described by Eddy.[26] This would help health care providers to decide the best, most efficient way to balance the benefits and harms of various treatments, along with the costs that people are willing to pay for these treatments. The capitated dollars would be allocated based on an unbiased cost-effectiveness analysis. The measure of the benefit must capture all the necessary information about all outcomes. This type of analysis parallels clinical judgment. Eddy also points out all outcomes of any treatment have two basic dimensions—an effect on length of life and an effect on quality of life. A common measure to roll these outcomes into a single measure for analytic purposes is "quality-adjusted life years" (QALY).[27]

WHO IS COLLECTING THE DATA?

In 1988, Roper et al. stated: "Federal health programs will no longer focus only on financing services, conducting medical research, implementing law, and administering bureaucratic rules. Federal agencies will also be involved in the collection of data and the distribution of information about health care itself—information on health outcomes that will influence medical practices."[28] As this role for the federal government gathered support, the Omnibus Budget Reconciliation Act of 1989 created the Agency for Health Care Policy and Research (AHCPR).[29] In 1992, this agency received $21 million to conduct treatment-effectiveness research, develop practice guidelines through the Medical Effectiveness Treatment Program (MEDTEP), and develop outcomes measures through the Patient Oriented Treatment Groups (PORTS). Numerous other federal agencies including the National Institutes of Health, the Centers for Disease Control and Prevention, the U.S. Food and Drug Administration, the Office of Technology Assessment, and the Physician Payment Review Commission (PPRC) use practice guidelines in the performance of their regulated responsibilities.

In the private arena, companies such as Value Health Sciences, Inc. (VHS) use a modified version of the RAND Corporation expert panel process to set appropriateness criteria for more than 34 procedures that are used by insurers, HMOs, utilization review forms, and others to identify via a computerized mechanism the indications for these 34 procedures. HPR in Boston, Massachusetts, has developed an episode-of-care profiling system to monitor the continuum of care across disease states. Tracking a care episode longitudinally—while capturing all the costs and data related to that episode of care and its related disease—has implications for consumers, payers, providers, employers, and insurers.

DISEASE MANAGEMENT

Another concept gaining strength and popularity is disease management or disease state management. The programs involved in this concept attempt to develop a clinical road map for total patient care with multispecialty input.[30]

Important aspects of disease state management are:

- identification of patients with a predisposition to a certain disease and those who have already developed that disease (e.g., diabetes, asthma, hypertension)
- use of evidence-based protocols with desired outcomes as end points, to help actively manage the patient's disease
- early intervention
- patient education
- getting the right information to the right decision maker at the right time[31]

THE DEMAND FOR OUTCOMES DATA

Employers are beginning to assume a major role in the growing focus on outcomes and accountability. In a recent edition of *Medical Economics*, Dwight McNeill, the health care information manager in GTE, states: "When Jose Canseco comes to bat everybody knows what his batting average is and the number of times he's been to bat. Yet we know nothing about the cardiovascular surgeon who wants to slit open someone's chest. Don't tell me consumers don't deserve to know how many times their surgeon has been at bat. Don't tell me you can't risk adjust so doctors' batting averages can be compared. Plans have to disclose this information, so employees can buy quality health care."[32] Also quoted in the same article, Peter Hayes of Hannoford Brothers, a Maine supermarket chain, states: "When we buy private-level cookies, we go to the factory to sample them, we give suggestions, and we continuously monitor the cookie for quality. Yet, I spend millions on health care and I don't know who gets treated and what the outcomes are. That's no longer acceptable."[33]

Intertwined in trying to make outcomes information available to all players demanding this data is the National Commission for Quality Assurance (NCQA), which reviews or accredits managed care organizations based on standards it has developed that measure the quality of care and service provided. NCQA reviewers use the standards (first promulgated in 1991 and revised in 1992)[34] to evaluate managed care organizations in the following areas:

- quality management and improvement
- utilization management
- credentialing
- members' rights and responsibilities
- preventive health services
- medical records

Emanating from the NCQA is the Health Plan Employer Data and Information Set (HEDIS). HEDIS is a list of performance measures that focus on patient satisfaction and indicators such as mammography rates, cholesterol screening rates, diabetic retinal exam rates, and immunization rates within the population served by the health plan. It should be emphasized that HEDIS measures are only indicators. For the most part, they are not even intermediate outcomes.

GETTING STARTED

Developing and implementing clinical outcomes research is a straightforward process. Like any research design project, the time frames, definitions, and goals of the project need to be decided upon and quantitatively defined. The purpose of developing the outcomes study should be addressed, and the right instrument must be developed according to the established timeline. It may be decided that the survey should capture data elements on both inpatients and outpatients, in order to accommodate an Integrated Delivery System. To that extent, choosing the appropriate methodology for capturing data along a continuum of care model will be vital to the success of the project. A good start then is understanding the differences among the various outcomes products and how they are used. Practice parameters and clinical guidelines (established by the Institute of Medicine of the National Academy of Sciences, Washington, D.C.) target the treatment of an illness from a practicing physician's interventions, while clinical pathways and CareMaps relate to a multidisciplinary team treatment effort. In addition, clinical pathways are used in a particular setting, while CareMaps use protocols that can be used in both an inpatient and outpatient setting. After the design has been selected, the purpose of the outcomes studies needs to be addressed. Ultimately, services need to be evaluated as appropriate or inappropriate interventions. Outcomes studies are not intended to rank physicians or hospitals, but to look at the effectiveness of treatment interventions.

It is also important to determine what data elements are to be collected and how those data are to be gathered and processed. Extracting data from a Physician Organization requires an information system that can track a patient's care along the continuum, and by a team of professionals. After the correct instrument and data elements have been decided upon, it is important to determine the process for collecting and managing the data. Ideally, the implementation of outcomes should be automated, not manual, because there is too much information to store and manage. An issue with an automated system is ownership of the data, and this should be explored prior to any agreement. Some of the packaged outcomes systems license the software, but own the data. Data extracted should be "clean," and the interpretation of the data should be valid. There should be a plan to ensure that the outcomes reports are used to improve care, thus keeping the process dynamic. A sample checklist for outcomes implementation is provided in Exhibit 12–3.

After the research design has been established, a committee should be formed that works on the outcomes project. One of its key responsibilities will be to select the medical departments in which the outcomes studies will be initiated, such as surgery, obstetrics and gynecology, and any high-volume and high-cost area. After the patient categories have been identified, the team should define the risk-adjustment factors and the outcome indicators. Outcome measurement categories include mortality, length of stay, discharge disposition, functioning status, devices present upon discharge, etc. The clinical risk factors that need to be defined include findings or distinguishing characteristics upon admission that adjust for severity. These elements include secondary diagnosis, chronic diseases, prior surgery, admission from the emergency room, neurological defects, previous medical conditions, lab work, blood pressure, etc. Once the elements have been defined, linking them with resources utilized and/or payment is ultimately part of the management process and the reason for investing in outcomes studies. If done effectively, outcomes studies can not only become part of the overall quality improvement process, but also establish cost-effective minimum standards of care.

FUTURE TRENDS

As outcomes databases become more widespread, they will be more useful in different areas. Payers, for example, may initiate the use of outcomes studies, instead of using existing performance indicators in reviewing appropriateness of care rendered in a delivery system. Outcomes studies could be used to measure the benefit of screening techniques employed by a Physician Organization. Current performance indicators do not measure the efficacy of screening techniques offered in a health plan. An outcomes system that followed a patient's course of health/illness through a continuum of care,

Exhibit 12–3 Developing an Outcomes Measurement Project—Checklist

Outcomes measurements are critical to identifying the efficacy of medical treatments and procedures both in terms of cost and effectiveness. The following is a checklist of steps that were followed at the Henry Ford Health System in designing its outcomes measurement project.

PRELIMINARY STEPS

1. Focus on issues of high utilization, cost, or variation in practice:
   - Issues that have yes or no answers are more apt to succeed.
   - Conditions or procedures that are part of a simple care delivery process are logistically easier.
2. Identify a physician leader to champion the project:
   - The project should be "owned" by the physicians.
   - Encourage education on outcomes measurement prior to developing the project.
3. Form a project team.
4. Designate a project coordinator.

DESIGNING THE OUTCOMES STUDY

1. Define the purpose of the outcomes study.
2. Determine what will be done with the data collected.
3. Determine the question you are trying to answer:
   - To define the data elements that are needed, consider if the goal is comparison, description, decision making, or quality improvement initiatives.
4. Define the criteria for enrolling patients in the study:
   - Define the type of patients involved in the study (acuity, age, etc.).
   - State the criteria for excluding patients within the selected subset.
5. Define the study timeline:
   - Define the event that observations are measured against.
   - Define the subsequent observational data that should be collected.
   - Define the windows of time within which you will accept data.
6. Develop the study instruments:
   - Determine whether data will be collected using existing databases.
   - Determine the means the data will be collected (mail, interview, phone).
   - Determine how the data will be identified (physician, patient, other).
7. Create the survey instrument:
   - Review literature or existing question databases for existing outcomes questions.
   - Design new questions if necessary.
   - Create a rough draft of the survey instrument.
   - Pilot the use of the instrument.
   - Edit the survey and develop a final version; be prepared for future editing if needed.
8. Collect the data:
   - Develop a protocol for the logistics of data collection.
   - Create a flowchart of all steps involved and try to simplify the collection process.
   - Consider when, how, where, and by whom the data are collected.
   - Develop a process that will not interfere with ongoing care delivery.
9. Manage the data collected:
   - If possible, use computer software to automate as much as possible.
   - Use software for patient tracking, survey development, and protocol implementation.
   - Consider where data will be stored and backed up.
   - Consider who owns the data.
10. Determine how the data will be used:
    - Develop a plan for data analysis.
    - Identify denominators or the patient population against which comparisons will be made at the time of data analysis.
    - Develop drafts of graphs that are desired.
11. Develop a plan for feedback and interpretation of the data:
    - Determine what reports are needed to present findings to physicians.
    - Develop a plan to achieve stated goals with the data collected.

Source: Henry Ford Health System, Detroit, Michigan, 1995.

including mortality rates, could replace the performance measure of system effectiveness in screening.

While outcomes research requires time, capital, and effort, this research is helpful for comparative analysis, particularly in reviewing physician performance. Instead of comparing physicians on overall utilization rates, outcomes analysis allows physicians to be compared on treatment rendered and resources utilized. It also substantiates the necessity to deliver the right amount of resources to a patient in a timely manner, thereby justifying the cost of treatment. Resource utilization data is being tied to outcomes data for this purpose.

Within a Physician Organization, the information system or the method for collecting, storing, and distributing data will be as important as the selected outcomes instrument. The ability to capture data along a continuum of care while still maintaining patient confidentiality will need to be addressed through technology. Key components of the new technology, which are discussed in more detail in Chapter 10, include the following:

- wide area and local area networking capabilities
- relational databases
- graphical user interfaces
- optical storage capabilities
- speech recognition software
- multimedia software

The ability to share information throughout an Integrated Delivery System will result in the standardization of outcomes methodology. Regionally or perhaps nationally driven efforts will establish industry standard databases and technology for storing, accessing, and retrieving information. The use of more advanced technology will assist the development and implementation of a more cohesive and comprehensive method of assessing quality and elevating standards of care.

Outcomes data must always be relevant, valid, and reliable. As outcomes research becomes more sophisticated, it should evolve toward a risk-adjusted system. Typical outcomes measurements have looked at mortality and morbidity. While these are important indicators, the information becomes more important when it adjusts for risk. Two cases of pneumonia are very different if one patient is a 75-year-old smoker and the other is a 28-year-old. In addition to risk-adjusted patient outcomes, quality measurements should include patient satisfaction and functional status.

Ultimately, financial information and resources utilized should be tied back into the intervention and the outcome. While cost has always been an important issue, particularly for employer groups and payers, quality is becoming increasingly important. The providers that can demonstrate better outcomes, even at higher costs, will become the preferred providers. Quality is the health care issue of the 1990s, as cost was in the 1980s. Once costs have been slashed and payment mechanisms have been established to control spiraling costs, the overall quality of a delivery system will become just as important—if not more important—to consumers.

NOTES

1. S. Schoenbaum, Toward Fewer Procedures and Better Outcomes, *Journal of the American Medical Association* 269 (1993): 794–796.

2. P.M. Ellwood, Outcomes Management: A Technology of Patient Experience, *New England Journal of Medicine* 318 (1988): 1549–1556.

3. J. Wennberg and A. Gittelsohn, Small Area Variations in Health Care Delivery, *Science* 182 (1973): 1102–1107.

4. L.L. Leape et al., Does Inappropriate Use Explain Small Area Variations in the Use of Health Care Services? *Journal of the American Medical Association* 263 (1990): 669–672.

5. M.R. Chassin et al., Does Inappropriate Use Explain Geographic Variations in the Use of Health Care Services? *Journal of the American Medical Association* 258 (1987): 2533–2537.

6. M. Holowecki, What Cook Book Medicine Will Mean for You? *Medical Economics* 66 (1989): 118–133.

7. Chassin et al., Does Inappropriate Use Explain Geographic Variations?

8. J.F. Piccirillo, Insights in Ololaryngology, *Outcomes Research in Clinical Practice* 8, no. 5 (October 1993): 1–8.

9. J.D. Kleinke, Medicine's Industrial Revolution, *Wall Street Journal*, 21 August 1995, sec. A, p. 8.

10. Kleinke, Medicine's Industrial Revolution.

11. Wennberg and Gittelsohn, Small Area Variations; Chassin et al., Does Inappropriate Use Explain Geographic Variations?; Piccirillo, Insights in Otolaryngology; Kleinke, Medicine's Industrial Revolution; A.S. Relman, Assessment and Accountability: The Third Revolution in Medical Care, *New England Journal of Medicine* 319 (1988): 1220–1222.

12. Picirillo, Insights in Otolaryngology; Kleinke, Medicine's Industrial Revolution.

13. J. Wennberg and A. Gittelsohn, Variations in Medical Care among Small Areas, *Scientific American* 246 (1982): 120; B. James, Congress in Health Outcomes and Accountability (Personal communication, 13 December 1995).

14. Ellwood, Outcomes Management.

15. *Health Outcomes Institute Newsletter*, 1 November 1993.

16. A. Tarlov et al., Medical Outcomes Study: An Application of Methods for Monitoring the Results of Medical Care, *Journal of the American Medical Association* 262 (1989): 925–993; Health Status Questionnaire Form 39, Health Outcomes Institute, Bloomington, Minnesota.

17. *Health Outcomes Institute Newsletter*.

18. D.A. Lane, Utility, Decision and Quality of Life, *Journal of Chronic Disease* 40 (1987): 585–591; A.M. Epstein, The Outcomes Movement: Will It Get Us Where We Want To Go? *New England Journal of Medicine* 323 (1990): 266–270.

19. E. Wagner et al., The Affect of a Shared Decision Making Program on Rates of Surgery for Benign Prostatic Hyperplasia: Pilot Results, *Medical Care* (official Journal of Public Health Associates) 33, no. 8 (August 1995): 755–782.

20. S.H. Woolf, Practice Guidelines, A New Reality in Medicine: II. Methods of Developing Guidelines, *Archives of Internal Medicine* 152 (1992): 946–952; D.M. Eddy, Clinical Decision Making: From Theory to Practice (Guidelines for Policy Statements: The Explicit Approach), *Journal of the American Medical Association* 263 (1990): 2239–2240.

21. Institute of Medicine Committee to Advise the Public Health Service on Clinical Practice Guidelines, *Clinical Practice Guidelines: Directions for a New Program*, ed. M.J. Field and K.N. Lohr (Washington, D.C.: National Academy Press, 1990).

22. American Medical Association, Office of Quality Assurance, *Attributes to Guide the Development of Practice Parameters* (Chicago, Ill.: American Medical Association, 1990).

23. K. Ihnagni, Are HMOs Really a Doctor's Best Friend? *Medical Economics* (January 1995): 26–33.

24. S.R. Hoffman, A Brief Guide to the Medical Paradigm Shift, *Surgical Services Management* 1 (1995):18–19.

25. S. Woolhandler and D.M. Himmelstein, Extreme Risk: The New Corporate Proposition for Physicians, *New England Journal of Medicine* 333 (1995): 1706.

26. D.M. Eddy, Cost-Effectiveness Analysis: A Conversation with my Father, *Journal of the American Medical Association* 267 (1992): 1669–1675.

27. D.M. Eddy, Cost-Effectiveness Analysis: Is It up to the Task? *Journal of the American Medical Association* 267 (1992): 3342–3348.

28. W. Roper et al., Effectiveness in Healthcare: An Initiative to Evaluate and Improve Medical Practice, *New England Journal of Medicine* 319 (1988): 1220–1222.

29. U.S. House of Representatives, *Omnibus Budget Reconciliation Act of 1989: Conference Report Accompanying HR 3299*, U.S. Congress, 21 November 1989.

30. G. Halpern, How to Develop Disease Management Protocols, *Managed Health Care News* (April 1995): S9–S10.

31. T. Hughes, Research in Managed Care: Outcomes Research in Disease Prevention and Management, *Journal of Management Care Pharmacy* (May/June, 1996).

32. A. Stomski, Employers to Doctors: It's Time for Real Savings, *Medical Economics* 72, no. 14 (July 24, 1995): 122–135.

33. Stomski, Employers to Doctors.

34. National Commission for Quality Assurance, 1350 New York Avenue, Suite 700, Washington, DC 20005.

Part IV

Managing Managed Care and Capitation

Chapter 13

Managed Care Contracting and Reimbursement for Physician Organizations in a Capitated and Risk-Sharing Environment

Richard Ferreira, M.D., J.D.

INTRODUCTION

Most physicians only encounter contracts when they venture into a financial arrangement with a bank or lending institution related to the purchase of a home, automobile, or similar investment. Since the advent of managed care, contracts for physician services as a whole and for individual specialists in particular have become a way of life. Unfortunately, most physicians are ill-prepared to deal with the issues that they need to face, and few understand the potential impact of the contract on their practice.

The earliest relationships between physicians and payers began in the mid to late 1960s when Blue Cross developed special programs that permitted Blue Cross to pay the physician directly. Prior to that, physicians had been required to bill the patient, who, in turn submitted the bill to the insurance company. The insurance company then paid the patient (plan member) the amount provided by the coverage in the contract. Payment to the patient was true, even if the insurance company accepted direct billings from the physician. In the late 1960s, Blue Cross and Blue Shield in several states offered to pay physicians directly from the company upon presentation of a timely and correct bill, completed in a proscribed manner. This offer was only applicable if the physician accepted what the company offered as payment in full. The days of discounting had begun. Again, this was the simplest of agreements, and the physician knew in advance the amount he or she would receive.

Beginning in the mid to late 1970s and continuing through to today, contracting has become an integral part of every physician's practice, particularly in managed care. To deal with the issues of contracting, the physician needs to appreciate the structure, intent, and content of the contract document.

The purpose of this chapter is to provide the physician or Managed Care Organization (MCO) with an understanding of contracts between the various parties. Specific issues reflecting the concerns of special parties are discussed in the various sections below.

CONTRACTS

The Contract As a Legal Document

Each contract is a legal instrument. To provide the greatest protection, the contract should be reduced to writing. The law recognizes other types of contracts such as oral agreements and implied contracts. The *oral agreement* is merely an agreement made verbally between parties wherein one promises to perform a certain task in return for consideration from the other. The court will uphold such an agreement and can apply a duty of performance on both parties when there is a problem. Such agreements are often hard to prove unless there are witnesses or some evidence that, outside some agreement, one party would not have acted in that way. The *implied contract* is a construct of law and is done to prevent the unjust enrichment of one party over another when no contract exists. This situation requires the act of a party that enriches another to the detriment of the first party, and under these circumstances the court can say an "implied" contract existed even though none was ever contemplated by either party. Neither oral nor implied agreements are commonly used in managed care, and they are mentioned only for the purpose of completeness.

Most written contracts follow a standard format:

- introductory paragraph
- recitals
- definition of terms
- obligations of the parties under the contract
- conditions of performance
- method and time of payment
- term of the agreement and termination
- notice requirements
- applicable law
- signature page

The *introductory paragraph* identifies the parties involved and normally states the date the contract is effective. This date may differ from the date of execution and should be specifically noted.

The *recital* begins with "Whereas" statements indicating the position and needs of the parties, and concludes with a "Therefore" statement respecting the reason for the contract. Generally speaking, this is a formality of the contract and not essential to the agreement.

In contrast to the recital, the *definition of terms* section is essential, and the physician needs to pay careful attention to the definitions provided. All definitions should be consistent with current practice and usage of the terms. Some definitions, in fact, define conditions of the agreement and need to have specific attention paid to them. Examples of such definitions might include:

- definition of an emergency service
- definition of authorization
- exceptions to those definitions

The need to carefully review definitions cannot be overly emphasized. The terms, when used in the agreement, will provide both parties with a clear understanding, irrespective of their particular perspective or who is subsequently reading the agreement.

The next area, *obligations of the parties*, may in fact be separated, with separate sections for each party involved. A mutuality of obligations is not uncommon, particularly in respect to issues related to legal requirements or obligations. The obligations related may address responsibilities going beyond the specific purpose of the agreement. In the case of medical services, such obligations can relate to the need to maintain records or to provide access to records for a specific period of time, the need for the parties to maintain their own liability and other forms of insurance, or the need to maintain certain availability or coverage requirements. Like the definitions, these terms require careful review on the part of the physician to ascertain the ability to meet the obligations.

Conditions of performance relate to specific circumstances under which the terms of the agreement apply or do not apply. For the most part, such conditions usually describe the circumstances under which the contract terms will apply, and by negation do not apply. The classic example in a managed care agreement is authorization for the service. Most agreements define the specific need for authorization and define how authorization will be provided. In some circumstances, conditions may extend a need to use certain individuals or providers of service. Conditions are very important for a clear understanding of when limitations may exist in the agreement.

Method and time of payment is an issue that receives a lot of attention. In reality, the primary concern is how much will be paid and within what "reasonable" time period. Many contracts will state payment in X days of receipt of a clean claim or absent notice of a defective claim. It is understandable that payment will be desired in the shortest period of time possible. However, each party must be forthright in their real expectations and abilities. A manually dependent claims system may only be able to reasonably deliver payments in 120 days after receipt, whereas, a claims system using computer technology may be able to deliver payment in 45 days. Each party should discuss the issue of timeliness of payment and come to an agreement on what is normally acceptable and what is outside the realm of acceptable or reasonable. The terms of payment are defined further by specifying the amount to be paid. This can vary depending on the methodology used and will be discussed later.

While this is a document stating an agreement, it is necessary to define a *term of agreement* and the *means of terminating the agreement*. Such a situation is often difficult, since both parties desire for the agreement to continue when all is well. Unfortunately, both parties will need to look at their desired needs and wants and come to an initial real term. It is not uncommon for this to be one year. A means of preserving an agreement on an ongoing basis is by virtue of an "evergreen clause." Such a clause states that the agreement with a term of X time will automatically renew if not notified of termination X days prior to termination. In this manner, both parties, if satisfied with the agreement, can permit the agreement to continue forward without further negotiations.

Termination of the agreement can occur as a result of cause, no cause, or as a constructive termination. *Cause* usually refers to a failure to perform under the terms of the agreement or a failure to meet specific required conditions of the agreement. A *no cause* termination is generally a mutual agreement that permits parties to terminate and usually reflects a circumstance when one of the parties acts in a manner that is inconsistent with the agreement but not a major breach of the agreement. Such an example may be the requirement that services be provided at a specific site but said site is not established. The other party is ready and able to perform but is not permitted to perform elsewhere. Failure to provide the specific site is a constructive limitation placed on the party willing to perform and may allow for a specific means of termination.

Much of what transpires when issues arise requires *notice*. The means of providing notice is usually to a specific individual or designated title at a stated location by a defined means (registered mail). This format of notice is recommended because it provides the most defined and specific means for the parties to correspond whenever an issue needs to be addressed. It does not mean that other communications are not met with success; however, formal means are required.

Applicable law refers to the law that will apply to the contract. Generally, the applicable law is the jurisdiction where the contract will be performed or carried out. It may, however, be the law of the jurisdiction of either party and it merely serves as notice of how matters of law will be resolved.

Finally, the *signature page*, where the involved parties affix their signatures, identifies their position or authority to sign and provides the date on which they execute the agreement.

Within each contract, there may be additional items or terms, which may depend on specific requirements imposed by local legislative enactment or regulatory requirements. These generally deal with public issues such as nondiscrimination, state-imposed obligations, or plan-imposed responsibilities. A common term is *arbitration*, meaning that disputes could be settled by a means other than suit through a disinterested third party. Such agreements for arbitration, unless the arbitration is accepted as binding, are generally not acceptable to many organizations. *Binding* simply means that the decision of the arbiter is binding on the parties; they do not have recourse through the courts even with an adverse decision.

Whenever the physician approaches a contract, the first item to determine is what is being contracted and between whom. Then, it is recommended that the document be read in its entirety to gain a flavor for the agreement. After the physician reads through the contract in that manner, it is recommended that the individual paragraphs or terms be read carefully, referring back to the definitions and/or related sections or other documents that are referenced or incorporated into the agreement by reference. In every circumstance, areas that are unclear or that do not appear to apply should be carefully noted, and specific questions respecting the issues should be drafted. It is helpful to place these questions in a written format that can be attached. A legal consultant may be costly, but having a contract expert review the document may, in fact, be the best investment for the uninitiated or apprehensive physician.

Almost all terms, with the exception of legal constraints or requirements, can be negotiated, meaning that each party can act in a manner to address the other party's concern and come to a mutually satisfactory agreement. Often, negotiations are dealt with in an adversarial manner, which is unfortunate and unnecessary. Negotiations are the opportunity for resolution of mutual needs by understanding what those needs are and how, through a process of give and take, each party assumes a position that is beneficial to the overall agreement. The attitude respecting a completed negotiation is that both parties should leave the table a little unhappy and neither should walk away with a broad grin on their face. This simply means that one party should not take advantage of the other and both will need to give in order to achieve an agreement.

Contracts with Health Plans

In managed care, the majority of relationships begin with contracts between the insurer (payer or health plan) and the purchaser (usually an employer). For the most part, physicians have little or no input at this level, as the issues deal more with employer cost expectations, union issues, benefit packages, and—today—measured value for each dollar spent. An exception to this rule of thumb could exist in cases where a self-insured employer goes directly to a group or MCO to arrange for health care coverage for the employees. While there has been considerable discussion of direct contracting in the literature and some expectation that it may increase, it now appears that the employer groups are seeking to band together into cooperatives and offer their combined populations to a successful bidding company. Obviously, these large cooperatives are seeking certain returns and a decrease in their costs.

The first level where physicians should be involved in contracts is in the contract between the MCO, no matter what its official legal structure, and the health plan where the physicians are accepting partial or total risk for a population of individuals. Much of the contract between the health plan and the MCO deals with issues of business, reporting obligations, divisions of liability, and formulas for calculating how capitation is paid on an age/sex basis. These issues may be of interest to some physicians, but to most, the explanation of the result by trusted administrative colleagues is all that is required.

Physicians need to concentrate on understanding *the scope of health care services* for which they are responsible. Such services go beyond simply the care provided by the physician directly in the office, the hospital, or elsewhere. The scope of such services may include certain requirements such as:

- compliance with a specific utilization protocol
- use of specific providers for defined services
- delivery of services not ordinarily offered by a physician's office
- inclusion of coverage not delivered by the physician

Most plans require the MCO to provide its own utilization processes. However, in some cases, the plan may reserve the final authority to approve hospital services or in some cases designate specific facilities for highly specialized tertiary or quaternary services. The degree of control exerted by the plan may create situations of discontinuity of care and increased costs. This can occur because the plan elects to use highly specialized services at academic centers or what have been termed "centers of excellence." Since these centers do not have established relations with the MCO, and since they owe their allegiance to the plan, communications respecting patient care may not be what is desired. This lack of communication can create a discontinuity of care and decrease overall quality. Physicians must have input into the responsibilities of such centers and their staff to be responsive to the local MCO. Another way in which these relationships can impact the MCO is when the plan contracts with the academic center for the institutional costs since these costs remain the plan's financial responsibility. The contract with the professional at that facility is of secondary importance, if at all. The charges generated and the number of intra-center professional or specialty referrals can be significant. Again, physicians should be able to have certain assurances provided by the center and/or the plan that would permit rapid development of mutually beneficial agreements.

Coverage issues in the health plan contracts should be detailed to a sufficient degree that questions that arise can be readily resolved. Many plans state that cosmetic services are not a covered benefit, but a closer review of the enrollee's information package could reveal that certain defects associated with birth and not of a functional nature are covered. In some states, such as California, breast reconstruction following any medically indicated removal of the breast must be included in the benefit package. Included in breast reconstruction is the reconstruction of the nipple, purely for cosmetic reasons. Items of this nature need to be explored so physicians are aware of what is included in the scope of their professional responsibility.

Wellness and preventive health care are issues of major concern to employers and, hence, to the plans. These issues should be of concern to physicians, but only if they take a broad, long-range view rather than a short-term, cost-saving view. The investment in a vaccination to prevent a future potential transplant (hepatitis) or major disease process with significant disabling sequelae (polio) is easily justified. However, the short-range view of not providing vaccinations to save a few dollars—since the patient would only be benefited in the distant future, when care will probably be delivered by another provider—may greatly increase future costs. This type of reasoning is counterproductive to the overall mission of health care. The purpose of this section is not to discuss the merits or costs of such a program, but to discuss how it can be affected in a contracting sense.

A number of issues in the area of wellness and preventive health can affect the physician involved in a managed care plan contract. Many plans provide additional capitation for specific wellness programs. These programs can include prenatal care instruction, stop smoking classes, stress and hypertension management, as well as other employee health education programs. For many MCOs and most independent physicians, such services have been ordered through community or hospital resources and have not been provided as a physician service. Under most managed care plans, education falls under direct physician liability.

In preventive health many educational issues arise, but physicians must be particularly aware of vaccinations. Over the past several years, several new vaccines have come onto the market, such as measles, chicken pox, and hepatitis. The issue here is not the value of the vaccine but the cost that accrues to the professional that was not contemplated at the time of the original agreement. The plans tend to define injectable medications given during an office visit as a professional expense. This creates a situation in which the public or enrollees through their employers have an expectation that these recommended services, which are not excluded, will be immediately provided. The plan, not wanting to lose business or have that business relationship threatened, supports the members and the employer groups to the detriment of the MCO. It is recommended that the MCO develop language that would provide for some reinsurance or shared costs of such new drugs or vaccines.

Contracts with plans also have numerous issues regarding various services that were contracted for by the plan or that are being carved out. Carve outs are health care services that are not included in the global service agreement. Patients needing these services are *carved out* from the rest of the insured population and required to receive treatment from a separate panel of providers. Frequently, carve-out agreements with providers are very limited in scope and focus on specific health care problems. *Carve out* is a dirty word in the southern California marketplace and should be throughout the industry. The classic carve out is mental health; although it may be easy on paper to identify a "mental health issue" versus a "medical issue," this is difficult to do with a living, breathing human being. Rarely does the patient with either a major mental health disorder or a major medical disorder not have some component of the other. The most common disorder in the United States is depressive disorder, which manifests itself in many and differing ways. Some patients present with a lack of appetite, others with headache, still others with vague symptoms of malaise; few will present stating they are depressed. Repeated medical evaluations may reveal no cause for the symptoms, which may be treated with various prescriptions until the disorder is properly recognized. Unfortunately, even if depression is recognized at the start, it is not uncommon for a carve-out company to refuse care until "medical causes" are ruled out.

Most carve-out companies offer services through their own group or providers, who are motivated not to provide services due to the limited resources available. Many carve-out companies develop their own hospital or facility relationships away from the primary MCO sites, and then use their referral patterns to address other issues of care not within their scope of coverage but "necessary" under the circumstances. These costs are passed back to the member's MCO, unless there is some accounting or acceptance for such care by the plan.

Another area for physician input in plan contracts relates to packaged rates, ancillary services, or special pharmacies that must be used. Often, the physician or group may be liable for the expense of such service or care if the enrollee is not directed appropriately or does not receive specific plan authorization. It is unlikely anything can be done to amend such a condition, but awareness of the issues involved and careful education of the MCO and its staff will go a long way to prevent such occurrences.

In summary, the health plan contract is a complex document for which legal evaluation is recommended. An experienced administrator or individual with group management experience should deal with the operational issues related to reporting and similar obligations. Finally, each MCO should involve a physician or group of physicians to deal with the issues related to the delivery of care. In the end, all should get together and prepare a summary or provide an explanation to the leadership of the MCO of major issues, particularly those that are new and impact the delivery system.

Contracts with Physicians

The agreements with physicians primarily deal with specialties, with primary care as the fundamental building block of the managed care delivery system. The first step in contract development is the definition of primary care, by specialty and then by responsibility or scope of care. Most groups accept family medicine, general medicine, general internal medicine, and pediatrics as primary care. A large number also include obstetrics for services related to pregnancy or well-woman care. (Recently, California enacted legislation that defined primary care specifically to include the specialty of obstetrics and gynecology [OB/GYN] unless the physician specialist does not desire to be defined as a primary care provider.)

Primary Care Physicians

The second step of this process is to define the scope of services or clinical responsibilities that are the responsibility of the primary care provider (PCP). Many groups have adopted or modified the guidelines put forward by Milliman & Robertson.[1] In order for any guidelines to be effective, there must be acceptance and adoption by the physicians involved. The following story exemplifies the effects of a lack of physician acceptance of established guidelines:

> A group of physicians practiced in a community where all foot care was provided by podiatrists, including normal care such as toenail clipping. The group had a significant number of elderly enrollees and routinely referred the enrollees for their foot care to the podiatrists, who saw all referrals and attended to all needs. There were no service issues or patient dissatisfaction. Unfortunately, this service was being paid for at a rate 10 times higher than the national figure in a fee market, and the podiatrists were capitated. No one involved—including the medical group, the plan, or even the podiatrists—could justify the cost. When the contract was terminated, an angry PCP who could not refer 26 patients with no medical problems for routine nail clipping called his utilization review director to find out why. When it was explained that this was now the responsibility of the PCP, he quickly responded with the fact that he was not trained to do so and did not have the necessary equipment. He was asked who clipped his nails. He then sent a nurse to buy a toenail clipper that would address the needs in 95 percent of the cases.

While the above story may seem humorous, it illustrates the point of concern and the expenses that can result if primary care providers do not have or have not accepted specific guidelines to their area of responsibility. Yet another issue, in the former fee-for-service world, is that many physicians refused to see patients under a certain age or over a certain age. Others refused to see patients for certain conditions or examinations (Pap smear, sigmoidoscopy, AIDS). While this may have been acceptable then and may still be accepted in some large groups, it is not generally acceptable for managed care. These patients will have to be dealt with by the group, and an individual physician's agreement may require modification if the full scope of responsibilities cannot be provided.

Many Independent Practice Associations (IPAs) do not have OB/GYN services included in their basic agreement with the PCP. They tend to contract with those individuals as specialists. A few groups treat pediatrics as a specialty and provide well-baby checks and routine child care through the family practice division. These are special circumstances and are best dealt with according to local community practices.

Specialists

Once primary services issues are resolved, or at least satisfactorily defined, the organization should address contracts for the delivery of professional services that the organization cannot provide itself. For the purposes of this discussion, the primary care physicians will be considered as accounted for through a basic employment agreement with some salary compensation mechanism or as capitated for a defined population.

The specialist community should be divided into separate groups:

- basic specialists
- tertiary or quaternary specialists
- hospital-based specialists

Basic Specialists. Basic specialists include cardiologists, general surgeons, oncologists, orthopedic surgeons, ophthalmologists, and urologists—with the latter three being especially important in organizations with a high number of senior enrollees. All other specialists would be tertiary or quaternary specialists. The reason for this separation relates to the relative speed with which the group requires a relationship and the general costs. The basic specialties constitute a larger percentage of specialists than the other specialty groups, but their costs may not be proportional. Following is a discussion of cost issues related to each group.

In general, contracting with specialists requires a document that addresses the needs of all physicians and not simply the needs of a single specialty. If a distinct document is developed for each specialty, the MCO would eventually have more than 60 different basic physician documents. A generic contract for all professional services requires some advance work on the part of the group to develop a manual or separate document dealing with the common issues that arise and the special issues that must be defined. Here, the issues generally relate to the circumstances surrounding the specialty and how it gains authorization, how it is compensated, and what is excluded from coverage.

Such issues would include a general statement of how authorizations are obtained and what process is required, followed by who is covered under the scope of the authorization. In the case of a patient with an authorization for a surgical procedure, the following specialists are included: the hospital radiologist, the pathologist, the anesthesiologist, and the surgical assistant. Other services are not included or are beyond the scope of the original authorization. Again, assume the surgeon has received authorization and the anesthesiologist provides routine surgical anesthesia. In this case, the anesthesiologist desires or is requested to provide a separate service of pain management. The language in the agreement should have already notified all parties that a separate authorization is necessary for services not covered by the original authorization, and it should indicate how such services will be reimbursed. Postoperative pain management is considered to be part of the surgeon's care and included in the fee. One means of dealing with the issue is to assign a portion of the surgeon's fee to the anesthesiologist for the service.

A particular area of concern for many groups is the various charges applied by billing agencies for emergency physicians. These charges can include:

- after-hours care (What is considered after hours for a facility open 24 hours a day?)
- Saturday, Sunday, or holiday charge (Is a physician expected to be present on those days?)
- special interpretations of laboratory tests, ECG, or X-rays (The fee for the particular visit itself contemplates that

such interpretation would be necessary and is included.)
- admission or separate charges for the patient being admitted

All specialties should eliminate certain charges such as those listed above, and all contracted physicians should know that these charges will not be paid. They must further recognize that they, or their billing agents, cannot separately bill any managed care (prepaid) enrollee for services that are not authorized. The issue of authorization can become muddied, because some patients seek care without an authorization. Unless that care is in response to a medical emergency or unless it would have been provided anyway, the MCO has no liability. The MCO must cover all medical emergencies, even when its physicians are available to provide the service and would have provided the service if given the option. The circumstances of care that would have been provided in any event is a matter of judgment and may or may not be accepted by the MCO. When the enrollee, of his or her own volition, elects to receive care outside of the MCO, it is unlikely that liability would be accepted. Under those circumstances, the provider may bill the patient directly. The only other exception to the policy of not billing a prepaid enrollee is for copayment or co-insurance responsibilities of the enrollee.

Tertiary and Quaternary Specialists. The issues dealing with tertiary and quaternary specialists, especially in the academic community, usually relate to the inability of those individuals to contract except through their organization (university practice group), their recognition that they are offering a "unique" area service, and the effect of managed care on the entire tertiary/quaternary area of care. Putting pricing aside, these physicians tend to work in a very tightly knit system; they use one another indiscriminately for consultation and support, even when such services can be offered by the MCO or themselves. Examples include routine laboratory needs, imaging, radiology, and supportive consultative evaluations available through the MCO. The common reason given is that the special tertiary or quaternary service is so unusual that only the university's laboratory, radiology department, or specialist colleagues are able to provide the service and ensure the quality of care. The simple reason is the referrals represent income to the tertiary and quaternary system. The issue is easily resolved when the service is packaged.

Hospital-Based Specialists. Hospital-based specialists have been difficult to contract with in the past, and they continue to represent the area of greatest difficulty in MCO contracting. The reasons for the difficulty are not of concern here, but the responses are. Many of these specialists try to avoid any and all contact with the MCO and its authorization process. Their attempts have varied from simple individual acts, to position papers of state and national specialty societies, to legislative acts or attempts at voter reform. An example of the latter was a recent attempt by a state society of anesthesiologists to place a referendum on the state ballot that would have declared anesthesia as primary care (for the unconscious). This attempt failed, but it reveals the extreme measures being taken.

Hospital-based specialists, unlike most other specialists, operate exclusively in the hospital (usually just one hospital). Usually the patient has no choice in the selection of the individual specialist providing that service, and the patient may never meet or speak to the individual. Often, the relationship between these specialists and the hospital is contractual and, in some instances, the specialists have created a closed staff that assures them exclusivity. The demand for these specialists' services has decreased as a result of decreased use of the hospital and the use of alternative sources of support, and hospital-based specialists have seen their control of the hospital patient and their incomes decline. Hospitals have been very sympathetic to these physicians but also are concerned about the hospital's ability to contract for managed care lives.

Some hospitals have altered their agreements with their hospital-based specialists so that the hospital has the final say on contracting with MCOs. Plans have begun to assign the liability of professional care by the four main hospital-based specialists to the hospital (radiology, anesthesia, emergency medicine, and pathology). Finally, entrepreneurial individuals have started specialty IPAs and are willing to buck the existing system for assurances of volume, usually under a capitation or risk-sharing agreement.

The responses of the hospitals and the plans, as well as the development of specialty IPAs, do not bode well for hospital-based specialists. While they may seem to have local control, this control is becoming less real. Many are finding themselves in positions that are subservient to organizational entities, and they are losing their sense of independence and cooperation with other physicians.

Resolving Contract Issues

Managed care participating physicians, IPAs, Preferred Provider Organizations (PPOs), health plans, and ultimately the purchasers will have to address all of the issues raised in this section. In most instances, the issues will be resolved among the physicians in the community and will not affect the plans or other entities.

Understanding the Needs of Both Parties

Every agreement must begin with an understanding. First, both parties have acknowledged a need for an understanding and—while they may not have any agreement as to the level of the understanding or they may be widely divergent in the appreciation of the value associated with the need—they begin seeking to define an agreement. Each discussion should begin by both parties identifying what they perceive as their need.

The need can be simple or complex in a business sense, which is not necessarily related to medical complexity. It is recommended that the individual complexities of the specialty, service, or site of delivery be put aside initially. Define the mutual needs as simply as possible. Take, for example, an MCO that requires a relationship with a transplant center for its enrollment. Medically, this is as complex as care can be, requiring special facilities, numerous specialists, usually an academic center, extensive postprocedure support services, and long periods of follow-up. The general needs might be defined as follows:

- The MCO wants the opportunity to provide patients to a defined group that responds to the group's and the patients' needs in a timely manner, provides necessary care, and reports back to the group for a "reasonable" cost.
- The transplant center wants all patients requiring that service referred to their center and their designated specialists with the agreed-upon payment made in a timely manner with the least amount of paperwork and red tape.

Having agreed upon each other's needs, both parties can begin to discuss their specific concerns or special needs. Although the list for the example chosen is very long, just a few will be listed for each:

- The MCO wants:
  1. a designated contact person at the transplant center

2. ability to support the center with MCO's own laboratory, X-ray, and support system whenever practical and efficient to do so
3. adherence to MCO requirements for authorization and delivery process
4. close communication with referring or primary care physician and return of care as soon as possible
- The transplant center wants:
  1. referral of all patients requiring the service to the center for primary evaluation
  2. use of the center's laboratory and other diagnostic services
  3. simplified or global authorization extending for time and staff

This example illustrates how, from a single simple understanding, specific needs can be identified on both sides. The process is called negotiation, and it should be looked on as an opportunity to solve mutual problems. Problem solving can be considered as accommodation or compromise, as long as patient service and true quality of care are not compromised in the process.

Needs will differ depending on the circumstances and the parties; but first they must be identified, then accepted by the other party, and finally discussed so as to reach a resolution. It may not always be possible to resolve each party's needs but at least an open and reasoned discussion will leave the opportunity for each party to return to the table at some later date.

REIMBURSEMENT METHODOLOGIES FOR MANAGED CARE

There are numerous reimbursement methods, some of which are very complex and involve the assignment of points or awards for differing units, which are then used for subsequent calculation of a fee or distribution of available dollars. The purpose of this section is not to get into these complex manipulations but to discuss the major and basic types of reimbursement. Basic to the entire discussion is the recognition that the payer—no matter if this is the purchaser, the plan, a group, or an IPA—will be paying based on a fixed number of dollars per member per month.

Standard Methodologies

The classic basis for payment is the fee charged for the service. Until the early to mid 1980s, the fee-for-service payment was the standard payment received except for Medicare and some insurers that had defined their own schedule, which was accepted as the full payment. In the market today, fee-for-service is no longer the standard, although it is still talked about. In essentially 100 percent of cases, some other basis is now used, and the MCO need not be concerned with fee-for-service except as it historically relates to the current payment method.

In shifting from fee-for-service payments, the first step taken by most payers and providers was to agree to a discount, initially expressed as a percentage off charges. The assumption was that the charges would equal the fee then in place for that service. However, this was not always the case. For example, a specialist was seeing certain patients of a physician group. Because the specialist was cooperative, available, and liked by the staff and patients who used his services, he was approached to enter into a contract in which, in return for added volume, he would provide a discount. At the time his fee was $40 a unit, and he agreed to a 20 percent discount off his charges. The group assumed payment would be $32 a unit. However, the specialist immediately raised his base charge to $60 a unit and expected $48 in payment, which was 20 percent more than what he had received in the past and 50 percent more than anticipated. Needless to say, this did not work out to the specialist's and the physician group's mutual satisfaction or benefit.

In spite of examples such as the above, percent discounts persist and are still being used. Hospitals were very reluctant to be involved initially except under such agreements. Many vendors of ancillary services still operate under such agreements. If such arrangements are to be used, there must be an agreement as to the base. A commonly accepted base is the Medicare reimbursement standard or another fixed standard.

The use of diagnosis-related group (DRG) for payment of hospital stays initially seemed to be an effective means of controlling costs, yet, as many discover, DRG often exceeds the charges when patients are carefully managed. As a result, hospitals are willing to accept fixed payments for each day of service, depending on the level of service with specific exclusions. This is known as a *per diem* structure. Per diems remain the main hospital compensation methodology used nationwide. However, many hospitals are now seeking to be involved in risk-sharing structures or capitation.

Per diems work well for routine, uncomplicated admissions for the hospital and the payer. The values are based on the hospital's experience related to the number of admissions and the length of stay. As hospital admissions decreased and lengths of stay were reduced by as much as two-thirds in mature markets, per diems became an ineffective means of compensation. In complicated cases, even with exclusion and stop-loss requirements, per diems fall short of the hospital's needs. In these cases, the hospitals consider the agreement a success if they meet their costs, which often is not the case. In response to these issues, hospitals in mature markets are moving to capitation agreements wherein they agree to share in savings of days with the payer.

Much has been said and written about *per case* rates, which are usually offered by tertiary centers for specialized services. Most often, these rates are developed as "loss leaders," with the intent of attracting other business from the payer. Usually, the payers have no need to use the facilities beyond that of the contracted service, and the hospital has to seek greater volume. Too often, this merely means offering the per case rate at a continued and increasing loss, since volume cannot make up for all costs by efficiencies of scale in a service-oriented business. Predictably, these facilities are now returning to the table seeking capitation relationships wherein they can share in savings.

Vendors of ancillary services are similar to hospitals, except they have been able to recognize their costs clearly and can effectively bargain on a discounted or per unit cost. With consolidation in the industry and the competition becoming more intense, vendors are similarly seeking capitation agreements. In their case, the reasoning appears to be development of stability, and long-term agreements are becoming commonplace.

Use of Relative Value Scales

Perhaps the most widely recognized means of physician reimbursement began with the establishment of a system to determine fees across the spectrum of care based on some agreed-upon formula. California's medical society developed the California Relative Value System (CRVS), which until 1974 was accepted widely throughout the country and used by a large number of physicians. The system was simple: each procedure or service was assigned a relative value when compared to other procedures or services in that service group. There was no single basic service to which all were compared but only related services within the specialties. Additionally, each specialty required a different conversion factor. Other state and private relative value scales (RVSs) all had the same deficiencies. In 1974, CRVS was declared illegal as a violation of antitrust and price fixing; it has never been reproduced or updated since then.

In spite of all the deficiencies associated with RVSs, they became the standard format for developing physician agreements and are still in common use. The methods involve an agreed-upon conversion rate, dollar per unit, to be applied to the RVS. The physician can bill that amount or any charge desired, but will only receive as payment in full the RVS times the agreed-upon conversion factor. Use of this methodology may require as many individual conversion rates as there are contracts and creates administrative concerns in claims processing.

Discounts off of an RVS system can exist if the MCO establishes a uniform conversion rate for general areas (surgery, anesthesia, radiology, and pathology) and then negotiates a percent discount from that base. This payment method is easier to administer in claims processing but creates issues for physicians.

Coding

Essential to effective use of any RVS system is the proper use of the codes associated with that system. Beginning with the initial RVS systems, CPT codes or similar codes were assigned to each procedure. Many procedures are combinations of other simple procedures. This is exemplified by total abdominal hysterectomy with bilateral salpingo-oophorectomy (TAH with BSO). The procedure involves removal of the uterus (including cervix), removal of both tubes and ovaries, and repair of the remaining vaginal defect. There is a single code identifying the procedure.

A creative surgeon submitted the following bill for TAH with BSO:

- exploratory laparotomy
- abdominal supracervical hysterectomy
- right salpingectomy
- right oophorectomy
- left salpingectomy
- left oophorectomy
- excision of cervical stump
- closure of vaginal defect
- reconstruction of pelvic floor
- lysis of adhesions (scar tissue)
- appendectomy (incidental and unrelated to procedure)
- closure of abdominal wall defect (incision used for procedure)
- plastic closure of skin (standard Pfannenstiel's incision)

Each procedure was individually charged at the agreed-upon conversion rate, and even if the agreed discount were applied it would have amounted to a reimbursement that was eight times greater than the full charge for a TAH with BSO. This case is an extreme example of the type of coding abuses that can occur. Others relate to the use of codes commonly reserved for unique or special circumstances such as after hours (for physicians called back to provide care), Sunday or holiday fees, interpretation fees (for radiology), history and physical for surgical cases (included in surgeon's fee), and postoperative care (also included in surgeon's fee).

The contracting parties should reach agreement on the use of codes, and both parties must agree to their proper utilization. To address certain common concerns—such as assisting at surgery, emergency care, and unusual care—modifiers were developed. Unfortunately, the modifiers were designed to address familiar but unusual circumstances and they were routinely used by many physicians to enhance compensation. Except for certain modifiers, the parties should agree to their limitation.

Resource-Based Relative Value Scale (RBRVS) as a Standard

In 1992, Hsaio completed a project that was undertaken for the federal government, the largest health care payer. The project was the development of a relative value system related to resource consumption and relative to a single procedure. That procedure was a simple or routine office visit, and all other procedures or services were related to it. There were three main considerations in the system for the value of a service:

1. physician work effort
2. business expense (nonmalpractice)
3. malpractice costs

When the three were combined, the result was the total relative value unit (RVU) assigned for the procedure, which when multiplied by a single uniform conversion factor would result in a relatively equitable reimbursement for all physicians and would not favor any specialist over any other or a procedure-oriented physician over a cognitive physician.

While that sounds like the ideal approach, it unfortunately was affected by its use by the Health Care Financing Administration (HCFA) for Medicare reimbursement and the politics involved. In the Medicare system, local factors are further considered; each of the above considerations is multiplied by a geographical adjustment factor (GAF), which differs for each consideration and for each Medicare area. Congress elected to impose this system in 1992 and, to lessen the impact of procedural specialists, a complex formulation for transition was put in place for procedures that were not within 15 percent of the payment made in 1991. Not satisfied that the system was complex, Congress abandoned the single care services in 1993, and one for nonprimary care, nonsurgical services (since anesthesia is not included under the system, one can argue there is a fourth).

Consider the benefits of RBRVS aside from the manipulations associated with Medicare and Congress:

- It is the only true relative value scale in which all services are related across the entire spectrum of specialties.
- It uses current CPT coding.
- It is updated annually.
- It has been developed by a third party, and physicians have had input and continue to have input.
- It is available to all in advance of implementation the following year.

Medicare Reimbursement

Whenever referring to RBRVS, it is recommended that the RBRVS system itself be distinguished from Medicare. If not done, many professionals will assume incorrectly that they will receive reimbursement equal to what is received from Medicare. Such an assumption will create certain difficulties when the professional receives a lesser amount. Even when the transition is completed, this will be true, since the GAFs will continue to be applied. These factors can add 15 percent or more to the total RVUs and final reimbursement.

Because there is such a great variability in the different geographic Medicare areas, because Medicare areas in larger communities can cut through the hospital staff depending on the individual professional's office location, and because professionals tend to discuss these issues over lunch or coffee, it is recommended that RBRVS be used as the base and modified upward or downward, using variable rates (conversion factors) or a percent discount up or down from the RBRVS base. Another factor in using RBRVS is that it is available on diskette; it can be downloaded to a computer and can greatly speed up claims handling. However, Medicare payments, handled by local intermediaries, are not easily downloaded. For this reason, claims handling and timeliness of payments can become an issue if Medicare payment levels are used. These claims frequently have to be manually handled; this can be done in a small system, but it becomes an administrative and time-consuming nightmare in a moderate or large system.

The rules applied to the Medicare payment system are available and have been incorporated into the RBRVS system. Use of these rules are suggested, since the rules in the CPT coding are more lax and less well defined. CPT code definitions are very clearly defined as opposed to the brief Medicare description, which may use the same descriptive phrase for five or six or more codes. Explain that CPT code definitions apply, but the rules of payment are as described through RBRVS and Medicare. In this way, there will be fewer conflicts and a clearer understanding. Even when questions arise, the answer will often be quickly provided by reference to RBRVS documents printed each year in the *Federal Register* (usually in late November, prior to the year of application).

Capitation

A great deal has been written about capitation, and it would seem that capitation carries with it some mystical powers to make everything work in the most effective manner available. Nothing could be further from the truth, and capitation must be understood if this mechanism is to be used effectively as a tool for managed care. An example of the misuse of capitation is seen in the following case:

> A diagnostic specialty (SPEC) was sought by a capitated professional group (CAP). While this group had the specialty in-house, a decision was made to contract out that diagnostic service to save money. CAP had 100,000 lives, and they wanted the service to be available to all of their enrollees. Put aside the issue of service and convenient sites (which cannot be done in real life), and the only issue of concern is cost. The prior year's costs for the service was $1.2 million. On a per member per month (PMPM) basis, the cost was $1 PMPM. The group negotiated a rate ($0.90 PMPM), which was less than their actual expense the prior year.

This was a 10 percent savings or $120,000 per year.

SPEC negotiated certain conditions, among which were that they would be able to control utilization and would provide the accounting for all services. In addition, they and the capitated group agreed on certain "national" norms of specific service utilization and that any increase in utilization greater than 8 percent would result in an increase of 10 percent in the PMPM going forward. CAP agreed and did not apply any form of utilization controls to their process for this service. Any of these diagnostic services could be ordered by any member of CAP (as well as by a significant number of contracted specialists), as long as the service was delivered by the diagnostic specialty provider.

In the first six months, SPEC demonstrated increased utilization greater than 8 percent and received a 10 percent increase. CAP was now paying $0.99 PMPM. At the end of the first year, the utilization was still greater than the agreed norms, and SPEC received another 10 percent increase (to $1.09 PMPM), and by the end of the second year, the amount was $1.20 PMPM.

At this point, SPEC served notice that they could not continue the agreement since they were losing money based on a utilization rate that was an average 20 percent greater than the "norm." As a result, they desired to reopen discussions regarding rates and put forth their proposal of $1.50 PMPM. Amazingly, CAP agreed to $1.35 PMPM. This was a cost savings of 10 percent according to the individual who finally signed the document based on current utilization. During this period, enrollment dropped by 20 percent.

There are a number of problems in the above case which will be referred to in the following discussion. Recall that two years earlier the costs were $1.00 PMPM, now the group had agreed to pay 35 percent more, and they called this a "cost savings." A review of the facts is as follows:

- The absolute dollars originally being spent for the service was $1,200,000 per year.
- The group paid $540,000 over the first six months.
- The group paid $588,000 in the second six months.
- In the second year, the group paid $1,152,000; and their total expense for the two years was $2,280,000 (5 percent savings over their projected costs at 100,000 enrollees).
- The reality is their total costs would have been $2,100,000, so the group spent 8 percent more than they would have under the original contract without an increase in the per member per month payment, based on utilization.

Capitation as Reimbursement

The best place to start is to think of capitation as a form of reimbursement. In capitation, based on some form of experience, the payment is received in advance of any service. There is no additional payment anticipated, aside from the obligations of copayment, which vary according to plan. Another essential concept is to recognize capitation as revenue and to treat it as principal and to preserve principal. CAP was correct in assessing the costs for services provided by their own specialists as compared to what could be purchased outside of CAP. Their opinion that they could preserve the capitation received was also correct when they completed negotiation. CAP established their expense or costs according to their own experience, and this is generally preferred. To this point, everything done by CAP with respect to paying capitation to SPEC was correct.

Determining the amount to be paid is critical to such a relationship. In this case, CAP selected their own experience, which is the preferred method. An alternative method would be to use someone else's data or actuarial data. Use of actuarial data is discouraged, since those data will not be pure "managed care" data; in the worst case, the data will be based on a mixture of managed care and nonmanaged care individuals, with different forms of utilization control applied. Actuaries tell us that there may be as much as a 20 percent variation from a standard over a period of time. Given all of these concerns, it is generally agreed that the best means for determining a capitation rate is with as much standardization as possible.

At this point, SPEC negotiated a standard by which to measure performance or utilization. They used a national standard developed through their own specialty for their services. In addition, SPEC negotiated what would occur if the variation from this norm was greater than 8 percent. SPEC was correct in seeking to establish a norm of performance, but CAP should have used their own data. In the case discussed, SPEC already knew the utilization by CAP was in excess of the "national" norms.

SPEC stated that they would apply utilization review to their services and would report utilization back to CAP. What SPEC proposed to do was to speed up the diagnostic process and complete evaluations in one visit. CAP appreciated their cooperative attitude and also welcomed the relief from having to conduct their own utilization review process. This unwillingness to perform utilization review is very common among the medical groups. Unfortunately, it represents a major downfall for the group. In this case, the group freely referred cases without any utilization review or tracking, and CAP's only data was supplied by SPEC.

Calculation of Capitation

To calculate how much capitation should be paid on a PMPM basis, the group should have data regarding its past experience or cost for a significant period of time. The shortest period recommended is one year, but two years or more is preferred. The calculation of PMPM costs would be based on the total member months for the measured period divided into the total costs for that period.

$$\frac{\text{total costs}}{\text{member months}} = \text{PMPM}$$

This calculation does not take into consideration several factors of importance:

- value of prepayment
- value of exclusivity or volume
- use of internal staff
- use of internal resources
- value of patient inconvenience

In the case of CAP, they did gain consideration for these factors, and we can accept that those considerations were accurate. Therefore, the amount agreed to between CAP and SPEC was reasonable, and each party was satisfied. The problem begins with the fact that CAP did not calculate the amount of referrals for this specialty as a rate per 1,000 enrollees or per 1,000 encounters. Had CAP done that, they may have recognized that the national data were not consistent with CAP's experience. This was CAP's first major error.

CAP's second error was not performing any utilization review or tracking on the number and types of referrals. This is a common error when groups capitate another party and it should be discouraged. The group should maintain its vigilance on utilization and, at the very least, it needs its own data to compare. SPEC provided all of the data, and CAP had no way of determining the appropriateness of the services provided individually except through a very time-consuming process that no one would undertake. The opportunity of control was lost, as was the opportunity to challenge SPEC on the appropriateness of the services rendered. In this case, one service (service A) was provided at a rate 10 times higher than in a carefully studied group of all senior members where the utilization was known to be excessive by any standard. CAP had less than 10 percent of its members in the senior population, and the utilization of these services by those under age 65 years is generally negligible.

Risk Is Opportunity

Risk as used in these discussions is another way to say *profit*, but that profit or opportunity is also the potential that costs may exceed the amount of service provided and hence be a loss. It is on this basis that groups take the position that they do not need to provide any utilization control for professionals who are capitated. The group thinks that the professional will do everything possible to reduce utilization and ensure a profit.

The group often forgets that the individual professional is convinced that the services provided under his or her direction are appropriate, necessary, and of the highest quality. In all negotiations with professionals, professionals will state that they will not accept a method that would impact the quality of service. Often this argument is used to defend a higher rate of compensation. Under these conditions, the group should expect the professional to continue to provide services in a manner consistent with the professional's normal and past practice. Given that expectation, the group should also recognize that, except in unusual circumstances, the individual professional's practice dedicated to the group is usually a small percentage of the professional's entire practice. In many instances, the professional's major practice is not related to managed care. None of these factors support the conclusion that the professional would alter past practices.

In this case, CAP was unaware of its existing overutilization as compared to a national norm, and SPEC was. This raises the question of why SPEC would agree to a lower rate—and the answer is that SPEC desired to get into a capitation relationship. In short, they were willing to take a loss while they built experience and obtained other contracts from other groups in the community. CAP then allowed all referrals (even from some nongroup physicians) to go directly to SPEC without any intervening review of authorization, and CAP did not track the referrals. SPEC, in the interest of patient service, provided a "complete evaluation," sometimes doing more than one procedure. In fact, about 50 percent of all of service A was directed by SPEC. (A subsequent separate review of just those cases revealed that 90 percent did not require the initial procedure or that service A was superfluous.)

SPEC took advantage of the opportunity. It realized it was protected against loss, and it had the incentive to increase utilization since it could gain greater reward and overcome the "losses." SPEC had already assured itself of a 10 percent gain after the first six months and another 10 percent gain at the end of one year.

Exclusivity and Volume

By capitating a professional, the group essentially agrees to provide the capitated professional with all cases referred for that service. This agreement is effectively an exclusive relationship between the parties and assures the capitated professional of a volume that justifies the discount agreed upon. In the capitation agreement between a plan and a group, the group accepts responsibility for all services covered by the agreement provided within a defined area, so long as the service is medically necessary or authorized by the group. This applies even if the group does not provide the service.

Many capitation agreements do not speak to the issue of the professional's responsibility for all services rendered. This may represent an issue, depending on the nature of services. In retrospect, this oversight may have created a real problem for CAP, because the service provided was commonly used and frequently provided by someone other than the group's employed specialist. This problem would go back to the PMPM determination. In fact, the SPEC contract did not cover any services provided by any other professional. When this information was taken into consideration, CAP had an additional $0.35 PMPM cost. To begin with, CAP had not properly constructed the agreement to include all services. The result is the original agreement assured CAP a 25 percent increase in their costs the moment they signed the agreement.

This agreement was not exclusive, except that all cases being electively tested would be referred to SPEC. SPEC had no obligation for services provided to enrollees for which it was capitated but did not provide.

In summary, this was a poorly constructed capitation agreement wherein CAP retained no control over the provision of services. The calculation of services was incomplete because CAP did not calculate its past utilization and measure it against the national standard. By relinquishing its control over utilization and tracking, CAP had no means of questioning the SPEC reports and ultimately paid a premium well over past expenses. CAP did not treat the capitation revenue like principal, and the group spent 70 percent more than the original costs.

In the end, this contract was terminated and an agreement was reached for capitation with the same provider for less than the proposed $1.35 PMPM and more consistent with the group's past experience. The provider, aware that they could lose more than 40 percent of the total revenue, became very active in the utilization review process, and the group permitted only authorized referrals to the provider. Both parties are now happy: the group is saving money and the provider is making a profit.

RISK SHARING

Understanding Risk Sharing

Risk sharing refers to a relationship wherein two parties agree to accept risk and work together to preserve a savings. The savings is then divided between the parties in an agreed-upon manner. The concept was introduced in managed care shortly after prepaid medicine began. In the 1970s and early 1980s, hospitals did not desire to take on this risk because they essentially had control. The insurance industry had difficulties with the hospital industry and was only able to gain agreements that were discounts off of charges.

The insurance plans then offered physician groups an opportunity to share in hospital savings. The groups would be able to do this more effectively because they controlled admissions to hospitals and could bring pressure on hospitals to lower the rates charged. Also, physician groups could expedite the care provided and reduce length of stay, as well as some admissions. In this way, groups were given incentive to work toward a common good for the plan and themselves and achieve a greater reward. Risk sharing provides an incentive that aligns both parties to achieve the same result.

Hospital Risk Sharing

The basic or initial risk-sharing model with respect to the hospital is described above. The gains were significant for the plans but were small by comparison for the group. The sharing agreement was a 50/50 split, but up to a maximum amount. The maximum applied as a percentage of the total capitation paid to the group, which would then be split.

An example of a typical relationship is as follows:

> Group's capitation = $1,000,000
> Risk share = 50% savings of a maximum of 15% of capitation ($150,000)
> Group's maximum potential = $75,000

During this period, hospital utilization was in the 400 days per 1,000 enrollees range, and utilization dropped to 300 days per 1,000 enrollees, a 25 percent reduction. Assuming the capitation on the hospital to be equal to that of the group, this could mean a savings of $250,000, of which the plan kept $175,000. Additionally, the groups were successful in convincing hospitals to move from discounts off charges to per diem rates, which produced another savings of 15 percent (another $150,000). All of this went to the plan, because the group had achieved its maximum reward. The plan retained $325,000 and the group $75,000. All that the hospital received was payment for services rendered.

In the mid to late 1980s two phenomena occurred. The plans began to allow groups to take on hospital risk (1) when they owned their own hospital or (2) when a hospital partnered with a group to take the risk. At this time, some hospitals did enter into such agreements, and the plans agreed to a risk-sharing agreement in which the entire savings would be shared between the hospital, the group, and the plan. These agreements always seemed to favor the hospital and plan, with the group receiving the smallest share. Hospital utilization days dropped significantly in this period to about 200 days per 1,000 enrollees. Following the same reasoning as above, this provided a savings of $500,000. Using a common formula, the plan and the hospital each gained $200,000 and the group gained $100,000.

Capitation and Risk Sharing

Capitating a group for all risks—hospital, pharmacy, out-of-area services, and so forth—would place the group in the best position to retain the greatest profit. This is the situation that groups owning their hospital found themselves in during the late 1980s and early 1990s. Trying to reduce costs (lowering per diems) or utilization (fewer days per 1,000 enrollees) was extremely difficult.

The concept of capitating the hospital and sharing the savings began in the early 1990s. Groups who were able to do this could then lower their costs (by about 15 percent) and lower days by another 15 percent (160 days per 1,000 enrollees). The result was that there was about $400,000 for each, with only $200,000 spent on hospital and other services related to the risk.

Other parties are attempting to take advantage of this opportunity, including drug companies who are entering the disease management services. In return for using more medication (usually a costly one), drug companies propose to save days and retain or gain a part of that savings. In reality, this is a naive approach to a complex problem and one that each group needs to think through carefully. In mature markets, it is unlikely that this approach will gain much favor.

Physician Opportunities

This chapter discusses the many opportunities for physicians engaged with a managed care group who can negotiate full-risk agreements with plans. For the most part, these opportunities will not exist for independent physicians or those who have avoided a relationship with an IPA.

Most of the concepts in this chapter were developed by physicians working with their administrative counterparts to structure a relationship that would be most beneficial to all involved. It is important to remember to structure a relationship that benefits both parties and not one over the other.

NOTE

1. Milliman & Robertson, Inc., *Health Cost Guidelines* (Denver, Colo.: 1995).

Chapter 14

Legal Issues Associated with Managed Care Contracting

Irwin M. Birnbaum, J.D.

EXECUTIVE SUMMARY

The purpose of this chapter is to introduce the reader to the various legal issues associated with managed care contracting. As such, this chapter addresses the variety of laws that affect the formation and operation of Managed Care Organizations (MCOs), as well as the managed care contract itself. The chapter concentrates on capitation and other risk-sharing arrangements, cautioning MCOs and providers against common pitfalls in such arrangements. Finally, the chapter identifies the major terms that should be considered for inclusion in every managed care contract and focuses on techniques of negotiation.

LEGAL ISSUES IMPORTANT TO COMPETITIVE POLICIES AND PROCEDURES

Federal Self-Referral and Fraud and Abuse Laws

The main federal laws relating to the financial arrangements between managed care organizations and physicians are the Fraud and Abuse (antikickback) statute,[1] and the two anti-self-referral statutes, Stark I[2] and Stark II[3] laws (so named after Representative Fortney H. ["Pete"] Stark, the former Chairman of the House Ways and Means Health Subcommittee and the primary sponsor of the anti-self-referral laws). The major principle of all these federal laws is that payments neither be made to nor received from physicians, directly or indirectly, on the basis of the amount of business they refer for various ancillary health care services either to themselves (i.e., entities in which a physician has a financial interest) or to third parties. In addition to the federal laws, many states have passed similar (and in some cases more restrictive) anti-self-referral and antikickback statutes. Every managed care contract should be reviewed to ensure that there is no violation of these federal and/or state laws.

Stark Laws

Stark I, which applies only to physician (or related family) owned clinical laboratory services to which the physician makes referrals, was signed into law in August 1993 and set out the standards governing physician

Note: The author wishes to express his appreciation to J. Elizabeth Scherl and Lori E. Harris for their assistance in the preparation of this chapter.

self-referrals. The regulations implementing Stark I became effective in the fall of 1995, and they further define some of the Stark I terminology and detail mandatory reporting requirements.[4] Amendment to the Stark law—the Physician Ownership and Referral Amendment of 1993 (also known as Stark II)—was passed in 1993 and became effective on January 1, 1995. Stark II offers the most significant and substantive changes affecting physicians (and other covered practitioners) under the Medicare and Medicaid laws since the sweeping 1977 anti-referral legislation. As yet, no Stark II regulations have been promulgated. The Stark II law follows the same framework as the Stark I law but applies the referral prohibition to a list of designated health services (DHSs). The Stark laws prohibit referral to providers in which a physician (or an immediate family member) has a financial interest, regardless of whether the physician's intent is to generate a profit for him- or herself. The following are considered to be DHSs under the Stark laws:

- clinical laboratory services
- physical therapy
- occupational therapy
- radiology (including MRI, CT, ultrasound, and other diagnostic imaging modalities)
- radiation therapy and supplies
- durable medical equipment and supplies
- parenteral and enteral nutrients, equipment, and supplies
- prosthetics, orthotics, and prosthetic devices
- home health services
- outpatient prescription drugs
- inpatient and outpatient hospital services

The Stark II law does not exempt or "grandfather" existing relationships. Furthermore, penalties for violations of Stark II are substantial: up to $15,000 per claim filed in violation, $100,000 for each circumvention scheme, refunds of paid claims, and possible exclusion from the Medicare and Medicaid programs.

The Stark law can be violated by making referrals to entities in which a physician has a financial interest, regardless of the physician's subjective intent. In essence, therefore, the Stark law functions as a strict liability law. This is in contrast to the antikickback statute (discussed in more detail below), which is a criminal statute under which intent must be proven in order to establish a violation. Under the Stark law, a *referral* is broadly defined to include a direct request for a health service and also a request for a consultation with another physician who, in turn, orders the DHS.

There are several major exceptions to the Stark II law. These include:

- *Radiology, pathology, or radiation therapy services.* The provision of radiology, pathology, or radiation therapy services, performed by radiologists, pathologists, and radiation oncologists is exempt from the general prohibition of Stark II if such services are performed by the requesting physician or under such physician's supervision pursuant to a consultation requested by another physician.
- *Physician in-office ancillary services.* An exception applies for in-office services when furnished by physicians (other than qualifying group practices) and by group practices. Services that are furnished by the physician or an employee under his or her direct supervision, provided that the services are provided in a building in which the physician furnishes other non-DHS services, and when the services are billed by the physician or an entity that is wholly owned by the physician, are exempt from the Stark II prohibition. The exemption from Stark II for group practices applies to those services furnished by the phy-

sician, a member of the same group practice, or by individuals employed by the group and under the direct supervision of a group physician, provided that the services are provided in the building in which the physician provides non-DHS services, in a building that the group uses as a central DHS facility, or in a building used by the group for some or all of its laboratory services. To fit the definition of a group practice, the group must meet the following additional standards:
1. The group must be legally organized as a type of group entity recognized under state law.
2. Each group member must provide substantially the usual range of services that such physician routinely provides.
3. Substantially all of the services of the physicians of the group must be provided through the group.
4. Billing and collection must be accomplished through the group.
5. Allocation of overhead and income must be in accordance with the methods previously determined by members of the group.
6. No compensation may be based on referral volume.
7. Members of the group in the aggregate must provide no less than 75 percent of the services provided by the group.

- *Ownership of securities in a publicly traded company.* In order to qualify for this exception, the ownership interest must be in publicly traded securities of a public company that has stockholder equity of at least $75 million. The securities themselves can be stock, options, or debt.
- *Rural providers and providers in Puerto Rico.* This exception covers hospitals in Puerto Rico or hospitals in which substantially all of the DHSs are provided to individuals who reside in a rural area.
- *Rental of office space or equipment.* This exception applies if the following conditions are met:
  1. There is a written agreement.
  2. The space or equipment is solely for the use of the lessee and does not exceed that which is needed for the lessee's legitimate business uses.
  3. The lease is for one year or more and the rent is for fair market value. (However, if the lease allows termination by either party without cause, it is questionable whether the one-year test is met.)
  4. The rent does not vary based on the volume of business between the parties.
- *Bona fide employment relationships.* If a physician is a bona fide employee, rendering physician services substantially full-time in facilities of another, then the presumption is that the person is an employee. The employment relationship must meet the following requirements in order to qualify as an exception:
  1. The employment must be for identifiable services.
  2. The remuneration must be fair market value and must not be related to the volume of referrals (while the volume of referrals cannot affect compensation, the volume of services performed personally by the physician can affect compensation).
  3. The compensation must be provided under an agreement that would be commercially reasonable even if no referrals were made to the employer.

Antikickback Statute

The antikickback statute prohibits knowingly and willfully offering, paying, soliciting, or receiving any direct or indirect payment, in cash or in kind, in return for referring an individual for Medicare or Medicaid services, or purchasing, ordering, or recommending such a service. A provider may face criminal penalties for violating the statute. The statutory language is quite broad, and brings within its reach many fairly innocuous arrangements. Thus, the Office of the Inspector General (OIG) in the U.S. Department of Health and Human Services has issued "safe harbor" regulations, which define conduct that is considered immune from prosecution or sanctions under the antikickback statute. (The fact that a particular set of facts does not fall within a safe harbor does not indicate that the conduct is illegal; it only takes away any immunity from prosecution, and may still be defended on a facts and circumstances basis.) The safe harbors may apply in numerous ways to managed care plans and should be reviewed prior to entering into any managed care arrangement. The overall impact of the safe harbors is to protect some beneficiary incentives, such as waivers of coinsurance and deductible amounts, and to protect certain kinds of price-reduction agreements between managed care plans (which include certain payers) and providers.

Safe Harbors. In 1991, OIG published a list of narrowly defined safe harbors[5] that include, but are not limited to, the following:

- investment interests in publicly traded entities with assets of $50 million (assets must be health care assets)
- two 60/40 rules:
  1. *60/40 ownership standard.* No more than 40 percent of the value of the investment interests of any "class of investments" in a nonpublicly traded or a smaller publicly traded company are held by investors in a position to either make referrals to the entity or furnish items or services to the entity. (An investor who may be in a position to make referrals may become untainted by signing a stipulation that he or she will not refer any business to the entity.) The services must not be marketed differently to passive investors than to noninvestors.
  2. *60/40 revenue standard.* No more than 40 percent of the revenue of an entity may come from referrals or business generated or items or services furnished from investors.
- space and equipment rentals if leases are written for a term of more than one year, are at fair market value, and are specific as to the item or premises to be leased
- certain personal service and management contracts between referral sources and the entities to which they refer
- certain discounts
- bona fide employment relationships
- certain group purchasing relationships
- certain Health Maintenance Organizations (HMOs) and Preferred Provider Organizations (PPOs)

New Development. A recent development has been the long-awaited appeals court decision in *Hanlester Network v. Shalala.*[6] In this case, the Ninth Circuit Court held that the limited partners/investors in a laboratory services venture did not violate either the "no solicitation" provision or the "no payment for referrals" provision of the antikickback law. The court found that the OIG could not show that the defendants had "knowingly or willfully violate[d] subsection (b)(2)," or that they "conditioned the number of shares sold on the amount of business that a physician agreed to refer." In *Hanlester*, in addition, dividends were paid to investors on the basis of their ownership interests, and not on the basis of the volume of referrals.

The court held that even though the defendants benefited from their referral relationship with a laboratory services provider, "the appellants [did not] intentionally" solicit or receive "remuneration . . . in return for referrals." The court ruled that the

Secretary's finding that appellants "knowingly and willfully" solicited and received remuneration in return for referrals is not supported by substantial evidence.

In short, the *Hanlester* decision has raised the standard of proof that the government must meet in order to show that defendants had the requisite intent to violate the antikickback statute.

Antitrust Considerations

The basic objective of the antitrust laws, broadly stated, is to eliminate practices that interfere with free competition. These laws are designed to promote a vigorous and competitive economy in which each business enterprise has a full opportunity to compete on the basis of price, quality, and service. For some time there was considerable confusion regarding the applicability of the antitrust laws to the health care industry. However, in *Goldfarb v. Virginia State Bar* (1975), the U.S. Supreme Court rejected the argument that there was an exemption from the federal antitrust laws for the "learned professions."[7] In 1976, the Supreme Court also rejected an argument that health care was neither in nor affected interstate commerce. Thus, at least since that time, there can be no question that health care providers are as fully subject to the antitrust laws as are any other businesses. Indeed, in 1993 and 1994, the Antitrust Division of the U.S. Department of Justice and the Federal Trade Commission issued Joint Enforcement Policy Statements relating to health care and antitrust.

Applicable Antitrust Laws

Three statutes give rise to most of the antitrust activity with respect to Managed Care Organizations. First, Section 1 of the Sherman Act, 15 U.S.C., Section 1, prohibits contracts, combinations, and conspiracies in restraint of trade. Proof of a violation of Section 1 requires: (1) an agreement, implied or explicit, by distinct entities (2) that has an unreasonably anticompetitive effect (3) in or affecting interstate or foreign commerce. Certain concerted practices are deemed to be so inherently anticompetitive that they are treated as *per se* illegal (that is, once the agreement is proved, no defense is available). These practices include price fixing, bid rigging, and the allocation of customers or markets.

Certain other joint activities, in particular group boycotts and tying arrangements, may have potentially plausible procompetitive benefits and thus are often subject to a modified *per se* analysis. This means that generally certain facts, such as whether the defendant(s) possessed market power, must be proved before the *per se* label will be applied to such activities. *Market power* is defined as the ability of one or more firms to affect price or output in a relevant market by their actions. (To illustrate: if there are three equally sized managed care entities in a relevant geographic market, likely none of them has market power alone. If A raised prices, B and C could undercut those prices and win A's customers; thus A would not raise prices unilaterally. Even if all three agreed to raise prices, while this would be an illegal agreement subject to *per se* treatment, the entities collectively might not possess market power if it is very easy for other firms to enter the market and undercut prices.)

Most types of restraints, however, are judged under the "rule of reason," which requires an in-depth examination of the nature, purpose, and effect of a restraint in a relevant product (or service) and geographic market (for example, the provision of managed care health coverage to employers and consumers in New York City). There must be a showing that the restraint causes actual and unreasonable harm to competition. Ordinarily, the existence of market power, measured by the structure of the market, the number and size of existing competitors, the ease of entry for potential competitors, and other relevant factors, is an essential element of proof of an unreasonable restraint of trade. However, where there is proof of actual anticompetitive effects, proof of market power based on market structure may be unnecessary.

Second, Section 2 of the Sherman Act, 15 U.S.C., Section 2, prohibits monopolization, attempted monopolization, and conspiracy to monopolize. The elements of monopolization are (1) monopoly power, generally defined as the power to control prices or exclude competition in the relevant market, and (2) willful acquisition or maintenance of that power, by predatory or illegal means, as distinguished from growth or development deriving from a superior product, business acumen, or historic accident. An attempt to monopolize consists of: (1) a specific intent to control prices or destroy competition in a relevant market, (2) predatory conduct designed to achieve the unlawful goal, and (3) a dangerous probability of success in achieving a monopoly.

Finally, Section 7 of the Clayton Act, 15 U.S.C., Section 18, prohibits mergers, acquisitions of stock or assets, and certain joint ventures where the effect may substantially lessen competition or tend to create a monopoly.

The remainder of this discussion will deal with the most important areas in which MCOs are affected by the antitrust laws, all of which arise under Section 1 of the Sherman Act. The following issues are discussed below: concerted refusals to deal, price fixing by providers, admission and termination of providers by MCOs, and exclusive managed care–provider relations. In addition, of course, price fixing, bid rigging, and allocation of markets or customers by Managed Care Organizations are violations of law. Section 1 of the Sherman Act is both a civil and criminal statue. Both firms and individuals are subject to criminal liability for price fixing, bid rigging, and allocation of markets. The law provides for fines for both corporations and individuals, and for imprisonment of individuals convicted of Sherman Act violations.

Specific Antitrust Concerns

Concerted Refusals To Deal with an MCO. An agreement among competitors that they will jointly refuse to sell to particular customers or buy from particular suppliers, or will do so only on jointly set terms, is referred to as a "concerted refusal to deal" or a group boycott. Generally, a concerted refusal to deal will be treated as illegal *per se* only when the competitors' agreement is designed to affect price or allocate markets and lacks a plausible procompetitive justification.[8] Although such circumstances are less likely, a concerted refusal to deal will also be treated as illegal *per se* where the competitors' activity succeeds in denying or persuading suppliers or customers to deny access to a supply, a facility, or a market that a competitor needs to compete, the boycotters possess a dominant market share, and there are no plausible arguments that the concerted refusal to deal was efficient or procompetitive.[9]

MCOs must avoid engaging in concerted refusals to deal. For example, if the MCOs in a relevant geographic market collectively refused to do business with a legitimate PPO because its members would not agree to one or more MCO's reimbursement rates, the agreement would be illegal *per se*. Individual MCOs are free, however, to make their own independent decisions whether to include that PPO as a participating group.

However, in most cases an MCO will be concerned about anticompetitive behavior by providers who seek to resist the discounted rates sought by MCOs. In a recent case, the Antitrust Division of the U.S. Department of Justice obtained a consent decree that prohibited eight Long Island hospitals from agreeing to refuse to do business with MCOs except on the best terms offered by an MCO to any one of the hospitals.[10] Classic Care was a corporation that the hospitals had formed to act as their exclusive bargaining agent with managed care payers and HMOs. Treating the corporation as essentially a sham, the government required the hospitals to make independent decisions concerning whether and at what rates to enter into contracts with managed care payers.

Where a group of providers agree that none of them will do business with an MCO so long as the MCO continues to do business with a competitor of the providers, the legality of the agreement will depend on the factors identified by the U.S. Supreme Court in *Northwest Wholesale Stationers*. In such cases, it is often not immediately obvious that there is an anticompetitive impact, particularly if the alleged boycotters lack market power and if their competitor can contract with other managed care payers. Nevertheless, the Federal Trade Commission has recently obtained a consent decree in a somewhat parallel situation where it is not clear that the alleged boycotters did have market power.[11]

Managed Care Challenges to Price Fixing by Providers. Price fixing occurs when two or more competitors agree, explicitly or implicitly, on the prices they will charge for services or goods. When providers negotiate reimbursement and pricing issues with a nonprovider-controlled MCO, there is no risk of illegal price fixing because the MCO is not in competition with the providers with whom it is negotiating.

A provider-controlled MCO, however, does face antitrust risks when setting provider reimbursement and bargaining with payers. Such an organization may be viewed as a horizontal conspiracy among competitors that acts as a mechanism for price fixing. In addition, where a group of providers who compete with one another negotiate with any MCO, the MCO should be alert to the possibility that the group is not a legitimate one but merely a cover to facilitate price fixing among its members in connection with negotiations with third-party payers.

In both cases, agreements among competitors in negotiating price, reimbursement rates, and other terms with third parties are lawful when the agreements are necessary consequences of a joint venture in which the competitors engage in genuine risk sharing. For example, if members of a PPO negotiate with an MCO for participation in a capitated program (physicians are paid a certain fixed amount per patient irrespective of whether a patient is treated), the physician members of the PPO share risk through participation in risk-sharing pools. In addition, they are encouraged to provide cost-efficient services and preventive health care measures to avoid treatment costs exceeding capitated payments. Risk sharing can also be achieved through a system of "withholds," in which part of the reimbursement pool is not paid until and unless specified performance criteria are achieved by the participating physicians.

Where there is such risk sharing, federal courts generally find that physician groups (or a provider-controlled MCO) are legitimate joint ventures, and analyze their activities under the rule of reason analysis.[12] The federal antitrust agencies have established a safety zone for physician joint ventures that provide services to MCOs. The agencies generally do not challenge a physician group that negotiates collectively for its members if the arrangement appears likely to yield lower prices for the consumer and lead to the institution of stronger utilization review. The agencies have established two standards that they believe would achieve these goals. (1) The joint venture should constitute 30 percent or less of the physicians in each specialty in the relevant market. (If the physician group received exclusivity, then no more than 20 percent of the physicians in a relevant market may join.) (2) The physicians participating in the network must bear "substantial" financial risk through their participation in the joint venture, such as through capitation payments or withholds.

Admission and Termination of Providers by MCOs. MCOs usually are selective in their admission of new providers, for reasons of controlling cost and enhancing efficiency. Additionally, they may terminate providers who do not follow their requirements. Such exclusionary actions against providers have the potential for creating antitrust liability. They may be challenged as a concerted refusal to deal if the MSO is provider controlled, or as an unreasonably restraint of trade or attempted monopolization if it is not.

Such actions, however, if properly conducted, will only rarely result in antitrust violations. The courts almost uniformly have found that provider selection based on cost-effectiveness rarely is anticompetitive in the context of litigation over hospital privileges for medical staff. That pattern of results should hold in challenges to provider selection by MCOs. In fact, the federal antitrust agencies are more concerned with the overinclusion of providers in any given program, due to the potential for increased market concentration and the ability of an organization that signs up most or all of the providers in given specialties to exclude competition by other MCOs in that area. If a managed care entity possesses market power and there is proof of an anticompetitive effect, a violation may be found.

A refusal by a provider-controlled MCO to admit a provider or a decision to terminate a provider might be challenged as a concerted refusal to deal by the provider members. The tests identified in *Northwest Wholesale Stationers* will be used to determine if *per se* or rule of reason analysis applies. In most cases, the MCO can avoid *per se* analysis, and the focus becomes the impact of its decision on overall competition in the relevant market. Two important considerations help to determine liability. (1) If providers are able to compete in a market notwithstanding their exclusion from a particular MCO, the plaintiff will be unable to show any injury. (2) The antitrust laws protect competition, not individual competitors. Thus, even if the members of a provider-controlled MCO who compete with the excluded provider have a reasonably significant market share (for example, 20 percent), the MCO's refusal to admit the provider is likely to be irrelevant to the state of overall competition. (As noted above, the federal enforcement agencies take the position that a physical joint venture should generally not include more than 20 percent of the providers in a given specialty in the area. A provider-controlled MCO would be considered to be such a joint venture.)

Exclusive Managed Care–Provider Relations. An exclusive dealing arrangement involves the agreement of one party (*A*) with another party (*B*) that *A* will be the sole provider of certain goods or services to *B*, thus eliminating the ability of *A's* competitors to sell to *B*. Thus, an exclusive dealing issue might arise if an MCO agreed to deal with only one hospital or group of physicians. Exclusive dealing is not *per se* illegal, but rather an unreasonably anticompetitive effect must be shown. As with all rule of reason analyses, a market analysis is required.

Once again, the federal enforcement agencies are concerned about overinclusive provider-controlled organizations, including PPOs and Independent Practice Associations (IPAs), where the organization's market power enables it to engage in exclusionary practices to prevent, exclude, or eliminate the development of competing alternative delivery systems. In a leading private case, a federal court held illegal a clause in a contract that prohibited physicians who provided medical services to the defendant IPA's subscribers from also participating in a Blue Cross program. In that case, almost all physicians in the area were members of the IPA. The court found that without the participation of at least some area physicians, Blue Cross could not operate. Thus, a prospective entrant was effectively shut out of the marketplace, and competition was stifled.[13]

Tax Issues

HMOs

The tax status of HMOs has evolved considerably in the last 15 years, largely as a result of the evolution of HMOs themselves and the changing views of Congress and the Internal Revenue Service (IRS) with respect to health-related organizations that operate similarly to commercial insurance companies.

Exemption under Section 501(c)(3) of the Internal Revenue Code. Section 501(c)(3) of the Internal Revenue Code (the Code) exempts from federal income tax entities that are organized and operated exclusively for charitable purposes. Historically, the IRS had taken the position that an HMO that provides medical services directly to its subscribers is not eligible for tax-exempt status under Section 501(c)(3).[14] In 1977, the IRS ruled that Sound Health Association, a staff model HMO, did not qualify for exemption under either Sections 501(c)(3) or (c)(4) of the Code, because, although the HMO provided some health services to the general public, it clearly accorded preferential treatment to its member-subscribers, which was insufficient to meet the community benefit standard. The U.S. Tax Court, however, disagreed with the IRS ruling and held that the association qualified for tax-exempt status under Section 501(c)(3).[15] The court in *Sound Health* applied the same standards for determining the tax-exempt status of the HMO as it would for determining the exempt status of hospitals and other organizations providing medical care. The court emphasized that the HMO's emergency room was available to all persons requiring emergency care, regardless of their ability to pay or their membership status. Further, the HMO had established a research program and an education program, had directed its ambulance company to bring emergency patients to the clinic, and was governed by a board of directors made up of prominent citizens of the community.

The IRS acquiesced in the Tax Court's opinion in *Sound Health*,[16] thereby reversing its earlier position in that case. In subsequent pronouncements regarding tax exemption for HMOs, the IRS has agreed with the Tax Court's analysis that the totality of an HMO's operation must be examined to determine whether the HMO serves primarily private or community interests.[17] Important characteristics for exemption include the actual provision of medical services at the entity's own facility, the provision of medical services to nonmembers on a fee-for-service basis, the provision of emergency medical services to individuals without regard to ability to pay, reduced rates for indigents, subsidized membership program, a community-represented board of directors, health education and research programs for the benefit of the community, and payment of primary care physicians on a salary basis. In addition, if the HMO is a membership organization, membership must be truly open—that is, the HMO must have a program to recruit individual members as well as employer groups, and the HMO must not impose any substantive age or health barriers to eligibility for membership on either individuals or groups.

More recently, a series of court rulings on a Pennsylvania HMO, the Geisinger Health Plan (GHP), has provided further guidance on HMOs' eligibility for tax-exempt status under Section 501(c)(3) of the Code. Initially, the IRS denied GHP tax exemption under Section 501(c)(3) of the Code, contending that it operated for the benefit of its subscribers and not for the community at large. GHP was affiliated with a number of hospitals, clinics, and physicians that all provided health care and were all part of the Geisinger System. The Tax Court disagreed with the IRS, ruling that the HMO independently qualified for exemption under Section 501(c)(3) of the Code.[18] The IRS then appealed to the Third Circuit, which held that GHP, standing alone, did not qualify for exemption under Section 501(c)(3) of the Code.[19]

The Third Circuit Court stated in *Geisinger* that there was no strict multifactor test that was appropriate when determining whether an HMO qualifies for tax-exempt status; rather, the totality of the circumstances must indicate whether the organization benefits the community in addition to its subscribers. According to the Third Circuit Court, GHP, unlike the HMO in *Sound Health*, benefited no one but its subscribers, because its requirement of subscribership was a condition precedent to any service. Even though the HMO had a subsidized dues program, the court found that it did not sufficiently benefit the community where only 35 out of 70,000 members received subsidies. The Third Circuit in Geisinger declined to address the merits of GHP's alternative argument that it should be tax-exempt as an "integral part" of the Geisinger System, which consists of various related organizations recognized as exempt under Section 501(c)(3) of the Code. This issue was remanded to the Tax Court. On remand, the Tax Court held that GHP was not entitled to tax-exempt status under the "integral part doctrine."[20]

Although not codified, the integral part doctrine has been recognized in regulations and cases as a basis for exemption under Section 501(c)(3) of the Code. The Tax Court relied on the Third Circuit's prior determination that GHP's activities served the private purposes of its members and concluded that GHP's operations were not so substantially and closely related to the exempt purposes of its affiliates that they would not constitute an unrelated trade or business. As a result, the Tax Court held that GHP was not entitled to exempt status under Section 501(c)(3) of the Code. On appeal by GHP, the Third Circuit affirmed the Tax Court's decision on the integral part doctrine, reasoning that GHP did not receive a sufficient "boost" from its affiliation with the tax-exempt organizations in the Geisinger System to warrant application of the integral part doctrine.[21]

Based on the foregoing, it appears that the opportunities for most HMOs to qualify as charitable organizations under Section 501(c)(3) of the Code are limited. An HMO would need to provide medical services directly to patients and take numerous steps to ensure that the community would benefit from its services.

Exemption under Section 501(c)(4) of the Code. Section 501(c)(4) of the Code provides for tax-exempt status for organizations operated exclusively for the promotion of social welfare. If a social welfare organization conveys benefits to only a closed-member group, then the community-based effect required to qualify for exemption under Section 501(c)(4) will not be satisfied. If, however, the benefits are available to a broad cross-section of the community, then the community benefit standard is likely to be met.

Before 1986, nonprofit HMOs may have been recognized as tax-exempt under Section 501(c)(4) of the Code because they were considered to be engaged primarily in promoting the common good and welfare of the community and not primarily in carrying on a business for profit. In 1990, the Office of the Assistant Chief Counsel of the IRS stated that the standards for exemption under Section 501(c)(4) of the Code should focus on a community benefit analysis, including (1) whether membership is open to individuals and small groups; (2) whether the HMO serves low-income, high-risk, or elderly segments of the community; and (3) whether the HMO uses community rating as opposed to an experience rating system.[22] Federal qualification under the Health Maintenance Organization Act (42 U.S.C., Section 300e), which requires quality assurance programs, community rating, and continuation of coverage, also would be a positive factor in determining tax exemption. In the General Counsel Memorandum (GCM), the IRS cautions, however, that no one factor is determinative.

Application of Section 501(m) of the Code to HMOs. In 1986 Congress added Section 501(m) to the Code, which provides that organizations otherwise described in Sections 503(c)(3) or (c)(4) of the Code can be tax-exempt only if no substantial part of their business consists of offering commercial-type insurance. While *commercial-type insurance* is not defined in the Code, the legislative history may be interpreted to suggest that Congress intended a general exemption from Section 501(m) for HMOs. However, Section 501(m)(3)(B) of the Code provides only that the term *commercial-type insurance* does not include "incidental health insurance provided by a health maintenance organization of a kind customarily provided by such organizations." It is unclear whether this exception was intended to apply to all types of HMOs or only to staff model HMOs, where medical care generally is provided in a single location by physicians who are employed by the HMO. The position of the IRS, as set forth in GCM 39829, is that this exception applies to all models of HMOs but that an HMO can be denied exemption under Section 501(m) of the Code either if (1) its principal activity does not consist of providing health care or (2) its provision of insurance is more than incidental to the provision of health care.[23]

In light of the movement of many HMOs toward managed care models that allow patients to consult physicians who are unaffiliated with the HMO, it may be difficult for HMOs to escape Section 501(m) of the Code by arguing successfully that insurance is only incidental to the provision of health care.

Independent Practice Associations

Independent Practice Associations (IPAs) generally are organizations (whether not-for-profit or for-profit) composed of health professionals who contract with prepaid health care plans, usually HMOs, to provide health services to members of the plan on a fee-for-service basis. Typically, IPA membership is limited to participating physicians in a particular geographic area. Association physicians agree to accept patients covered under the contract between the IPA and the HMO and to bill the IPA for services performed according to a fee schedule established by the IPA. The HMO then reimburses the IPA in accordance with its contract with the IPA.

In 1982, the IRS Chief Counsel issued a GCM in which it concluded that IPAs do not qualify for tax exemption because their primary activity is conducting a business similar to organizations operated for profit and they operate primarily for the benefit of their physician members.[24] The IRS formalized this position in 1986, declaring that an IPA will not qualify for tax-exempt status, that an IPA serves the interests of its physician members by acting as a billing and collection service, and that the formation of an IPA generally has no effect on the availability or quality of medical services in the community.[25]

The IRS Chief Counsel also has concluded that an IPA-model HMO does not qualify for tax exemption under the Code.[26] In that GCM, the IPA was found to serve primarily the interests of the physicians rather than the community and to offer no direct benefit to a sufficiently broad segment of the community.

Corporate Practice of Medicine Issues

Many state laws contain what is commonly referred to as a corporate practice of medicine restriction. In general, this doctrine is grounded in state statutes that prohibit the unlicensed practice of medicine. Typically, the statutes forbid the practice of medicine by anyone other than a licensed professional and therefore prohibit corporations from hiring physicians. The statutes are enforced either directly, by prohibiting business corporations from practicing medicine through licensed employees, or indirectly, by prohibiting business corporations from obtaining profits derived from the provision of physician professional services.

The policies underlying the doctrine are varied, but ultimately are grounded in a perceived interest in the patient's well-being. Some states focus on the theoretical underpinnings of the practice of medicine, including the sanctity of the doctor-patient relationship and the independence of the physician's professional judgment from lay control. Other states seek to preserve the unquestioned commitment of the doctor to the patient, free of competing loyalties to a corporation.

The specific statutes and case law applicable to the corporate practice of medicine doctrine vary from state to state. A few states have clearly established statutes and case law that go so far as to prohibit hospitals (with exemptions for certain types of hospitals) from employing physicians. Other states do not have any clearly delineated doctrine. Between these two extremes are states that provide exemptions from the general prohibition for groups of licensed professionals (whether in a corporation, a partnership, a limited liability company, or employer-employee relationship), not-for-profit hospitals, employee health clinics, and state-approved HMOs. As might be imagined, the inconsistencies in this doctrine cause special difficulties for those MCOs considering providing health care services across state lines.

In general, with the emergence of Integrated Delivery Systems, MCOs, and large-scale mergers between various health care providers, many states now consider the corporate practice of medicine doctrine to be an antiquated rule based on an outdated understanding of the medical profession and the business of health care. Therefore, while some states have maintained the rule, others have eliminated, altered, or weakened it, or provided exceptions applicable to many types of large health care providers. Some states have simply declined to enforce the rule.

Most states have, at least, provided exceptions for hospitals, nonprofit organizations, and HMOs. Although some of these entities might be organized as corporations and therefore fall within a corporate practice of medicine restriction, these types of institutions do not, in general, raise the same concerns for courts and legislators that other for-profit businesses raise.

In short, MCOs and providers must review, on a state-by-state basis, any applicable corporate practice of medicine restrictions prior to offering services in a particular state.

The Business of Insurance

Providers furnishing health services for a capitated price or otherwise assuming financial risk may be deemed, pursuant to a particular state's law, to be engaged in the business of insurance. *Black's Law Dictionary* defines insurance as a contract whereby, for a stipulated consideration, one party undertakes to compensate the other for loss on a specified subject by specified perils. The party who agrees to make the compensation is sometimes called an *insurer*; the agreed consideration for the contract is the *premium*; and the subject, right, or interest to be protected is the *insurable interest*.[27]

The provision of capitated health care services potentially fits within this definition of insurance in that the provider or MCO accepts a premium, in exchange for which the provider or MCO then agrees to provide care for the insured if there is the occurrence of an illness or injury. Therefore, a critical issue for each provider who provides capitated services will be whether the particular state's laws require the provider to become licensed as an HMO, an insurance company, or other licensed entity. Many states do not directly address the issue of when a provider that provides capitated health services must become licensed, since many of these laws were enacted prior to the expansion of MCOs. However, some states do address such issues either via statute or advisory opinions.

For example, New York Insurance Laws provide as follows: "An organization which provides health care services for a periodic fee paid in advance but which does not comply with the provisions of article forty-four of the public health law [regarding HMOs] shall be deemed to be engaged in the business of insurance and may not operate without being licensed under this chapter [the Insurance Law]."[28] This broadly worded provision might appear to prohibit an entity from furnishing prepaid health services unless it is licensed as an HMO or an insurer. However, Article 44 of the New York Public Health Law permits HMOs to contract with providers for the provision of health services to its enrollees pursuant to "risk" contracts. Therefore, this suggests that a provider is permitted to provide health care services to an HMO's enrollees for a periodic fee paid in advance (without being licensed as an HMO or an insurer) if the arrangement is in compliance with the New York Public Health Laws.

MCOs and providers must carefully review these issues on a state-by-state basis to ensure compliance with a particular state's laws.

UNDERSTANDING THE MCO CONTRACT

The Managed Care Organization functions efficiently only when all of the components of the managed care system are in place and operating effectively. In order to ensure efficient operation, all contracts pertaining to the MCO must be carefully negotiated and reviewed.

The variety of contracts that are required to form an MCO vary, depending on the degree of integration that is desired and acceptable by the hospital and the providers. The degree of integration may vary from a very loose affiliation of coordinated managed care contracts to a system where a hospital seeks to employ the physicians and to own all ancillary services.

Basic Checklist for Understanding and Negotiating Managed Care Contracts

Below is a basic checklist for understanding and negotiating managed care contracts:

1. **Evaluate the payer's financial solvency.** Obviously, care must be taken before entering into a contractual relationship with a financially unstable organization.
2. **Monitor your own performance.** Understand the costs incurred by the provider and determine whether the payment method adopted by the plan is reasonably anticipated to cover those costs and provide some profit. (See Chapter 15 for a more detailed discussion on monitoring internal performance.)
3. **Select your negotiating team.** Make sure it includes the appropriate decision makers.
4. **Understand the terms of the contract.** Fully understand what covered services the providers will be expected to provide, and be sure the providers are able to do so. Understand the process by which a patient's enrollment in the plan must be verified, whether there are any practice protocols that must be followed, and how the utilization review process works.
5. **Review relevant documents.** Do not sign any agreement until all relevant documents have been reviewed and understood, including any exhibits to the contract or any other documents referenced in the agreement.
6. **Ask questions and negotiate where possible.** Unless the provider is a large, multispecialty group or provides a specialty of critical importance to the managed care plan, the likelihood of having negotiating leverage with well-established managed care entities is remote. These entities often have form agreements and a sufficient number of

providers willing to participate. Smaller or start-up MCOs may be more likely to negotiate.

7. **Obtain written confirmation of any oral representations.** Any provisions orally represented by managed care agents will not be binding unless in writing and specifically integrated into the agreement.
8. **Review the final agreement.** The provider and provider's attorney should review the final agreement to be sure it includes important terms, accurately reflects discussions and negotiations with the entity, and does not contain any surprises.

Negotiating the Contractual Terms

Preparation is one of the most important preliminaries to the successful negotiation of a managed care contract between a provider and a payer. Prior to beginning the negotiations, the provider must identify its key objectives in order of importance. Providers should look to the following issues: maintaining a patient population base; developing the managed care program; protecting revenue; and maintaining relationships with payers. In addition, a key element of capitation is that some of the financial risk is shifted from the payer to the provider. Therefore, from the provider's perspective, the success of any negotiations may hinge on the provider's ability to manage the care within the contract's payment constraints. A provider that has limited experience—either with a payer, a patient population, or a payment arrangement—should try to structure a contract that allows for a period during which the provider's financial risk is limited or subject to modification.

Prior to entering into any managed care contracts, providers must carefully evaluate whether the elements of the managed care system are in place, the identity and financial stability of the contracting parties, and the distribution of risks and responsibilities. In addition, the provider must perform due diligence to assess the MCO. The provider organization should do the following:

- Understand how the MCO is organized and owned. (Is it owned by a commercial insurance company? A national managed care company? A Physician-Hospital Organization [PHO]? Some other entity?) Understand whether the MCO contains the appropriate legal structure to enter into the contract.
- Research the financial stability of the MCO, including identifying the MCO's financial resources and its experience with and commitment to managed care. Examine the MCO's annual report for the past several years and attempt to evaluate its stability and record of performance. Also, investigate the financial stability of the payer, if different than the MCO.
- Investigate the MCO's reputation in the community or with other providers. (What is the MCO's relationship with the community or other providers? What is the MCO's history with respect to managed care?)
- Examine the MCO's market influence and future plans. Does the MCO have an adequate number of patients? What are its plans for growth (regionally or locally)? What is the MCO's current service area?

The various agreements comprising a managed care arrangement often need to be negotiated and renegotiated (e.g., on an annual basis). The negotiating process can be one of the most important factors in determining the success of the managed care plan, because the results of negotiations—the terms of the agreements between the MCO, the payer, and the provider—determine the success of the MCO. Prior to beginning to negotiate the contract, the provider organization must have clearly defined goals and a clearly defined method to accomplish these goals.

The Negotiation Process

The negotiation process involves a tremendous amount of preparation as well as give-and-take between the parties in the move toward resolving important issues. Normally, there is a great deal of conflict between the parties, since the only common goal is the desire to provide health care services to a particular population. For example, the managed care plan seeks to spend as little money as possible for its obligation, while the providers seek to maximize reimbursements. Troublesome negotiation points include such issues as reimbursement, timing of payments, exclusivity provisions, and patient volumes. Each party should approach the negotiations with the idea that there must be a fair amount of give and take for the mutual benefit of the parties.

One of the first decisions involves the location of the negotiations. This is not usually the most important factor in the success or failure of the negotiations. Some negotiating teams may feel strongly, however, that conducting the negotiations in their own environment may offer certain advantages and increased comfort. Each negotiating team will likely probe the limits of the other team's authority very early during the negotiation process. Many negotiators expect the members of the other negotiating team to be able to conduct a give-and-take exchange without checking each point with other persons in their organization who have the ultimate authority. On the other hand, for tactical reasons, a negotiating team may wish to defer authority to those who are not involved in the day-to-day negotiations. The early give and take of the negotiation process will establish the authority of each team.

Each team should make careful records of the entire negotiation process. The notations for the process should reflect the following: date and location of negotiations, names and titles of participants and observers at each negotiating session, important terms of proposals that have been made by either party, points made during the discussion of the various proposals, agreements made by the parties, and areas of disagreement. These notes will help to ensure that each member of the negotiating team precisely recalls what has transpired during the process and what items remain to be discussed.

The Negotiating Team

The team for the provider organization should consist of at least the following members: the chief financial officer, the controller, the contract manager, and legal counsel. The chief financial officer and the controller are integral members of the team since contracting with a managed care plan involves detailed negotiations about financial issues. Some organizations may have a designated contract manager; it is presumed that this individual has experience with managed care contracts and therefore should be a part of the negotiating team. The legal counsel, who is also presumed to have experience with managed care contracting, will help to identify approaches to a variety of issues, as well as to identify and advise regarding pertinent legal issues.

Each member of the team should have a clearly defined role, which should be discussed in advance of any negotiation. Each member of the team will perform better when they understand the role of each of the other members. A team approach permits a division of labor and an ability to add special expertise to the negotiating process. In general, though, it is recommended that one or two people should direct the negotiations.

The members of the negotiation team should try to find out as much as possible about the members of the other party's negotiation team. This should include research of the other negotiating team's professional backgrounds, training, and educational experience. This will help the team to understand the style of negotiations used by the other party.

The team must have a sense of what it hopes to accomplish throughout the negotiations and should prepare a list of objectives for the process. This list should serve as a guide throughout the negotiation process.

In addition, the team's preparation must include a thorough review of the parameters of the proposal and any acceptable trade-offs.

Negotiating Styles and Tactics

There are two basic types of negotiating styles—confrontational and collegial. Some parties believe that the aggressive and confrontational approach, where the focus is on the real or perceived differences between the parties, is the best approach. Other parties believe that the collegial style, where the negotiators attempt to build a consensus between the parties via a "give-and-take" approach, is best because it is well suited to the concept that the outcome of the negotiations represents the beginning of a relationship between the parties. There is no clear right or wrong style, although experienced negotiators tend to prefer one style over another.

The negotiating team for the Physician Organization must have an idea of what they hope to accomplish through the negotiation progress. In addition, the team must have a full understanding of the strengths and weaknesses of its own organization, as well as the strengths and weaknesses of the other party's organization. This is especially important, because inevitably the other party will be familiar with the Physician Organization's weaknesses.

The Core Items

The basic items of the MCO contract have been previously identified and defined. They include such issues as the following: covered services, eligible persons, payment mechanisms, medical necessity, experimental treatment, emergency procedures, credentialing of providers, and utilization and quality review.

The Nonnegotiable Items

Certain nonnegotiable items must be included in the contract because they involve issues of compliance with federal and/or state laws. These include such issues as the following:

- compliance with federal and state fraud and abuse laws
- compliance with federal and state antitrust laws
- compliance with federal tax-exempt laws
- certificate of need requirements
- state licensure requirements
- state freedom of choice or willing provider laws
- state corporate practice of medicine laws

All managed care contracts must be reviewed with these laws in mind to ensure compliance.

Payment Mechanisms

Overview

The provisions for payment are a key element of the managed care contract. The managed care contract must clearly describe the payment mechanisms (e.g., nature and amounts) designed to compensate the MCO, the hospital, the physicians, or other providers. In addition, all payment mechanisms must be carefully scrutinized for compliance with applicable laws, such as the federal and state fraud and abuse and antireferral laws.

Of course, payment mechanisms, standing alone, cannot accomplish efficiencies and cost savings in the provision of health care. Payment mechanisms designed to enhance efficiencies must be complemented by other managed care techniques including provider selection, utilization management, and quality measurement. Still, payment mechanisms are an extremely important element in achieving the desired results in a managed care program. Essentially, there are only a few different types of payment mechanisms: fee-for-service payment, per diem payment, per case or diagnosis-related group reimbursement, capitation, and percentage of premium paid. The level of scrutiny adopted by the contracting parties regarding the remaining contractual terms may be influenced by the extent to which the provider and payer are expected to share the financial risk associated with guaranteeing a certain level of care for fixed premium amounts, copays, and deductibles. For example, a physician group asked to participate as provider in an HMO for a global capitation amount will need to pay closer attention to the stability and market power of the HMO and less attention to the definition of certain terms, such as *emergency services*. On the other hand, an IPA negotiating a fee-for-service discounted rate on behalf of its physician members should be more concerned with those contract provisions that can create a financial risk for the physicians, such as eligibility of members for certain services, the definition of emergency care, and the member-authorization process.

Types of Payment Methodologies

Fee-for-Service. Fee-for-service is the traditional method by which providers of health care are compensated for their services. Under this method of payment, providers are usually required to submit a standard list of charges to the MCO for approval. This list of charges would then be used as a basis for reimbursement. The reimbursement will usually be limited to the lesser of the billed charges or the usual, customary, and reasonable amount as determined by the payer. A variation of the fee-for-service payment mechanism is the discounted fee-for-service mechanism, whereby the provider agrees to provide covered medical services at a discount of standard charges. The discount generally applies to the lesser of the standard charge or the usual, customary, and reasonable amount.

Per Diem. Under the per diem payment method, the hospital provider receives a fixed payment per day of hospital service required by the beneficiaries of the plan, which is significantly discounted from the hospital's posted charge. Usually, there are variations in the per diem charge for different levels of service. Under this type of payment, since the hospital is usually significantly discounting its fee, it is at risk for unforeseen financial losses. Therefore, an important negotiation issue under this type of payment mechanism includes protection against catastrophic cases, such as a stop-loss threshold or a dollar amount that is sent in advance so that, if charges exceed that level, the provider will be reimbursed by an alternative method, such as a discount off the standard charges. MCOs tend to prefer a discounted per diem payment methodology, since they directly benefit from any efficiencies in delivery of health services (e.g., reduced length of stay). Because per diem charges may encourage a provider to increase a patient's length of stay, the payer usually insists on stringent controls or incentives to protect such increases.

Possible variations from the flat per diem model include a per diem charge that varies according to the patient's length of stay and service needs. Additionally, the per diem charge for the first day of hospitalization can be priced higher than subsequent days. Also, the provider can avoid some amount of risk by successfully negotiating a separate payment method for certain high-cost services, which would then be excluded from the per diem charge. Another risk-averting technique that providers may adopt is to negotiate for a stop-loss threshold, requiring the payer to pay separately for charges in excess of a specified amount.

Per Case or Diagnosis-Related Group (DRG) Reimbursement. Under this type of payment mechanism, payment is prospectively based on the diagnosis code for a particular patient. Under this mechanism, it is important for the hospital provider to obtain some type of stop-loss protection if the charges for a patient with a particular diagnosis exceeds a set dollar threshold because of longer lengths of stay or extraordinary costs for that particular hospital admission. Per case charges create somewhat more of a risk to providers than the per diem method, because increased length of stay will not generate additional reimbursement. However, MCOs sometimes try to avoid DRG reimbursement since they do not benefit from any efficiencies in the delivery of care (e.g., reduction in length of stay).

Capitation. Under the capitation payment mechanism, the provider receives a fixed payment per member per month. In exchange for receiving the fee, the provider will provide all or certain specified covered services to the enrollee and, in the case of a primary care physician, will make referrals and arrange for hospital and specialist physician services only pursuant to the parameters in the provider agreement. In a capitation model, the provider assumes the risk that the cost of services required by covered enrollees could exceed the capitation payment received by the provider to furnish such care. Due to its risk-transferring nature, MCOs often prefer the capitation methodology. However, providers must enter into such arrangements with caution and with legal counsel, since the more risk that a provider assumes, the greater the possibility that state law would deem the provider to be an insurance company, subject to applicable state licensing and regulation. Additionally, capitation may be an inappropriate payment arrangement for providers who lack the financial and/or administrative means to assume risk, or if the patient base is not large enough to dilute that risk effectively.

Capitation plans often appear as one of three models: ordinary capitation, global capitation, or intermediary capitation. Each model impacts differently upon the risk assumed by the provider. Thus, providers must first understand how each model operates:

1. **Ordinary capitation.** Under ordinary capitation, the MCO makes a capitation payment to a physician, physician group, or other provider as compensation for the professional services that the particular provider is expected to furnish to patients. As with any of the three models, certain services may be "carved out" of the capitation agreement. For example, a hospital may agree to accept a capitated rate to provide inpatient and outpatient services to covered members, but may negotiate for a separate payment scheme (e.g., fee-for-service or discounted fee-for-service) for emergency room services.
2. **Global capitation.** Under the global capitation model, the MCO's capitation payment compensates a provider not only for that provider's professional services, but also for other services rendered by other providers. For example, a group of primary care physicians may accept a capitated payment in exchange for providing or arranging for all covered services needed by an enrollee of the MCO, including specialty services, ancillary services, and inpatient services. The physician group is then on the hook to contract with and compensate the other providers for their services.
3. **Intermediary capitation.** Under this model, the payer (i.e., HMO, insurer, or self-insured employer) pays a capitated amount to an intermediary entity (i.e., PPO, PHO, IPA, or management company). Or, the intermediary may agree to accept a percentage of the premiums

collected by the payer from enrollees. Either way, the intermediary organization assumes the risk and separately contracts with providers or provider groups to furnish the necessary services. The intermediary may or may not pass the risk along to the individual providers.

Once providers become familiar with the alternatives, they must understand which, if any, of the models is compatible with their purposes and goals in managed care contracting. That judgment will be affected in part by the provider's knowledge of, and level of comfort with, the MCO and its ability to remain financially solvent, maintain sufficient enrollment, and provide incentives for patients to utilize the provider's services over those of competitors (e.g., a PPO that provides financial incentives to members who stay "in plan").

The provider's willingness to accept any of the capitation models will also depend in part upon the provider's ability to provide services and undertake the responsibilities imposed by the plan. Thus, before assuming financial risk in a managed care arrangement through capitation or otherwise, a contracting provider should become familiar with the patient population in the applicable community. The provider's investigation must include determining whether the plan includes a disproportionate number of high-risk patients, which would obviously increase the risk factor to the provider.

A provider accepting capitation need not necessarily be entirely without protection. For example, some providers successfully negotiate a stop-loss limitation, meaning the provider will not be at risk for costs in excess of a certain amount over the capitation payment. A contract providing a provider with stop-loss protection should clearly identify the stop-loss amount and how that amount is calculated. Also, certain high-risk or expensive procedures can be carved out of the capitated payment and paid separately on a fee-for-service or other basis. Again, the contract should be specific regarding the circumstances under which a service or services will be carved out of a capitated arrangement.

Percentage of Premium. Under the percentage of premium payment, which is essentially another form of capitation payment, the provider receives a percentage of the plan's monthly premiums in return for the provision of all covered services to enrollees. Again, the provider is at total risk under this type of payment mechanism.

Risk Pools. In those cases where reimbursement is not a capitation or percentage of premium basis, the MCO may require that the provider set aside a certain percentage of the provider reimbursement during the term of the agreement. This arrangement is referred to as a risk pool. The "withhold amount" is placed in a fund that will be used to protect against the utilization risk assumed by the providers under the agreements. When the utilization and resulting cost of providing care is less than anticipated, there is a surplus in the withhold fund, and this amount is then distributed to participating providers. The fund may also be used at the end of the year to bring providers to a contractually agreed-upon reimbursement rate. When the costs exceed projections, those amounts will be used to pay for the excess costs, amounting to a reduction in the reimbursement for the providers.

A managed care contract that includes a provision for withholds should clearly describe the treatment of withheld funds. The contract should address how and when the funds will be withheld, where they will be deposited, and under what conditions the withholds are to be distributed. The funds should be held in interest-bearing accounts, with interest accruing to the providers if and when the conditions for the return of the withholds are satisfied. In addition, the contract should address whether, and under what circumstances, the provider may ever be at financial risk beyond the withhold amount and, if so,

Selecting a Payment Mechanism

Not all services need to be provided under a single rate or methodology. The contract may state that different types of services are covered under different rates or payment methods. In such a case, the contract should explicitly state how services are covered and under which rate. For example, the Federal Trade Commission recently approved (for antitrust purposes) a provider network that combines several payment mechanisms. A group of hematologists/oncologists in Pittsburgh, Pennsylvania, formed a nonexclusive provider network to contract on their behalf with third-party payers such as commercial health insurers and self-insured employers. The network, which includes 35 physicians, will offer hematology/oncology services to the payers in exchange for a capitated fee. However, drug therapy will be carved out of the capitation; instead, the network will provide drug therapy under a modified fee-for-service structure. Participating providers will be reimbursed by the network using relative value scale standards. The network will set aside 20 percent of its monthly capitated payments to cover expenses, management fees, and incentive compensation to physicians who meet certain cost, quality, and utilization standards set by the network's board of directors. Physicians are free to provide services outside of the network, but they may not refuse to participate in agreements negotiated by the network.

Clearly, it can be difficult for the emerging MCO to select the appropriate payment method. During the negotiation process, there are many questions that need to be addressed, including how the payer establishes its payment rates; whether payment rates will be renegotiated or increased during the year (e.g., an automatic renegotiation based upon certain conditions); when payment will be made; what type of billing forms will be utilized; how billing will occur for hospital-based physicians (i.e., separately or as part of payment to the hospital); billing patients for noncovered services or not medically necessary services; appeal mechanisms for disputed claims; retroactive denials; who (if anyone) gets billed if services are mistakenly provided to an ineligible person; and the available remedies in the event that the payer does not pay. The payment portion of the contract should also specify the time frame for payment; whether there is a waiver if a claim is not filed by a certain date; the date from which the payment obligation measures (i.e., from the date of submission of the claim or from the date of approval of the claim); the time limit (if any) for the payer to challenge a bill; whether the payer is responsible for any late payment penalty; limitations on payer recoupment of alleged overpayments; and protocols for denials of claims, which should include an explanation by the payer and a right of appeal by the provider.

Provisions of the Contract

As a preliminary matter, all of the necessary contract terms should be simple, clear, and precise. In addition, care must be taken to ensure that the standard contract provisions do not conflict with one another. During the negotiation process, thought must be given to what each party promises and contracts to perform and also to whether the parties are able to do what they promise. The definitions section of most managed care contracts is one of the most important parts of the agreement. Some of the basic components of the managed care contract are defined in the definitions section, including for example, covered services, medically necessary services, experimental treatment exclusions, and eligible persons. Careful negotiation and attention to the definitions section can help to minimize timely and costly appeals processes, alternative dispute resolution, and litigation.

Covered Services and Medically Necessary Services

The basic obligation under any managed care contract is to provide covered services to the enrollees. Therefore, the scope of services to be provided by the provider to the enrollees must be explicitly set forth in writing. In some cases, a payer may require that a provider provide all services to enrollees. On the other hand, a provider may need to limit its obligation to provide services. An example of such a limitation is a provider who does not wish to provide emergency transport services. The provider will be bound by the definition of covered services that is provided in this section of the contract; hence, the definition of covered services under the contract is a key provision.

The definition of covered services in the managed care contract should include a list of benefits, including any special limitations or conditions that apply to a particular benefit—such as a dollar limit, a visit limit, a preexisting condition limitation, a referral or preauthorization requirement, or a requirement that particular types of providers render a specific service. Any ambiguities in this portion of the contract will be construed against the MCO in favor of the insured. In addition, the provider may wish to include some flexibility in the definition of covered services, in case the provider needs to cut back on the range or types of services provided. Therefore, the contract should include some type of notice provision and/or renegotiation provision that permits the provider to change the services that are provided.

Furthermore, some managed care contracts may define covered services as those services that are medically necessary. As such, the term *medically necessary* should also be defined explicitly and clearly in the managed care contract, and should be consistent with the definition of medical necessity that is used in the utilization review program.

Experimental/Investigational Treatments

Whether an MCO provides coverage for experimental and/or investigational treatment is an area that has been extensively litigated. Courts have held that in order for an experimental or investigational exclusion to be upheld, it must be clearly stated in the coverage plan contract that a particular provision is excluded. As such, the managed care contract should provide not only a list of covered services, but also a list of excluded services. In addition, the contract should outline the appeals process for both the patient and the provider to address any disputed issues.

Emergency Procedures

Emergency services are usually treated quite differently from nonemergency services in terms of the applicability of certain utilization review requirements. The contract should state who determines whether emergency services are required and whether there is a waiver of preauthorization in the event of an emergency. From the standpoint of the provider, it is beneficial for the contract to state that there is some discretion for providers to treat emergency situations and be assured of payment without fear of retroactive reclassification of the services rendered from emergency to nonemergency. Furthermore, any provisions for emergency services must be consistent with the Emergency Medical Treatment and Active Labor Act[29] and any applicable state law requirements.

Eligible Persons

During the negotiation process, the MCO will decide what persons are eligible for services from the MCO. Factors to be considered include age mix, socioeconomic mix, male/female mix, and health status. Once an individual is covered by the MCO, the contract should provide for a clear mechanism for the providers to check the identification and eligibility of individuals. These mechanisms can include, for example, identification cards and/or telephone verification of eligible persons.

In general, the provider should place the burden on the payer to accept the responsibility for identification of beneficiaries and verification of their eligibility and coverage through a clearly defined identification and verification process. The payer should provide weekly and/or monthly listings of eligible persons. In addition, the contract should clearly state that the provider may rely on such identification in emergency situations, as long as he/she acts reasonable (such as, for example, accepting another form of verification). The payer should be restricted as to the time by which a payer may notify a provider of a "retroactive" disenrollment of an insured and should be limited as to the imposition of retroactive financial consequences.

Credentialing of Providers

The method of credentialing providers should be addressed in the managed care contract. The parties to the contract must specify who is responsible for the credentialing of physicians who participate in the MCO. Although, in general, hospitals must credential physicians before granting them medical staff membership or clinical privileges, the MCO should separately credential physicians for participation in the MCO.

Utilization and Quality Review

Utilization and quality review programs are key features of the cost containment activities of the MCO. The purpose of such programs is to ensure that beneficiaries of managed care plans receive only necessary and appropriate services. The contract should identify all aspects of the utilization review and quality assurance programs, including the appeals process and quality assurance procedures, which includes a review of patient care, as well as credentialing, monitoring, and discipline providers. These programs include preauthorization or preadmission review, concurrent review, and retrospective review.

Preauthorization or preadmission review typically consists of examining the record and the provider's recommended treatment protocol for the diagnosis. The preadmission reviewer then determines the necessity for the hospitalization or treatment. It is possible for the contract to specify that this type of review is to be applied only to high-cost procedures and/or to those procedures usually performed on an outpatient basis. The definition of medical necessity is crucial to this determination. It is also important for the contract to specify the time period within which utilization review decisions must be made and, if there is no response within the requisite time period, then authorization should be deemed granted. In addition, telephone authorization should be deemed to be binding.

Concurrent review seeks to review the duration of treatment and/or hospitalization to ensure that it does not exceed a certain time period. It also covers second surgical opinions, early discharge, and locations for outpatient procedures. This type of review can be difficult unless objective criteria exist to minimize disputes. Again, telephone authorization and timely response should be required as part of the managed care contract. The MCO should try to negotiate a contract provision that requires the payer to make payment for services through the date of discharge if eligibility for hospitalization ends during the course of inpatient treatment. In addition, this section of the contract should be explicit and specify the types of admissions and services that are subject to review, the frequency of the review, and the information that the provider must provide to the payer for the review.

Retrospective or retroactive review identifies possible costly patterns of treatment by physicians, diagnosis, or unit. It is hoped that this type of review enables the MCO to take corrective action to prevent future losses. This type of review can pose a real financial risk to the provider if the contract permits the payer wide discretion to deny payment retroactively for any service.

Typically, the utilization review process is managed by the payer either directly or through a third-party utilization company. As such, the providers should negotiate to ensure that the scope of utilization review and quality assurance programs is clearly defined in the contract. Also, the provider should try to share in the control of the utilization review and quality assurance programs.

It is important for the MCO to ensure that the review procedures clearly identify the reviewer, the standards for the review (e.g., the definition of medical necessity should be consistent with the definition of medical necessity in other places in the managed care contract), and the appeal rights after utilization review decisions. For example, the initial utilization review may be performed by a nurse; however, if there is a recommendation to deny a claim, then the claim should be reviewed by a physician.

The contract should clarify the appeals process, which should be timely and reasonable. In addition, the treating physician, hospital or facility, and patient should all be allowed to appeal. Appropriately licensed specialists should review all appeals, and adequate communication must be maintained with patients and physicians during the appeals process.

A significant change in the utilization review and quality assurance plans should require advance approval by the other parties to the contract or, at a minimum, notification and an opportunity to comment. Providers should insist upon an ability for an early termination in the event of an amendment to utilization review or quality assurance that the provider has not agreed to. Finally, there should be procedures in place for review of the utilization review and quality assurance programs.

Medical Records/Confidentiality

The contract should address which parties to the contract have access to the patient records and who bears the costs of copying records. It is wise to state a specific maximum (and reasonable) cost for photocopying of medical records in the managed care contract. In general, it is usually the provider who owns the physical record that documents services and has the legal duty to maintain the confidentiality of the records. However, the contract should specify this. Furthermore, a payer does not necessarily have an automatic right to these records and must, in most cases, obtain some type of specific consent to access such records.

Several federal laws address confidentiality of medical records, and most states have laws that address this issue. The provisions in the managed care contract should be consistent with applicable federal and state laws.

Term/Termination Provisions

The term/termination provisions of the managed care contract are extremely important. The term of the contract (i.e., whether the contract is a short-term or long-term contract) will typically be a business decision on the part of the contracting parties. Various factors, such as the degree of commitment to the arrangement and the level of confidence in the MCO will enter into this decision.

In general, in determining the term of the contract, the provider should consider the following factors: the nature of the payer, the volume and nature of the payer's enrollees, the provider's experience in managed care plans, and the particular payment at issue. The obvious benefit of a short-term contract is that it gives the parties a chance to become comfortable with the arrangement. On the other hand, a long-term contract permits the parties to work together in the MCO without continually renegotiating the contract.

A provider should review the contract termination clause to ensure that it allows for adequate flexibility in terminating the contract before the completion of the stated term. Most contracts permit two types of termination: with cause and without cause. When termination without cause is permitted, the notification requirement to the other party is usually substantial.

Typically, termination for cause is permitted in the following circumstances: loss of licensure, certification, or accreditation; financial instability; cancellation of insurance or reinsurance; changes in the law that affect the contract; failure to make timely payments; sale of assets, merger, or change of control of the MCO; failure to provide the required services; and noncompliance by provider or payer with stated billing procedures.

Each party should have the right to terminate the contract in the event of a material breach by the other. It may be appropriate to include a time period within which the breaching party can cure before the termination of the contract. The cure period should be considered in those places where the cure can be objectively measured, such as failure to make timely payments, failure to provide the required services, or noncompliance with the stated billing procedures. In addition, contracts that contain an opportunity to cure breaches of the contract (such as a 30-day opportunity to cure) should also include some type of protection against repetitive breaches.

There are times when termination without an opportunity to cure is appropriate. These situations include failure to comply with state or federal certification or registration requirements or the loss of such certificate, registration, or license; the provider's loss of certification in the Medicare or Medicaid programs; or a situation involving gross negligence. It is prudent to include in the contract a clause that requires the parties to be in compliance with applicable laws and regulations. Furthermore, a party should be able to give notice to another party of a suspected violation. In addition, it is prudent to include a provision allowing the parties to reevaluate or terminate the contract in the event of significant legal or reimbursement changes. Disputes over the sufficiency of the stated cause and the completeness of any cure may be resolved by the dispute resolution process.

In addition, the contract should address whether the renewal is automatic or must be renegotiated. It is wise to include a notification provision that requires the MCO to provide advance notice of the end of the contract term. The contract should also contain a provision for the payment of post-termination obligations. For example, the MCO may have responsibility for payment for services rendered and for care initiated prior to the termination of the contract. There must also be an acceptable protocol in place to address the issue of patients who are receiving care at the time of termination; these issues include notice to patients, payment for services rendered after termination, and patient transfers. In addition, federal and state laws may affect a provider's ability to terminate care in the event of termination of the contract.

Potential Liability, Insurance, and Indemnification

Unfortunately, potential liability is one of the costs of doing business for any business, including MCOs. There are many aspects of the operation of an MCO and of the MCO contracts that give rise to liability. In recent years, litigation has focused on malpractice committed by employed professionals, refusal to render treatment on the grounds that such treatment is experimental, physician credentialing, and utilization and quality review activities.

Quality review activities are an important area of concern for the MCO. Courts have increasingly held MCOs liable for negligent actions by physicians providing services to enrollees or for coverage decisions resulting in failure to provide services to an enrollee.

The landmark decision in this area was a California case, *Wickline v. State of California*, where the court stated that a third-party payer can be liable when medically inappropriate decisions result from its cost containment efforts.[30] The *Wickline* decision further stated that the physician cannot escape liability by simply complying with the limitation imposed by the third-party payer. Although this case was limited to its specific facts by a later case, quality and utilization review activities are clearly a source of potential liability for the MCO.

Another area of concern is physician credentialing. The contract should clearly distinguish between physician credentialing for hospital privileges or participation in a provider network and the credentialing process for physician participation in a managed care plan. In addition, the contract should reflect which party (the MCO or the payer) is responsible for evaluating ongoing physician performance and for implementing any corrective action or disqualification for contract participation.

Due to the liability for both providers and payers that may arise during the course of a managed care relationship, the managed care agreement should include specific and mutual obligations with respect to insurance and indemnification. The contract should obligate all parties to obtain, at their own expense, insurance policies (or to establish self-insurance funds) covering that party's general and (if applicable) professional liability. The insurance requirement should identify the minimum acceptable limits of coverage per occurrence and in the aggregate.

In addition to insurance coverage, an indemnity clause can often protect the contracting parties against liabilities, expenses, or other losses suffered as a result of another party's behavior. A common problem, however, with indemnity clauses is their breadth and vagueness. Providers are often asked to indemnify the MCO against any type of loss without regard to whether the MCO's actions contributed to that loss, without any limit on the provider's financial exposure, and without any limits to the time period in which the MCO must seek indemnification for a loss. Also, a standard MCO contract often fails to provide for *mutual* indemnification. A well-drafted indemnification provision should require each party to indemnify the other against costs (including legal fees and judgments) arising solely by reason of the indemnifying party's acts or omissions. Further, the indemnity obligation should not exceed the limits of the indemnifying party's general and professional liability insurance.

Dispute Resolution

There are various types of disputes that can arise during the operation of an MCO: patient grievances (this usually involves the scope of coverage); provider grievances (this usually involves payment and credentialing issues and utilization review decisions); and disputes between the organization and the payer (this usually involves disputes surrounding the terms of the contract). All MCO contracts should contain a mechanism to deal with such disputes. It is imperative that disputes be resolved quickly and economically. Alternative dispute resolution procedures, such as arbitration or mediation, are often an appropriate substitute to litigation. Litigation is lengthy and expensive and often leads to unpredictable results. Alternative dispute resolution procedures are advantageous in that there is usually less acrimony, protection of continuity of health services, prevention of long and costly appeals, and increased procedural flexibility. In the managed care area, there is much to be gained where speed in resolving a dispute increases the likelihood of successful treatment and, in most cases, satisfies the needs of the parties who wish to continue to foster their long-term relationship. Some states mandate that certain resolution procedures be included in the managed care plan contracts.

Disputes in the managed care area tend to surround the following issues: coverage questions, emergency treatment, experimental treatment, beneficiary verification, utilization or quality review, and claims or payment disputes. Coverage disputes include such issues as whether a particular treatment is medically necessary. To protect against such a dispute, the contract language should establish preauthorization as a condition for coverage of elective or nonemergency treatments and prohibit subsequent payment denial on the basis of lack of medical necessity for services that were preauthorized. Another area that is frequently disputed is emergency medical care. The contract should clearly define any policies and procedures relating to emergency medical care. Experimental treatments should be clearly defined in the contract. Such a determination is often left to the payer's discretion; when this is the case, such a determination should be made in a timely manner with the involvement of a qualified health professional.

With regard to beneficiary verification, disputes may arise regarding enrollee eligibility, the manner of eligibility verification, or the responsibility for verifying eligibility. Such issues should be clearly addressed in the contract. Utilization or quality review disputes arising under the payer's utilization review procedures can have serious economic implications for providers, since they may result in payment disallowance or reduction of payment for services rendered. To minimize such disputes, an effective utilization review program should be timely and provide for input from provider representatives and physicians. With regard to claims and payment disputes, clear contract language and familiarity with contract procedures reduce the number and seriousness of these types of claims.

There are essentially three different types of alternative dispute resolution methods:

1. **Interim determinations** are usually made by the payer and include an initial determination of such issues as extent of coverage, beneficiary eligibility, and experimental treatment modalities. The MCO contract should permit an appeal of these initial determinations, preferably to a neutral review panel.
2. **Nonbinding dispute resolution** assists the parties to resolve their dispute by agreement. This process can vary from an informal meeting, to structured negotiations between the parties, to mediation. This type of proceeding often encourages the parties to resolve their disputes without resorting to arbitration or litigation.
3. **Arbitration** is a more formal type of dispute resolution in that the parties agree to permit the arbitrator to resolve the dispute and the findings are binding. The arbitration clause should specify the procedural rules that the parties will follow, the method for the selection of an arbitrator, and the governing state law pertaining to the arbitration proceedings.

Stop Loss

A stop-loss provision protects a provider from unanticipated events such as an unanticipated volume of patients or an unanticipated change in the intensity of services. Typically, these provisions involve setting a threshold, beyond which the payment method changes to either a standard or discounted charge.

CONCLUSION

The key to successfully negotiating the many legal and business issues associated with managed care contracts is preparation. The emerging Physician Organization must be familiar with the various types of Managed Care Organizations, such as Health Maintenance Organizations, Preferred Provider Organizations, Independent Practice Associations, Management Services Organizations, and Physician-Hospital Organizations.

In addition, the Physician Organization should retain legal counsel who is knowledgeable about the laws that affect the formation of MCOs. These laws include the federal self-referral and fraud and abuse laws, antitrust considerations, tax issues, corporate practice of medicine restrictions, and business of insurance issues.

Finally, the Physician Organization must prepare to negotiate the various contracts that form the MCO. Successful negotiation of these contracts requires understanding the key terms of such contracts, preparing the negotiation team, and implementing a negotiation strategy. With this preparation, it is hoped that the Physician Organization will enter into a relationship with an MCO that is mutually rewarding.

NOTES

1. Social Security Act, sec. 1128B(b), codified at 42 U.S.C., sec. 1320a–7b.

2. Omnibus Budget Reconciliation Act of 1989, Public Law No. 101-239, codified at 42 U.S.C., sec. 1395nn.

3. Omnibus Budget Reconciliation Act of 1993, Public Law No. 103-66, codified at 42 U.S.C., sec. 1395nn.

4. *Federal Register* 60 (August 14, 1995): 41914.

5. *Federal Register* 56 (July 29, 1991): 35952.

6. *Hanlester Network v. Shalala*, 51 F.3d 1390 (9th Circuit, 1995).

7. *Goldfarb v. Virginia State Bar*, 421 U.S. 775 (1975).

8. *Federal Trade Commission v. Superior Court Trial Lawyers Association*, 493 U.S. 411 (1990).

9. *Northwest Wholesale Stationers, Inc. v. Pacific Stationery and Printing Co.*, 472 U.S. 284 (1985).

10. *United States v. Classic Care Network, Inc., Federal Register* 59 (December 30, 1994): 67719.

11. See Medical Staff of Good Samaritan Regional Medical Center, *Federal Register* 59 (September 23, 1994): 48889. In this case, medical staff at one Phoenix hospital allegedly conspired to withhold patient admissions unless the hospital closed its multispecialty clinic.

12. See *Hassan v. Independent Practice Assoc.*, 698 F.Supp. 679 (D. Mich. 1988). The court found that a capitated IPA arrangement was lawful because physicians shared the risk of loss through capitation payments; the plan did not dictate what participating physicians could charge to nonplan patients; and the plan constituted a new product, namely guaranteed comprehensive physician services for a prepaid premium different from fee-for-services.

13. *Blue Cross of Washington and Alaska v. Kitsap Physician Services*, 1982-1 Trade Ca. (CCH), 64,588 (W.D. Wash. 1981).

14. See, for example, GCM 37043 (March 14, 1977).

15. *Sound Health Association v. Commissioner*, 71 T.C. 158 (1978).

16. 1981-2 C.B. 2.

17. GCM 39828 (August 30, 1994); GCM 38735 (May 29, 1981).

18. *Geisinger Health Plan v. Commissioner*, 62 T.C.M. (CCH) 1656 (1991).

19. *Geisinger Health Plan v. Commissioner*, 985 F.2d 1210 (3d Cir. 1993).

20. *Geisinger Health Plan v. Commissioner*, 100 T.C. 396 (1993).

21. *Geisinger Health Plan v. Commissioner*, 30 F.3d 494 (3rd Cir. 1994).

22. GCM 39829 (August 30, 1990).

23. GCM 39829 (August 30, 1990).

24. GCM 38894 (September 3, 1982).

25. Rev. Rul. 86-98, 1986-2 C.B. 74.

26. GCM 39057 (November 9, 1983).

27. *Black's Law Dictionary*, 5th ed., p. 721.

28. New York Insurance Law, sec. 1109(b).

29. 42 U.S.C., sec. 1395dd.

30. *Wickline v. State of California*, 192 Cal. App. 3d 1630, 239 Cal. Rptr. 810 (1986).

Chapter 15

Critical Issues in Negotiating Capitated Contracts

Kerry McDonald

INTRODUCTION

The devil is in the details. In this chapter, the details of capitation contracting are discussed. The contracting process is looked at from a negotiating perspective discussing contracting strategy, language details, rate development, and their impacts on operations. The reader should become familiar with the language before the first approach to entering negotiations, as well as key clauses contained in capitation contracts and their operational/business meaning. This chapter also presents guidelines for acceptable terms for common clauses. The rate development information takes the reader through the process of developing a capitation rate from raw utilization data, and describes common sources for that data.

After reading this chapter, the reader should be able to engage in the contract negotiating process without being intimidated by the length of the contract or lack a starting point for the process. This chapter should also enable the reader recognize the operational impact, cost, and increase or decrease in risk associated with particular terms. Used as a practical guide to the business process of capitation contract negotiations, this chapter will prove a valuable resource.

THE BUSINESS ENVIRONMENT

To effectively discuss the critical issues of negotiating capitated contracts one must understand the business environment in which the organization will be operating. The medical service delivery, administrative, and financial approaches necessary to be successful in a managed care, capitated environment are dramatically different from those used in a traditional fee-for-service environment.

The Fee-for-Service Environment

In the fee-for-service environment, the health care provider emphasizes increasing visits, or utilization, in order to increase revenues and profits. Cost plays a secondary role to increased utilization. Even if costs increase on a per unit basis, the practice, or facility, can still increase profits if it increases utilization. For example, if a practice can increase the ancillary service utilization, it can offset an increase in the per unit cost caused by moving to a larger, more expensive space or hiring more personnel. The option of increasing utilization, or simply increasing price to offset increases in cost, is no longer available to providers in a capitated environment. Even if providers have no, or few, relationships with Managed Care Organizations, their ability to contract successfully with these organizations will depend on the efficiency of their operation.

The Managed Care Environment

To be successful in managed care, providers must emphasize reducing costs and becoming more efficient. Revenues will depend on the type of contract that the provider negotiates with the managed care organization. In capitated arrangements, revenue is essentially fixed and profitability is affected solely by reductions in cost. Reducing utilization increases profits, as long as costs decline with the reduction in utilization. Under capitation, providers' compensation is based on a fixed monthly payment related to the size of the total population served, with little regard to actual utilization or provider costs. The payer's determination of the capitation is based on reducing costs and putting the provider at risk for increased, or failure to reduce, utilization. Under capitation, both providers and management focus on *cost and efficiency*.

This change in the external business environment necessitates changes in the internal thought process. It requires providers to rethink the relationships between charge and visits, ancillary utilization and visits, and patient visits and profit. Transition from the traditional fee-for-service incentives to capitated incentives requires a commitment from upper management, both physicians and administrative. Not only must the way in which success is viewed change, but the way in which service is delivered, tracked, and marketed must change.

Reduced cost/increased efficiency = profitability and desirability in the marketplace

PREPARING FOR NEGOTIATIONS

Prior to entering into capitated contract negotiations with a payer, the provider organization must look inward and make strategic decisions relating to its preparedness and strategy for future involvement in capitation. These decisions are unique to each organization. They are driven by the organization's resources, market position, market opportunities, market stage of managed care development, and the commitment of the individuals in the organization to convert to some level of capitated business. There must be a commitment on the part of the providers to make capitation contracting work. The organization should not approach contracting as a defensive mechanism to protect what the organization currently has, but as a proactive strategy to ensure success in the future. If it is not proactive, the organization may have short-term success, but it will not invest in the necessary systems for long-term success.

There are two basic categories of capitation or risk contracting available to providers: (1) providers can pursue contracts that limit their risk to only those services that they provide, or (2) they may pursue contracts that include risk for services beyond their organization's scope. Organizations that are initiating their managed care strategy may want to limit their scope of risk until such time as they have the proper infrastructure and confidence to manage risk outside their organization. This decision will define the type of contract the organization will pursue. For some organizations, this decision will be dictated by their specialty; for others, it may mean commitment to a growth strategy that will assemble the necessary resources to compete for more global risk contracts. In any case, assembling the infrastructure necessary to manage utilization and cost is a key to success.

A later section of this chapter addresses specific issues related to cost and administration in preparing for the successful negotiation of capitation contracts, tracking performance against payment, and positioning the organization for renegotiating these contracts.

STRATEGY FOR THE NEGOTIATIONS

All completed contract negotiations should produce a "Win-Win" situation between the provider and the payer. Prior to entering into capitation contract negotiations, the organization must determine its strategy for proceeding through the different stages of negotiations. Often, when physicians receive a managed care contract, they go directly to the compensation section to see what rate is being offered. In the case of fee-for-service contracts, this may establish a financial basis for proceeding with the negotiations. However, this strategy does not provide the necessary information to make a financial decision when negotiating a capitation contract. Because a capitation amount is an all-encompassing rate for a specific scope of service, knowing what scope of services is included in the capitation and relating the organization's specific cost of producing those services to the capitation is necessary to determine the adequacy of the rate.

Knowing the scope of services, the organization's ability to perform those services, and the true level of risk requires the organization to change its strategy from negotiating the rate to negotiating the language and scope of services first and then negotiating the rate. It is possible to accept any rate proposed by a payer, if the services to be offered and level of risk are appropriate for that per member per month (PMPM) capitation amount. By reviewing the contract language and proposing the elimination of services or reduction of risk to a level that the capitation payment would support, the organization is now prepared to discuss the additional cost of providing these services, or accepting the level of risk. For example, a requirement for the provider to institute and conduct preventive medicine programs, such as weight loss and smoking cessation classes, as defined and directed by the payer, clearly carries a cost to the provider. If the capitation rate is generally comparable to other rates being offered that do not include this requirement, the provider must receive an addition to the capitation to organize and provide these programs, along with some control over the number and frequency of these programs. Specifics relating to the number and frequency of these services must be spelled out in the contract. If an organization does not already offer such programs and have the related personnel and printed materials in place, there is a start-up cost in addition to the ongoing cost to provide the programs. A clear definition of the organization's responsibility for such service will allow the organization to provide quality service, while preventing it from breaching the contract through nonperformance, due to a lack of funds or lack of understanding the payer's expectations.

NEGOTIATING THE LANGUAGE

Identifying the areas of the contract that carry cost or risk is key to negotiating the language of the contract. The following items are common contract clauses that require scrutiny and possible negotiation.

Definitions

The provider should read the definitions carefully to ensure that they are clear and represent the provider's understanding of the key terms being defined. The definitions contained in the final contract will have to be lived with. For example, the definition of *out of area* or *provider service area* should correspond to the geographic area in which the provider has some influence over the treatment site of the patient. The area could be defined by ZIP codes, counties, or other common boundaries. It is not appropriate for the provider service area to be defined as "anywhere in the state." Under such a definition, should a patient be admitted to a nonparticipating facility in the provider's service area, those costs would be attributed to the provider. Additionally, the provider would want to transfer the patient to a participating facility is in the provider's service area as soon as is medically appropriate, so that the provider can treat the patient within its referral system. Other definitions that are important to review include *emergency services, primary care and specialty provider definitions,* and *medically necessary services.*

Provider Performance Provisions

The provider performance provisions are the obligations of the provider under the contract. These provisions are of paramount importance, since the provider organization will be required to perform all of the tasks designated in these provisions. Typical performance requirements include the following:

- Provide corporate documents: articles of incorporation, bylaws, possibly financial statements.
- List provider data: names, tax ID, license numbers, Drug Enforcement Agency numbers, Medicare certification number, business hours, list of subcontracting providers, and regular updates of this information.
- Secure a medical director.
- Specify conditions under which a subcontracted provider would be terminated.
- Provide notification of a subcontracting provider's contract termination.
- Meet credentialing requirements for contracting organization providers and subcontracting providers.
- Provide a list of hospitals where providers have staff privileges. The payer may require the providers to secure privileges at specific participating hospitals.
- Specify amounts and provide proof of malpractice insurance. These amounts should relate to state law and/or community standards and not be excessive.
- Comply with the benefit plans when providing services. The provider should acquire a copy of these benefit plans and perform an analysis so as to determine the potential cost relating to the capitation offered.
- Comply with the quality assurance and utilization review plans. The provider should acquire copies of these programs, along with the grievance procedures, and perform an analysis to determine the cost to the organization of implementing additional systems needed to comply.
- Comply with the plan's drug formulary. Providers should obtain and review a copy of the formulary to determine the impact on their practice patterns and the potential effect on patient care. Most payers are very strict regarding compliance with the formulary; therefore, any questions or problems should be raised during the negotiations.
- Provide 24-hour, 7-day coverage. The organization must have a sophisticated on-call system in place if it is going to accept risk for services other than those it directly provides. The 24-hour, 7-day coverage is generally nonnegotiable.
- Do not discriminate between plan beneficiaries and the provider's other patients. Payers expect their patients to be treated the same, without separate waiting rooms, treatment areas, appointment availabilities, and access to providers.

- Make referrals only to participating providers. In many cases, the contract will require the provider organization to pay for any referrals to nonparticipating providers. This clause should be negotiated to reflect that there is a participating provider who has the required service capability and will see the patient within the medically necessary time frame and that the provider "knowingly" makes the referral.
- Report encounter data. Although this requirement is generally imposed by insurance commissions, the contract should be modified so that this information can be delivered to the payer with the least cost to the provider. Generally an agreement that the payer and provider will implement a system to accept the provider's encounter data electronically can be achieved. Make sure that the format is specified and that the payer will modify its programming to achieve compatibility. Work out all of the details during the negotiations; a surprise programming bill can be costly to the provider organization.
- Specify how to handle new or additional benefits. Make sure that the provider organization has the right to negotiate compensation for these new benefits.

This list is not all-encompassing. Depending on the contract format, additional items may be included, which will be covered later in this chapter. There may be additional provisions that are not included in this chapter. However, armed with this list, a provider organization should be able to identify provisions that expose the organization to cost or risk, or jeopardize the quality of care.

Compensation

This section of the contract specifies the *capitation methodology*, if not the rate. Some contract formats specify the rate in an addendum specific to the benefit plans that will be serviced under the contract. In addition to the capitation rate, this section of the contract also includes provisions on billing and payment, if any services are to be billed. Payers increasingly restrict the time frame for submission of a claim. In many cases, they require a claim to be submitted within 60 days of the date of service. This section should also include a provision for the time frame for payment of a claim, usually 30 days. Make sure that the type of days used for both of these limits are the same—a calendar day is not equal to a working day. For example, submission in 60 calendar days and payment in 30 working days gives the payer approximately 45 calendar days in which to pay, while the provider is strictly limited to 60 calendar days.

The compensation section generally specifies *penalties* for deficiencies in the provider's performance provisions. If the provider is penalized, make sure that a reasonable period for correction occurs first, usually 30 days, and that the payer is also penalized for deficiencies (such as 1.5 percent per month interest) on late claims and capitation payments, prorated by days. Additionally, look here to enforce the payer-provided reports and timeliness of risk-pool settlements. Payers are notorious for their late reports and risk settlements. Even with a top-of-the-line information system, the information supplied by the payer is vital to reconciling the provider's data with the payer, since the payer will use its data for all payments to the provider. Late risk-pool settlements impact cash flow and carry a lost time value of money and lost opportunity cost. These are real dollars.

Many contracts address *reconciliation of membership* in this section. Membership reconciliation is of vital importance, since revenue depends on the membership count on the day the capitation check is cut. There will be new members, deletions for people who were disenrolled when the last payment was made but were not recorded in the enrollment file, and additions for people who were enrolled but not recorded in the enrollment file. The delay in entry is normal and many times is due to employers not reporting staff changes in a timely manner. The provider organization must reconcile the membership monthly with the capitation payment and the provider's enrollment file. Negotiation of the electronic transmission of the enrollment update is vital. Updating the provider system manually is extremely labor intensive and costly. Electronic transmission of the enrollment updates should be negotiated in a fashion similar to the electronic payment of claims. However, the fields to update should be chosen carefully. If the provider organization is asking patients at the time of patient visits about their address, coinsurance, phone numbers, and other demographic data—as they should be—the provider may have the most recent data. It is not necessary to update all fields when a member enrollment file is updated. The enrollment file should be updated and checked against the capitation list at least bimonthly. If this task is done less frequently, particularly if the plan is experiencing rapid growth, the provider will have patients calling for care who are not in its enrollment file. The retroactive disenrollments should be limited to 90 days or less; however, if the provider can negotiate an open-ended retroactive enrollment, this is favorable.

This section should specify collection of *copayments*, conditions for compensation for excluded services, coordination of benefits, application of third-party recoveries, and compensation for occupational illness and work-related injury. All copayments should be collected at the time of service. Copayments have already been calculated into the capitation rate, thereby reducing the rate as the copay increases. The provider should be able to bill and collect from the patient for noncovered or denied services, and from the payer for services excluded from the contract. Coordination of benefits (COB) is the collection for the provider's services when a member has another primary insurance. This has also been included in the calculation of the premium and, therefore, in the capitation rate. Billing COB is performed just like billing for fee-for-service patients; however, after the primary insurance has paid, the capitated provider becomes the secondary insurer and writes off any balance. In a general population, COB can represent up to 7 to 9 percent of the total medical cost of the benefit plan. Obviously, the hospital piece of this is a significant percentage. Subrogation, or third-party recoveries, are reimbursable to the provider under much the same theory as COB. However, the primary insurance is an auto insurance policy or a property and casualty policy. Subrogation occurs when a third party is responsible for the injury or illness. Workers' compensation is also a subrogation. Make sure that the contract allows for the provider organization to bill these other insurances for the services provided. Some Health Maintenance Organizations (HMOs) have excluded subrogation from their contracts, telling providers it is part of their capitation. If a payer makes this claim, the provider should require proof that the capitation has already been increased. Proof would require an actuarial report to show the prior year's recoveries and how they were included in the rate.

Last, but certainly not least, this section should include a *beneficiary hold harmless clause*. In most cases, the insurance commission not only requires this clause, but also specifies the language. A beneficiary hold harmless clause requires the provider to look only to the payer for payment of covered services. This is nonnegotiable. It includes all causes for nonpayment, including insolvency and bankruptcy of the payer. For this reason, it is important to contract with payers who have financial strength. The provider should also negotiate the ability to request a book and record check of the payer, requiring access to a payer's books and possibly the submission of periodic financial statements. Having the ability to review the payer's books will allow a provider organization to verify the solvency of the HMO or, more importantly, a Managed Care Organization (MCO). MCOs are not regulated the same as HMOs, if they are regulated at all. HMOs are required to report to the insurance commission on a periodic basis, at least annually. However, an MCO may only be required to report to the HMO.

Term and Termination

This section of the contract should be straightforward; however, there should be a termination at will that is bilateral and requires only 60 days, or so, notice. Any other termination provisions should also be bilateral. In many cases, the insurance commissions have specified terms that survive the contract. This language may require the provider to continue treating patients until such time as they can be transferred to new providers. Be sure to negotiate the rate and type of payment for services provided after termination of the contract. A long delay by the HMO in transferring patients to a new provider can be costly if no rate and type of payment is previously agreed upon.

Records, Audits, and Compliance with Regulatory Agencies

This section of the contract should be self-explanatory. However, some issues require negotiation. The notification period prior to an on-site visit to review medical, financial, or other records should be at least 48 hours, and 72 hours if possible. If there is not a provision for payment to the provider for record copying, it should be negotiated. The cost to the provider to copy hundreds of pages can be significant. A charge of $0.25 per page is reasonable, which should also cover the labor cost. This section also generally specifies that the medical records of all plan members belong to the plan. When terminating the contract, the provider must be able to retain a copy of the medical record for liability reasons. Many payers attempt to exclude this from the copying charge. This should be resisted. Probably the most costly and most important aspect of the medical records is compliance with a defined structure that requires dividers and a specified order to the chart. The insurance commission will check member charts during its annual inspections; more importantly, if the HMO wishes to receive National Committee for Quality Assurance (NCQA) certification, the medical records will be heavily scrutinized. Care and preparation should be taken to meet NCQA standards for the chart format and the provider documentation. Proof of this can increase the provider organization's desirability to HMOs and MCOs.

General Provisions

Additional provisions may be found in this section of the contract, or they may be in sections with more specific titles. Other titles may include marketing, risk pools, indemnification, covered services, primary care services, or some other category. The most important provisions are addressed below.

Marketing

It is important to understand the marketing techniques used by the payer. During the marketing process, the payer may be overselling services. For example, the payer may be generating a demand for specific services, such as annual comprehensive physical exams, that will impact the operation of the provider offices. Or, the payer may require the provider to open it offices to give tours to prospective members, push preventive medicine programs, or any number of other techniques that will affect the operation and cost of the provider organization. Understanding these techniques and providing for them in the contract can save the provider time and money.

Risk Pools

This section can be relevant not only in a fee-for-service contract or single-specialty capitation contract, but also in a global capitation agreement where the payer and the provider share in the savings from hospital or facility costs. Make sure that the calculations are clearly understood and that the limits of risk are at least equal to those of the rewards.

Indemnification

This is a provision whereby the payer requires the provider to hold the payer harmless from any litigation arising out of the treatment of patients or an incident by which someone is injured at a provider facility. This clause should be bilateral, and the provider organization should send a copy to its malpractice carrier to ensure that it does not violate the malpractice contract and leave the provider exposed to increased liability. This clause should be negotiated with language that is approved by the professional liability insurer. The provider should require proof of coverage by the payer for professional liability and/or errors and omissions insurance.

Covered Services

Somewhere in the contract, all services for which the provider is responsible should be described in detail. Services that are covered benefits but excluded from the provider's responsibility should also be described in detail. This is the part of the contract in which limitation, reinsurance, stop loss, carve outs, membership guarantees, and limits of utilization covered by the cap are negotiated. All types of services must be carefully considered. The provider should attempt to negotiate removal of services that it cannot control from the contract. Examples include out-of-area treatment (including children away at college), organ transplants, extracorporeal membranous oxygenation (ECMO) treatments, and ambulance and transportation, to list just a few. Home health care and outpatient surgery facility services should be grouped with the inpatient hospital services.

Reinsurance. Reinsurance is a policy that the provider purchases, or the payer provides, that limits the total claims responsibility for members. It can be done through a specific (member-specific) claims limit designation above which the provider is not responsible for payment, or pooling, of the cost. This clause is referred to as a stop-loss provision. All contracts should contain a stop-loss provision with a reasonable limit of around $35,000. Specific diseases can be negotiated at a lower limit—such as AIDS, cardiac surgery, premature births more than a specific number of weeks early, and other known high-cost conditions over which the provider loses control. Additionally, an aggregate policy can be purchased that will limit the total aggregate claims cost of the covered lives. This limits total exposure.

Carve Outs. The carve-out provision should specify any and all areas of coverage that have been capitated separately and apart from the provider's contract. Examples include mental health benefits and durable medical equipment, and may include pharmacy, home health care, laboratory, or regional-centers-of-excellence services (such as transplants).

Membership Guarantees. If the provider organization is negotiating to open a new location for the payer, some form of base membership guarantee payment is in order to cover the development costs. In some capitation agreements, the provider is paid discounted fee-for-services until the membership reaches a threshold level that reduces the risk of capitation.

Utilization Covered by the Capitation. This particular clause is especially important to specialists. Once capitated, there is a tendency to refer anything that remotely fits the specialty to that specialist. Also, utilization can change drastically from one year to the next. For example, the birth rate can double or triple from one year to the next in an area with many young couples. Conditions or treatments that can be quantified on a per 1,000 member basis or that are high-cost and out of the provider's control should be limited to a specific utilization level.

Other Issues in Negotiating the Language

After a thorough reading and analysis of the contract, the provider organization should list all of the points to be negotiated in the language stage of the negotiations. In addition, the provider organization should ask the payer for utilization data specific to the demographics of the population to be served. Remember that the payer reports these data at least annually to the regulator. The payer may say that this information is not available. However, persist and indicate that this alone could be a deal breaker. If the payer continues to insist that the data are not available, look more closely at utilization limitations as a method to limit risk, until such time as the data can be collected, independent of the payer.

NEGOTIATING THE RATE

Once the language and its relevance to the rate and cost have been addressed, the provider should prepare to negotiate the rate. Managed care is a business of contracts and information. As such, any claims made by either side—but particularly the providers—will require substantiation. Independent information is available on each HMO. It can be acquired from the insurance commission or from any number of independent organizations who rate the performance of the HMO/insurance industry (e.g., Moody's, Standard and Poors). The information desired includes the following utilization and cost data: inpatient days per 1,000 members; admissions (or discharges) per 1,000 members; number of visits per member per year; total hospital costs; total physician costs; total pharmacy costs; total outpatient facility costs; premiums for each benefit plan offered; medical loss ratio (total costs of medical care), administrative cost ratio (total costs of administration); gross revenues; total expenses (with a break out of depreciation); net profit; and any other financial, utilization, or statistical information about the payer. Because MCOs may not be required to report independently, this information may be harder to find for them. More and more HMOs and MCOs are becoming public companies, allowing anyone access to their annual report and 10Q filings with the Securities and Exchange Commission. These reports provide a wealth of information on costs, utilization, and even business strategies. If the benefit plans include Medicare or Medicaid, utilization data for these organizations is independently available (most easily Medicaid).

For the purposes of demonstrating the development from raw data of capitation rates that relate to a specific contract risk level, the annual report of the Maryland Medicaid system was acquired for 1994, containing 1993 data. The following is a description of the steps followed to arrive at some baseline capitation rates for a contract with the following terms:

- a global capitation contract with the provider group fully at risk for all physician services, both primary care and specialty, including inpatient, outpatient, and office services
- a 50/50 risk-sharing arrangement with the HMO for the outpatient and inpatient facility fees, including home health
- full risk for pharmacy fees
- full risk on dental services
- HMO limited to an 85 percent medical loss ratio
- guarantee of payment for 3,500 members, because the provider was to open a new site with no membership to transfer in at opening

This type of arrangement is typical of global capitation contracts, with the exception that dental and some other specialties, such as mental health, are usually carved out.

Table 15–1 represents the abstraction of membership data from the Maryland Medicaid report. These data are broken down by

Table 15–1 Assumptions and Statistics

Membership	Male Mem	Female Mem	Potent HMO Mem	% Males	% Females
Under 1	14,262	13,737	27,999	3.67%	3.53%
1–5	36,828	35,652	72,480	9.47%	9.17%
6–14	40,293	39,590	79,883	10.36%	10.18%
15–20	12,692	26,912	39,604	3.26%	6.92%
21–44	33,927	94,896	128,823	8.72%	24.40%
45–64	14,855	25,268	40,123	3.82%	6.50%
65–74	5,251	14,102			
75–84	3,757	11,934			
+85	1,632	8,218			
Total	163,497	270,309	388,912	39.30%	60.70%

Reprinted from the Maryland Medicaid Annual Report of Costs, 1994.

age and sex. Because utilization patterns vary greatly according to age and sex, the analyzer should attempt to obtain the data from the payer in a format that allows for the breakdown by age and sex. Columns 2 and 3 represent the actual membership levels found in the raw data. Column 4, "Potent HMO Mem," represents an abstraction of the raw data that considers the age groups of individuals in Medicaid programs, such as Aid to Families with Dependent Children (AFDC), who would be potential members of an HMO plan. Medicaid administers programs that pay for nursing home/long-term care not seen as potential managed care programs. The last two columns represent a percent analysis of these age groups, compared to the total population of these age groups. This information will become important in later calculations.

Table 15–2 represents a combination of abstracted data and calculated statistics. This table develops the basic utilization statistics for this Medicaid population. Columns 1 and 2, "Membership & Visits" and "1993," are the abstraction of visit data specific to the current Medicaid HMO programs, which include members in the age groups targeted in Table 15–1. Note that the bulk of the utilization, 81.5 percent, is from the AFDC members. Because of the high ratio of AFDC members to the total Medicaid population, the readily available breakout of this group's data, and Medicaid's efforts to enroll these members in managed care, this analysis uses this population as the basis of the analysis. It is important for providers to ask: What kind of visits are these, and how do they compare to the kind of visit my organization will be providing service for? When comparisons are made, it is vitally important to compare "apples to apples." In this case, *visits* represent visits to HMO physicians reported to the Medicaid program. A phone call to the Director of the Managed Care Program in Maryland's Medicaid managed care office revealed that, although there were some inadequacies in their HMO data collections program, the visit data are fairly accurate (and, thus, the 1.44 visit per member per year figure is fairly reliable). It is also important to know that many Medicaid members seek their primary care in the emergency department, and that these visits were not part of this count.

Following columns 1 and 2 to the bottom of the top chart reveals a gross breakdown of the total Medicaid membership, as compared to the AFDC population. Moving to the "Visits (AFDC)" column, the visit data for all categories available is displayed. The total payments, or costs, for these same categories are displayed in the "Total AFDC Costs" column. Note that there are no costs

Table 15-2 Utilization Statistics

Membership & Visits	1993	Visits (AFDC)		Total AFDC Costs		
Average HMO Mem	69,346	Tot Inpt Admits	28,087	Inpatient	139,385,167	46%
HMO AFDC Visits	81,479	Tot Hosp Days	109,261	Outpatient	63,702,103	21%
HMO APTD Visits	4,395	Tot Outpt Visits	97,419	Tot Phys Cost	73,802,873	25%
HMO STD-1 Visits	4,008	Tot Phys Visits	380,974	PC Costs	42,847,348 (14%)	
HMO SOBRA Child Vis	7,755	Tot PC Visits	221,180	Spec Costs	30,955,525 (10%)	
Tot HMO Visits	100,072	Tot Spec Visits	159,794	ER Costs		0%
HMO Vis/Mem/Yr	1.44	Tot ER Visits	37,743	Pharmacy Costs	20,068,671	7%
		Tot Pharm Visits	141,234	Dental Costs	3,237,848	1%
Total MA Mem	433,805	Tot Dental Visits	39,976	Total:	300,196,662	100%
AFDC Tot Mem	249,128		179,782			

Utilization	1993	Cost				
Admits/1000 Mem	156	Inpt Ave Per Diem	1,275.71			
Inpt Days/1000 Mem	608	Outpt Cost/Visit	653.90			
Days/Admit	3.89	PC Costs/Visit	112.47			
Outpt Visits/Mem/Yr	0.54	Cost/Spec Visit	193.72			
PC Visits/Mem/Yr	1.23	ER Cost/Visit				
Spec Visits/Mem/Yr	0.89	Per Pharm Vis Cost	142.10			
ER Visits/Mem/Yr	0.21	Dental Costs/Visit	80.99			
Scripts/Mem/Yr	0.57					
Dent Visits/Mem/Yr	0.16					
Tot Phy Vis/Mem/Yr	2.87					

Reprinted from the Maryland Medicaid Annual Report of Costs, 1994.

for emergency department visits; these costs are bundled into the outpatient costs, since the hospital outpatient departments bill for these services. It was not possible to determine the percentage of outpatient costs attributable to emergency department visits. As a general point of interest, the total 1993 cost for AFDC patients in the state of Maryland (which has a population of about 4.5 million) was over $300 million. The redistribution of these dollars, based on a more efficient utilization of resources, cannot help but to provide savings and profit to a managed care system.

The lower portion of Table 15–2 represents the calculated statistics using the data provided in the upper portion of the table. These statistics are important not only to the process of calculating a capitation rate, but also to the ongoing management of a capitation contract. In columns 1 and 2, the inpatient days per 1,000 members and the visits per member per year for each of the reported categories are computed. The cost per visit computations are found in columns 3 and 4.

Table 15–3 reports the published capitation rates from Medicaid to the HMO. These rates are equivalent to the premiums paid by an employer for a commercial health plan. This information can be acquired from the HMO for the commercial plans, Medicaid, and Medicare plans. This table also projects the age and sex mix based on the percentage found in Table 15–1, with the total equaling the 3,500 members guaranteed in the contract. The last column, "Total Cap Payment," calculates the capitation rate for each age group as a monthly payment to the payer. In this case, the payer would receive $597,317 per month for a typical population mix of 3,500 AFDC members.

Table 15–4 shows the payer capitation rate, less the 15 percent that equals the 85 percent medical loss ratio guaranteed in the contract. The medical loss ratio of an insurance company is the percentage of premium revenues that the insurance company paid for actual medical services. This ratio is available from a number of sources; the insurance commission may make this statistic available, or it is available from Moody's or Standard and Poors, and many industry rating or watchdog publications. When this reduced rate is extended and broken down by age group and sex for the guaranteed population, a total monthly payment of $507,720 is available for payments to medical service providers.

Table 15–5 represents an analysis of the total payments by major category, by adult

Table 15–3 Published Capitation Rates Paid by Medicaid to the HMO

	AFDC Rates		Potential Members		Total AFDC Cap Payment
Age	Full M Cap Rate	Full Female Cap	Males	Females	
Under 1	$408	$359	128	124	$96,801
1–5	93	83	331	321	57,160
6–14	86	52	363	356	49,748
15–20	80	262	114	242	72,626
21–44	191	244	305	854	266,771
45–64	102	178	134	227	54,211
75–84					
+85					
Total			1,376	2,124	$597,317

Reprinted from the Maryland Medicaid Annual Report of Costs, 1994.

Table 15-4 Capitation Rates and Payments

			Site Mem Guarantee:	3,500
Age	Male Cap Rate Less 15%	Female Cap Rate Less 15%	Cap Pmt Males	Cap Pmt Females
Under 1	$347.11	$305.19	$44,551	$37,730
1–5	78.69	70.14	26,081	22,505
6–14	73.09	44.29	26,504	15,781
15–20	67.92	222.85	7,758	53,974
21–44	162.75	207.33	49,691	177,064
45–64	86.86	151.57	11,612	34,467
		Tot Cap Less 15%	**$507,720**	

Reprinted from the Maryland Medicaid Annual Report of Costs, 1994.

Table 15-5 AFDC Adult and Child Payment Breakdown

	AFDC Payments	Percentage of Total Payments	Capitation Payment Breakdown
Tot Inpt Hosp Child	$87,997,098	29.31%	$42.52
Tot Inpt Hosp Adult	51,388,069	17.12%	24.83
Tot Outpt Hosp Child	31,957,849	10.65%	15.44
Tot Outpt Hosp Adult	31,744,254	10.57%	15.34
Tot Phys Child	44,362,230	14.78%	21.44
Tot Phys Adult	29,440,643	9.81%	14.23
Tot Pharm Child	8,783,207	2.93%	4.24
Tot Pharm Adult	11,285,464	3.76%	5.45
Tot Dental Child	2,685,672	0.89%	1.30
Tot Dental Adult	552,176	0.18%	0.27
Total Payments 1993	**$300,196,662**	**100.00%**	**$145.06**

Reprinted from the Maryland Medicaid Annual Report of Costs, 1994.

or child. The category payments are shown as a percentage of the total payments, so that the average capitation rate, calculated by taking the total capitation (less 15 percent) from Table 15-4 and dividing by the 3,500 guaranteed members, can be broken down by these major categories. This table provides the breakout of the capitation by inpatient hospital, outpatient hospital, physician, pharmacy, and dental. This information can be further analyzed to determine additional components of the global capitation contract. This type of analysis will become routine for all segments of a globally capitated organization's membership.

Table 15-6 shows the breakdown of all physician costs using the same techniques as Table 15-5. The "PMPM Cost" column derives the capitation rate for each of these detailed categories. This information is important in establishing the capitation requirements for both primary care and specialty care physicians. The physician capitation from Table 15-5 is used as the base total physician capitation to which the appropriate percentage is applied. The "To-

Table 15-6 Physician Cost Conversion to Capitation

	% Total Costs	Total Cost in $	PMPM Costs	Percentage of Total Care
Primary Care				
Office	47.99%	718,900	17.12	
Inpt	4.56%	68,332	1.63	
Outpt	0.13%	1,963	0.05	
Physical Exams	3.78%	56,589	1.35	
X-ray	1.59%	23,765	0.57	
Total Primary Care		869,549	20.70	58.06%
Specialty Consults				
Office Consults	0.51%	7,576	0.18	
Outpt Consults	0.15%	2,314	0.06	
Inpt Consults	1.41%	21,161	0.50	
Surgery				
Inpt	13.28%	198,962	4.74	
Outpt	3.14%	47,021	1.12	
Anesthesia	3.30%	49,421	1.18	
Pathology	0.33%	4,886	0.12	
Radiology				
Inpt	1.68%	25,144	0.60	
Outpt	2.28%	34,164	0.81	
Other Services				
Lab	0.71%	10,678	0.25	
Emerg Room	2.29%	34,231	0.82	
Other Specialty				
Office	6.86%	102,752	2.45	
Inpt	3.83%	57,313	1.36	
Outpt	1.09%	16,400	0.39	
Drugs Dispensed	1.08%	16,191	0.39	
Total Specialty Services		628,215	14.96	41.94%
Total Physician Cost Capitation	100%	1,497,764	35.66	

Reprinted from the Maryland Medicaid Annual Report of Costs, 1994.

tal Physician Cost Capitation" at the bottom is calculated by adding $21.44 for child physician costs plus $14.23 for adult physician costs (Table 15–5), and multiplying the sum by the 3,500 members guaranteed in the contract.

It is now possible to determine how much money is available to operate the primary care site, how much is available to employ or contract with specialists, and the costs of certain, specific pieces of the care (such as inpatient surgery physician costs, or outpatient surgery physician costs).

Table 15–7 contains an analysis of the outpatient facility costs that is similar to the analysis of physician costs in Table 15–6. The difference is that the physician group is at risk for the total amount of physician costs, while the risk on these outpatient facility costs is being split 50/50 with the payer. In this case, each specific category had to be reviewed to determine whether it was part of the outpatient facility or physician costs, according to the specific definitions given in the language of the contract. (Negotiate the language first!) The provider organization is at risk for 100 percent of physician costs, and outpatient facility costs had to be halved to determine the amount charged to the provider group. This analysis determined an

Table 15–7 Outpatient Hospital Costs

Department	% Tot Costs	Total $	PMPM Costs	Group Responsibility	Contract Outpatient	Contract Specialty
Clinic	12.18%	157,477	3.75	3.75		3.75
Emergency Room	14.50%	187,451	4.46	4.46		4.46
Operating Room	8.78%	113,523	2.70	1.35	1.35	
Anesthesia	0.72%	9,295	0.22	0.11	0.11	
Delivery Room	2.85%	36,793	0.88	0.88		0.88
Laboratory	14.49%	187,308	4.46	2.23	1.99	0.24
Radiology	16.36%	211,539	5.04	5.04		5.04
ECG, EEG	2.82%	36,449	0.87	0.87		0.87
Pharmacy	3.23%	41,707	0.99	0.50	0.50	
Blood/Transfusions	0.49%	6,303	0.15	0.08	0.08	
Supplies	4.54%	58,646	1.40	0.70	0.70	
Psych Day Care	1.60%	20,642	0.49	0.49		0.49
PT/OT	3.30%	42,690	1.02	1.02		1.02
Other	14.16%	183,014	4.36	2.18	2.18	
Total Outpt Costs:	**100.00%**	**1,292,837**	**30.78**	**23.64**	**6.91**	**16.75**

Reprinted from the Maryland Medicaid Annual Report of Costs, 1994.

additional $16.75 specialty physician capitation and a $6.91 outpatient facility provider group capitation.

So far, we have determined that the primary care capitation should be $20.70 PMPM (Table 15–6), the specialty rate should be $14.96 PMPM (Table 15–6) + $16.75 PMPM (Table 15–7) totaling $31.71 PMPM, and the total outpatient capitation should be $13.82 PMPM, with the provider group responsible for $6.91 PMPM (Table 15–7).

Exhibit 15–1 ties together the analysis of all of the other tables to give a comprehensive summary of the capitation rates, as they apply to a Medicaid contract (remember this is data from the state of Maryland) and to the specific terms of this global capitation contract. Since all payers in the state of Maryland are compensated based on this data, one well-performed analysis can be used for all payers. Please note that the inpatient hospital rate has been calculated and the adjustment to the outpatient rate appears in the difference between the second and third sections of the exhibit. The third section also shows the result of a 10 percent reduction in the inpatient days per 1,000 members, in days per 1,000 and admissions per 1,000. This is the beginning of the projection portion of a capitation analysis. Once the rate has been determined, the provider organization should analyze the utilization so as to target the areas where utilization is high and can be reduced. This is the beginning of the process of budgeting for profit. However, this analysis is beyond the scope of negotiating the contract; it is a capital budgeting issue.

In summary, the capitation rate for a global capitation contract with these terms should pay the provider organization $104.24. The annual revenue generated by this contract will be $4,378,265. With a simple 10 percent reduction in the inpatient days per 1,000 members, using the per diem of $1,275.71 (Table 15–2) and the inpatient days rate of 608 days per 1,000 members (Table 15–2), there is the potential for, all other things being equal, 60.8 days reduction times 3.5 (3,500 members) = 212.80 fewer inpatient days times $1,275.71 = $271,471.08 times .5 = $135,735.54 profit, or 3.1 percent. Obviously this is a very simplistic profit analysis; however, it demonstrates the point that these contracts can be lucrative at this stage of the market transition.

How does this analysis affect the negotiation of a capitation contract? The key to ne-

Exhibit 15-1 Capitation Analysis

	Ave Cap Pmt	Monthly $		
Site Guarantee	3,500			
Admin % for HMO	15.00%			
Tot Cap Pmt to HMO	170.66	597,317		
Average Cap Payment	145.06	507,720		
Combined Cap Rates	Total Cap	Outpt Risk Shr	50% Risk Shr	Total Group Cap
Inpatient Hospital	67.35		33.68	33.68
Outpatient Hospital	30.78	13.82	6.91	23.64
Physicians	35.66			35.66
Pharmacy	9.70			9.70
Dental	1.56			1.56
Total	**145.06**		**40.59**	**104.24**
	PMPM Pmt	Monthly $*		
Capitation Payments				
Inpt Hospital	33.68	117,870		
Outpt Hospital	23.64	82,745		
Primary Care	20.70	72,462		
Specialty Care	14.96	52,351		
Pharmacy	9.70	33,942		
Dental	1.56	5,476		
Total Cap	104.24	364,847		
Tot Monthly Rev	364,855			
Tot Annual Rev	4,378,265			
Utilization Reductions		Days/1,000	Admits/1,000	
Inpt Days/1,000	10.00%	546.97	140.61	
PC Visits/Mem/Yr	3.75			

*at 3,500 members

Reprinted from the Maryland Medicaid Annual Report of Costs, 1994.

gotiating anything is to be loaded with information about your needs, acceptable ranges of compensation, and the position and needs of the other party. In many cases, the payer will tell the provider organization that it does not have available the utilization data that the provider requested. U.S. Healthcare, in a recent negotiation in Connecticut, told the provider group that it did not set its capitation rates based on utilization, and, therefore, did not keep these data. A provider group that searches the available sources of statistics on payers (insurance commission offices, Moody's, Standard and Poors, and other trade groups that track payer performance) will be armed with data that can be used at the bargaining table or used simply to reject a payer who is offering a rate that is too far out of line. The more that is known about the other party, the better job of negotiating one can do.

PREPARING THE ORGANIZATION FOR CAPITATION NEGOTIATIONS

This discussion of capitation has not approached any issues from the traditional fee-for-service perspective. The opening section of this chapter discussed the need for provider organizations to change their perspective from "increased revenue = increased profit" to "reduced cost/increased efficiency = profitability and desirability in the marketplace." For this reason, it is imperative to look at the operations of providers' offices and facilities from a cost perspective. This is the only way to determine pricing and product mix, and to project profits and sales to Managed Care Organizations. To understand the cost perspective of operating a practice or hospital, it is necessary to look at some cost accounting and finance concepts. Applying these concepts to the everyday management systems found in these businesses will give management the tools to begin to realize the increases in efficiency and cost control that are necessary for success in capitation. It will also provide the last piece of vital information needed at the negotiating table: What is the organization's cost base? (See your costs, see your profits. Don't see your costs, don't see your profits!)

Appendix 15–A of this chapter contains definitions that are important to the following discussion. It is advisable to have them handy as a reference.

Preparing for the New Business Environment

When preparing to enter the capitated business environment management should convert the usual financial information format from

revenue − expense = profit

to

revenue − variable costs = contribution (to fixed costs and profit) margin

This margin becomes more important than the traditional gross margin. Management should review all costs, but particularly fixed costs. Every attempt should be made to find ways to convert fixed costs to variable costs. Shifting the traditional fixed to variable cost ratio to increase the variable cost component is a key to the success of the organization. Some calculations are as follows:

revenues − variable costs − fixed costs = operating income

unit contribution margin = unit price − unit variable costs

breakeven point = fixed costs/unit contribution margin

number of lives to achieve a certain operating income = (fixed costs + target operating income)/unit contribution margin

How do these calculations relate to pricing a capitation contract? Since the contribution margin is the contribution to fixed costs and profits, at the point in the year that all of the annual fixed costs have been paid the remaining contribution margin is the annual profit. The classification of a cost as either a fixed or variable cost is extremely important when determining the cost structure of providing the services. Health care providers are essentially faced with a short-term pricing problem, since capitation contracts are generally for a one-year period. However, to effectively renegotiate the rate and track the profitability of this piece of business, it is necessary to have a detailed data gathering and analysis system in place.

If costs are miscalculated and they do not cover the full costing of the service, it does not mean that the organization has lost money. Since the organization is using the contribution margin as one of the bases in costing the service, and assuming that the organization is getting patients that it would not have gotten without the contract (very important), as long as the price is greater than the variable costs, the organization is putting more profit on the overall bottom line than it would have, had it not contracted. Obviously, the closer the organization is to covering not only the variable costs, but also the fixed costs and achieving a full costing profit, the better. To limit the risk on the first capitation contract, the organization should consider negotiating a limited-risk contract, rather than a full-risk contract. If the nature of the contract is to capitate the organization only for the services it specifically provides and to share in a risk pool for the services that it does not specifically provide, the organization has a limited-risk position.

In addition to looking at overall costs, the organization needs to develop carefully derived standard costs. The organization should go through the following general process to prepare for these negotiations:

1. The costs of providing services need to be divided into fixed and variable costs. The easiest costs to assign are direct service costs, which tend to be variable costs. The following are variable costs related to general patient care:
   - **Direct labor.** Using an allocation base of labor hours per patient per delivery unit (visit or day), applied against an average hourly cost, individually for the appropriate labor provider (nurses, aides, unit clerks, unit managers, receptionists, billing clerks, referral clerks, etc.), will give the most accurate direct labor cost.
   - **Direct materials.** Using an allocation base of dollars per patient per delivery unit (visit or day) for the appropriate nonlabor costs (such as general nursing supplies, including medical supplies laboratory/drawing supplies, forms, laundry, and personal patient supplies) will give the most accurate direct materials cost. These supplies exclude medications.
   - **Direct pharmacy costs.** Using an allocation base of dollars per patient per delivery unit (prescription) for all medications dispensed or administered at the cost to the organization will give the most accurate cost.
   - **Other ancillary costs.** These should be allocated on a similar basis, an appropriate allocation base per patient per delivery unit, to determine the variable costs. These categories should cover the direct service costs.
2. Other costs that have a variable component are: housekeeping, maintenance, dietary, marketing, and administration. Costs that are basically fixed include land, building, equipment, and depreciation and amortization, and utilities. There are also fixed components to the housekeeping, maintenance, dietary, marketing, and administrative costs.
3. A variable costing income statement format will help to calculate a contribution margin that represents the organization's contribution to fixed costs and profit. The more specific its costing methods, the better the organization will be able to track performance and profit. This format can be used both on an overall cost basis and on a standard cost basis. The format of the variable costing income statement can be found in Appendix 15-B of this chapter.

The source of data to derive the costs of providing care are the costs over the past year for each category, broken down on a per unit of sales basis. This would include costs from payroll, accounts payable, depreciation schedules, etc. After deriving the costs of providing each level of care, a break-even point should be calculated for the contract. A target operating income should then be determined that will leave some room for negotiation, without being too high to scare away the payer. Keep in mind that these should be new patients, because fixed costs have been covered by the current patient base; therefore, the pricing must cover the variable costs, but does not have to cover both fixed and variable costs to make a profit. Additionally, when negotiating a new capitation contract, management should consider negotiating a guaranteed base membership that makes the break-even and target operating income analysis relevant. If management costs out the contract thoroughly, the price can be adjusted for the volume very quickly.

While developing the organization's standard costs and pricing for managed care contracts, a great deal of consideration should be given to the changes in the cost drivers that produce a lower per unit cost and to adjusting the fixed to variable cost ratio. A serious look at the delivery system and productivity levels of its components should help management to identify changes in the way business should be done, which will lower costs. For example, achieving a physician productivity level of 3.0 patients per hour, changing the way nursing care is delivered in order to change the nurse to patient visit or nurse to physician ratio will impact cost. Changing the delivery system for pharmaceuticals, or the procurement system, will impact cost. These are the types of changes that are necessary for success in managed care.

This may seem like a rigorous process to determine pricing for these contracts; however, when dealing with Managed Care Organizations, the whole relationship is cost-oriented. Payers cost account their medical loss ratio in great detail, as a matter of routine. Their whole business is cost driven; their decisions and their profits are cost driven, and they expect providers to operate from a cost-driven perspective. Whenever providers experience problems with their managed care contracts, it is because they did not have a thorough understanding of their costs and cost drivers. That is why some providers are very successful with managed care contracts and others are not. As the health care system moves to managed care, the successful providers will develop sophisticated cost accounting systems that will allow them to provide services for competitive prices. This is the whole basis of managed care.

Implementing Management Systems for Capitation

After signing the contract, it must be managed. This requires the proper infrastructure, information system, and accounting system to track costs against the proper revenue. This requires the use of an accrual method of accounting. An accrual accounting system is defined as matching revenue and expense to the period in which they occur. This means that instead of counting the phone bill paid in January as a January expense, it must be booked back to December, the period in which the expense was incurred. To understand the systems necessary to be successful, it is necessary to address the issues outlined below.

Difference in Management Perspective

When managing a capitated contract, it is necessary to view some common processes in a very different way. In the fee-for-service world, physician groups and hospitals tracked referrals to determine where their patients came from. In managed care, referrals are tracked to determine where patients are going. In the fee-for-service world, referrals were viewed as generating revenue. In managed care, referrals generate expense. The portion of the information system that currently tracks referrals for fee-for-service arrangements cannot track referrals properly for management of a capitated contract. This hints that new infrastructure will be necessary to manage in the capitated environment. Knowing this cost is important to negotiating rates for future business.

In the fee-for-service world, utilization review is used to justify the care that the organization wants to provide. If approval is received from the payer, the organization will benefit from providing additional services and the corresponding increase in revenue. In managed care, utilization review and case management are used to determine whether the proposed care is necessary and appropriate. If it is, then providing the care is a necessary and appropriate expense. Fee-for-service incentives reward the determination that service needs to be provided in the highest-intensity setting possible. In managed care, the least intensive setting that can provide the appropriate level of care is the most desirable. Care plans to move the patient to the lowest-intensity setting have necessitated the creation and development of new, less intensive settings for care. This brought about the wave of development in home health care and outpatient procedures. New areas, such as subacute care, should be further explored and developed.

In the fee-for-service world, the focus of management has not been to become more efficient, but to make sure that all services and supply charges have been captured and charged in such a way that reimbursement is maximized. This system allows management to begin with a known, the service that was provided, and concentrate on tracking and collecting for that known. In managed care, management is beginning with an unknown, the total utilization of the population. This requires management to develop new systems of delivery that will make providing care more efficient. Providers in the fee-for-service world are concerned with the quality of care and efficiency of their own operations. In managed care, providers must be concerned with the productivity, quality, efficiency, and outcomes of all of the providers in the continuum of care. They are now, more than ever, required to police their peers and make definitive decisions about whether to work with them.

The transition from the fee-for-service environment to the capitated environment requires the management of provider organizations under two diametrically opposed incentive systems. In practice, this can become very confusing to the providers and management. In the fee-for-service physician's practice, elements of productivity include the following:

- average charge per visit
- number of ancillary services provided, as a revenue generator
- number of admissions and length of stay, as a revenue generator
- number of procedures performed, as a revenue generator

The analysis of whether to purchase a new piece of equipment is based on the number of patients that can be charged for that particular service.

In the managed care world, elements of productivity include the following:

- patients seen per hour
- number of referrals made (should be tracked against some standard, such as per 100 encounters)
- number of admissions and patient days per 1,000 capitated members, as a gauge against utilization assumptions as an expense
- number of procedures performed in-house that might have been performed outside in the past, as a savings because of the lower cost to the group

The analysis for the purchase of a new piece of equipment now focuses on whether the group will be able to save on the total cost of providing that particular service to the capitated population. The group will want to know, for example, how many procedures were performed by outside providers, what was the total cost, and how much will it cost if the group buys that equipment and provides the service in-house (vertical integration).

To manage both fee-for-service and capitated populations properly, management must have the capability of tracking the necessary information and understanding when to apply the appropriate philosophy. For providers it is more complex. Their compensation is generally tied to the method of incentive and, therefore, they have a more difficult time working in both directions. Management's ability to deal with the resulting frustration becomes a key element in the success of the organization. Additional tracking statistics can be found in Appendix 15–C.

Operational Issues

Management must confront many operational issues when converting to capitation management systems. The results of detailed cost accounting must lead the provider organization to produce a more efficient operation. Areas that can be looked at initially include the following:

- In the past, physicians may have had their own nurse to assist them with their patients. Now the staffing structure will need to be formed around a patient-flow system that produces a more consistent and higher physician productivity level without reducing time from the direct physician-patient contact. This could mean different members of the nursing staff assisting the physician on the same patient.
- The use of midlevel providers should be considered to relieve the physician of patients who can appropriately be treated by a nurse practitioner or physician's assistant.
- Triage systems should be set up to determine the necessity of a particular patient's request to be seen, at what level, and by whom. The on-call system must be able to determine if a patient needs to be seen in the emergency room, or the appropriateness of denying that level of care and requiring the patient to be seen in the office the next day.

Management must develop systems to track all of these contacts with patients; record them; and, when necessary, assign costs to them.

One of the most important areas of managing a capitated contract is the accounting system. The cash method of accounting is no longer appropriate and can be destructive. A true accrual method is required, along with a sophisticated cost accounting system. This—along with increased information system requirements, contract analysis, and negotiation—requires the recruitment of management with a higher level of skill than was previously necessary. One of the reasons for the high level of merger and acquisition activity in the physician practice market is this increase in management and infrastructure costs.

Management must understand that it is being paid in advance for providing services that it may not know the actual cost of until much later. This requires management to track incurred but not reported (IBNR) costs. Managing the IBNR is difficult for experienced managers, and it should not be assumed that someone can quickly be trained to perform this task. The decisions relating to the IBNR can be the difference between success and failure.

Depending on the type of capitation contract and the relationship with the HMO, the physician group may be required to pay the claims it generates from its referrals. If this is required, a new system, new level of expertise, and new positions are required. The payment of claims is a complex system that, essentially, is designed to ensure that only necessary services are paid and that only appropriate charges are paid. This means that many of the revenue-enhancing techniques that an organization has used in the past must be undone when paying the claim. This function is extremely important to the success of the organization; therefore, only experienced people should be hired.

The management of the utilization review/case management system and the referral system must be clearly delineated. A utilization review/case management nurse position should be created and filled by an experienced person. The physicians will also have to decide how they want their referral system to work. In general, hospital admissions and outpatient surgeries must be approved by the HMO and certified for a length of stay. Many physician groups employ a similar strategy for their general referrals. The more experienced, or senior, physicians review all nonemergency referrals before they are approved and the appointments are set. At the very least, they set referral guidelines. All HMO contracts require the group to set up a quality assurance committee, have regular meetings, keep minutes, and discuss relevant topics. They also require the review of medical records—both by the group, as a quality assurance function, and by the HMO at random times. Even the forms and order of the medical record are specified and reviewed. There are site inspections both by the HMO and the state insurance entity. These committees and systems are key checks and reviews to ensure that appropriate and efficient care are being provided. Through these mechanisms, inefficient providers and systems of providing the appropriate level of care are identified.

Hospitals have similar operational issues to consider when taking on a capitated contract. The traditional utilization review functions require changes. In the past, cases were reviewed from the perspective of having to get length-of-stay approvals and extensions from some other utilization management entity. Under capitation, the utilization management function of the hospital will focus on whether the patient is being treated at the best intensity level of care. If the patient is being treated on an inpatient basis at an acute care facility and he or she could be treated at a subacute level or at home, then the system is misallocating resources to that patient. Hospital utilization departments will have to determine the appropriate level of intensity required by the patient and allow that to drive the decision-making process. Utilization management will have to coordinate the transition of the patient to home health care more expeditiously than generally occurs now. The extra day spent in the acute care unit is extra cost for the hospital and a loss of potential profit.

Hospital administrators will also have to look at their service delivery systems, including the following:

- Open a subacute care facility within the hospital, which will allow a patient to be stepped down to a lower level of care as soon as it is appropriate.
- Implement a home health care operation.
- Examine the pharmacy system from several perspectives:
  1. Can a formulary be set up for the capitated patients that can be agreed upon by the admitting physicians?
  2. Can the hospital purchase the medications for the capitated patients at a lower cost than their fee-for-service patients (since the hospital will not be retailing these medicines)?
  3. How many days' supply of medicine is appropriate to dispense to the floor for a patient at one time?
  4. Pharmacy has been a very difficult area of health care for Managed Care Organizations to control; however, if a hospital is to thrive under capitation, it must be creative in structuring and operating its pharmacy department.

Hospitals will have to apply the new tests of successful operations to all of their ancillary departments. New ideas will be needed that use capitated incentives to manage operations, service delivery, and the appropriate care setting for patients.

How do all of these operational issues relate to the negotiation of a capitation contract? This is a valid question whose answer management should keep in mind through the transition and beyond. To payers, the most desirable provider organization is one that can provide the required service in the most efficient, lowest-cost, highest-quality way. When competing with other provider organizations, the organization must distinguish itself by the sophistication and maturity of its managed care systems.

CONCLUSION

Provider organizations must make many changes in the way they operate their businesses to remain viable as managed care and capitation increase in the marketplace. This chapter has concentrated on critical issues in negotiating capitation contracts. It is important to remember that negotiating the language first is critical to setting the stage for negotiating the rate. Additionally, converting the organization to a cost-based management system and collecting information on the payer, prior to negotiations, will position the organization not only to be competitive, but also to avoid the narrow-margin or no-margin contracts that some payers are circulating in the marketplace. Knowing your cost, knowing their cost, and knowing your exposure are critical elements of successfully negotiating a win-win business relationship and a capitation contract.

Appendix 15–A

Cost System Definitions

A cost system's purpose is to collect data in a form that provides a reliable basis for predicting the economic consequences of decisions, such as:

- Which services should we continue to offer or discontinue?
- Should we provide a particular service, or should we acquire it from another company? (the classic make or buy decision)
- What price should we charge? (What is the required capitation, per diem, or diagnosis-related group [DRG] price?)
- Should we buy or lease the proposed equipment? (the classic lease or buy decision)
- Should we change our service delivery methods?
- Should we expand a particular department?

Activity-based accounting: An accounting system that has activities as the fundamental cost objects, rather than departments, products, etc.

Average cost: Computed by dividing some total cost by some measure of volume that is most closely related to the total cost incurred. Unit costs are average costs and must be interpreted with caution. For decision-making purposes, the fixed cost per unit must be distinguished from the variable cost per unit. (Examples include cost per patient per day, cost per operating room procedure, cost per emergency department visit.)

Break-even point: That point of volume where total revenues and total expenses (costs) are equal.

Contribution margin: The excess of sales over *all* variable costs, including marketing and administrative.

Cost accumulation: The collection of cost data in some organized way through an accounting system.

Cost allocation: A general term that refers to identifying accumulated costs with or tracing accumulated costs to cost objects, such as departments, activities, or products. (Examples include costs of maintenance department, personnel department, or accounting department. These departments are cost centers and do not relate directly to the profit centers. Their costs must be allocated through some rational method to the profit centers to determine the true cost of providing the service.)

Cost driver: Any factor whose change causes a change in the total cost of a related cost object. Drivers are causal factors whose effects are increases in total costs. (Examples of cost drivers for providing inpatient care include number of RN hours, number of aide hours, number of medication orders, number of supplies used, and number of patients.)

Cost object: Any activity or item for which a separate measurement of cost is desired. A synonym is *cost objective*. The cost objects are chosen for decision-making purposes, not for their own sake. (Examples include activities or operations, products or services, projects, departments, programs.)

Direct costs: Costs that can be identified specifically with or traced to a given cost object, in an economically feasible way.

Fixed cost: A cost that does not change in total, despite changes of a cost driver. A fixed cost is fixed only in relation to a relevant volume range (usually large) and a given time. In a strict sense, if tomorrow there were no more patients to treat, fixed costs would be the ongoing costs that the organization is committed to. In a liberal sense, if a particular department were closed, fixed costs would include costs charged to the department that would continue, such as a supervisor. (Examples of fixed cost include the rent, the debt service on a bond issue to build a new operating room.)

Flexible budget (or variable budget): A budget that is adjusted for changes in the unit level of the cost or revenue driver.

Gross margin: The excess of sales over the specific cost of the goods or services sold. This cost includes only the direct cost of providing the service, not marketing and administration.

Indirect costs: Costs that cannot be identified specifically with or traced to a given cost object, in an economically feasible way. These are the costs that are allocated.

Payer mix (sales mix): The relative combination of quantities of services paid by specific payers.

Revenue driver: Any factor whose change causes a change in the total revenue of a related service. (Examples include the number of members the group or hospital is capitated for, and the ages of those members if the capitation is age specific.)

Standard costs: Carefully predetermined costs that are usually expressed on a per-unit basis. Standard costs help managers to build budgets, gauge performance, obtain "product" costs, and save recordkeeping costs. Standard costs are the building blocks of a flexible budgeting and feedback system.

Variable cost: A cost that changes in direct proportion to changes of a cost driver. (Example: the cost of pharmaceuticals changes in proportion to the number of admissions.)

Appendix 15–B

Variable Costing Income Statement Format

Revenues (or revenues/unit):			XXX
Variable costs:			
Direct labor:	XXX		
Direct materials:	XXX		
Direct overhead:	XXX		
Variable cost of services sold:		XXX	
Variable marketing and administrative costs:		XXX	
Total variable costs:			(XXX)
Contribution margin:			XXX
Fixed costs:			
Fixed service provision overhead:		XXX	
Fixed marketing and administration costs:		XXX	
Total fixed costs:		XXX	(XXX)
Net income:			**XXX**

Appendix 15–C

Data Sources, Elements, and Specific Statistics

Managed Care Organizations require increases in the amount, kind, and detail of information to manage their capitated contracts properly. Physician groups will no longer be gauging their success by the average revenue per visit and the number of visits. Physicians will need to track and use the following data in their decision-making process:

PHYSICIAN PRODUCTIVITY DATA

- number of patients seen per hour
- number of referrals made per 100 encounters (gives a method of comparison to other physicians)
- specialties and specialists referred to
- breakdown of the specific lab tests ordered (physicians should become aware of the cost differential between ordering specific tests and ordering profile or panel studies)
- number of inpatient admissions, length of stay, total hospital days (these cases should be compared to similar types of admissions)

OUTSIDE REFERRAL STATISTICS

Controlling the outside referral costs is not only a function of reducing utilization (the actual number of referrals, and the referral rate per 1,000 members) but is also a function of the services that can be provided in-house and the contracts that have been negotiated with the specialist panel (discounted fee-for-service, fee schedule of the capitated group, DRG, or subcapitation carve out). The capitated group should look for a system of management that strives for continual improvement in the utilization and contractual relationships with its specialist network. This requires a flexible system of information retrieval from a data collections system that tracks both referral information and claims payment information. The specific reporting needs will vary, depending on the specific area being analyzed. In general the organization should monitor the following:

- number of referrals by specialty, with total and average costs, separated by outpatient and inpatient, with length of stay for inpatient

- number of referrals to each outside provider, by specialty, with total and average costs, separated by outpatient and inpatient, with length of stay for inpatient
- number of referrals per 1,000 members
- number of admissions per 1,000 members
- number of total patient days per 1,000 members
- PMPM costs by specialty, outpatient, inpatient

Part V

Taking Leadership

Chapter 16

Developing and Operating Physician-Driven HMOs

John Pollard, M.D.

INTRODUCTION

Control of the health care industry in the United States is shifting from providers to payers—that is, to health insurance companies and government. This is very unsettling to physicians who recognize that change in control is occurring, and distressing to physicians who feel the effects of this change. As a result, some physicians are joining together to become payers and creating managed care insurance companies that they control.

Change in control is being driven by the growth in managed care insurance in the United States. Patients enrolling in Health Maintenance Organizations (HMOs) are increasing dramatically, and growth in managed care insurance is expected to continue for the foreseeable future. In fact, predictions suggest that 95 percent of the U.S. population will be enrolled in managed care within the next 10 years. This growth in managed care is a response to the generally held opinion that too much money is spent on health care in the United States. As health care insurance companies try to control costs while providing high-quality care, they begin to control how physicians care for patients. Needless to say, this control rankles physicians.

In addition to their concerns about being told by managed care insurance companies how to manage patients, physicians have concerns about the quality of care provided their patients and the reduced financial return they receive for their work. One obvious answer to these problems is for physicians to create their own managed care insurance companies. Many physicians are doing just that.

Examples of physicians who have established their own managed care insurance company include the physicians of the Fallon Clinic in Worcester, Massachusetts; the Ochsner Clinic in New Orleans, Louisiana; the Scott and White Clinic in Temple, Texas; and the Carle Clinic in Urbana, Illinois. The Carle Clinic developed its own managed care insurance company in 1980, in response to the physicians' concern that the control of health care was moving from the provider to the payer. The Carle Clinic physicians started by establishing an HMO called CarleCare, which was marketed initially in the local community. From this small beginning, the company has evolved into a managed insurance company that offers a wide variety of managed care insurance products throughout Illinois.

BASIC REQUIREMENTS

Certain basic requirements must be met if a group of physicians is to develop a managed care insurance company. These requirements are:

- development of a champion
- interested physician group
- primary care physicians
- governance structure
- management structure
- adequate capital

The very first requirement is the development of a champion. The champion, preferably a physician, must work hard without compensation to overcome the many obstacles of creating a physician-driven managed health care organization. Fortunately for physicians, these champions do exist. The next requirement is a group of interested physicians. These physicians must recognize that it is in their best interest to take the unfamiliar step of creating a health insurance company. Gaining commitment from a successful group of physicians is particularly difficult, yet they must act while they are successful. It is much easier from a business perspective to create the new company before managed care competitors become active in the market and before the physicians are affected financially by becoming providers for someone else's HMO. By the time the need to act is obvious, the optimal time is past. These physicians must be educated to a new vision of future medical practice, and then convinced to do what they must to succeed in this future.

The group must have an adequate number (50 percent or more) of primary care physicians to be successful in operating a managed care insurance company. Primary care physicians provide the bulk of care to enrollees in successful managed care plans. In general, they manage patients more cost-effectively than specialists, without sacrificing quality.

Carle Clinic was fortunate to have developed a strong primary care base by the 1980s. Internal medicine and pediatrics had long been strong departments of the group practice. Family practice was added to the clinic in 1975, and by the 1980s was the fastest-growing department of the clinic. Since then, it has become the largest department.

As an interested group of physicians begins to develop, the issues of governance and management surface. Usually it is not difficult to establish a board to govern the emerging organization. On the other hand, it is very difficult to get physicians to accept the management that is necessary to create a successful physician-driven managed care insurance company. Physicians are independent and see the changes management is likely to require as an infringement on their rights. Still, physicians must agree to be managed, or the organization will not be successful. The final and most important requirement is that the group must have the capacity to bear financial risk if they are to create a health insurance company. Capital must be adequate to satisfy government regulators and to withstand the negative financial impact of potential "bad medical experience." An example of bad medical experience is one or more patients requiring a heart transplant early in the development of the company. The expense of the treatment could bankrupt the young company if capitalization is not adequate. Because physicians seldom have capital, often a partner is needed. The local hospital with its capital base may become that partner. In seeking capital or a capital partner, it is important to develop a business plan. This plan outlines the financial needs of the company, as well as the anticipated income and expenses and expected cash flows for the first several years.

Carle Clinic did not follow this step in establishing its physician-owned managed care insurance company. Carle relied on the "reserve" present in the group's ability to provide most of the needed care and its ability to reduce physician compensation to meet capital requirements as necessary (although this was undesired). Fortunately for the Carle physicians, who had to learn to practice in a managed care setting, the percentage of their practice that was capitated was small initially. As the percentage of patients in managed care grew, the Carle doctors' ability to provide high-quality care in a cost-effective way improved. Clearly, though, there was an unmeasured cost to this learning curve.

Physicians already in group practice when the champion emerges are better able to meet the requirements of establishing a managed care insurance company than physicians in individual practice. Usually governance and management structures are in place. Even so, physicians already in a group will resist the additional management of their medical practice required to be financially successful in caring for HMO patients. Furthermore, it is unusual for a group practice to have a strong capital base. A capital partner may still be needed.

If physicians are able to meet these requirements and move to the next step, the company can be very successful and enable physicians to provide high-quality care and to have a satisfying practice.

INITIAL STEPS

Once the requirements for establishing a physician-driven managed care insurance company have been met, the next steps can be undertaken (see Exhibit 16–1). Assessment of the market is the first task. This involves determining how many potential enrollees are already in managed care plans and how many and what plans are available. In addition, the number of companies in the marketplace and their size and characteristics must be determined. The new managed care company must determine how many are likely to offer the managed care plans that it wants to develop. If employers have had experience with managed health care, the market is probably competitive, and it will be difficult for a new managed care company to market its products. On the other hand, if employers are not familiar with managed care, there will be less competition, but time must be spent educating employers and employees about the benefits of managed health care. In any case, an assessment of the market is essential.

Exhibit 16–1 Initial Steps

- Conduct market assessment.
- Hire experienced executive.
- Develop and price benefit plans.
- Develop underwriting criteria.
- Contract for provider services.
- Develop information system.
- Comply with government regulations.

If after assessing the market the decision is to proceed, an experienced HMO executive must be hired. Executives with experience in managed care are in high demand, so the position will be difficult for a developing company to fill. Nonetheless, this is an essential part of starting a managed care health insurance company. Once the proper executive is hired, benefit plans must be developed and priced so they can be marketed to employers and to individuals. Naturally, the richer the benefit plan, the higher the price. Since most employers are concerned about cost, managed care health plans are often bare-bone plans to begin with so the price can be low. The exact trade-off of price and benefits will depend on the market assessment.

Many different benefit packages can be created at different prices. The usual product of a managed care insurance company is an HMO. This product offers health care provided by a designated group of physicians and institutions for a preset monthly payment. Usually, copayments and deductibles are part of the plan; they are set high enough to discourage patients from seeking care for minor ailments, but low enough so as not to deter enrollees from seeking care for significant illnesses. Except for emergencies when they are away from home, enrollees are not covered when they seek care from nondesignated providers.

A point-of-service (POS) plan functions in a manner similar to an HMO when enrollees seek care from their primary care physicians. Copayments and deductibles increase if the enrollee goes directly to a plan specialist, and they increase further if the enrollee seeks care from a nonplan physician. Copayments and deductibles can be structured so that the plan is indifferent to where the enrollee seeks care. The enrollee has a financial incentive to see his or her primary care physician and to use specialists designated by the plan.

A Preferred Provider Organization (PPO) offers discounts in return for "steerage" of patients to designated providers. The greater the steerage and the larger the group, the greater the discount. Administrative services only (ASO) is a contract between the managed care insurance company and an employer for the managed care insurance company to provide administrative services to the employer. The employer is at risk for payment of the health care services provided to employees. The managed care insurance company is not at risk in an ASO. In certain mature managed care markets, employers are moving away from capitation to self-insurance and contracting for services with low-cost provider systems that demonstrate high quality.

A thought that often occurs to physicians forming a physician-driven managed care insurance company is to limit enrollment so they can test the managed care market with a small group of patients. This sounds reasonable, but there is a problem with this approach. In any group, the first people to sign up for managed care if the provider group is of high quality are the ones with medical problems. If the enrollee group is not of sufficient size to include a large number of healthy people, the cost of providing care to the members of the group will be high. Therefore, if a managed care product is offered to a group, enroll as many of the group as possible (no limit), so healthy people as well as people with medical problems are included. This will ensure that the cost per enrollee of providing care is reasonable. The development of underwriting criteria is important. Often in physician-driven managed care companies, the underwriting is not as strict as it needs to be. Physicians are patient advocates by training, which can result in too liberal an underwriting approach. An example is to permit the adult son or daughter of a prominent member of the hospital board to enroll in the plan because of political pressure, even though that individual has a known serious medical condition such as Hodgkin's disease in remission. It is important in a small, developing plan to have strict underwriting. If done properly, this will result in initial good medical experience and help the fledgling company get off to a good financial start.

Developing contracts with other health care providers is an important initial step. Health care services not available from physicians sponsoring the plan must be provided via contracts with other providers. Hospital services, home care services, home infusion services, and so forth must be provided via contracts. In addition, it is important to have a relationship established with a tertiary care center so that patients with complex illnesses who cannot be treated locally can be managed in a high-quality, cost-effective way by a tertiary care center. Usually, discount for services based on the volume of referrals can be arranged. Often the volume of referrals will include not only patients in the managed care plan, but also other patients referred from plan physicians to the tertiary care center.

Having a first-rate information system is essential as a managed health care company begins operating. Accurate information presented in a timely, understandable manner is essential for proper operations. The information system must be able to handle financial information for plans offered to various employers. Financial feedback is important for proper management and pricing of the plans.

In addition, the information system must be capable of providing physicians information about their own resource utilization as well as the resource utilization of all physicians in the plan. Permitting physicians to compare their use of laboratory and X-ray examinations, the emergency department, hospital days, and so forth, with the entire group will help them improve the way they practice and improve cost-effectiveness of the care provided.

Initially, the physicians will doubt the accuracy of the data presented. Naturally, every effort must be made to make sure the data are correct and useful to physicians. Even though physicians are defensive at first, over time their practice patterns begin to change. It is interesting to note that even the most cost-effective physicians—as well as the least cost-effective ones—improve as data are provided.

The final step before beginning operation is to seek necessary governmental approvals. The requirements vary from locale to locale. Generally, each state has regulations affecting the operation of a managed care insurance company, depending on the products offered.

When these initial steps have been taken, the plan is ready to begin operation.

START-UP

Now the physician-driven managed care insurance company is ready to begin operations. It needs to generate its revenue flow by marketing itself. The three marketing strategies for enrolling members are:

1. Market to companies.
2. Market to individuals.
3. Market to Medicare enrollees.

The first strategy is to market the products that have been developed to employers. The goal is to have employers offer only the products the company offers. Often, however, the company's managed care products are offered side by side with other managed care products or indemnity health insurance products. Benefit package, price, and the perceived quality of the providers in the plans are the basis for competition, and these factors influence the decisions made by employees as they sign up for health insurance plans. Employee groups of 40 or more generally are not underwritten. Smaller employee groups require underwriting.

At the same time, marketing to individuals can be undertaken. This is more difficult and is more expensive per enrollee. Still, it is a valuable way to increase the number insured by the managed care insurance company. Two types of products can be offered to Medicare enrollees. A Medicare wrap-around and a Medicare risk contract. A Medicare wrap-around product provides health insurance for the costs of health care services not covered by Medicare. This is an appropriate product in most markets. With the Medicare risk contract, the insurance company receives 95 percent of adjusted average per capita cost (AAPCC) and is financially responsible for total cost of providing health care to the insured Medicare enrollees. (Simply put, the AAPCC is Medicare's average cost per person of providing medical care to enrollees). A Medicare risk contract is only feasible in markets where there is a high AAPCC.

Many states are encouraging health care providers to assume risk for providing care to Medicaid enrollees. This is a very different type of managed care product and should be undertaken with caution or not at all. In many states, the individuals enrolled in Medicaid change from month to month. Furthermore, communication with Medicaid enrollees is very difficult. Financial incentives to encourage enrollees to seek care in appropriate settings are not available either.

Still, several companies have solved the problems of Medicaid risk contracts and find them profitable.

OPERATIONAL ISSUES

The physician-driven managed care insurance company is now operational. Ten thousand people have been enrolled, and growth continues. What are the main problems? As Pogo says, "We have met the enemy and he is us." The main problem is managing physicians.

Exhibit 16–2 lists the operational issues that must be addressed by all successful physician-driven HMOs. As the physician-driven managed care insurance company is developed, all the physicians interested usually become participants. Fortunately, most of the physicians will be good participants, but a few bad ones will be part of the group. Both good physicians and bad physicians will need to change.

As the company begins functioning, information on the quality of care provided and the cost-effectiveness of providing that care will become available. Obviously, physicians with quality problems must be encouraged to improve to maintain the reputation of the plan providers. If they do not improve, they must be removed as providers from the plan.

All physicians must improve the cost-effectiveness of providing care. The first step is to reduce hospital utilization; bed days per 1,000 enrollees must drop from approximately 500 to 300, and then gradually to under 200. Physicians must be encouraged to talk with one another to determine how to maintain high-quality care while reducing the cost of providing that care. Developing clinical guidelines for managing common problems is helpful. The number of prescriptions written and the cost of the drugs used are important issues. In summary, physicians will have to change the way they practice. This is a difficult change to accomplish, but it can and must be done.

To help physicians become more cost-effective while maintaining quality, the managed care insurance company must use the services of an active medical director. This should be a physician who is respected for clinical skills and is a good communicator. The medical director must be able to work with physicians to educate them about the changes they must make. He or she must encourage physicians to work with one another to seek high-quality, cost-effective ways to manage patients' medical problems. Guidelines developed by Milliman and Robertson can serve as a basis for this physician education.[1]

In addition to educating physicians about the changes that must be made to practice in a managed care setting, the organization must offer physicians financial incentives to incorporate these changes into their practice. In other words, the proper method of compensating physicians for their work must be in place.

While physicians receive approximately 20 percent of the health care dollar for the care they provide, they control 80 percent of health care expenditures. Thus, the financial incentive plan that is in place must reward physicians for providing high-quality, cost-effective care themselves and for utilizing resources in an appropriate manner. There are many different models for physician compensation; the most important aspects of any of these models include proper incentives, and feedback to physicians about the resources they use in providing high-quality care to their patients. The feedback, coupled with suggestions by the medical director in consultation with colleagues, will

Exhibit 16–2 Operational Issues

- Maintain quality.
- Be cost-effective.
- Educate physicians.
- Establish financial incentives for physicians.
- Educate patients.
- Establish the right size.

enable physicians to improve their resource utilization over time.

Just as physicians are educated to change the way they practice, so, too, must patients be educated to utilize medical services properly in a managed care environment. Patients must be encouraged to seek care from their primary care physicians rather than self-referring to specialists or nonplan providers. They must be educated to use the emergency department only for emergencies. They must be educated about how best to care for themselves. Preventive care has always been a goal of the medical profession. Now, with managed care, there is finally a financial incentive to keep patients healthy. Good patient education has a payoff in a managed care setting. Smoking cessation programs; weight control programs; and good methods of controlling hypertension, hypercholesterolemia, and diabetes all become financially beneficial as well as medically beneficial preventive health programs.

One very good way to help patients assess health care in an appropriate manner is to develop a telephone advisory nurse (TAN) program. With TAN, plan enrollees can call a nurse 24 hours a day to seek medical advice. The nurse guides the patient by suggesting home remedies, a routine or same-day appointment with the physician, or an emergency department visit, depending on the severity of the medical problem. The enrollees/patients receive their care in an appropriate setting and generally are very satisfied with the service. The telephone advisory nurse improves the quality of the service while improving cost-effectiveness.

As the physician-driven managed care insurance company grows, the question of expanding the market arises. Can the company grow by providing services to patients in a wider geographic area? This requires adding physicians to provide services in the new areas. Generally, this is worth doing because the larger the enrollment, the lower the administrative expense per enrollee. On the other hand, the new physicians added must be of high quality and be willing to adjust their practice patterns to the managed care environment. Expanding markets also permit contracts with multilocation employers that might not otherwise be possible.

Competition may or may not be present in the market as the company develops. Certainly it must be faced at some point. Competition will be on the basis of price, benefit package, and quality of providers. It is hoped that the quality of the company's providers will give an advantage to the physician-owned company initially, as its products are marketed. In the long run, however, all competitors will be offering a quality product, and the principal factor will be price. This begins to squeeze the profits of the company.

Contracts with other managed care insurance companies become an issue for physicians. Because the competition is initially based on the providers, it is important that the company physicians contract with as few other managed health care insurance companies as possible. As the physician-driven company grows, it is hoped that the involved physicians can stop contracting with other health insurance companies. This will help increase the number of enrollees in the physician-driven company.

An issue for multispecialty clinics and other physician groups as they grow more cohesive is the ratio of primary care physicians to specialists. As the managed care percentage of the practice increases, this issue becomes more significant. For 100,000 enrollees, 45 to 50 primary care physicians are needed. Many fewer specialists are needed per 1,000 enrollees. Since, in most settings, more than enough specialists are available, "rightsizing" the organization is a difficult issue. However, to stay competitive, rightsizing must occur. The physician provider group must have the appropriate percentage of primary care specialists, cardiologists, orthopedists, and so forth to survive in the long run.

MISCELLANEOUS ISSUES

Several additional issues of significance must be addressed once a group of physicians begins participating in managed care. These issues are:

- effect of managed care on medical practice
- competition with other companies
- physician control

The first of these issues is the effect of managed care on the fee-for-service practice. As physicians change the way they care for patients enrolled in the HMO, they begin to change the way they care for non-HMO patients. The goal of high-quality, low-cost care is the same, no matter what the payer class of the patient. The physician does not develop two or three practice styles depending on the payer class, but rather evolves toward providing high-quality, cost-effective care to all patients.

There are minor exceptions to this general rule. The exceptions occur at the margin. For example, a 40-year-old, asymptomatic man who wants a stress test will not receive one as a member of an HMO. If he is a fee-for-service patient who wishes to pay for the stress test, the test will be ordered. Still, the core practice is internally consistent, and the care is the same for patients from all payer classes: all patients receive high-quality, low-cost care.

A second, peripheral issue is the possibility of large, nationwide PPOs or HMOs using the provider network established by the physician-driven managed care insurance company. Usually these HMOs or PPOs want to contract for services at a discount. Whether to contract with such a company needs to be considered carefully. The new company may bring additional patients at a reasonable discount, or the new company may simply reduce the potential market for the physician-driven company without providing new patients. The risks and benefits of such a contract must be carefully considered.

The same is true for contracting with other local HMOs. Hopefully, the physician-driven company will be able to develop enough market share so its providers do not need to contract with other managed care insurance companies. This gives the physicians control and keeps competitors from growing. To achieve this degree of market strength may take time in a competitive market.

The final issue, but maybe the most important, is physician control. *Physician control* sounds better than it actually is. The term suggests that physicians will be able to do as they believe best for their patients without constraints. This is not true, because the market brings constraints. In order to sell health insurance, contracts must be priced competitively and must have competitive benefits. The same constraints the market places on other insurance companies will be placed on the physician-driven company. Still, it is generally easier for physicians to accept constraints that they apply to themselves rather than constraints from non-physician-driven insurance companies, and these self-imposed constraints are usually more patient friendly.

CONCLUSION

Developing and operating a physician-driven managed care insurance company is difficult, but very rewarding. It gives physicians the opportunity to provide their patients the best quality care possible in a managed care setting. It permits physicians to receive the financial rewards for their work. The rewards come from the practice of medicine and from the profits of the health insurance company. Finally, and maybe most importantly, it gives physicians greater control of their future.

NOTE

1. Milliman & Robertson, Inc., *Health Cost Guidelines* (Denver, Colo.: 1995).

Chapter 17

Organizing and Managing Specialty Networks for Capitation

Richard W. Krohn, M.B.A.

INTRODUCTION

The landscape of health care delivery is changing, and nowhere is this change more evident than in the terms of physician contracting. These changes throughout the U.S. medical market are not to the complete advantage of physicians, particularly specialists. Many forces, including professional practice management companies, the investor-driven initial public offering (IPO) market, and the "urge to merge" are introducing change at accelerating rates in unforeseen ways. Mature managed care markets fail to provide much insight into the reordering of physician services; it is becoming increasingly clear that the West Coast experience is no longer a reliable indicator of market transition elsewhere.

Like other providers, specialists are challenged by new and unfamiliar contracting methodologies. At the same time, specialists are confronted with a paradigm shift in health care services, away from specialty medicine and toward primary care. This double whammy —risk-based contracting and surplus specialist capacity—has fostered the growth of specialty networks. The advent of primary care as the focus of health care delivery is a transitory phase, and eventually the multispecialty providers will become the preeminent source of physician services. Before this shift in physician focus can occur, specialists must develop the clinical and business capabilities to manage risk and outcomes, and must introduce effective risk-contracting delivery systems. The focus of this chapter is on the specialist as a risk contractor and as a participant in a risk-contracting specialty network.

SPECIALTY NETWORKS—DEVELOPMENT AND STRATEGIC CHOICES

Specialist physicians, like their primary care colleagues, are faced with formidable challenges in positioning themselves, both individually and collectively, for managed care. Until recently, it was widely believed that specialty networks were unproven and probably unworkable, due to lack of cohesiveness and primary care primacy. But it is now clear that single-specialty and multispecialty networks can succeed in a risk-based environment, and that they confer distinct market advantages to their members. By definition, risk contracting transfers responsibility for contract management to provider organizations. The ultimate success of a specialty network in the world of capitation is a function of the networks' ability to capture patient volume at a fair price, and then to manage patient care competently through medical management and professional management. The specialty network allows each provider to share marketing power, to share data, to establish single utilization management and quality assurance standards, and to share administrative expenses.

But no single specialty network model is suited to every local market, and the mere formation of a specialty network does not guarantee success as a risk contractor. To be successful, the clinical composition of the network must first be determined. The culture of the network should be characterized by physician leadership, clinical excellence, acceptance of shared control, and a willingness to work with managed health plan payers. Physician members should strongly endorse the adherence to practice guidelines and patient relations. There should be an experienced medical director with outstanding communications abilities, knowledge of risk contracting, and strong management capabilities. A clearly defined purpose of networking must be defined and acknowledged by all members. Ideally, the network should be more than a contracting vehicle. It must be a cohesive group that implements utilization and quality standards, clinical and management information services, marketing, purchasing, and shared administration. Payers are particularly looking for specialty networks that are geographically diverse, can provide measurable episodic care, and do not experience wide variations in utilization among members.

As a risk contractor, the specialty network must determine its strategic direction and marketing posture. More advanced specialty networks have radically departed from the accepted approach of subordination to primary care leadership, and they are contracting directly with payers and purchasers. These networks do, however, cultivate primary care relationships as a parallel strategy. The central strategic objective of the network is to capture volume within defined carve-out contracts—and to do so at an acceptable level of reimbursement. Obviously, the closer the specialty network can get to the source of the capitation dollar—the payer—the greater the leverage the network will have in negotiating capitation.

The specialty network must answer a market need, in that network services must be constructed to meet the needs of payers and purchasers, and the characteristics of the network must support those needs. For instance, the network should be selective with specific criteria for quality and cost-effectiveness, and the coverage area should reflect a geographic diversity that corresponds to the demographic and patient access requirements of payers and purchasers. Similarly, the local market should be scrutinized for potential contracting opportunities. A thinly populated region with small businesses as the major purchasers is unlikely to support a specialty network. A more densely populated region is likely to yield aggressive payers interested in seeking efficient networking relationships. There needs to be deliberate product development effort geared toward defining the scope of services to be provided, and member practice must undergo in-depth practice assessments and reengineering in order to deliver care that can meet quality and cost objectives.

The first step in establishing the service orientation of the network is to conduct a "history and physical" of participating practices, to determine the clinical capabilities, risk contracting resources and experience, and operational characteristics of each practice. This process defines the baseline service capabilities and product development criteria for the network. Key results are a common contracting strategy, common fee schedules, and common risk management processes. The cumulative service profile of the practices must be merged into a network structure that supports the mission of the network. For instance, a network that wishes to bundle services or offer case rates might best be served by a "messenger" network model, while an aggressive risk-contracting network might opt to establish a committed model Independent Practice Association (IPA). In each instance, the network model should directly support a product—whether that product is packaged services, carve outs and carve ins, disease management, or shared gatekeeping.

Depending on the services and product to be delivered, the specialty network must establish partnerships with other providers to market a broader range of services to payers and purchasers. The linkage to primary care is fundamental to success as a network, but additional relationships with acute care and ancillary services may also strengthen the marketability of the network. The correct mix and identity of these partners is a function of the local market, but each partner should possess the same characteristics of efficiency and managed care mentality that define the network itself. Each potential partner should be validated in terms of their risk-contracting readiness, service capabilities, culture, and infrastructure.

Exhibit 17–1 describes a progressive process of network development that first establishes broad goals and expectations, and then defines the operational characteristics that meet these criteria. This is not a sequential process, because many of the activities of network development occur simultaneously and collaboratively. Neither is it a straight path, because the activities and strategic direction must conform to an evolving mission.

Once the framework of the specialty network and its capabilities are established, the risk-contracting strategy must be determined. At the least, the network will contract for the clinical services of its members, either directly with payers or as a subcapitation of a larger contract held by others. This is the lower end of the contracting pyramid and yields lesser reimbursement for lesser risk. Among more ambitious and more integrated specialty networks, shared risk arrangements with payers confer greater risk to the network (overhead, utilization) specific to covered specialty services. More mature specialty networks have developed case rates and package pricing for services such as cardiac care and oncology services. And finally, at the higher end, global risk transfers all utilization and financial risk for covered services to the network. The correct risk-contracting strategy is a function of the network internal risk management capabilities, the managed care sophistication of participating physicians, the strength of utilization and financial controls throughout the network, and the stage of managed care in the local market.

Exhibit 17–1 Steps in the Development Process for Specialty Networks

- Define clear vision and mission.
- Educate physicians.
- Establish physician leadership.
- Define governance, legal structure, ownership.
- Establish committee and define services.
- Build physician panel and service capabilities.

Ultimately, the correct network structure is defined by the local market and the service capabilities of the network. A single-specialty network may not attract the same interest in a smaller market as a multi-specialty network, and a selective-panel network may be more successful than an open-panel network. The size and clout of the specialty network is also a function of capitalization and legal limitations. A poorly capitalized network will be weak and of diminished capacity, and legal restrictions may be placed on "closed" or selective networks. Regardless, it can be safely assumed that in more mature managed care markets, capitation will require more advanced practice sophistication, in terms of clinical care and business management, and more selective physician membership. The more closely integrated physician networks, with a reputation for quality care, cost management, and access, will prevail.

THE FRAMEWORK OF SPECIALTY RISK CONTRACTING

Generally speaking, there are two predominant types of risk-contracting specialty networks: the IPA model, consisting of independent physicians and groups serving a local or regional market, and the network model, consisting of integrated practices across a broad geographic range. The IPA model is prevalent and has proved to be successful among physicians whose aim is to retain control of their practices while gaining the collective benefit of patient volume and advanced practice management. This approach also serves as the springboard for further integration of practices and alliances with other specialties and primary care partners. The evolution of practice integration occurs through shared information services, shared medical management, shared long-term contracts, and shared practice management services. Not all IPAs are alike. Some are more integrated with advanced information systems, and others are loose affiliations with no management infrastructure.

The network model tends to be prevalent among for-profit corporations, public and private, that are in the business of purchasing practices and employing physicians, or providing practice management services to Physician Organizations. The key marketing advantage of this model is the adherence to cost and utilization standards, which is the result of sophisticated information systems, selective recruitment, and strong practice guidelines.

Within the general network framework of risk contracting, there is still further definition of specific specialty services. In the broadest setting, multispecialty networks offer a varying range of medical services, based on membership and need. The contracting posture of the multispecialty network is a function of market need, available services, and internal management. The networks with greater managed care savvy are able to accept higher levels of risk and to manage that risk effectively. Typically, a multispecialty network will contract for a defined range of services and, if necessary, subcontract or subcapitate covered services in the contract that are beyond internal capabilities or preference.

A second type of specialty network is the single-specialty carve out. The contracting strategy of the carve-out network is to offer specific specialty services, either within a single specialty or among related specialty services. This network tends to be wide in geographic scope, because a central objective is to drive volume through a select cadre of specialty providers, to the exclusion of other providers within the same service area. Again, the effectiveness of the carve-out network lies in its ability to manage the financial and utilization components of risk, and its ability to demonstrate that effectiveness to payers. Currently, the most active areas of carve-out risk contracting are in such specialties as behavioral health, ophthalmology, cardiology, orthopedics, oncology, and chronic care. On a more limited scale, specialty networks have signed capitation contracts in areas such as catastrophic care; urology; ear, nose, and throat (ENT); and podiatry. As a class of payer, Medicare Health Maintenance Organization (HMO) risk contractors appear to be the most aggressive in developing specialty carve-out relationships.

A key measure of network efficiency, at least in the eyes of payers, is the clinical composition of the specialty network. Payers expect specialty networks to be selective in member recruitment and broad in geographic access. They want proven, efficient providers located in areas in which their plan members live and work that are guided by experienced medical directors. There is a further expectation that risk-bearing networks will possess the internal management capability to conform to the payers' utilization and information reporting standards. A strong network medical director and management support infrastructure are key to meeting these expectations and delivering the services that meet patient needs without bankrupting the specialty network.

MAKING RISK CONTRACTING WORK IN SPECIALTY NETWORKS

Evaluating Whether the Specialty Is Suited to Capitation

Although many Physician Organizations possess the internal expertise and tools to manage risk contracts successfully, it is not immediately clear that accepting risk is practical or even desirable. Capitation contracts cover, within a defined scope of services, the health of patient *populations,* and the capitation rate makes assumptions about the health behavior of that population. This is basically a numbers game. By accepting capitation, physicians are accepting responsibility for the provision of care to a population, in the belief that such care can be delivered at manageable cost, with an acceptable margin for profit.

The keys to making this equation work for the physician are *rate* and *volume;* the number of covered lives must be sufficient to make the actuarial estimate of cost and patient population behavior work. In addition, there must be a complete understanding of the operating costs of the network. Further, physicians must anticipate unexpected utilization and maintain insurances (stop loss, reinsurance) to protect themselves against this possibility. Logic would indicate that success in capitation is the result of predictable, measurable patient behavior. But specialty medicine is not uniformly suited to such measurement. This is why actuarial assumptions of service costs and utilization are so important, along with actual data on the patient populations that will be served under risk arrangements.

Payers are looking for networks of subspecialists that provide appropriate, cost-effective, episodic care. From a cost standpoint, specialties that do not experience wide variations in patterns of patient treatment and practice lend themselves best to networking and risk contracting.[1] Capitation of general surgery, for instance, is more difficult because of the overlap in services. Specialties such as neurosurgery are not as well suited, due to the limited volume, variable service cost structure of the specialty. Generally speaking, the specialties that can quantify the costs of specific services within a defined range, and can manage appropriate utilization of those services within acceptable parameters through wellness, patient intervention, and disease management techniques, are most likely to be successful in risk contracting.

It must also be remembered that risk contracting as a strategy is specifically intended to drive patient volume, not enhance patient revenue. It is almost certain that specialty risk contracting will entail reduced service revenue per episode of care, and this trend must be factored into the overall national trend of reduced specialty revenue (and compensation).

Deciding Whether To Be the Lead Contractor or To Follow As the Subcontractor

Once the specialty network has accepted that capitation is a necessary strategy, it must determine how that contract will be established. Should the network carve out specific specialty services or subcapitate with a primary care network or other entity that holds a risk contract for full medical risk? Conceptually, the greatest benefit from capitation is derived by capturing the greatest share of the premium dollar. This means that if the network can contract directly with payers and purchasers for a range of specialty services, and eliminate the layers of cost between provider and patient, the greatest percentage of the dollar associated with that care can be retained. At this level of risk contracting, the risk component tends to be more advanced, and the administrative requirements of the contract are more pronounced. Ultimately, the risk profile of the capitation contract must conform to the internal risk management capabilities and medical services of the specialty network and the tolerance of specialists to risk.

By contracting directly with a payer; by accepting risk; and by providing its own insurance, medical management, and other contract management services, the specialty network can capture a significant share of administrative and mark-up revenue that would otherwise accrue to the payer or other providers in a subcapitated arrangement. However, a sophisticated infrastructure, managed care–savvy management, and excellent information systems are necessary to perform these functions successfully. Often, specialists are satisfied to subcapitate from another provider group, limit their risk exposure and administrative responsibilities, and concentrate on utilization management within a narrowly defined range of covered services.

Knowing How Much Is Too Much

It has been mentioned that some specialties are more suited to risk contracting than others, and even then the question remains: How much risk should the specialist accept? The short answer is, of course, do not accept risk over which one has no control. For instance, an oncologist might be unwilling to accept the risk of hospital expense related to advanced cancer treatment if he or she cannot influence hospital utilization practices. A similar concern is the ability of the network to manage the financial risk of the contract successfully, through professional management, information systems, clinical guidelines, and utilization management. But the lower the risk accepted, the less revenue that will be realized from the contract. Whether the contract stipulates risk sharing or risk transferral to the network, the risk assumed must be complemented by both a clinical and administrative capability to manage that risk effectively. Exhibit 17–2 describes the types of covered services typical to an ophthalmology carve-out contract. Within each category of service described, specific procedures and units of services are defined by Current Procedural Terminology (CPT) code. According to the terms of the contract, each of these services, at the CPT code level, must be made available to each plan member, in exchange for a defined, capitated per member per month (PMPM) payment.

Matching the Market

The risk-contracting strategies of a specialty network should reflect the overall mission and market positioning of the network. Risk contracting should serve first as a vehicle to gain entry to the market for managed health care delivery. Second, risk contracting should provide the network with market leverage in establishing strong provider alliances. Payers prefer to limit the number of provider groups they must work with; and a strong, geographically diverse, well capitalized, and clinically efficient specialty network possesses a distinct advan-

Exhibit 17–2 Sample Ophthalmological Covered Services—Ophthalmology Carve-Out Contract

- general ophthalmological services
- special ophthalmological services
- ophthalmoscopy
- other specialized ophthalmology services
- procedures (invasive diagnostic, surgical)
- contact lens services

tage in capturing volume. The specialty network can use this advantage to establish alliances with primary care groups and networks, acute care and ancillary providers, vendors, and management services. Ultimately, however, the specialty network must craft a strategic plan that is supported by these alliances, whether that plan is to become part of a "one-stop shopping" network, to become a dominant regional specialty organization, to carve out specific specialty services, or to maximize control of the premium dollar.

Maintaining Volume and Cost-Efficiency

Regardless of the strategic direction of the specialty network, risk contracting must be considered a primary tactical approach to maintaining—and even expanding—market share. For specialty medicine, capitation is unlikely to increase revenue on a per encounter basis, and it should not be pursued with this end in mind. This truth must be considered within the overall context of managed care and the predisposition of payers to shift utilization to primary care medicine or enhance prevention.

The name of the game is to be an efficient and appropriate provider, and to establish efficiencies throughout the entire network before a rival provider group does. The health care "pie" devoted to specialty medicine is shrinking, and the future belongs to those specialists who seize the initiative to meet the market demand and work cooperatively with the purchasers of specialty services.

UNDERSTANDING THE CAPITATION CONTRACT

To manage both the financial and utilization components of a capitation contract successfully, the specific risk-bearing provisions of the contract, including accountabilities, must be firmly understood by network physicians. To minimize the network's exposure, an awareness of risk-contracting methods and group preferences should be brought to the contract negotiations. Risk provisions in the contract, both of a financial and clinical nature, should be considered topics of negotiation and consensus. Part of this exercise includes evaluating the payer. What is its professional reputation? What is its history of risk sharing and surplus distribution? Grievance resolution? Marketing strategy? Physician relations? It is also at this point that an understanding of risk related to mutual accountabilities and contractual responsibilities of each party must be clearly defined. What are the specific covered services? How is the rate calculated? What are the risk-sharing provisions? Is the contract assignable? Is there a minimum enrollment guarantee? What are the patient demographics of the patient panel? What are the termination provisions of both parties? It is vital that the network physicians clearly understand the scope of service accountabilities of the contract, as well as the financial impact of providing those services.

Complementing the payer and service definition process should be an evaluation of the pool of payers that comprise the network's contracting base, and the types of risk the network is willing to accept. Clearly, no network should rely on a single contract to provide a significant source of revenue; the loss of the contract, for whatever reason, can have serious consequences. Conversely, contracting with every payer available can stretch the network's resources beyond reasonable capacity and can introduce a nightmarish web of conflicting, payer-induced clinical and administrative requirements. A balance must be established between the network's need to diversify payer exposure as a function of revenue and the practical service limitations in a capitated environment.[2]

The Capitation Schedule

Regardless of the context of specialty risk contracting, the essential reimbursement feature of the agreement is the capitation schedule. This section of the contract describes the specific services being capitated and the payment that will be made on a PMPM basis. It is this section that determines the service parameters of the contract, as well as the gross revenue that will be derived from the provision of those services. The capitation rate must satisfy the cumulative costs of providing care to a population of patients, comprised of people of varying health care requirements. The rate must also cover the related administrative costs of providing care—including personnel, supplies and equipment, occupancy, capital acquisitions, repairs, and the like. Further, the "rate times panel size" equation must provide an acceptable risk cushion against catastrophic cases, outliers, and unexpected utilization. In other words, the capitation rate(s) must be supported by a sufficient patient panel size to provide a minimum actuarial probability of profitability. Table 17–1 describes the relationship between covered services and PMPM reimbursement. In column A, covered services are identified at the CPT code level. Before entering into a risk contract, the covered services and CPT-specific reimbursement rates must be thoroughly examined and understood. The exact composition of units of service included in the contract is a subject of negotiation. Specialists must either subcontract or exclude service units that are beyond service scope or cannot be provided economically. Column B describes a fee schedule for each unit of service. Column C describes a factor of expected service utilization per 1,000 members. Column D is the calculated PMPM rate, based on fees and utilization. This process underscores the need for the specialty network either to develop or gain access to accurate, local, normalized clinical cost data.

Physician Accountability

Within the text of many capitation contracts, clauses can be found describing physician clinical responsibilities, reporting requirements, credentialing, insurability, continuing care, records retention, and utilization review (UR)/quality assurance (QA) compliance. Additional training and education must be anticipated in complying with the unique clinical and administrative requirements of each capitation agreement. Often, a dedicated personnel resource must be allocated for determining eligibility, precertification, reporting, and working with physician relations personnel. Physicians must determine if the parameters of clinical practice as outlined in the contract are compatible with their personal professional ethics. Sample questions the physician must ask include: Can capitated patients be treated in the same manner as fee-for-service patients? What are referral restrictions? Can an in-house lab be used? Is the practice reimbursed for patient education? These types of issues should be addressed before a contract is signed.[3]

Table 17–1 Sample Capitation Rate Development

(A) Procedure	(B) Cost	(C) Annual Utilization (per 1,000 members)	(D) PMPM Rate
99211	$26	0.12363	$0.27
99212	$39	0.28017	$0.91
99213	$45	0.88788	$3.33
99214	$61	0.21326	$1.08
99215	$92	0.14407	$1.10
		Total	**$6.69**

Note: All values are for illustrative purposes only.

Specialty Risk Pools

The risk component of the specialty capitation contract is found within the managed health plan risk pool, which is basically a series of reserve allocations, including withholds, insurance coverages (stop loss, excess), and utilization risk. Among the various shared risk features common to capitation agreements, contractual withholds provide the greatest potential for financial benefit or liability. The potential benefit occurs as a result of the efficient performance of the provider in accordance with the terms of the contract. The liability occurs to the extent that plan service targets have not been met, and the resulting shortfall must be funded from the withhold funds.

The basic mechanism for the determination and measurement of the plan's withholds is the risk pool budget. This budget can incorporate reserve allocations for a number of potential liabilities, including service risk, referral risk, and insurance risk. The specific elements of a risk pool budget are a function of the capitation agreement (that is, the range of services being prepaid). The risk pool is further adjusted for age, sex, primary diagnosis, and outlier factors specific to the patient panel. Typically, but not universally, the risk pool budget ranges from 10 percent to 17 percent of the total capitation. Figure 17–1 illustrates a common division of risk under a global risk arrangement. Notice the risk-sharing relationships between primary care physician/specialist, and hospital/specialist. In this example, it can be seen that referrals and admissions exercise a strong influence on the specialty risk component of the contract.

Capitation Incentives and Penalties

As a component of capitated payment, withholds are incentive funds that are disbursed to the provider at the end of the reporting year, subject to a number of provisions. First, risk pools are shared risk arrangements; all parties to the pool share

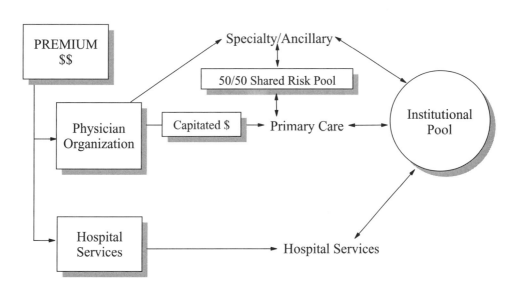

Figure 17–1 Sample risk pool distribution and allocation flow. Courtesy of Medical Alliances, Inc., Alexandria, Virginia.

in the performance-based rewards and penalties. Second, disbursements are subject to a number of conditions that affect the ultimate cash settlement. For instance, disbursements generally cannot exceed 50 percent of gross capitation payments for the reporting period. Additionally, a deficit in one risk pool (e.g., referral risk pool) is offset against any other withhold surpluses. Finally, a formulated disbursement ceiling is calculated, beyond which the provider is not entitled to further benefit, regardless of performance.

As a negotiating strategy, the specialty network wants to capture as much financial risk as the payer will yield, presuming that such risk can be capably managed. A more conservative risk-contracting posture is to negotiate risk corridors, which limit the upside and downside exposure of the network. In either case, professional assistance is required to implement the risk-contracting strategy of the network. This assistance includes actuarial analysis of historical clinical and financial performance of the network and its members, consulting assistance in constructing the internal capabilities to manage the risk accepted, and operational analysis of the network and its sites.

INFRASTRUCTURE REQUIREMENTS OF SUCCESSFUL RISK CONTRACTING

Medical Management

In addition to managing the financial risk of capitation, the group must manage the medical risk of the contract. This risk is a function of standards of care throughout the group panel, referral patterns, access to information, physician communication, and the culture of the Physician Organization. To manage utilization successfully, there must be educated physician leaders and members who are well informed on the quality and financial issues associated with capitation. Specifically, this involves the identification and provision of appropriate care, through the formal establishment of clinical protocols and procedures. In addition, there must be clinical and administrative guidelines governing referrals. These policies and procedures must be established, and they must be respected, as well.

Physicians must be made aware of their clinical performance, its impact on group profitability, and the need to serve a common goal. It falls within the role of the medical director and management support systems to coordinate these activities and to implement them effectively. Communication among physicians is vital, and when necessary, the means to enforce clinical guidelines must be established. There is often a learning curve that physicians must traverse to understand fully the relationship between individual clinical choices, quality, appropriate patient care, and financial viability, and this learning should be encouraged and supported by the group through education and dialogue.

To the extent that the specialty network can manage utilization, the capitation risk pool is favorably affected. Ultimately, the risk pool surplus or deficit is subject to the performance of the entire physician panel and operational efficiency. Smaller panels tend to be more effective at managing this risk, because individual physician performance has greater impact on cumulative performance, and because utilization and costs can be more closely monitored and corrected. In larger panels there tends to be the "free rider" problem, in which individual physicians do not willingly modify their clinical behavior in the belief that their impact on total panel performance is marginal.[4]

From Production to Performance

Once the contract is in force, the key to successful risk management is the establishment of clinical and administrative efficiencies. Clinical efficiencies can be promoted through practice guidelines, clinical protocols, peer review, outcomes measurement, and patient satisfaction surveys. A number of proven management tools can be employed to meet the utilization goals of risk contracting. Clinical performance can be favorably influenced by practice guidelines, clinical protocols, best practice standards, disease state management techniques, outcomes measurement, patient satisfaction, and peer review. Programs such as wellness, patient education, community health education, provider extenders, demand management, and case management can also serve the overall goal of appropriate utilization in the most cost-effective setting.

Physician extenders (physician assistants and nurse practitioners) have proved to be effective in conducting initial patient intake and patient assessment, and these functional roles free up the physician for actual patient care. Further efficiencies can be created through innovative approaches to care delivery, including self-care products, telephone reminders, patient education and wellness programs, and a bias toward primary care and home health. Emerging technologies such as interactive telemedicine, both for diagnostic and triage purposes, are particularly useful in gaining needed efficiencies. Similarly, the electronic stethoscope and such techniques as the electronic electrocardiogram and peak flow meter (asthma) can be conducted remotely, in the patient's home. Disease state management is becoming increasingly common as a technique of managing a defined disease condition proactively and providing a course of treatment that intervenes earlier and encourages care delivery in ambulatory settings. In this environment, each physician is evaluated according to his or her clinical performance, as found in encounter data, payer claims and financial reports, and internal management analyses. Finally, the culture of the group must make the conceptual leap from production-based to risk-based reimbursement, from individual clinical autonomy to network accountability, and from individual to common network goals.

Risk Management Skills

In addition to the clinical responsibilities transferred to providers by capitation, contract management skills must also be conspicuous among managers and staff. Familiarity with managed care payment systems, insurance, marketing, staff development, cost analysis, and strategic planning are all relevant skills to risk contracting that may or may not command equivalent priority in the fee-for-service world. In-house staff skills must be available to manage the various aspects of capitated risk successfully. Under capitation, a heightened business sophistication is mandatory in controlling the financial and utilization components of risk. The tool of risk management is clinical and financial information.

The business operations of the group must support clinical efficiencies, primarily through resource allocation, information access, and procedural compliance. Network resources—including personnel, equipment, and space—must be allocated according to the greatest dollar value derived. This rule must govern capital spending, staffing, practice location, and clinical partnerships. Staffing should be driven by productivity, which means eliminating duplication and maximizing process efficiency. The essential truth of this process is that staff should be equipped to do more with less. Capital spending should be linked to profitability and efficiency, and clinical partnerships should augment service capacities and geographic reach.

Information Management

Information is the linchpin of effective care delivery and medical management, and often this entails the introduction of advanced, sophisticated information systems. Fundamentally, such a system must accurately capture service costs, as represented by utilization, as well as the attendant administrative costs of providing those services. Moreover, the system must provide the tools to measure the efficiency of these costs, and the means to correct inefficiencies.

At a minimum, clinical and financial recordkeeping, as well as internal policies and procedures, must be consistent with the information requirements of each contract. Capitation contracting is information intensive, and reporting requirements are conferred upon the provider. The specialty network information management system should possess clinical reporting capabilities including the following:

- patient tracking
- referral tracking
- utilization review
- case management
- quality and outcomes measurement
- productivity reporting

Additionally, the information management system must include a sophisticated accounting system with data maintenance and flexible reporting capabilities for the following:

- accrual basis accounting
- cost accounting (including rate analysis)
- incurred but not reported (IBNR) and ancillary service cost tracking[5]

As a rule, the information requirements of single-specialty networks are more focused than multispecialty networks, due to the more narrowly defined services and liabilities of single-specialty risk contracting.

SUCCESS FACTORS OF RISK-BASED SPECIALTY NETWORKS

Have a Clear Network Mission

Too often, physicians embark on a specialty networking initiative without a clear sense of the network's true purpose or capabilities. Managing member expectations and establishing common goals among participating physicians from the outset is critical to the success of the network. The network must provide, at the very least, competitive advantages in marketing and payer contracting. The network must firmly establish its membership as the premier provider network within a geographic region and must ally with complementary Physician Organizations, such as primary care groups/networks and other noncompeting specialty organizations to have sufficient negotiating leverage. The network must deliver on its goals of appropriateness, cost-effectiveness, and quality. Finally, the network must be a representative organization—that is, the governance and equity structure must offer all members significant participation and financial equity.

Obtain Adequate Capitalization, Either Internally or with Partners

A chronic error made by physician networks is the underestimation of the true costs of launching a functional network, and of introducing practice management services. Undercapitalized networks suffer one of two fates: either they never truly evolve into a functioning entity, or they are so constricted by lack of capital that they cannot effectively develop infrastructure and services that would differentiate them in the eye of the purchasers. The specialty network should develop a comprehensive business plan, including detailed five-year financial projections, which identifies its purpose and the estimated costs of achieving that purpose. Financing the venture then becomes a central issue and the decision to self-fund, borrow, or accept outside investment determines the strategic course of the network and the practical limits of its operations.

Accept Only the Amount of Risk That Can Be Effectively Managed

The rule here is simple: the network must not accept more risk than it can comfortably absorb with internal resources, or confidently off-load to subcontractors. Service areas in which the network is not capable should be carved out of the contract, and all aspects of risk (financial and medical) must be professionally managed. Among more advanced specialty networks, case rates and package pricing are becoming increasingly common. This risk-bearing strategy assures the network of a baseline revenue stream across a defined range of specialty services. The challenge for the network is, of course, to match professional resources to the clinical requirements of the packaged services efficiently and profitably. A fundamental purpose of the risk-contracting network is to capture an increasing share of the premium dollar, evolving from partial risk contracting to percentage of total premium contracting.

Gain Member Volume, Not Patient Volume

From a risk-contracting standpoint, there is a single, overwhelming purpose of the specialty network—to capture member volume. Notice the distinction between patient volume and member volume, because profitability in a risk-contracting environment relies in large part on managing the patient care provided to a defined membership, by providing the most appropriate care in the most cost-effective setting. The larger the volume of patients assigned to each physician through a network contract, the greater the actuarial probability that the contract can be managed successfully, barring adverse selection or excessive outliers. As a contract-negotiating position, the network must insist upon a minimum enrollment guarantee to protect each participating physician from excessive exposure due to adverse patient panel characteristics.

Establish and Maintain Payer Diversity

The same principle that governs minimum enrollment applies to contracting with few payers. Unless the market presence of one or a few payers dominates the market, it is prudent to diversify the contracting relationships of the network. A single payer can terminate a managed health plan risk contract, experience sudden and dramatic reversals in profitability and enrollment, alter provider utilization requirements, or adjust capitation payments—all on relatively short notice. The specialty network must be positioned to accept changes in payer relationships, to replace unprofitable payers with more lucrative ones, and to retain a greater share of control in contracting relationships.

Be the Quality, Efficient Provider

The basic premise of capitation is that the cost of care of a patient population can be managed efficiently and in a manner that maintains financial viability. This is true only to the extent that the health characteristics of the patient population are not adverse, that utilization and referrals do not exceed actuarial expectations, and that practice administrative costs are in alignment with industry standards. Managing the financial aspect of risk contracting requires strong cost accounting skills, contract negotiation and rate analysis skills, and contract management skills. Similarly, internal clinical and administrative policies governing utilization, referrals, and functional roles are vital to the management of cost. Case management also plays a vital role in identifying and managing outliers and high-cost services. Careful allocation of functional responsibilities is particularly important, because it has been demonstrated that many clinical tasks can be successfully conducted by physician extenders. These functions include routine exams and inoculations (physician assistants and registered practical nurses), telephone triage (nurses), and self-care and patient education (nurses).

The withhold aspect of capitation is directly affected by the network's ability to manage cost of care efficiently. Risk pool distributions are subject to the cumulative performance of the physician panel. This dilution of physician performance tends to reduce the effectiveness of withholds as a physician utilization management tool. For this reason, individual physician performance bonuses are replacing withholds as part of physician compensation (and incentive) plans.

Develop and Use Information Tools

Although discussed previously, it bears mentioning again that one of the linchpins of successful risk contracting is information. Successful risk contracting relies on the ability of the network to meet or exceed expected clinical and financial performance targets. These targets must be specific, fair, measurable, and consistent. Most stand-alone physician practice billing systems are not equipped to handle the information demands of risk contracting, and the network should develop, as a core capability, managed care information services.

Ally with Other (Noncompeting) Physician Organizations

Like it or not, primary care is gravitating toward the center of the health care universe, and becoming part of that delivery system is crucial in capturing volume and referrals. Primary care physicians are forming integrated networks, merging, and selling into publicly traded management companies. They are broadening their range of covered services to include both single-specialty and multispecialty provider groups, in order to accept greater levels of risk and appeal to payers seeking a single source network. The nature of these alliances may take a variety of forms, from simple contractual agreements to shared equity in a practice management company. Single-specialty networks in particular should pursue alliances with multispecialty groups in addition to primary care providers. See Chapter 1 for more information on these alliance issues and options.

Exercise Network Panel Selection and Deselection

A precept of managed care is that there is, in gross terms, excess capacity among specialty providers. Payers can and do insist on stringent utilization and quality standards among their participating providers, and enforce those standards through contractual withholds. Payers are seeking efficient specialty providers, and can "cherry pick" specialists to fill out their regional panels. Increasingly, specialists across the country are getting pink slips or being deselected by payers. The specialty network must address this reality by not overloading its panel (as is inevitably the case in the IPA model), and by recruiting specialists of proven clinical efficiency and managed care mentality. New members should exhibit practice patterns that are consistent with the contracting requirements of the network, and new members' patient relations should enhance the image, reputation, and marketability of the network. The network must also, from the outset, establish a mechanism to remove physicians whose clinical performance or personal disposition undermines the image or cumulative efficiency of the network.

Support Network Efficiencies through Practice Management Services

As an adjunct to the need for information in the specialty network, one of the most pressing needs of providers engaged in risk contracting is effective management of their practices. This need extends beyond managing the clinical and financial aspects of risk and includes facilities management, staffing, internal policies and procedures, purchasing, marketing, recruitment, clinical and functional reengineering, and education. The specialty network should offer, through a Management Services Organization (MSO) type structure, individually tailored practice assessment services, group purchasing, in-house consulting services in areas such as reengineering and practice operations, clinical and staff recruitment, records retention and waste disposal, as well as other commonly requested services.

Member practices of specialty networks face fundamental choices about contracting with the MSO versus merging practice assets and turning over the entire management of their medical practices to the network MSO. When assets are merged, overall value of the MSO is significantly increased, due to its control over the revenue stream of the medical practice. For each physician, the decision to buy or merge proceeds from consideration of a number of options. Services can simply be contracted from the network (or other vendors) on an à la carte or bundled basis. Alternately, physicians may choose to transfer partial or total assets of their practice in exchange for equity in the MSO company.

The specialty network can exploit a real opportunity to recruit and integrate physicians by offering, through an MSO, not only a menu of services but an equity participation vehicle that aligns the goals of the network membership. The flexibility of this approach will appeal to a broad spectrum of physician cultures.

Empower Physicians with Knowledge

It is often the case in specialty network development efforts that participating physicians are spread along the learning curve in terms of business, financial, and managed care sophistication. Many physicians participate only reluctantly, and are conceptually opposed to any change in practice style or reimbursement that is unfamiliar and may be less lucrative. These same physicians must be educated about two major issues: (1) the emergence of managed care and its impact on their future livelihood, and (2) the need to position their practices to succeed in a shrinking specialty service environment. This educational process is an ongoing one and must be reinforced through formal educational programs that discuss the main themes of risk contracting and managed care practice operations. Clinical reengineering also plays a prominent role in positioning physicians, through education and information, for the transition to a managed care environment.

THE BOTTOM LINE—WHAT SPECIALISTS SHOULD EXPECT FROM THEIR NETWORK

Enhanced Physician Influence

The specialty network shifts control in relations between provider and payer toward the provider. Because the network can deliver on cost, quality, geographic diversity, and patient access, payers are more flexible in negotiating contracts and less able to terminate specialist relationships on short notice. For the network's part, it can strike more advantageous contracting terms, expressed both in capitation rates and in utilization standards. Just as important, where a proven ability exists to manage the risk component profitably, the network may selectively contract for the type and level of risk with which it is comfortable. Procedures that are not desirable may be carved out, and progressively more advanced levels of risk can be accepted as the network gains experience as a risk contractor.

Competitive Advantage through Aggressive Marketing

From the perspective of the payer, there is a clear disposition toward working with large, proven networks of specialty providers, each working within a single, defined set of clinical performance criteria, all credentialed and selectively chosen, all adhering to a managed care mentality, and covering a wide geographic region. The network must create an organization that affirms this image and must then aggressively market the network to payers. The marketing posture of the network emphasizes the selective credentialing, clinical standards, managed care sophistication, information systems, and geographic coverage of the network. This image should be promoted in marketing presentations, through advertising, through professional associations, and through personal relationships within the medical community. The purpose of this effort is to establish a brand identity and product recognition directly associated with the network.

Compensation Systems That Emphasize Performance

Compensation among allied physicians can easily become a contentious issue, and it is important to establish a clear, equitable, and fully enforced compensation policy for all participating members of the network. There is a noticeable shift taking place in risk-based compensation, away from withholds and payer-induced incentives and toward internally controlled bonus programs. This approach rewards individual physicians for satisfactory performance as measured by a series of utilization indicators, and makes physicians eligible for incentive pay based on individual performance, not cumulative panel performance. The formula is as follows. Each physician is guaranteed a base salary, based on specialty, volume, and competitive factors. Increases in salary are determined by performance, as measured by panel size rather than productivity. In addition to the base salary, each physician may receive bonus payments based on the individual contribution toward the network clinical goals (productivity) and financial profitability. Representative of this approach is Exhibit 17–3, which describes a hybrid model of physician compensation. The components of compensation incorporate a guaranteed base salary, based upon a multiple input methodology, and a series of incentive options that encourage the alignment of physician and network goals.

The key to gaining an equitable physician compensation program is to align the incentives for all participating members of the network. Physicians should be rewarded for financial performance, quality of care, patient satisfaction, and clinical efficiency. The changed incentives include demand management of specialty care, reduction in admissions, promotion of self-care, disease

---

Exhibit 17–3 Sample Specialty Network Compensation Model

Components

1. Base salary
   A. Individually determined by market and historical factors
2. Individual productivity (incentive)
   A. Aligns personal and network goals
   B. Determined by measurement tools (Resource-Based Relative Value Scale, Ambulatory Care Groups, etc.) and covered services
3. Managed care effectiveness (incentive)
   A. Practice efficiency (particularly under capitation)
   B. Measurement tools include utilization budgets, satisfaction surveys
4. Service benefit to the network (incentive)
   A. Participation in the governance and administration of the network
   B. Mentoring newer physicians

Courtesy of MGMA Research, Englewood, Colorado.

state management, and preventive medicine. These internal performance systems should be aligned with external measurement systems such as Health Plan Employer Data and Information Set (HEDIS) 2.0. Purchasers are holding managed health plans accountable to these process indicators, and the plans expect compliance from their provider networks.

Outstanding Business Services

One of the greatest irritants in a practicing physician's professional life must be the mountain of paperwork and procedural issues of payer contracting that interfere with time devoted to clinical care. One of the core capabilities of the specialty network is the assumption of these contract management responsibilities. The network negotiates and manages the nonclinical aspects of each risk contract on behalf of participating physicians, and works with practice staff to meet the information and reporting requirements of payers. The network helps participating physicians improve the business sophistication of their practices, through advanced information services, policies and procedures, reengineering, and human resources. The network can also provide practice support services such as records storage, waste disposal, group purchasing, patient education materials, and the like. Figure 17–2 describes a full range of practice support services offered by a single-specialty practice management company. The product lines of this company span both medical and practice management. Additionally, the company offers capital and practice development capabilities. Comprehensive practice support services, both clinical and operational, provide real marketing leverage to the physician market.

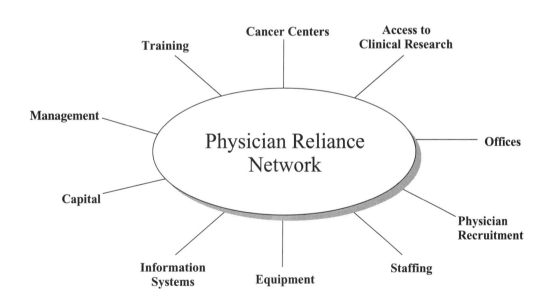

Figure 17–2 Specialty network service lines, Physician Reliance Network. Courtesy of Piper Jaffray, Inc., Minneapolis, Minnesota.

Excellent Risk Contract Management Services

At a minimum, the specialty network should serve as a clearinghouse for risk contracting among a committed group of providers. The network should evaluate payers, negotiate contracts, and once in force, manage the administrative component of each contract. This function may take one of two forms: either the network contracts on behalf of the member physicians as a single provider unit; or the network negotiates multiple contracting arrangements, based on specialty, risk profile, and geographic need. For instance, a truly integrated (and clinically efficient) network of specialty providers could compete for global risk contracts, serving a defined geographic population, for multiple payers. Alternately, the specialty network might also compete for more narrowly defined risk contracts on behalf of the entire network, and carve-out contracts for specific providers, with perhaps a separate risk profile and geographic coverage. This tiered approach to contracting is not without its problems; some participating providers may conclude that the true benefits of contracting through the network are accruing to a select few, while the expense of generating those contracts is being spread among the entire membership.

Superior Medical Management and Practice Management

A core capability of successful physician networks is sophisticated medical management and practice management services. Medical management services define the clinical guidelines that govern physician behavior and provide the framework for standardization of utilization behavior. These standards are a synthesis of practice guidelines, best practice protocols, outcomes measurement, and patient satisfaction.

Practice management services allow participating physicians to accomplish two goals: (1) allocate less time to paperwork and administrative issues at the expense of clinical care, and (2) create cost efficiencies that allow the physician to profit in a risk-bearing practice environment. These services can range from contract management, to centralized staffing, to information systems, and the unifying theme of each service is efficiency.

A SUCCESSFUL SPECIALTY CARVE-OUT NETWORK —SALICKNET

SalickNet, formed in 1992, is a wholly owned subsidiary of the publicly owned Salick Health Care (SHC) based in Los Angeles, California. SalickNet provides at-risk specialty services in oncology and catastrophic care, in seven regions, located in five states. The parent company, SHC, has experienced dramatic growth in the past three years, thanks in part to mergers and expanded operations. Assets have risen from $146 million as of August 31, 1993, to $209 million as of May 31, 1995. Revenues have increased correspondingly from $115 million in 1993 to $112 million in the first nine months of fiscal 1995. Net income during the same period has been somewhat depressed by costs associated with acquisitions and the recent acquisition of 50 percent of SHC outstanding stock by Zeneca Pharmaceuticals. Strategically, SHC has focused on quality, reputation, cost containment, clinical outcomes, alternative delivery, and strong capitalization as core ingredients of sustained growth.

SHC facilities include freestanding outpatient centers, academic hospital-based clinics, satellite physician offices, and home care programs. SalickNet augments SHC delivery capabilities with networks of contracted providers. SHC uses a staff model or MSO approach at the facilities it owns and operates. SHC also uses the hub-and-spoke approach, with the cancer centers serving as the focal point for regional cancer treatment services, including physician services, radiation therapy, and home infusion. This control of the physical and process components of care is considered vital in successfully managing capitation of catastrophic illness.

Salick controls costs and utilization across the continuum of cancer treatments—from physicians, to nurses, to case managers, to social workers, to home health aides, to facilities. Quality and outcomes are key aspects of the comprehensive treatment program designed for each SalickNet patient. Physician incentives are based on outcomes, quality of care, and patient satisfaction.[6]

The central clinical concept of the SalickNet approach is disease state management, a system in which focused, comprehensive, integrated treatment is directed to a specific disease or illness. This program of treatment is patient specific and continually refined to optimize clinical outcomes. SalickNet has built an outpatient-based delivery system that treats cancer from a quality, cost, and outcomes approach (i.e., a team of professionals collaborates in providing an entire course of treatment). The clinical profile of this treatment is determined by guidelines established by SalickNet and designed to yield the best outcome at the most efficient cost. Patients are treated in the most appropriate setting—be that an outpatient center, physician office, or the home—and case managers keep the treatment program focused and outcome oriented.

SalickNet is a capitated provider, and physicians are partners in these risk contracts. Physicians are responsible for implementing and adhering to clinical guidelines established by Salick, including cost control, quality, and outcomes. Currently, the capitation includes all professional fees, chemotherapy, inpatient services, radiation therapy, diagnostic imaging, home care, emergency department visits, nutritional counseling, infusion services, hospice, and social services. SalickNet also offers tailored fixed fees, case rates, and outpatient visit group pricing. These services are marketed directly to HMOs and Preferred Provider Organizations (PPOs) as a cancer carve out. Figure 17–3 illustrates a typical capitated flow of funds in a specialty network. The gross capitation is reduced by general and administrative fees, planned withhold, and risk pools. Typically, physician compensation is determined through a combined methodology of resource utilization (ex., Resource-Based Relative Value Scale [RBRVS]) and efficiency (the withhold).

Like other providers, SHC has had to contend with declining reimbursements for outpatient treatments, particularly in Medicare. This phenomenon will become increasingly acute as government health programs make the transition to risk products. SalickNet has faced the challenge of maintaining profitability in this environment by increasing volume at existing sites, expanding geographically, diversifying payer mix, and implementing cost reduction strategies and controls.

Despite the high cost and resource-intensive nature of cancer treatment, SalickNet has prospered as a carved-out, capitated provider. According to Bettina Kurowski, Ph.D., executive director of SalickNet, cancer lends itself to a carve-out approach for several reasons:

- There is a growing population for cancer treatment. At current incidence and mortality rates, about 40 percent of the population will eventually develop cancer.
- Cancer is a high-cost disease. Payers are looking for ways to reduce the overall costs of cancer treatment.
- Cancer is an easily definable, clearly assignable disease. There is not a conflict as to which provider should assume control of the patient once a diagnosis is made.
- There is a clear beginning and end to treatment.
- Demonstrated improvements in quality are attainable through standardization of protocols and consistency of treatment. Uniformity of treatments leads to improved outcomes.

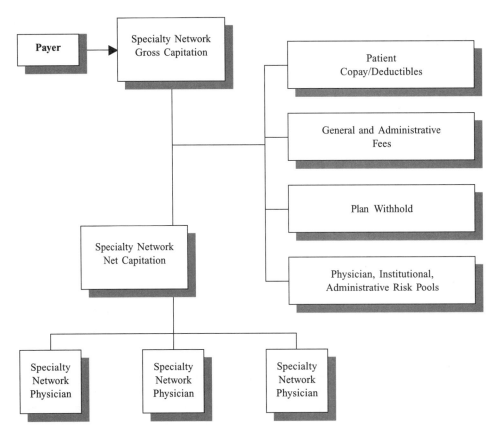

Figure 17–3 Sample specialty network flow of funds.

- Costs are predictable. The incidence and prevalence of cancer among an adult population can be accurately measured (and services priced accordingly).

Successful execution of a carve-out network requires a sophisticated program of care. According to Kurowski, successful specialty carve-out networks possess a number of key attributes:

- **Scope of services and program coordination.** Disease management requires that the efforts of multiple providers and resources be harnessed efficiently and cover an acceptable geographic region.
- **Communication and information exchange.** Because multiple providers are involved and each course of treatment is patient specific, effective communication is necessary between primary care physicians, specialists, case managers, and payers.
- **Referrals.** For carve outs, referrals should be general, authorizing all appropriate diagnostic and treatment services. This streamlines the process and places the final decision for care in the hands of the case manager, medical director, and treating physician.
- **Capitation contract provisions.** Policies and procedures must be explicit regarding out-of-area care, follow-up treatment, continuing care, and other utilization issues that affect the capitation rate.
- **Clinical guidelines.** These should be established and refined through clinical research and network experience.

- **Outcomes measurement.** These include morbidity and mortality, patient satisfaction, patient access, and quality of life.
- **Case management.** This must be utilized, both in developing treatment plans and monitoring effectiveness and outcomes.[7]

These attributes illustrate the growing recognition that mature, successful specialty networks must possess internal risk management capabilities. These capabilities must be matched with the efficient use of clinical resources and the efficient management of multiple delivery sites.

WINNING THROUGH ADAPTATION

The SalickNet approach is representative of a growing trend in specialty contracting. By assuming risk and introducing internal capabilities to manage costs and utilization, organizations like SalickNet are finding capitation a profitable form of reimbursement. Further, by replicating the success of this approach with selected physician, health system, and capital partners, these organizations are building successful, nationwide specialty networks. It is a safe bet that as managed care captures an ever-growing segment of the health care market, specialist organizations that are proven managers of risk will be well positioned to capture covered lives and, in so doing, ensure their own future.

The key to continued success is adaptation. The network must constantly be in touch with its customers at the local level and anticipate changes in market demand. Once identified, these market demands must be met with a "bias for action" in developing and implementing products. The network membership must also be adaptive to changing clinical resource requirements. The fundamental clinical goal of the network is to be the efficient provider of care, through careful selection, education, and a shared clinical culture. The fusion of these operating principles will contribute markedly to the ongoing success of the specialty network.

NOTES

1. American Health Consultants, Physicians Boost Managed Care Clout by Forming Single Specialty Networks, *Physicians Marketing and Management* 6, no. 120 (December 1993): 2.

2. R.W. Krohn, Minimizing Risk in Capitation Contracting, *Group Practice Journal* 44, no. 4 (November/December, 1995).

3. R.W. Krohn, Eight Essential Rules of Capitation Contracting, *Group Practice Journal* 44, no. 4 (July/August 1995): 42–44.

4. R. W. Krohn, *Success in Managed Care: Improving Performance in a Capitated and Risk Sharing Environment* (Alexandria, Va.: Medical Alliances, Inc., 1995), 19–30.

5. *Capitation: The Future of Health Care Reimbursement* (Washington, D.C.: The Advisory Board Company, July 1993), 11.

6. American Health Consultants, Salick Health Care Makes a Run at Large Scale Cancer Capitation, *Physician's Capitation Survival* (October 1994): 12–15.

7. B. Kurowski, President, SalickNet, 1995.

Chapter 18

Multispecialty Physician Organizations: The New Force in Medicine

Nancy McDermott, Charles Hollander, M.D., Richard Garber, M.B.A., and Steven Wolfson, M.D.

INTRODUCTION

Historically, the term *multispecialty organization* has been used to describe a Physician Organization mainly comprised of specialists. In this chapter, *multispecialty organization* refers to a new force in the health care arena, an organization that is primary care–based and includes the appropriate mix of specialists who are linked by asset integration or long-term contract to meet the market's needs. Multispecialty group practices are growing in numbers as payers, and the dictates of efficiency, are demanding more coordinated care between primary care physicians and specialists. In a stage 1 or 2 market, the managed care environment is fragmented; primary care physicians are the gatekeepers for delivering health care services, controlling if and when a patient is referred to a specialist. However, as markets become more integrated, the emphasis changes to coordinated, efficient delivery of a continuum of care with a generation of outcomes measurements. In this context, primary care physicians are best served by forming partnerships with chosen specialists.

In a multispecialty Physician Organization, the patient's doctor (at different times either primary care or specialist) and the demand management system are the care facilitators, ensuring that the patient receives the most appropriate care in the most cost-effective setting. With the development of advanced demand management systems and integrated provider networks, it is clear that the time of primary care physicians is too valuable to be absorbed by gatekeeper duties. The specialist not only provides health care services specific to his or her specialty, but also becomes a consultant to the primary care physician. In the consultant role, the specialist becomes involved in an episode of care earlier in the process rather than later. As mentioned in earlier chapters, outcomes research is increasingly showing that certain acute conditions are treated more cost-effectively, with better outcomes, if specialists are involved earlier. In the treatment of myocardial infarction, for example, the mandate that all care flow through a primary care gatekeeper slows the care delivery process with adverse consequences for the patient.

This chapter focuses on multispecialty Physician Organizations as a way to meet market needs and shows how physicians can develop a primary care–based, multispecialty organization with a management company, group practice, and integrated practice association components. It profiles two physician groups in Connecticut, one primary care, the other specialist, who recognize the value of creating a multispecialty alliance and are now collaborating on statewide network building, contracting, and care delivery.

THE BENEFITS OF A MULTISPECIALTY ORGANIZATION

Purchasers want access, convenience, quality care, and low cost. Payers want to contract with providers who have demonstrated low utilization rates, fewer inpatient days, and improved outcome measurements. In addition, many payers want one-stop contracting, so they can reduce expenses related to network operations, which in turn would allow them to lower premiums below those of other health plans. Primary care physicians are seeking a steady flow of income; control over how health care is delivered; and incentives that recognize efficient, effective patterns of care and controlled operational costs. Specialists are looking for continued patient referrals, contracts with a broad range of covered services, a competitive advantage in a fragmented market, and reduction in the hurdles placed in the process of care delivery by traditional managed care.

Exhibit 18–1 outlines the characteristics of multispecialty organizations necessary to align and satisfy diverse goals. Because they provide a wide range of medical services, manage application of practice protocols, and provide internal management data, multispecialty Physician Organizations are in an advantageous position to satisfy payers and purchasers' demands for accountability. Consequently, they carry more clout during contract negotiations and have access to more contracts than smaller, single-specialty organizations or primary care–dominated organizations. For instance, in Connecticut the primary care–based networks with little specialist integration are finding it difficult to lure contracts away from functional Physician-Hospital Organizations (PHOs) that deliver primary care, specialist care, and hospital services under one package. Also, multispecialty organizations benefit from operational savings due to economies of scale—savings that can be passed on to both patients and physicians.

Exhibit 18–1 Characteristics of Multispecialty Physician Organizations

- **They are conducive to quality of care.** A broader physician base generates more resources and can offer the diversity of clinical staff and information systems necessary to support physicians in maintaining high standards.
- **They develop and manage physician-driven medical management programs.** These programs include risk management, infection control, preventive health care, and provider and patient education.
- **They follow an organized approach to growth and physician specialty mix.** Specialties are recruited based on the needs of the service areas, quality of care, willingness and ability to function within a care team, as opposed to a haphazard accumulation of physicians.
- **They integrate clinical care relationships.** Multispecialty Physician Organizations link primary care and specialist physicians based on their history and ability to collaborate in care delivery.
- **They are responsive to patient wants.** The focus of the organization is ease of access to the doctor who can treat a sports-related injury, skin disease, or heart condition with the minimum of red tape and delays.

Improved Patient Care

Patients are the ultimate benefactors or victims of change in the delivery of health care. In the world of managed care, a patient often represents a statistic rather than an individual and is frequently referred to as a "covered life" or "per member per month." When an employer changes its health plan or a Managed Care Organization changes its physician panel, those covered by the plan must find a new physician if their family physician is not on the new plan's physician panel. Little regard is given to the trust and familiarity built up between an individual and his or her own family doctor. This also has an adverse impact on patient care, because continuity of care is often a critical element of effective and speedy diagnosis and treatment of both serious and minor illnesses.

Obtaining care can become a tedious, frustrating experience for the patient covered by a traditional managed care gatekeeper plan or a primary care model. When an individual becomes ill, he or she first must call or visit the primary care physician. If the primary care physician thinks the condition warrants specialist care, the patient is given a referral. A referral is often very specific as to the treatment and number of visits approved. For example, a man with an unusual skin rash must first see his primary care physician. The primary care physician examines him, concludes he should see a specialist, and gives him a specialist referral for two visits. Then, the patient must make the first appointment with the specialist. He has two visits with the specialist and the condition requires additional treatment. He must then call or return to the primary care physician for another referral. These procedures require significant time and energy on the part of the patient, and also the primary care gatekeeper. The result is fragmented care and, often, delays in receiving treatment.

Multispecialty organizations are able to eliminate many of the disadvantages experienced by patients under managed care plans. In a multispecialty Physician Organization, the delivery of care is managed by physicians assisted by advanced demand management systems that integrate care managers with databases of services and interactive nurse triage. In most cases, when treatment from a specialist is necessary, it can be obtained directly from specialists who are part of the multispecialty organization. The time and energy expended by patients obtaining referrals, going back and forth between the primary care physician and the specialist, are eliminated by the multispecialty organization. Also, when treatment is provided within the organization, the physicians are better positioned to collaborate on the patient's care and provide the patient with more coordinated treatment. In fact, the primary care physician can consult with the specialist to determine the care needed even before a referral is given. Finally, through their advanced information systems, multispecialty organizations have immediate access to outcomes data and are able to use this readily available information to the benefit of the patient.

Because a multispecialty organization can provide primary care and specialist services to a patient through an integrated information system, the organization is able to compile, interpret, and report on the patient's continuum of care and outcomes. These reports are generated on a regular basis and distributed to the physicians in the organization. They are used for many purposes, one of which is peer review and in-house education. Often physicians are able to learn from the experiences of their colleagues and voluntarily adjust their practice style for the betterment of the patient. The patient and the managed health plan benefit from the organization's enhanced quality of care.

Reduced Premium Costs

Health Maintenance Organizations (HMOs) and other payers are contracting with Physician Organizations willing and capable of assuming financial risk for the provision of health care services. They are holding providers accountable for accessibility, quality service, outcomes, patient satisfaction, and cost-efficiency. Multispecialty organizations, like large, single-specialty organizations, have the financial depth to fund risk contracts and the information systems needed to manage these contracts. However, single-specialty organizations are not able to service full-risk contracts on an integrated basis equal to the multispecialty organization. Consequently, if a managed health plan contracts with a single-specialty organization for a broad range of services, it must rely on the ability of the single-specialty practice to manage its outsourced services or recruit and negotiate additional contracts with other caregivers in order to provide a full spectrum of care to the insured patients. When a managed health plan contracts with a multispecialty Physician Organization, it does not need to negotiate additional contracts. The multispecialty entity already provides the diversity needed to serve patients and the in-house management systems to manage its contracts. This reduces the resources of the managed health plan devoted to contract negotiation and management.

Physician Control over Delivery of Care

While the majority of physicians are beginning to realize that managed care and capitation are here to stay, they are concerned that some of the policies and procedures employed by managed health plans have been detrimental to the physician-patient relationship. Many physicians believe that they have an obligation to their patients, and to their profession, to embrace managed care, learn its intricacies, and empower themselves to protect the patients' care and their professional integrity. In fact, this is one of the reasons most often cited for forming alliances, groups, or other types of Physician Organizations. As part of a multispecialty organization, physicians are better able to control and consequently affect the quality of care and standards of health. They are able and willing to assume financial risk out of their commitment to the health of their patients.

Physicians also benefit from collaboration with their peers on a patient's care. Because primary care physicians and specialists are members of the same team, they are more inclined to consult with one another on a patient's treatment. In this way, the specialist becomes involved in the patient's care, sometimes without the need for a formal referral. This efficiency translates to better care for the patient and increased savings to the group.

Like large, single-specialty groups, multispecialty organizations are able to provide useable, current data related to the organization's delivery of care through advanced information systems. The added benefit afforded by multispecialty organizations is that these data are not single-specialty oriented. They include information on the patient's entire program of care. Physicians are able to review these data, along with outcomes measurements, and apply the acquired knowledge to care delivered to other patients. But, why is this any different than outcomes data available throughout the industry? First, data generated in-house are very current. Outcomes data published for the medical profession must withstand a lengthy review and verification process. This process, coupled with standard editorial and publication procedures, means that the data reported are usually a year or more old. Also, physicians tend to accept more readily information that is based on the experiences of their partners, because they see on a daily basis how their partners practice medicine, and they are less likely to question the quality or source of the data compiled from their work.

Exhibit 18–2 highlights the benefits of a multispecialty organization that is well organized and patient focused.

CREATING MULTISPECIALTY ORGANIZATIONS

Organizational structures for multispecialty organizations do not differ from the

Exhibit 18–2 Benefits of Multispecialty Physician Organizations

---

Patients

- managed continuum of care with clinically integrated physicians
- increased quality and continuity of care
- improved accessibility through one-number customer service

Payers

- fewer contracts to negotiate and manage
- better reporting data and claims management according to Health Plan Employer Data and Information Set (HEDIS) measures
- consolidated approach to key service lines, high-volume procedures, and cost quality

Physicians

- continuity of physician-patient relationship
- control over the delivery of care
- enhanced collaboration on episodes of care
- useful management data and feedback on practice performance
- effective integration with demand management and customer service extenders

---

equity organizational models discussed in Chapter 1, and include organizations with linked Independent Practice Associations (IPAs), group practices, management companies, and other alliances through joint ownership and governance of a single Physician Practice Management Company (PPMC) that is serving the business and managed care needs to the different entities. An example of the latter exists between two Physician Organizations located in Connecticut. CHCPhysicians P.C., a primary care integrated group practice, and SpecialtyNet, a limited liability specialty group, have recognized the benefits of aligning with other health care providers to offer a broad spectrum of services to the patient and the payer. They are involved in joint efforts to offer educational programs for physicians on a statewide basis, build an expanded provider network, negotiate and service managed care contracts, and expand a management company formed from the restructuring of a staff-model HMO.

Less than one-third of the total health care market in Connecticut is currently penetrated by managed care. Total lives exceed 3.2 million (3,279,116)[1] and managed care lives are just under 1 million (872,528 lives).[2] As of 1995, capitation was not a major payment mechanism, although payer research identified a significant trend toward capitation as the managed health plans develop the information and management infrastructure to support risk sharing. Connecticut has a shortage of primary care physicians and a surplus of specialists; therefore, the Connecticut managed care market is dominated by the IPA-model HMO, capturing 85 percent of the market. No single player controls the managed care market; however, the "homegrown" physician-driven products remain popular in the state, as evidenced by the enrollee growth of MD Health Plan and Physicians Health Services (PHS), with enrolled growth of 53 percent and 200 percent over the last couple of years, respectively.

CHCPhysicians P.C. is a group practice of over 55 primary care physicians and midlevel practitioners who have a long history of managing capitated contracts as staff physicians to Community Health Care Plan (CHCP), a staff-model HMO. It has a competitive advantage over other primary care organizations in the area because its physicians have been practicing under managed care, including capitation and risk sharing, for more than 20 years. The CHCPhysicians P.C. strategic plan includes growing into a statewide organization by expanding its group to include primary care physicians located in other regions in Connecticut and enhancing its services by developing alliances with specialty groups.

SpecialtyNet LLC was organized in early 1995 by multispecialty physicians in the New Haven region. Its mission is to become a vehicle for premier specialists throughout Connecticut to meet the challenge of delivering high-quality and cost-effective medical care. Its primary function is to extend managed care contract negotiation, contract management, and medical management services to specialist physicians. As of December 1, 1995, approximately 60 physicians were members of SpecialtyNet. To accomplish its mission, SpecialtyNet has set out to:

- Obtain and administer joint managed care contracts.
- Seek to partner with high-quality, cost-effective primary care physicians.
- Facilitate risk sharing, including capitation, consistent with the delivery of quality care.

SpecialtyNet LLC is a committed model integrated network. The board of managers can commit the entire membership to risk-bearing managed care contracts. The organization expects rapid growth, as physicians across many specialties continue to seek the advantages of integrated health care delivery in partnership with primary care physicians. It is actively working to develop networks of specialists in other labor markets in the state, offering to "clone" its corporate structure and share integrated statewide managed care contracting. Figure 18–1 shows the organizational relationships between SpecialtyNet LLC and its alliance partners.

Finding Common Ground

Over the years, many SpecialtyNet LLC physicians have provided capitated specialty services to CHCP patients and consequently have an established relationship with the newly formed CHCPhysicians P.C. In early 1995, representatives from both organizations began discussing collaborative initiatives that would enhance their services. Because of their prior work together, it was not surprising that they are similar in culture and standards of quality. Both groups

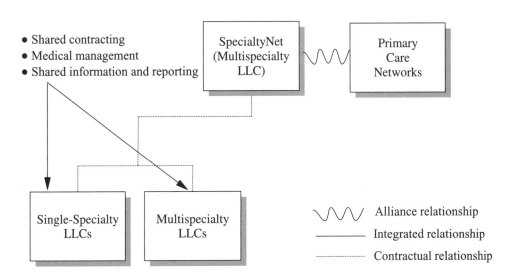

Figure 18–1 Organizational relationships: SpecialtyNet and alliance partners. Courtesy of Medical Alliances, Inc., Alexandria, Virginia.

operate from an underlying foundation based on the following beliefs:

- Patients can best be treated and their interests defended in physician-driven organizations.
- Effective delivery of managed care requires the coordinated efforts of all physicians—primary care physicians and specialists.
- The infrastructure of physician coordination should direct information and decision making to doctors and patients, not to the bureaucracy.
- Managed care requires the development of new organizations and new ethical emphasis.

The relationship of CHCPhysicians P.C. and SpecialtyNet LLC is somewhat unusual, in that they have not experienced turf wars between primary care physicians and specialists. Both organizations realize that it is in their best interest, and the best interest of their patients, to develop strong alliances with each other. They have found common ground through their efforts to meet the challenge of finding ways for physicians to manage care. One alliance is common ownership of a single management company. Instead of quarreling over who should be the gatekeeper, they have agreed that care should be directed by the appropriate physician, at the appropriate time, to be dictated by the status of the patient.

Collaborative Initiatives

CHCPhysicians P.C. and SpecialtyNet LLC have identified and embarked on a number of collaborative efforts that can be grouped into the following categories:

- physician education and relationship building
- network building
- joint managed care and risk contracting
- organizational integration of Management Services Organization (MSO) operations
- patient education

Education and Relationship Building

To drive the education and relationship building component, CHCPhysicians P.C. and SpecialtyNet LLC have established the Institute for Quality and Managed Care. The purpose of the institute is to offer educational programs to physicians on physician equity structures and on how to ensure quality patient care despite significant reductions in health care expenditures by government, business, and HMOs. The programs include a series of interactive educational forums on managed care issues that affect the operational, clinical, and financial components of providing quality care and overall physician practice management.

The first conference was held in November 1995 and featured a nationally renowned physician leader in managing effective Physician Organizations. Representatives from CHCPhysicians P.C. and SpecialtyNet LLC participated in the program presentation. Over 350 physicians attended this program. This series has been successful in offering to physicians statewide the opportunity to increase their understanding of the changes in health care and how these changes specifically affect their practices. It has also proven to be an effective tool for CHCPhysicians P.C. and SpecialtyNet LLC to create a presence in the state. Subsequently, a number of the attendees at the conference have either called CHCPhysicians P.C. or SpecialtyNet LLC to express an interest in the statewide expansion of this concept, or have been the focus of recruitment. In addition, the success of the seminar generated subsequent media interest and a favorable atmosphere for collaborative efforts. Several potential institutional strategic partners suddenly took notice of the efforts of these two physician groups and have suggested collaboration.

Network Building

The strategic plans for both CHCPhysicians P.C. and SpecialtyNet LLC are to expand their organizations statewide. The number of physicians in CHCPhysicians P.C. is projected to grow to approximately 128 physicians by the end of year 2 and approximately 180 physicians by the end of year 3. This expansion through merger is intended to enhance market leverage and competitiveness, making CHCPhysicians P.C. a larger entity that will be an effective risk-bearing network able to achieve profitability within a declining health care premium market. CHCPhysicians P.C. is the largest primary care group practice in the state and intends to maintain that position to ensure greater negotiating strength and enhanced financial benefits from managed care contracts.

SpecialtyNet LLC plans to expand its multispecialty care base through recruitment of other specialist physicians, group practices, IPAs, and limited liability corporations (LLCs) willing to manage risk associated with capitation contracting. It is also supporting the development of a series of single-specialty networks to whom SpecialtyNet LLC will provide managed care contracting services, including negotiations, contract management, utilization review, and quality reporting. Cardiology is the first specialty to begin development of a network. It is anticipated that network will seek an alliance with SpecialtyNet LLC. SpecialtyNet LLC also plans to develop relationships with other Physician Organizations to integrate contractually a network of specialists.

The current relationship between CHCPhysicians P.C. and SpecialtyNet LLC is not an exclusive relationship. Like the framers of the U.S. Constitution, each group's focus has been protected. However, because of the goodwill between the two groups, as they are developing their own organizations they are also seizing opportunities to promote and provide partnership referrals to the other group.

Joint Contracting

While CHCPhysicians P.C. and SpecialtyNet LLC are pursuing their own contracts, they are also jointly negotiating contracts. Currently, CHCPhysicians P.C. is in the final stages of negotiating a provider services agreement with Blue Cross Blue Shield of Connecticut to exclusively provide care for a fully capitated population of 37,000 lives. SpecialtyNet will provide the specialty care needed to service this contract.

Organizational Integration of Management Company Operations

The fourth area of activity is focused on expansion of a Management Services Organization, Physicians Health Care Alliance (PHCA). PHCA is the management company that is supporting the development of the statewide delivery system. It provides all of the management and operational services necessary to manage the diverse, multilocation medical practice network provided by CHCPhysicians P.C., including personnel, information systems, contracting expertise, accounting, financial analysis, purchasing, and capital equipment acquisition. It is anticipated that PHCA will also provide the managed care contracting and select management expertise for SpecialtyNet LLC, and single and multispecialty efforts around the state: thereby earning management fees of 10 to 15 percent of contract revenues for negotiation, contract management, and medical management services (see Figure 18–2).

PHCA's long-term objective is to provide a variety of operational services to physicians, ancillary service providers, PHOs, and other health care service providers in the state. The management team of PHCA was formed by the former management team from Community Health Care Plan. The fundamental strategy for growth of the manage-

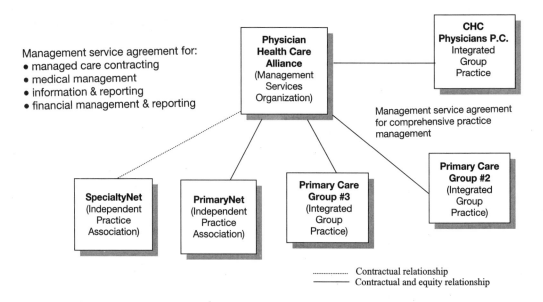

Figure 18–2 Organizational chart for PHCA and related entities. Courtesy of Medical Alliances, Inc., Alexandria, Virginia.

ment company is to expand the Integrated Group Practice (CHCPhysicians P.C.), the specialty network (SpecialtyNet LLC), and the larger risk-bearing network of contracted physicians.

BRIDGING THE GAP BETWEEN PRIMARY CARE PHYSICIANS AND SPECIALISTS

Creating any type of Physician Organization, whether primary care, single specialty, or multispecialty, is an intricate, multilayered process requiring strong leadership with a vision. It is a process of dealing with conflict as new and old health care organizations deal with the shifts in the traditional power structure. It is a process that is nearly impossible to design from the top down; although it can be facilitated and guided, it does not always have a predictable, clean, neat outcome. Integration is the process of dealing with conflict and resolving the issues through a series of progressive decisions that lead to the legal, financial, and operational integration between alliance partners.

Common wisdom suggests that a multispecialty organization should be comprised of 60 percent primary care and 40 percent specialists. However, market demographics such as age, geographic diversity, occupational mix—and, most important, politics, capital, and past relationships—will determine the actual makeup of the Physician Organization. During the relationship-building stage, it is important to identify and address the obstacles or challenges to creating the organization. Build the framework for the relationship on established shared objectives. Some of the objectives will be obvious, such as promoting physician leadership, enhancing accessibility and quality of health care, improving outcomes, and protecting revenue stream. Other common objectives may not be as apparent. Flush out these hidden objectives, as they can be as solidifying as the ostensible objectives. Structure the organization to reflect new, redefined objectives, with the primary care physicians and specialists collaborating on the organization's structure and operations (such as governance, contract negotiations, rate setting, compensation/bonus plan, practice goals, and peer review). Always respect the inherent differences of the groups.

In markets across the country, multispecialty Physician Organizations are setting up their own management companies and acquiring capital through a minority sale of equity to other alliance partners who could be a health system, managed health plan, or public or private investor.

NEW RELATIONSHIPS SPROUTING FROM MULTISPECIALTY ORGANIZATION DEVELOPMENT

When CHCPhysicians P.C. and SpecialtyNet LLC embarked on their development processes, they had a natural affinity for collaboration due to their history of cooperative caregiving and underlying trust. CHCPhysicians P.C. did not carry a grudge against the specialists. They realized that as primary care physicians they needed the specialists. They realized that they could not "stick it to" the specialists during the day and then expect to call a specialist at 3 A.M. to request that the specialist get out of bed and go to the hospital to treat one of the primary care physician's patients. SpecialtyNet LLC also saw the wisdom in allying with quality primary care physicians, particularly a group of physicians experienced in treating patients under the auspices of managed care. Because of the solid relationship between the two groups, during the November 1995 educational program the primary care physicians found themselves promoting the specialists and the specialists found themselves promoting the primary care physicians.

SUMMARY

The key success factors for any rapidly evolving physician health care organization are:

- physician leadership
- management
- risk-taking spirit by physicians
- clinical integration
- information systems infrastructure

The steps for creating successful multispecialty Physician Organizations are many and progressive. Recognize the leadership roles in each group. Understand the political forces and strategically balance them against one another. An organization can do everything else correctly, but if it does not have strong, effective leadership, the group will not succeed. The leaders from each group should have credibility not only within their own group but also in the physician community. In addition, leaders for diverse groups must be able to recognize the strengths of each group, communicate clearly, and build consensus. Second, it is important to do market research, business planning, and execution at the same time. These should be concurrent processes. Delays will lead to the loss of competitive advantage. Be sure to understand the political forces and implement strategies to enhance the positioning of the Physician Organization. Build a solid management and clinical infrastructure to support the organization and its alliances. Most importantly, ally with physicians who are similar in culture and hold their physicians to the same standards of delivering quality care to patients.

NOTES

1. U.S. Bureau of the Census, Connecticut Office of Policy and Management, 1992.
2. Connecticut State Department of Insurance, 1994.

Chapter 19

Creating The Future through Today's Vision and Actions

Douglas Goldstein

INTRODUCTION

One lesson from the front lines of physicians organizing throughout the country, is that . . . Nike was wrong . . . "Just Do It" is not enough in today's competitive managed care environment. Physician and health care leaders must be committed to . . . "Doing It Better."

The accelerated rate of change in the health care and Physician Practice Management industry demands that executive and physician leaders look beyond the surface of any merger and consolidation opportunity and examine fundamental principles and systems.

COMPETITIVE ADVANTAGE THROUGH SYSTEM BUILDING BLOCKS

The information in the previous chapters presented critical information on the system *Building Blocks* necessary to survive and prosper in a new health care world characterized by price competition, capitation, and an emerging emphasis on outcomes. The implementation of critical paths and other aspects of the *Outcomes Databases* Building Block lays a foundation for the clinical reengineering necessary to manage health not just treat illness. This reengineering focuses on improving practice guidelines, measuring results, giving feedback to physicians, and applying disease management to targeted medical conditions. It is an approach that is patient and disease focused, yet takes into account the whole person.

Interactive patient technologies from online health services such as *Thrive* (the joint venture between Times Warner and America Online), to telephone-based demand management systems supports patient *Self Care and Empowered Consumers* to make better health care decisions. *Information Systems* and Intranet connectivity using the Internet are the central nervous systems for the health system of the future and are vital to enhancing access and lower costs. *Multispecialty Networks* will incorporate powerful customer service and demand management functions to ensure that patients get the right care in the most appropriate setting at the lowest cost.

An improved health care delivery system depends on building trust, cooperation, intelligence, and a caring culture committed to solving problems and managing capitation ready organizations through advanced financial, clinical, and operational systems. The characteristics necessary to create a caring and healthy future depend on all the system *Building Blocks*. Most importantly, it requires an alliance attitude and physician leadership.

TRACK TRENDS AND NEWS IN THE EXTERNAL ENVIRONMENT

Timely, accurate information is a competitive advantage. The Internet, with its on-line services, Newsgroups and World Wide Web, offers unlimited opportunities to gain information faster than ever before and to link with associates across the world trying to solve the same clinical or management problems. Get on-line and search news daily. Check out Physician Practice Management Companies or Health Maintenance Organizations (HMOs), or telemedicine. Register with a quality or disease management *listserv* or *Newsgroup* and communicate with colleagues all over the world on how to solve critical problems. Discover critical market intelligence and knowledge that will deliver a competitive advantage to your organization.

Timely information will help spot market opportunities and the evolution of the following trends which are clearly evident in the market driven restructuring of the health care system:

- *Larger Purchasers and Increasing Demand for Cost Effectiveness*—The clout of purchasers is growing due to their size and organization. Businesses are developing purchasing cooperatives to directly contract with Integrated Delivery Systems. The national HMO management companies are growing as they acquire regional HMOs throughout the country. The purchasers of health care are getting larger, so the providers of health care must grow larger.

- *Multispecialty-Driven Care Management Systems Will Replace the Gatekeeper*—Primary care physician–driven *gatekeeper* functions will be abandoned. Instead, large multispecialty Physician Organizations will operate advanced triage and access software programs for customer service and demand management. These systems are essential to guide patients in the effective use of the health care system. The Physician Organizations with effective demand management systems can generate additional fees for administrative services.

- *Transition of Power To Provider-Based Delivery System*—Under capitation every component of the delivery system is a cost center. When physician leaders and clinical systems drastically reduce the number of hospital days and lower the use of specialists, the next biggest cost center is the managed health plan which may be taking 20 percent to 30 percent or more of the health care dollar for sales, marketing, benefit design, administration, and profit. Providers are organizing and launching HMOs and provider service organizations (PSOs). New federal legislation promises to accelerate this trend because many provider based HMOs operate with lower overhead than the for-profit HMO management companies.

- *Shifting Physician Compensation*—While specialist care will be essential to quality, cost-effective care, specialist demand and specialist compensation will decline. As organizations recognize the value of primary care physicians, their incomes will increase, then level off. As price competition increases in markets, physician base salaries will be impacted.

- *Increasing Competition for the Hearts, Minds, and Revenue Streams of Practices of Primary Care and Specialist Physicians*—Hospitals and managed health plans will increasingly vie for the attention and commitment of physicians under long-term management agreements or acquisition. There are numerous variations on the Physician Equity Alliance and most seek control of the cash flow of the medical practice and related ambulatory health services.

- *Rapid Growth of the Physician Practice Management Industry*—In 1993, the market value of publicly traded practice management companies was less than $500 million. In 1996, the total market capitalization of publicly traded practice management companies is greater than $10 billion, and there are two companies that have over $1 billion in annual revenue. This is a major new force in the health care industry.
- *Virtual Integration, Not Vertical*—Vertically structured organizations are too bureaucratic, expensive, and difficult to operate for a cost-driven, competitive market. Network structures with a degree of financial consolidation and virtual integration through the information superhighway will win the day. Virtual structuring must be a prime focus of Physician Organizations as they create organized systems of care that function as a integrated network linked electronically.

To develop leading edge strategies, leaders must take these national trends into account and adjust for regional market conditions, so that competitive goals, strategies, and actions can be tailored to a specific market. There is a tremendous need for changed leadership and empowerment management. As health care restructuring continues to depend on local, community-based action, organizations will more frequently seek out leaders who can manage change and empower others. The environmental slogan, "Think globally, act locally" fits the challenge faced by physicians and health care executives.

The real action in health care restructuring is at the regional level. The state and federal governments have the obligation to structure the right incentives. But only physicians, health care workers, executives, and consumers can manage costs and use resources wisely. Consumers who use the health care system must remain conscious of quality and cost. Physicians and executives must set aside self-interest and put patients and community first as they build alliances among providers, payers, and consumers.

The fate of health care restructuring depends on what transpires in local communities, health systems, and medical practices. The clearest path to efficient, cost-effective, prevention-oriented approaches to health care delivery depends on the creative thinking and wise decision making of physicians, nurses, and health care executives.

COMPETITIVE ADVANTAGE THROUGH THINKING AND LEADERSHIP

To overcome the numerous challenges faced by executives and physicians, discovering how to do something better, different, and faster is essential to secure competitive advantage, avoid knock-offs, or duplicates of another organization's strategies. In the integration game, the advantage will go to networks and systems with quality physicians capable of managing health and treating illness. Remember to apply lessons learned from other organizations. Understanding how managed care evolved in other markets is necessary, keeping in mind that every market is different. What worked in California two years ago will not work in New York state in the year 2000 and beyond. Physicians, health system executives, and managed care executives should apply the lessons of the California Health Care Wars and intimate knowledge of the local environment to develop innovative approaches to creating sustainable health care delivery systems.

Development and expansion of clinical physician leadership is the first step toward integration. Physicians must assert their position in new, evolving health care organizations by choosing physician partners and setting *Guiding Principles* for other physicians to emulate. Develop an aggressive growth business plan for Physician Organizations. Invest some capital in your own future. All key stakeholders—physicians, trustees, health care executives, and insurance executives—must learn new communications skills, create new information systems, ensure patient care quality, and create a seamless delivery system.

Physician leaders will be successful if they inspire and involve others to take responsibility for changing the organization and delivery of care. The goal is to guide and nurture progressive change, not to demand, dictate, or impose new structures. Remember, every new evolving health care organization is the result of a series of mergers, consolidations, and growth. Even more important, every Integrated Delivery System, Physician Practice Management Company, Physician Equity Alliance, and Physician Organization is a work in progress. Leaders who can empower their colleagues to meet the challenge of change will be winners in creating *sustainable* health care systems in the patient's best interest.

Index

A

Access Health Marketing, 44
Accountability
  advanced physician management system, 91
  outcomes research, 221
  and specialty networks, 324
Accounting
  activity-based accounting, 301
  cost accounting system, 125
Activity-based accounting, definition of, 301
Adjusted average per capita cost (AAPCC), 105–106, 313
Administrative services only (ASO), 312
Advanced physician management
  care management, 92–93
  clinical performance measures, 96
  disease management, 93–94
  governance/management role of physicians, 88–89
  health status management, 91–92
  Lovelace Health Systems (LHS) model, 88–94
  management performance measures, 95–96
  medical practice board support, 89–90
  performance measures, 94–95
  physician group incentives, 91
  physician profiling, 96–98
  physician report card, 91
  physician training, 89
  population–based measures, 95
  primary care initiatives, 90
  specialists initiatives, 90
Advanced physician management systems
  budget for, 208–210
  change management, 213–214
  conversion to new system, 210–212
  financing of, 210
  future needs, 215
  information systems principles, 208
  planning principles, 208
  requirements analysis, 207
  steering committee for, 206–207
  strategic plan for, 206
  strategic plan maintenance, 207–208
  training for new system, 212–213
  value added by, 214–215
  work plan for, 213
Advanced practice management system, capabilities of, 38
Adventist Health System, 80
Aetna Health Plans, 44, 77
Aetna Healthways Health Centers, 150
Agency for Health Care Policy and Research (AHCPR), 41, 223
Ambulatory care groups, 131
Ambulatory information system, selection of, 204
American Clinical Management, 22
American Group Practice Outcomes Management Project, 41
American Health Network, 24, 30
America Online, 50
Antikickback statute, 253–255
  components of, 181
  recent developments, 254–255
  and safe harbor, 254
Antitrust, 255–258
  admission/termination of providers by MCOs, 257–258
  exclusive managed care–provider relations, 258

353

and independent practice associations
  (IPAs), 175–177
 laws applicable to managed care, 255–256
 and mergers, 168–170
 nonexclusivity, indications of, 176
 and price fixing, 257
 and refusals to deal with MCO, 256–257
Arbitration, 276
Asset transfer agreement, 122
Atlantic Health Network, 4, 24

B

Baltimore Medical Group, 4, 24, 30
Baptist Health Care System, 84
Bay Physicians Medical Group, 84
Beneficiary hold harmless clause, capitated contracts, 283–284
Benefit plans, and mergers, 164, 168
Blue Cross, 85
Blue Cross & Blue Shield, 150
Blue sky laws, 170
Boland Healthcare, 80
Boot, 165
Break–even point, definition of, 301
Budget, for advanced physician management systems, 208–210
Built to Last: Successful Habits of Visionary Companies (Collins and Porras), 65
Business development. *See* Expansion process
Business form, 172–174
 limited liability company, 173–174
 nonprofit corporation, 174
 professional corporation, 172–173
Business Healthcare Action Network, 160

C

California Health Network, 80
Capital
 capital expenditures, types of, 153
 and expansion process, 123–124
 and growth of company, 151
 internally generated, benefits of, 154
 minority investors, pros/cons of, 157
 necessity for growth, 150–151
 for physician health system joint venture (PHSJV), 10
 for physician practice management company (PPMC), 13–14
 for physician regional network, 7
 sources for physician equity alliance, 23
 for specialty services network, 16
 for strategic alliances, 153
 for venture medical management company, 21
 working capital, 153
Capitated contracts
 beneficiary hold harmless clause, 283–284
 capitation methodology, 282–284
 carve outs, 285
 coordination of benefits, 283
 copayments section, 283
 covered services, 285
 definitions in, 280–281
 and geographic area, 280–281
 indemnification, 285
 and marketing methods of payer, 284
 membership guarantees, 285
 negotiations strategy, 280
 penalty section, 282
 preparation for capitated business environment, 294–296
 preparation for negotiations, 279–280
 provider performance provisions, 281–282
 rate negotiation, 286–293
 reconciliation of membership section, 282–283
 regulatory compliance, 284
 reinsurance, 285
 risk pools, 284–285
 for specialty networks, 323–326
 term/termination, 284
 utilization covered by capitation, 285
Capitation, 245–248, 268–269
 calculation of, 246–247
 exclusivity and volume, 248
 global capitation, 268
 intermediary capitation, 268–269
 management systems for, 296–298
 misuse of, 246
 operational issues, 298–300
 ordinary capitation, 268
 PMPM basis, 246, 280
 as reimbursement, 246
 risk and profit, 247–248
 and risk sharing, 249–250
 types available to providers, 279
 See also Capitated contracts
Capitation management, computerized, 194
Capitation methodology, capitated contracts, 282–284
CareAmerica, 74
Care management, 92–93
 for continuum of care, 93
 goals of, 92–93
 and high-risk populations, 93
 resource management, 93
 therapeutic alliance, support of, 93
CareMaps, nature of, 48–49, 225
Caremark, 80, 147, 149
Carle Clinic, 310–311
Carve outs
 capitated contracts, 285
 single–specialty, 320
Case management, computerized, 194
Case–mix management, by database, 193
Catholic Healthcare West, 80
CHCPhysicians, 24, 342–347

Churning, 130, 135
Classic Care, 256
Clayton Act, 169, 256
Clinical pathways, nature of, 48
Clinical performance measures, 96
Clinical practice guidelines, 39–41
  examples of, 48
Clinical practice improvement (CPI)
  and advanced physician management, 87, 89, 90
  physician commitment to, 90
  processes in, 90
Clinical protocols, computerized, 193–194
Coastal Health Care Group, 16, 123, 144, 147
Coastal Physician Group, 28, 76
Coding, relative value scales (RVS), 243, 245
Communication/information systems, 34–38
  advanced practice management system, 38, 125–126
  ambulatory information system, 204
  application program interface, 195
  barriers to, 38
  benefits of, 34–35, 98
  for capitation management, 194
  for case management, 194
  for case-mix management, 193
  for contract management, 193
  desktop computers, 195
  electronic data interchange (EDI), 35–36
  electronic medical record (EMR), 38
  for eligibility/enrollment function, 193
  future view, 100
  installation requirements, 36–38
  on Internet, 196
  local-area networks (LAN), 195
  management information system functions, 198
  management information system selection, 203
  multimedia capabilities, 196
  new information systems, functions of, 99
  object-oriented programming, 195–196
  open systems, 195
  optical storage technology, 196
  physician involvement in, 98–99
  point-of-care devices, 196
  regional/national systems, 192–193
  relational database management system, 196
  selection of system, 197–202
  structured query language (SQL), 196
  for treatment profiles/protocols, 193–194
  types of systems, 38
  types of technologies in, 35
  for utilization/cost management, 193
  vendor analysis of service/cost, 201
  wide-area network (WAN), 195
Communication with physicians, 59–71
  acknowledgment of mistakes, 68–69
  feedback in, 66
  flexibility in, 67
  and guerilla management, 69
  implementation of change by organization, 66
  and input by physicians, 64
  lack of by physicians, 56
  leadership building for physicians, 64–65
  and learning by physicians, 65–66
  listening, importance of, 66
  meetings, content of, 70
  people-oriented organization, 69
  problem-solving in, 67–68
  resposiveness of organization, 66–67
  sharing of data, 64
  solutions versus fads, 67
  and stabile relationship, 64
  and time for reflection, 71
  trust in, 63–64
  values focus, 65
  and visibility, 70
Community Health Plan, 82
Compensation. *See* Physician compensation
Comprehensive practice management MSO, operation of, 28
Compuserve, 50
Computerization. *See* Advanced physician management systems; Communication/information systems
Concurrent review, under managed care contract, 272
Confidentiality, under managed care contract, 273
Continuous quality improvement (CQI), 48–49
  clinical reengineering, 48–49
  steps in process, 48
  tools of, 48–49
Continuum of care, elements of, 93
Continuum Care Corporation, 22
Contracts, 263–276
  checklist for understanding of, 263–264
  contract management, computerized, 193
  core items of, 266
  negotiating styles/tactics, 266
  negotiating team, 265–266
  negotiation process, 265
  nonnegotiable items, 266
  See also Capitated contracts; Managed care contracts
Contribution margin, definition of, 301
Coordination of benefits, capitated contracts, 283
Copayments section, capitated contracts, 283
Corporate practice of medicine, issues related to, 261–262
Corporate subsidiary
  advantages/disadvantages of, 158–159
  and strategic partner, 157–159
Cost accounting system, 125
Cost accumulation, definition of, 301
Cost allocation, definition of, 301
Cost approach, valuation of business, 109
Cost driver, definition of, 302
Cost management, 54–55
  and communication with health plan, 55
  computerized, 193

importance of, 54–55
incurred but not reported costs, 55
variable-costing income statement, 54
Cost object, definition of, 302
Cost reduction, 54
Cost system, definitions in, 301–302
Covered services
capitated contracts, 285
under managed care contract, 271
Credentialing of providers, under managed care contract, 272
C reorganizations, 165–168
Critical pathways, nature of, 48
Current Procedural Terminology (CPT) code, 8, 322

D

Daughters of Charity Health System, 16
Debt, types of, 152
Demand management, 43–46
effectiveness of, 44–45
elements of, 43
teleservices in, 44–45
Designated health services (DHS)
Stark law criteria, 252
under Stark laws, 252
Diagnosis-related groups (DRGs), 59
and reimbursement, 242
reimbursement by, 268
Direct costs, definition of, 302
Discounted future cash flow, valuation of business, 10
Disease management, 46–47, 93–94, 223–224
cost savings from, 47
diseases covered by, 94
elements of, 46–47, 224
episode of care approach, 94
lead organizations in, 46
Dispute resolution
alternative methods, 276
under managed care contract, 275–276
Doctors Healthcare, 24
Due diligence, and mergers, 114, 162–163

E

Electronic data interchange (EDI), 35–36
cost of, 36
cost savings from, 36
integrated hub-and-spoke system, 35–36, 192
point-to-point system, 35–36, 192
Electronic medical record (EMR), 37, 38, 124
Eligible persons, under managed care contract, 271–272
Emergency Medical Treatment and Active Labor Act, 271
Emergency procedures, under managed care contract, 271
Employment agreement, physician/shareholder, 122
Empowerment of consumers, 45, 55–56
and self-care, 55–56
Encounter data, reporting of, 282
Episode of care approach, disease management, 94
Equity principles and expansion, 108–109, 118–122
common stock, 120
preferred stock, 120
Excess earnings method, valuation of business, 110
Expansion process
and action-oriented research, 104–107
advanced medical management systems, 124
aggressive business development, 107–108
ambulatory management infrastructure, 124–126
business/practice valuations, 109–111
capital sources, 123–124
equity structure, development of, 118–122
equity transaction, understanding of, 108–109
execution of expansion, 126
legal agreements, 122–123
mergers, 111–118
purchaser needs, identification of, 106–107
Experimental treatments, under managed care contract, 271

F

Fallon Clinic, 130
physician compensation, 135–136
Fee-for-service
nature of, 267, 278–279
transition to capitation, 297–298
FHP of California, 4, 82
Fixed costs, definition of, 302
Flexible budget, definition of, 302
Focus Health Services, 12
Foundation Health Plan, 74, 82
Friendly Hills Medical Group, 30, 73, 80
Front Range Medical Management, 12

G

Gatekeeper functions, 349
Geisinger Health Plan (GHP), 259
Global capitation, 268
Goldfarb v. Virginia State Bar, 255
Goodwill, and valuation of business, 111
Graphical user interface (GUI), 195
Grateful Med, 50
Gross margin, definition of, 302
Group Health Plan, 82
Group practice, legal criteria, 253
Group Practice Compensation Trends and Productivity Correlations, 142
Group practice without walls, 6

H

Hanlester Network v. Shalala, 254–255
Harriman Jones Medical Group, physician compensation, 134–135
Hart-Scott-Rodino Act, 169
Harvard Community Health Plan, 47, 56, 131
Health Futures, 73–74
Health Maintenance Organization Act, 260
Health maintenance organizations (HMOs)
   prices, downward trend, 74
   taxation of, 258–261
Health Online, 50
Health Plan Employer Data and Information Set (HEDIS), 39, 40, 41, 122, 224
HealthSource, 82
Health status management, 91–92
   database for, 92
Health Status Questionnaire, 133
Hill Medical Group, 73, 80, 82
Horizontal integration, example of, 160
Hub-and-spoke system, information systems, 35–36, 192

I

Iameter, 41
Income approach, valuation of business, 109
Income Distribution, 142
Incurred but not reported costs, 55
Indemnification
   capitated contracts, 285
   under managed care contract, 274–276
Independent practice associations (IPAs), 4
   antitrust, 175–177
   form of business, 172–174
   insurance regulation, 177–178
   network participation agreement, 175
   organization of, 174–175
   securities, 177
   specialty networks, 320
   state regulations, 178
   taxation of, 261
Indirect costs, definition of, 302
Information management, specialty networks, 327–328, 330
Information systems. *See* Communication/information systems
Insurance, 262–263
   definition of, 262
   terms related to, 262
Insurance companies, purchase of medical practice management companies, 25
Insurance regulation, independent practice associations (IPAs), 177–178
Integrated delivery systems
   alternative methods of, 85
   characteristics of, 72, 82–83
   market forces in, 82

   merger of. *See* Mergers
   partnership models, 84–85
   payer–driven networks, 83–84
   provider–sponsored systems, 84
   time factors in managed care stages, 81–83
   variations of, 73
Integrated hub-and-spoke system, electronic data interchange (EDI), 35–36
Integrated Physician Services, 12
Integration
   horizontal, 160
   virtual integration, 73
Interim determinations, dispute resolution, 276
Intermediary capitation, 268–269
Internet services, 49–54, 196
   benefits to use of, 51, 52, 54
   health care related elements, 50
   Web sites for physicians, 51–54
InterStudy, 75
Investigational treatments, under managed care contract, 271
Investment
   growth/revenues in health care field, 147
   in physician organizations, 25, 29

J

John Deere Health Care, 46
Joint ownership
   business entity, 183
   corporate practice of medicine, 185
   fraud/abuse, 185–186
   hospital contribution, 183
   operating agreement, 183
   physician contribution, 183
   securities, 185
   Stark law (anti-referral), 186
   tax-exempt status, 183–185

K

Kaiser Health Plan, 77, 80

L

Leadership, physicians, 43, 57, 149–150
Legal issues
   antikickback statute, 253–255
   antitrust, 255–258
   contracts, 263–276
   corporate practice of medicine issues, 261–262
   insurance, 262–263
   Stark law (anti–referral), 251–253
   taxation, 258–261
Letter of intent
   lock-up language, 162
   mergers, 114, 162
Liability, under managed care contract, 274–275
Limited liability corporation (LLC), 6, 7, 8, 10, 16

elements of, 173–174, 183
joint venture LLC, 183
Listening, and communication, 66
Local-area networks (LAN), 195
Lovelace Health Systems (LHS)
  advanced physician management model, 88–94
  medical delivery health model, 91–94

M

Managed care, evnironment of, 279
Managed care contracts
  content of contract, 232–234
  contract issue resolution, 240
  contracts with health plans, 234–237
  covered services, 271
  credentialing of providers, 272
  dispute resolution, 275–276
  eligible persons, 271–272
  emergency procedures, 271
  experimental/investigational treatments, 271
  format of contract, 232
  implied contract, 232
  indemnification, 275
  medically necessary services, 271
  medical records/confidentiality, 273
  and needs of all parties, 240–241
  potential liability, 274–275
  with primary care physicians, 237–239
  with specialists, 238–240
  stop-loss provision, 276
  term/termination provisions, 273–274
  utilization and quality revies, 272–273
Managed care stages, 75–83
  aggressive stage, 77–78
  domination stage, 78–80
  integrated delivery system stage, 81–82
  network war stage, 80–81
  stage 1 markets, 75–76
  stage 1 strategies, 76–77
  stage 2 markets, 77–78
  stage 2 strategies, 78
  stage 3 markets, 78–79
  stage 3 strategies, 79–80
  stage 4 markets, 80–81
  stage 5 strategies, 82–83
Management and asset acquiring MSO, operation of, 28–29
Management performance measures, 95–96
Management of physician organizations
  continuous quality improvement (CQI), 48–49
  cost management, 54–55
  cost reduction, 54
  demand management, 43–46
  disease state management, 46–47
  integrated communication/information systems, 34–38
  Internet services, 49–54
  of multispeciality physician networks, 42–43
  outcomes research/reporting, 38–39, 41–42
  physician leadership, 57
  preventive medicine, 55–57
  process measures, 39–41
  See also Advanced physician management
Management services organizations (MSOs), 4, 9, 11, 134
  composition of, 26
  comprehensive practice management MSO, 28
  fraud/abuse statutes, 181–182
  growth of, 25–26
  legal documents, 180
  management and asset acquiring MSO, 28–29
  safe harbor, 182
  service bureau MSO, 28
  services of, 26, 28
  Stark law (anti–referral), 182
Market approach, valuation of business, 109
Market power, definition of, 255
Mayo Clinic Health Book, 56
McGraw–Hill Relative Value Set, 130
Medical delivery model
  care management, 92–93
  disease management, 93–94
  health status management, 91–92
Medical Director/Vice President for Medical Affairs, 64
Medical Effectiveness Treatment Program (MEDTEP), 223
Medical Information Line, 44
Medically necessary services, under managed care contract, 271
Medical Network Enterprises, 20
Medical Outcomes Study (MOS), 220
Medical Practice Board, 88–89
Medical records, under managed care contract, 273
Medicare reimbursement, relative value scales (RVS), 244–245
Medicare Resource–Based Relative Value Scale, 130
MediQual, 41
MedPartners, 16, 25, 30, 49, 144, 147, 149
Meetings, content of, 70
Membership guarantees, capitated contracts, 285
Mergers, 111–118
  antitrust, 168–170
  articles of incorporation, 163
  asset components of, 114, 116
  benefit plans, 164, 168
  bylaws, 163
  due diligence review, 114, 162–163
  key operating statistics, 117
  letter of intent to merge, 114, 162
  merger agreement, 164
  merger briefing book, 113–114
  partner screening checklist, 113
  physician employment agreement, 164
  practice merger data request, 115–116
  securities, 170
  shareholders' agreement, 163–164

Stark law (anti–referral), 170–172
steps in, 113–114
tax aspects, 164–168
Meridia, 85
Milliman and Robertson, 40
Montana Associated Physicians, 4
Morale of physicians, and compensation, 128–129
Mullikin Medical Centers, 4, 16, 25, 30, 49, 73, 80, 82, 144, 147
Multimedia, 196
Multispeciality physician networks, 42–43
benefits of, 42–43, 339–341
characteristics of, 338–339
collaborative initiatives, 344–346
and delivery of care, 341
development of, 341–343
education component, 344–345
goals of, 43
joint contracting, 345
management company operations, integration of, 345
meaning of, 338
network building, 345
and patient care, 339–340
physician leadership in, 43
primary care/specialties, combination of, 346–347
and reduced premium costs, 340–341
relationship building component, 344
relationship building from, 347
trends related to, 42

N

National Cardiovascular Network, 18, 20
National Committee for Quality Assurance (NCQA), 39, 224, 284
Negotiation
for capitated contracts, 279–280
of contracts, 265–266
Network of networks, operation of, 19
1994 Physicians Compensation Survey, 142
Nonbinding dispute resolution, 276
Nonprofit corporation, elements of, 174
Northwest Wholesale Stationers, 257, 258

O

Object-oriented programming, 195–196
Ochsner Clinic, 4
Omega, 20
Open systems, 195
Optical storage technology, 196
OPTUM Nurseline, 44
Ordinary capitation, 268
Outcomes management system, 219–220
Outcomes research, 38–39, 41–42
accountability, 221
American Group Practice Outcomes Management Project, 41

application of, 221–223
benefits of, 42
on clinical practice guidelines, 39–41
current position of, 218–219
data collection survey, 220
data collection vehicles, 223
demand for data, 224
development implementation of research, 224–225
disease management, 223–224
elements for tracking, 39
funding for, 41
future view, 225, 227
health attributes measured, 220
history of, 217–218, 219
nature of outcomes research, 41
outcomes data, nature of, 219–220
outcomes measurement project checklist, 226
patient preferences, utility measures, 220–221

P

PacifiCare, 82
Pacific Physician Services, 16, 25, 30, 144, 147, 149
Partnership models, 84–85
elements of, 84–85
Patient management information system, 197
Patient Oriented Treatment Groups (PORTS), 223
Patient satisfaction surveys, 132–133
Payer-driven networks, 83–84
elements of, 83–84
Payer mix, definition of, 302
Payment methods, 266–270
capitation, 268–269
diagnosis-related groups (DRG) reimbursement, 268
fee-for-service, 267
per case payment, 268
percentage of premium, 269
per diem payment, 267–268
risk pools, 269–270
selection of, 270
Pediatrix, 20
Penalties, and capitated contracts, 282, 325–326
Per case payment, nature of, 268
Percentage of premium, nature of, 269
Per diem payment, nature of, 267–268
Performance measures
clinical performance measures, 96
management performance measures, 95–96
new measures, 95
physician profiling, 96–98
population-based measures, 95
Per member per month (PMPM) basis
capitation, 246, 280, 322, 324
and capitation rate/payment, 290, 292
PHP Healthcare, 25, 30, 123
PhyCor, 16, 25, 26, 28, 29–30, 76, 123, 144, 147, 149

Physician compensation
    changing compensation plans, 140–141
    compensation consultants, use of, 128
    Fallon Clinic, 135–136
    and group citizenship, 133
    and group growth, 129
    Harriman Jones Medical Group, 134–135
    incentive aspects, 129
    income distribution scenarios, 136–139
    market-based salaries, 129–130
    and morale of physicians, 128–129
    and panel size, 131
    and patient satisfaction, 132–133
    productivity-based, 130–131, 141
    and quality of care, 133–134, 141
    resource materials on, 142
    utilization statistics in, 131–132
Physician Compensation and Production Survey, 142
Physician-driven HMOs
    competition aspects, 316
    effects on medical practice, 316
    initial steps, 311–313
    operational aspects, 314–315
    physician control in, 316
    requirements for, 310–311
    start-up marketing, 313–314
Physician equity alliance, 24
    capital sources of, 23
    examples of, 4, 24
    goals of, 24
    issues for physicians, 25
    lines of business, 24
    management of, 24
    operation of, 4, 22–23
    ownership of, 23
    revenue generation, 24
    and strategic alliance partners, 155–157
    systems used by, 24
    variations on, 24
Physician equity models
    growth of, 4–5
    physician equity alliance, 22–25
    physician health system joint venture (PHSJV), 9–12
    physician practice management company (PPMC), 12–16
    physician regional network, 6–9
    specialty services network, 16–20
    venture medical management company, 20–22
Physician extenders, 327
Physician Health Care Alliance, 4, 24
Physician health system joint venture (PHSJV), 9–12
    capital sources, 10
    examples of, 12
    goals of, 10
    governance, 10
    income distribution, 11–12
    lines of business, 11
    management of, 10–11
    operation of, 9
    ownership of, 10
    revenue generation, 11
    situations for use, 12
    systems used by, 11
    variations on, 12
Physician-hospital organizations (PHOs), 73–74
    economic limitations of, 4
    elements of, 73–74
    goals of, 61, 73, 74
Physician Network Statement, 176
Physician organizations
    evolution of, 29–31
    goals of, 31, 60–61
    growth principles, 32
    management of. *See* Management of physician organizations
    See also Physician equity models
Physician Ownership and Referral Amendment, 252
Physician Practice Management Companies Newsletter, 147
Physician practice management company (PPMC), 3, 4, 12–16, 144
    and business expansion, 108, 109
    capital sources, 13–14
    examples of, 16
    expansion of, 145–149
    financial aspects, 150–153
    goals of, 14
    governance of, 14–15
    income distribution, 15
    lines of business, 15
    management of, 15
    newsletter on, 4
    operation of, 4, 12
    ownership of, 13–14
    and physician leadership, 149–150
    revenue generation, 15
    situations for use, 15–16
    strategic alliance options, 153–160
    systems used by, 15
    variations on, 16
Physician profiling, 96–98, 222
    benefits of, 96
    elements of, 97–98
Physician regional network
    capital sources, 7
    goals of, 7
    governance of, 7
    income distribution, 8
    lines of business, 7–8
    management of, 7
    operation of, 6
    ownership of, 7
    revenue generation, 8
    situations for use, 8
    systems used by, 8
    variations of, 9

Physician Reliance Network, 19
Physician Resource Group, 20
Physicians
 lack of communication by, 56
 leadership profile, 57
Physicians Online, 50
Point-of-care devices, computers, 196
Point-to-point system, information system, 35–36, 192
Population-based performance measures, 95
PPMC: Market, Financial and Operating Statistics for Physician Practice Management Companies, 4
Practice parameters, nature of, 48
Preauthorization/preadmission review, under managed care contract, 272
Preferred provider organizations (PPOs), 75
 discounts by, 312
Preventive medicine, 55–57
 consumer interest in, 56–57
 and empowerment of consumers, 55–56
 publications on self-care, 56
Price fixing
 legal aspects, 257
 situations for, 257
Primary care physicians
 contracts with, 237–239
 initiatives for, 90
PrimeHealth, 22, 80, 84
Process measures, 39–41
 Health Plan Employer Data and Information Set (HEDIS), 39, 40, 41
Prodigy, 50
Productivity, physician compensation based on, 130–131, 141
Professional corporation, elements of, 172–173
Provider performance provisions, capitated contracts, 281–282
Provider-sponsored systems, 84
 hospital-led systems, 84
 physician-managed networks, 84

Q

Quality, continuous quality improvement (CQI), 48–49
Quality of care
 definition of, 133
 and physician compensation, 133–134, 141
Quality measures, number used, 39

R

RAND Health Insurance Experiment, 218, 220, 223
Reengineering, for clinical improvement, 48–49
Referrals, legal definition, 252
Reimbursement methods
 capitation, 245–248
 diagnosis-related groups (DRGs), 242
 relative value scales, 242–245
 standard methods, 241–242
Reinsurance, capitated contracts, 285
Relational database management system, 196
Relative value scales (RVS), 242–245
 coding, 243, 245
 Medicare reimbursement, 244–245
 resource-based relative value scale, 243–244
Relative value unit (RVU), 8
Report cards, for physicians, 91
Research, for business expansion, 104–107
Resource-based relative value scale, 243–244
Resource Base Relations ValueScale (RBRVS), 8
Retrospective/retroactive review, under managed care contract, 272
Revenue driver, definition of, 302
Risk management
 and outcomes research, 222–223
 specialty networks, 326–328
Risk pools
 capitated contracts, 284–285
 nature of, 269–270
 specialty risk pools, 325
Risk sharing
 and capitation, 249–250
 by hospital, 249
 meaning of, 248–249
 and physician opportunities, 250
Rule of thumb methods, valuation of business, 110

S

Sac Sierra Medical Group, 4
Safe harbors
 and 60/40 ownership standard, 254
 and 60/40 revenue standard, 254
 impact of, 254
 management services organizations (MSOs), 182
SalickNet, 20, 334–337
 Scripps, 80
Selective panel single–specialty network, operation of, 18–19
Self-referral. *See* Stark laws
Sentara, 73
Service bureau MSO, operation of, 28
Sharp HealthCare, 80
Sheridan Healthcare Group, 22
Sherman Act, 169, 255, 256
Single-specialty carve–out model, 320
Sisters of Providence, 73
60/40 ownership standard, and safe harbors, 254
60/40 revenue standard, and safe harbors, 254
Sound Health Associates, 259, 260
Specialists
 basic specialists, 238–239
 contracts with, 238–240
 hospital-based specialists, 239–240

initiatives for, 90–91
tertiary/quarternary specialists, 239
SpecialtyNet LLC, 342–347
Specialty networks
    aggressive marketing of, 332
    business services of, 333
    capitalization of, 328
    and capitation incentives/penalties, 325–326
    capitation schedule, 323–324
    compensation model, 332–333
    education process, 331
    efficiency of, 320–321
    example of, 334–337
    information management, 327–328, 330
    IPA model, 320
    as lead contractor or subcontractor, 321–322
    medical management, 326
    medical/practice management, 334
    network mission for, 328
    and network panel selection/deselection, 330
    physician accountability, 324
    relationship with noncompeting physician organizations, 330
    and risk contracting, 321–323
    risk contract management services, 334
    risk management, 326–328
    single-specialty carve–out model, 320
    specialty risk pools, 325
    steps in development of, 318–320
    success factors related to, 328–331
    suitability to capitation, 321
    volume/cost-efficiency, maintenance of, 323
Specialty services network, 16–20
    capital sources, 16
    examples of, 19–20
    goals of, 17
    governance of, 17
    income distribution, 18
    issues for physicians, 20
    lines of business, 18
    management of, 17
    operation of, 16
    ownership of, 16
    revenue generation, 18
    situations for use, 19
    systems used, 18
    variations on, 18–19
Standard costs, definition of, 302
Stark laws (anti-referral), 251–253
    designated health services (DHS) criteria, 252
    exceptions to, 171–172, 252
    group practice, criteria for, 252
    joint ownership, 186
    management services organizations (MSOs), 182
    mergers, 170–172
    and reorganization chart, 171
    self-referral prohibitions, 170–171

Stark I, 251–252
Stark II, 252–253
Starr, Paul, 5
State regulations, independent practice associations (IPAs), 178
Stock
    independent practice associations (IPAs), 177
    joint ownership, 185
    and mergers, 170
    types of, 120
Stop-loss provision, under managed care contract, 276
Strategic alliances, 153–160
    capital needs, 153
    and corporate subsidiary, 157–159
    physician decisions about, 159–160
    and physician equity alliances, 155–157
    structure of equity, 154
Structured query language (SQL), 196
Sutter Health System, 73

T

TA Associates, 22
Taxation, 258–261
    of HMOs, 259–261
    of independent practice associations, 261
    and mergers, 164–168
    Section 501(c)(3) exemption, 259–260
    Section 501(c)(4) exemption, 260
    Section 501(m) application to HMOs, 260–261
    tax-exempt status, joint ownership, 183–185
    tax-free reorganization, 164–165
Telephone nurse advisory (TAN) program, 315
Teleservices, 44–45
    elements of, 45
    health advisory hotlines, 44
    leaders in, 44
Tel-Patient Network, 44
Term/termination provisions
    capitated contracts, 284
    under managed care contract, 273–274
Thrive, 348
Total care management, 44
Transformation of American Medicine, The (Starr), 5
Treatment effectiveness, meaning of, 218
Treatment efficacy, meaning of, 218
Trends, tracking of, 349–350
Triple-option point-of-service plans, 88

U

Unified Medical Group Association, 131
Uniform Clinical Data Set (UCDS), 41
UniHealth, 73, 80
Union-like specialty care network, negative aspects of, 18

United Health Care Corporation, 44, 82
U.S. Healthcare, 77, 82
Utilization and quality review
   concurrent review, 272
   under managed care contract, 272–273
   preauthorization/preadmission review, 272
   retrospective/retroactive review, 272–273

V

Valuation of business, 109–111
   cost approach, 109
   discounted future cash flow, 10
   excess earnings method, 110
   income approach, 109
   market approach, 109
   rule of thumb methods, 110
   tangible and intangible assets and liabilities, 110–111
Value Health Sciences (VHS), 223
Variable costing income statement, format of, 303
Variable costs, definition of, 302
Venture medical management company, 20–22
   capital sources, 21
   examples of, 22
   goals of, 21
   governance of, 22
   lines of business, 22
   management of, 22
   operation of, 20–21
   ownership of, 21
   variations on, 22
Viva, 20
Volunteer Hospitals of America, 80

W

Wellpoint, 82
Wickline v. State of California, 275
Wide-area network (WAN), 195
World Wide Web (WWW), 49–54
   Web sites for physicians, 51–54